THE ABOLITIONIST MANIFESTO

SLAVERY
GONE FOR GOOD

Black-Book Edition

~ 2024 ~

Cory Edmund Endrulat

Epilogue by
William H. Douglas

Table Of Contents

"No wonder that the slaves themselves, who have always been enslaved, do not understand their own position, and that this condition in which they have always lived is considered by them to be natural to human life, and that they hail as a relief any change in their form of slavery; no wonder that their owners sometimes quite sincerely think they are, in a measure, freeing the slaves by slacking one screw, though they are compelled to do so by the over-tension of another. Both become accustomed to their state; and the slaves, never having known what freedom is, merely seek an alleviation, or only the change of their condition; the other, the owners, wishing to mask their injustice, try to assign a particular meaning to those new forms of slavery which they enforce in place of the older ones." *- Leo Tolstoy, Author, Philosopher (1828)*

Please sit with your conscience.
The most important topic for the evolution of humanity.
Quotes provided for clarity, regardless of who said them.

Quotes Are Associated With Parenthesized Birth-Date
Universal, Timeless, Nonpartisan, Independent, Anti-Slavery, Educative
Slavery: Gone For Good (2.0, The Black Book Edition)
Copyright 2024 Cory Edmund Endrulat   ISBN 9798324231378

Why Talk About Slavery?

Simply put, if you *care* about freedom, then slavery is the antithesis. Therefore, by understanding what is slavery, you can understand what is freedom. This process of knowing what is, from what is not, is known as **Apophasis**. The subject of slavery may be touchy for humankind, yet it is a necessary one to address, considering the fact it has existed for thousands of years, despite many *moral* disputes and implications. How could that be? Additionally, if we want to end all forms of injustice in the world, it would help for us to understand one that humanity has long struggled with. We cannot expect slavery to be merely *"abolished"* as we will discover upon observing the the very nature of slavery.

Frederick Douglass, Former Slave, Abolitionist (1817) - "I did not know I was a slave until I found out I couldn't do the things I wanted" *related to* "If I could have convinced more slaves that they were slaves, I could have freed thousands more" disputed quote attributed to *Harriet Tubman, Former Slave, Abolitionist (1822)*

Leo Tolstoy, Author, Philosopher (1828) - "Not only the greatest sages of the world, the teachers of humanity, Plato, Aristotle, justified the existence of slaves and proved the legality of it, but even three centuries ago men who wrote of the imaginary society of the future, of Utopia, could not imagine it without slaves... Slavery was contrary to all the **moral principles** which were preached by Plato and Aristotle, and yet neither the one nor the other saw this, because the negation of **slavery destroyed all that life which they lived. The same happens in our world.**"

Frederick Douglass, Former Slave, Abolitionist (1817) - "America is false to the past, false to the present, and solemnly binds herself to be false to the future"

What Is Slavery?
The **claim** of **ownership** over the life of another individual or their **property**; or the **involuntary** servitude of an individual's labor to another; or the **control** over the life of another by threat of **violence**.

From *The Etymology Dictionary*: 1550s, "severe toil, hard work, drudgery;" "state of servitude, condition of a slave, entire subjection to the will and commands of another." A slave, from the late 1200s, is defined as a "person who is the chattel or property of another." *(Old French escalve, Medieval Latin sclavus, Italian schiavo, Spanish esclavo)* Originates with "slav" due to the many "Slavic" people being sold into slavery due to conquering and war. Slav is defined as "one of the people who inhabit most of Eastern Europe," a shortening of *sloveninu* or *slovo* meaning "word" or "speech" which suggests the representation of people who are "foreign," "of a different voice" or "dumb," more specifically different in both race and language. Related to robot, from *Old Slavic rabu* meaning "slave." Slave-holder or slave-master is defined from 1776 as "one who owns a slave or slaves." Slave-driver is defined from 1807 as "overseer of slaves at their work" or as "cruel or exacting task-master" from 1854.

Slavery is known to have different forms, for instance, **chattel slavery** is the form many people are familiar with, due to the **abolitionist movement** in the 19th century.

Ralph Waldo Emerson, Abolitionist, Author (1803) - "Slavery it is that makes slavery; freedom, freedom. The slavery of women happened when the men were **slaves of kings**."

Kevin Bales, Professor (1952) -
"Slavery is **theft** – theft of a life, theft of work, theft or any property or produce, theft even of the children a slave might have borne."

Ayn Rand, Philosopher, Author (1905) -
"The man who produces while others dispose of **his product**, is a slave."

Leo Tolstoy, Author, Philosopher (1828) -
"The necessity to do what other people wish against your **own** will is slavery. And, therefore, as long as any **violence**, designed to compel some people to do the will of others, exists there will be slavery."

Henry Clarke Wright, Abolitionist (1797) -
Slavery is the "**submission or subjection** to control by the will of another being"

EndSlaveryNow.org -
"Slavers and human traffickers grossly violate **human rights** since they claim **ownership**, **labor** and/or the humanity of another human being."

William Batchelder Greene, Abolitionist (1819) -
"What is it to be a Slave? It is to have the inward **knowledge** of that which is great and holy, and to be **constrained** to do tilings that are small and base. It is to be a person consciously capable of self-government, and to be, at the same time, subject to the will of another person. It is to be, a full-grown person whose actual **rights** are those

of a child only. It is to see the Blazing Star, and not be **permitted** to **follow** it.”

Francis Dashwood Tandy, Philosopher (1867) -
“The savage found it to his advantage to spare the life of his enemy in order to make him a slave.

What Is Chattel Slavery?
The complete **ownership** of one individual by another; the claim over 100% of somebody’s labor or **property**; the use of **involuntary** free labor. Individuals under this condition are under **duress**, or the continued threat of **violence**. This form is also known as **overt physical slavery**, or “ball-and-chains” slavery.

From *The Etymology Dictionary*: “chattel” comes from the early 13th century *chatel*, meaning “property, goods.” Also *Old French chatel*, “wealth, possessions, property, cattle.” The word “cattle” also means **“property” of any kind**, including money, land, or income, *(Anglo-French catel, Medieval Latin capitale)* also from Middle English as “movable property, livestock.”

Ralph Waldo Emerson, Abolitionist, Author (1803) -
“Slavery is an *institution* for converting men into monkeys”

One of the most notorious Abolitionists in the 19th century was William Lloyd Garrison, who was the main editor of *“The Liberator” newspaper* which he held for thirty-five consecutive years without missing a single weekly edition, and he wrote this in regards to the *aggregate* end of chattel slavery within the United States due to his efforts: “We commence a new decade with the same confidence in the **principles** we espouse, the same assurance of success in the cause we advocate, that we felt at the commencement of our labors, only greatly strengthened by the experience gained, and the progress made toward the goal of final victory. It has been a long, desperate, and (humanly speaking) most unequal struggle with the organized religious sentiment, the political power, the combined wealth, the recognized respectability, the popular feeling, the business selfishness, the satanic malignity, and the universal brutality and ruffianism of the country; but, from the hour the bugle of freedom first sounded its notes in favor of *immediate and universal emancipation*, the movement has advanced with *slow but irresistible* power, under Divine guidance, confounding the wisdom of the wise, contemning the might of the strong, taking the cunning in their own craftiness, unmasking the *hypocritical*, swallowing up all the rods of the magicians, breaking sects and parties into fragments, vanquishing all opponents, its poverty more than a match for all the wealth of the land, its spirit sublime and unconquerable, its truths *self-evident*, and its results glorious in the annals of historic achievement; and still, 'Against the wind, against the tide, It steadies with upright keel' outstripping all competition, and with the haven of righteousness and peace full in view." Garrison was willing to speak of "controversial" topics in regards to suffering laborers, school systems, women's rights, capital punishment, the treatment of Indians, animal rights, alcoholism and much more. To be reminded of this passion and strife, we may become inspired for what change may be needed in the modern day.

During the times of 19th century abolition, pro-slavery advocate Sen. Hammond, of South Carolina stated, "the great strength of the South arises from the harmony of her political and social institutions. This harmony gives her a frame of society, the best in the world, and an extent of political freedom combined with entire security, and as no other people ever enjoyed upon the face of the earth... In all social systems there must be a class to do the mean duties, to perform the drudgery of life — that is a class requiring but a low order of intellect and but little skill… Such a class you must have, or you would not have the other class which leads progress, refinement and civilization. It constitutes the very mud-sills of society and of political government... Fortunately for the South, she has found a race adapted to that purpose to her hand. A race inferior to herself, but eminently qualified in temper, in vigor, in docility, in capacity, to stand the climate, to answer all her purposes. We use them for the purpose, and call them slaves. We are old fashioned in the South yet; it is a word discarded now by ears polite; but I will not characterize that class at the North with that term; but you have it; it is there; it is everywhere; it is eternal. Northern Laborers are but Slaves." Many pro-slavery newspapers would attack the efforts of Abolitionists, such as the *N.Y. Courier & Enquirer*, having an article titled "Shall the Government be Preserved, or the Abolitionists Have Their Will" saying "do you, fellow citizens, feel this disregard for the constitution of your country? Are you ready to do an act that from the very nature of things must plunge this great nation into confusion and disaster, and then stand with impious lips to charge the calamity upon your God! We trust not — we will not suffer ourselves to entertain so foul a suspicion of our countrymen."

What Is Your Property?
Your **Own** Life *(future)*
Your **Own** Freedom *(present)*
The products of your Life and Freedom *(past)*
also said as "the fruits of your labor"

What Is NOT Your Property?
Another's **Own** Life

Another's **Own** Freedom
Another's **Own** Property, *unless* **voluntarily** *traded*

In Other Words...
You do **NOT Own** the Life or Property of anyone else,
You Are **NOT the Source** of Freedom for others
...otherwise that *is* Slavery

What Is Ownership?
Having responsibility, control of usage or rightful
possession of property that belongs to you.

Self-Ownership is the specification that you own you and
that I own me. In other words, nobody has a higher claim
over your own life, other than you; no other person or group
of persons owns your life, and nor do you own the lives of
others. Therefore, to practice self-ownership would mean to
not give away ownership over to others, for that of which
only you can truly have ownership over; similarly, to not
give away responsibilities to others, for that of which only
you can truly be responsible for.

Frederick Douglass, Former Slave, Abolitionist (1817) -
"Where **justice is denied**, where poverty is enforced,
where **ignorance** prevails, and where any one class is
made to feel that society is an organized conspiracy to
oppress, rob and degrade them, neither **persons nor
property** will be safe."
"**The first work of slavery** is to mar and deface those
characteristics of its victims which distinguish men from
things, and persons from **property**. Its first aim is to destroy
all sense of high **moral and religious responsibility**. It
reduces **man to a mere machine**. It cuts him off from his
Maker, it hides from him the **laws of God**, and leaves him
to grope his way from time to eternity in the dark, under the

arbitrary and despotic control of a frail, depraved, and sinful
fellow-man."
"It is, then, the first business of the enslaver of men to blunt,
deaden, and destroy the central **principle** of human
responsibility. **Conscience** is, to the individual soul, and
to society, what the law of gravitation is to the universe. It
holds society together; it is the basis of all trust and
confidence; it is the pillar of all **moral** rectitude. Without it,
suspicion would take the place of trust; vice would be more
than a match for virtue; men would prey upon each other,
like the wild beasts of the desert; and earth would become
a hell."

What Does Slavery Have To Do With Morality?
In talking about property and freedoms that people *naturally*
have, people talk about the notion of "natural rights" or a
"natural moral law" and what is right or wrong. This was the
main argument of conscience or **moral suasion** used by
Abolitionists to end chattel slavery after thousands of years.
Though exact definitions may be disputed, and our
application may be contradictive, around the world most
people have a general basic morality, which author C.S.
Lewis details from every culture in his book, *"The Abolition
of Man."* He additionally warns us about the dangers of
moral relativism, that which disregards morality, and states
that humanity will abolish itself without such long-held
teachings. Among those teachings may be shared *The
Golden Rule* as "do unto others what you would have done
to yourself," or *Karma* as "you reap what you sow", or *the
Law of Attraction* as "the energy you emit is the energy you
attract," "energy flows where attention goes," "as you think,
feel and act, so you shall be," or *the Law of Cause and
Effect* as "effect invariably follows cause," "for every action,
there exists an equal and opposing reaction." It is often
understood that a wrong action is that which results in

harm, is involuntary, is any form of theft or a violation of property and self-ownership or an act of violence. Abolitionists similarly appealed to **"god's government"** or "higher laws" as the reason why man is not to be a slave to another man. This became even more apparent when the American government in the 19th century passed **the Fugitive Slave Act** which made it further illegal for slaves to run away from their masters, reimbursing those who can capture runaway slaves and threatening those citizens who do not help this initiative with jail-time and fines. The fines being $1000 in 1849, would be $30,000 in 2009. Such acts only further enraged the Abolitionists. Hence, **Morality is not legality**. Just because something is "legal," does not make it right. Wrong actions include murder, assault, rape, theft, trespass, coercion and willfully lying. In understanding each of these actions, we may understand how they violate ownership, therefore reinforcing slavery. Murder is the theft of one's *Own* Life which is not rightfully ours to take, assault is the theft of one's *Own* well-being without right, rape is the theft of one's *Own* free-will sexual association, theft is the stealing of one's *Own* property, trespass is the theft of the security of one's *Own* living domain, coercion is the theft of one's *Own* free-will choice via violence or duress, willfully lying is the theft of necessary information which negatively impacts one's *Own* ability to engage in their *Own* informed decision making. In this sense, some form of property is always being stolen when a wrong action is committed, hence the saying *"no victim, no crime."* If we use *apophasis* knowing what is wrong of us to do or have, we have the right to our *Own* property, and the right to do anything that is *not* wrong. Another saying goes "your rights end where the rights of others begin" as an emphasis of self-discipline, for which temperance is often associated with justice. It is no surprise during the 19th century, many Abolitionists, while challenging one big institution, they would find themselves at odds with others therein; they were promoting temperance, or self-discipline regarding alcohol, as well as promoting free love (notably later Angela and Ezra Heywood, Moses and Lillian Harman), women's rights, land freedoms, octagonal houses, spirituality and more. Only you can be truly responsible for your own actions, you must own up to your ownership. Historically, slaves do not know or act on behalf of their *(natural)* rights, since they are trained into obedience; therefore, their "rights" are rather privileges *(man-made)*, based on moral relativism or the whims of their masters.

William Lloyd Garrison, Journalist, Abolitionist (1805) - "Enslave the liberty of but one human being and the liberties of the world are put in peril"

The Liberator, Abolitionist Newspaper (1831) - "Its spirit and purpose—**the higher law**, in its supremacy over nations and governments as well as **individual conscience**—the Golden Rule, in its binding obligation upon all classes—the Declaration of Independence, with its self-evident truths—the rights of human nature, without distinction of race, complexion or sex."

John Lind, Philosopher (1737) - "How came there to be slaves in your land of liberty? Are **rights**, which can neither be forfeited by conquest, nor ceded by compact, nor purchased by obligation alienable by a change in the colour of the skin? Why did not these sons of liberty restore their slaves to rights, which the one could not acquire, nor the other alienate?"

Henry David Thoreau, Abolitionist, Philosopher (1817) -
"If the alternative is to keep all just men in prison, or give up war and slavery, **the State** will not hesitate which to choose."

Lysander Spooner, Abolitionist, Lawyer (1808) -
"The pretense that the 'abolition of slavery' was either a motive or justification for the war, is a fraud of the same character with that of 'maintaining the national honor.' Who, but such usurpers, robbers, and murderers **as they**, ever established slavery? Or what government, except one resting upon the sword, like the one **we now have**, was ever capable of maintaining slavery? And why did these men abolish slavery? Not from any love of liberty in general —not as an act of justice to the black man himself, but only 'as a war measure,' and because they wanted his assistance, and that of his friends, in carrying on the war they had undertaken for **maintaining and intensifying that political, commercial, and industrial slavery**, to which they have subjected the great body of the people, both white and black. And yet these imposters now cry out that they have abolished the chattel slavery of the black man — although that was not the motive of the war—as if they thought they could thereby conceal, atone for, or justify that **other slavery which they were fighting to perpetuate**, and to render more rigorous and inexorable than it ever was before. There was no difference of principle—but only of degree—between the slavery they boast they have abolished, and the slavery they were fighting to preserve; for all restraints upon men's natural liberty, not necessary for the simple maintenance of justice, are of the nature of slavery, and differ from each other only in degree."

Frederick Douglass, Former Slave, Abolitionist (1817) -
"Power concedes nothing without a demand. It never did and it never will."
"Liberty is meaningless where the **right** to utter one's thoughts and opinions has ceased to exist. That, of all rights, is the dread of tyrants. It is the right which they first of all strike down."
"I was just as well aware of the **unjust, unnatural and murderous** character of slavery, when nine years old, as I am now. Without any appeal to books, to **laws**, or to authorities of any kind, it was enough to accept God as a father, to regard slavery as a **crime**."
"The **morality of the act** I dispose of as follows: I am myself; you are yourself; we are two distinct persons, **equal** persons. What you are, I am. You are a man, and so am I. God created both, and made us separate beings. I am not by **nature** bond to you, or you to me. Nature does not make your existence **depend** upon me, or mine to depend upon yours. I cannot walk upon your legs, or you upon mine. I cannot breathe for you, or you for me; I must breathe for myself, and you for yourself. We are distinct persons, and are each equally provided with faculties necessary to our individual existence. In leaving you, I took nothing but what **belonged to me**, and in no way lessened your means for obtaining an honest living. Your faculties remained yours, and mine became useful to their **rightful owner.** I therefore see no **wrong** in any part of the transaction."
"It is only when we contemplate the slave as a **moral and intellectual** being, that we can adequately comprehend the unparalleled enormity of slavery, and the intense **criminality** of the slaveholder."
"To be a slave-holder is to be a **propagandist** from necessity; for slavery can only live by keeping down the under-growth **morality** which **nature** supplies."

Angelina Grimke, Abolitionist (1805) -
"One who is a slaveholder at heart never recognizes a human being in a slave."

Auberon Herbert, Philosopher (1838) -
"Chorus — Each man shall be free, whoever he be, And none shall say to him nay! There is only one rule for the wise and the fool — **To follow his own heart's way**. For the heart of the free, whoever he be, May be stirred to a better thing; But the heart of the slave lies chill in its grave, And knows not the coming of spring."

Walter E. Williams, Author (1936) -
"How does something **immoral**, when done privately, become **moral** when it is done collectively? Furthermore, does **legality** establish morality? Slavery was legal; apartheid is legal; Stalinist, Nazi, and Maoist purges were legal. Clearly, the fact of legality does not justify these crimes. Legality, alone, cannot be the talisman of moral people"

Etienne de La Boetie, Philosopher (1530) -
"Even if liberty had entirely perished from the earth, such men would invent it. For them slavery has no satisfactions, **no matter how well disguised**"

Stephen Pearl Andrews, Abolitionist (1812) -
"It cannot be rightly said that any man has a **right to do wrong**; but every man has the right to the **freedom** to do wrong. In other words, he has the right not to be interfered with in the exercise of his own judgment of right, although it may lead him to do what all the world pronounce wrong, provided only that he acts at his own cost, that is, that he do not throw the burdensome consequences of **his acts** on others."

"The full and final abolition of slavery can not but be regarded, by every reflecting mind, as prospectively certain."

From the N.Y. Evangelist newspaper (1856) -
"In this republic the government proclaims Slavery as the universal law. It hunts the fugitive, and seizes him for his master; it fastens his fetters, and holds the key of his prison-house."

Henry Clarke Wright, Abolitionist (1797) -
"There is nothing on the records of the world more shocking to humanity, than is this transaction, from beginning to end. The facts touching their arrest, their return to Washington, fettered and bound, and guarded like felons; their mock trial; their incarceration; the cruelty practiced on them by the officers of the United States; the sale of the recaptured slaves, especially some of the young females — one of the victims being a slave of the widow of President Madison; the sundering of domestic ties; children sold from parents, and parents sold from children; all this done in the capital of this Republic, and through the instrumentality of the federal Union... And there are men and women in Britain and Ireland, who are lending their direct influence to sustain these horrors among us. God forgive them!"

C.S. Lewis, Philosopher (1898) -
"I am very doubtful whether history shows us one example of a man who, having stepped outside traditional morality *(Tao)* and attained power, has used that power benevolently."
"Either we are rational spirit obliged for ever to obey the absolute values of the Tao [natural law], or else we are mere nature to be kneaded and cut into new shapes for the pleasures of masters who must, by hypothesis, have no

motive but their own 'natural' impulses. Only the Tao provides a common human law of action which can over arch rulers and ruled alike. A dogmatic belief in objective value is necessary to the very idea of a **rule which is not tyranny or an obedience which is not slavery**."

How Can Slavery Be Right? How Was It Justified?
Slavery can only be a legal "right," but it can not be morally right. Since it is a condition of *duress*, it may be considered *the worst form of wrong*, since it is wrong guaranteed and repeated. To reiterate, another being and their property does not belong to you. Morality is not consistent in it's principle or use, if it is based on privileges that can be "granted" or "revoked" at any time and based on fluctuating opinion, or the idea that one person can be *the source* of morality for others. Who are we to impose our will on another human being, if we have equality and humility? If we did, we would be in contradiction to *the golden rule*, and right would simply be dependent upon might. However, as evident upon reading *Right is Might by Richard Wetheril* for reference, one can only *claim* to be the sole moral arbitrator and they may *attempt* to convince others that it is legitimate. Therefore, through another perspective, legality is merely imposed morality, and this is the theft of one's *Own* moral compass, conscience and freedom of choice. For when legality *is* aligned to morality, there begs the question as to it's necessity, if it's actually helping to enforce morality, or if it is rather providing space for exception and legitimizing other evils. The "radical" Abolitionists like one of the most prominent figures, William Lloyd Garrison, deeply understood this concept. Frederick Douglas said about him, that "he rose not by the power of the church or the state, but in bold, inflexible and defiant opposition to the mighty power of both." For instance, if we are under "god's government" then what use is there for

human government? And why would the devoted follower of God support slavery, or the state? Despite seemingly like a strange question during the time of Abolition, it is written about extensively at the same time period, 1845, as when *philosophical anarchism* began. Interestingly enough, the first anarchists in history were considered religious, be it for example, Christian or Taoist. In correlation, famous psychologist Dr. Carl Jung shares with us in his book *The Undiscovered Self*, about how religion *can* be the greatest bulwark against the power of the government or what he calls "state doctrine," if it is used in challenging it's *authority*. One may be curious to see how many modern religious-followers would so bravely adopt this point of view. The Abolitionists mainly utilized this position in giving them leverage over the slave-masters who claimed *authority* over their fellow man for the many reasons they used as a justification, whether it was racially or economically; in truth, the morality mattered most at the end of the day, for when the governments at the time supported chattel slavery, many Abolitionists additionally challenged the authority not just of the slave-masters, but of the government. Such principles ended many Abolitionists in jail, with censorship of their material, as well as slander from the media, warning the world of their "revolting" positions. Having to fight all fronts, they dealt with a world that was justifying an age-old practice that was held mainly due to the superstition and fear that came from conformity, despite knowing in their heart what was truly right. Today we may understand, it does not matter how people have justified slavery in the past, because the act itself is a claim of ownership over somebody who does not belong to the claimant.

Justification comes from the Latin noun *jus*: "right" and the Latin verb *facere*: "to make, to create", meaning "to *create* a right", even if it isn't *actually* right.

Carl Jung, Psychoanalyst (1875) -
"The State has taken the place of God; that is why, seen from this angle, the socialist dictatorships are religions and State slavery is a form of worship. But the religious function cannot be dislocated and falsified in this way without giving rise to secret doubts, which are immediately repressed so as to avoid conflict with the prevailing trend towards mass-mindedness. The result, as always in such cases, is overcompensation in the form of *fanaticism*, which in its turn is used as a weapon for stamping out the least flicker of opposition. Free opinion is stifled and moral decision ruthlessly suppressed, on the plea that the end justifies the means, even the vilest. **The policy of the State is exalted to a creed, the leader or party boss becomes a demigod beyond good and evil, and his votaries are honored as heroes, martyrs, apostles, missionaries. There is only one truth and beside it no other.** It is sacrosanct and above criticism. Anyone who thinks differently is a heretic, who, as we know from history, is threatened with all manner of unpleasant things. Only the party boss, who holds the political power in his hands, can interpret the **State doctrine** authentically, and he does so just as suits him."

"The performance of a 'magical' action gives the person concerned a **feeling of security** which is absolutely essential for carrying out a decision, because a decision is inevitably somewhat one-sided and is therefore rightly felt to be a risk. Even a dictator thinks it necessary not only to accompany his acts of State with threats but to stage them with all manner of solemnities. Brass bands, flags, banners, parades and monster demonstrations are no different in principle from ecclesiastical processions, cannonades and fireworks to scare off demons. Only, the suggestive parade of State power engenders a collective **feeling of security** which, unlike religious demonstrations, gives the individual no protection against his inner demonism. Hence he will cling all the more to the power of the State, i.e., to the mass, thus delivering himself up to it psychically as well as morally and putting the finishing touch to his social depotentiation. The State, like the Church, demands enthusiasm, self-sacrifice and love, and if religion requires or presupposes the 'fear of God,' then the dictator State takes good care to provide the necessary terror."

"The goals of religion – deliverance from evil, reconciliation with God, rewards in the hereafter, and so on – turn into worldly promises about freedom from care for one's daily bread, the just distribution of material goods, universal prosperity in the future, and shorter working hours. That the fulfillment of these *promises* is as far off as Paradise only furnishes yet another analogy and underlines the fact that the masses have been converted from an extra-mundane goal to a purely worldly *belief*, which is extolled with exactly the same *religious fervor* and exclusiveness that the creeds display in the other direction."

"In order to free the *fiction* of the sovereign State – in other words, the whims of those who manipulate it – from every wholesome restriction, all sociopolitical movements tending in this direction invariably try to cut the ground from under the religions. For, in order to turn the individual into a function of the State, his **dependence** on anything beside the State must be taken from him."

"But it is possible to have an attitude to the external conditions of life only when there is a point of reference outside them. The religions give, or claim to give, such a standpoint, thereby enabling the individual to exercise his judgment and his power of decision. They build up a reserve, as it were, against the obvious and inevitable force of circumstances to which everyone is exposed who lives only in the outer world and has no other ground under his feet except the pavement. If statistical reality is the only reality, then it is the sole *authority*. There is then only one condition, and since no contrary condition exists, judgment and decision are not only superfluous but impossible. Then the individual is bound to be a function of statistics and hence a function of the State or whatever the abstract principle of order may be called. **The religions, however, teach another authority opposed to that of the 'world.'** The doctrine of the individual's *dependence* on God makes just as high a claim upon him as the world does."

"Science supplies us with, instead of the concrete individual, the names of organizations and, at the highest point, the abstract idea of the State as the principle of political reality. **The moral responsibility of the individual is then inevitably replaced by the policy of the State** *(raison d'état)*. Instead of moral and mental differentiation of the individual, you have public welfare and the raising of the living standard."

"The goal and meaning of individual life (which is the only real life) no longer lie in individual development but in the policy of the State, which is thrust upon the individual from outside and consists in the execution of an abstract idea which ultimately tends to attract all life to itself. **The individual is increasingly deprived of the moral decision** as to how he should live his own life, and instead is ruled, fed, clothed and educated as a social unit, accommodated in the appropriate housing unit, and amused in accordance with the standards that give pleasure and satisfaction to the masses. The rulers, in their turn, are just as much social units as the ruled and are distinguished only by the fact that they are specialized mouthpieces of the *State doctrine*. They do not need to be personalities capable of judgment, but thoroughgoing specialists who are unusable outside their line of business. State policy decides what shall be taught and studied."

"The policy of the State is the *supreme principle* of thought and action. Indeed, this was the purpose for which he was enlightened, and accordingly the mass man grants the individual a right to exist only in so far as the individual is a function of the State. The believer, on the other hand, while admitting that the State has a moral and factual claim, confesses to the belief that not only man but the State that rules him is subject to the over-lordship of 'God' and that, in case of doubt, *the supreme decision will be made by God and not by the State*... The individual who is not anchored in God can offer no resistance on his own resources to the physical and moral blandishments of the world. For this he needs the evidence of inner, transcendent experience which alone can protect him from the otherwise inevitable submersion in the mass. Merely intellectual or even moral insight into the stultification and *moral irresponsibility* of the mass man is a negative recognition only and amounts to not much more than a wavering on the road to the atomization of the individual. It lacks the driving force of religious conviction, since it is merely rational."

Former Slave (from online audio) -
"You can't give me the **right** to be a human being, I am born with that right. Now you can keep me from having that if you got all the policemen and all the jobs on your side, you can deprive me of it, but you can't give it to me because I was born with it just like you was."

Lysander Spooner, Abolitionist, Lawyer (1808) -
"Slavery, if it can be legalized at all, can be legalized *only* by positive legislation. Natural law gives it no aid."

Percy Shelley, Author (1792) -
"Conformity and obedience, Bane of all genius, **virtue**, freedom, truth, makes slaves of men and of the human frame, a *mechanized automaton*."

Ayn Rand, Philosopher, Author (1905) -
"If some men are entitled by **right** to the products of the work of others, it means that those others are deprived of rights and condemned to slave labor. Any alleged 'right' of one man which necessitates the violation of the rights of another, is not and cannot be a right. No man can have a right to impose an unchosen obligation, an unwarranted duty or an **involuntary** servitude on another man. **There can be no such thing as the right to enslave.**"

Henry Clapp, Jr., Abolitionist (1814) -
"Might is right, is the corner stone of all slavery."

The Liberator, Abolitionist Newspaper (1831) -
"The American press is, to a fearful extent, in the hands of a cowardly, mercenary and *unprincipled* class of men, who have no regard for truth in dealing with what is unpopular; who cater to the lowest passions of the multitude, and caricature every movement aiming at the overthrow of established **wrong**; who are as destitute of all fairness In controversy as they are lacking in **self-respect**; and whose columns are closed against any reply that may be proffered to their libellous accusations. It is true, these men represent the prevailing public sentiment, either in the locality in which they reside, or in the country at large; but, fearfully *demoralized* as that sentiment is, in many particulars, they aim to make it still more corrupt, rather than to change it for the better. They not only publish all the lies they can pick up, in opposition to the struggling cause of humanity, but they busy themselves in coining lies, which they

audaciously present to their credulous readers as reliable truths. There is no end to their deception and tergiversation. Such men are far more dangerous to society than burglars, incendiaries and highwaymen. Occupying a position of solemn trust, and almost awful *responsibility,*—exerting a potent influence over a large class of ignorant and unreflecting minds, who look up to them as teachers and guides, however deficient in brains or vicious in *morals,*— they have it alike in their power and in their disposition to deceive, mislead, circumvent, and *demoralize,* to a ruinous extent. Each of them is a local *authority*; and of their many readers, comparatively few think of questioning the authenticity of what is laid before them, from day to day, or from week to week. In what part of the country—in what town or village—can an anti-slavery meeting be held, of an uncompromising character, even after a struggle of twenty five years, without being basely misrepresented by the press, or treated with silent contempt? Yes, for a quarter of a century, **abolitionism—the denial of the right to make man the property of man**—has been lampooned, anathematized, vilified, unceasingly and universally, by the journals of the day, both religious and secular—its advocates have been held up as crazy fanatics and wild disorganizers—and its meetings represented as unworthy of countenance by sane and decent men! We feel competant thus to arraign the American press generally— first, because we have been familiar with its course for the last forty years—and second, because we have the consciousness of publishing a free, independent, impartial journal, in the columns of which all sides have ever been allowed a fair hearing, and which seeks to make known the truth, the whole truth, and nothing but the truth, at whatever cost or hazard. How such a paper—advocating the noblest cause that can engage the attention of man, and giving auxiliary support to other great reformatory movements—is appreciated and sustained, is seen in its petty subscription list, in its limited circulation, in the covert and open effort every where made for its *suppression*; and how other papers, which espouse the side of the oppressor, make falsehood and jesuitism their stock in trade, and resist every attempt to reform society by removing old abuses, are encouraged and upheld, may be seen in the wide circulation and richly remunerative income of Bennet's Herald, the New York Observer, the Journal of Commerce, and many others of a similar stamp. What does all this indicate as to the state of the country?"

William Lloyd Garrison, Journalist, Abolitionist (1805) - "The wealth, the enterprise, the literature, the politics, the religion of the land, are all combined to give extension and perpetuity to the Slave Power."
"The tremendous power of the Government is actively wielded to 'crush out' the little Anti-Slavery life that remains in individual hearts, and to open new and boundless domains for the expansion of the Slave system."
"The North has as much to do with Slavery (not slaves) as the South. The North does as much to support it, protect it, and extend it, as the South."

John Quincy Adams, Philosopher (1767) - "The first was the immunity, for twenty years, of preserving the African slave trade; the second was the stipulation to surrender fugitive slaves – an engagement positively prohibited by the **laws of God**, delivered from Sinai; and thirdly, the exaction, fatal to the *principles* of popular representation, of a representation for slaves – for articles of merchandise, under the name of persons. To call government thus constituted a democracy, is to insult the understanding of mankind. It is doubly tainted with the infection of riches and slavery. Its reciprocal operation upon the government of the nation is to establish an artificial majority in the slaves representation over that of the free people, in the American Congress, and thereby to make the preservation, propagation and perpetuation of slavery the vital and animating spirit of the national government.'"

Leo Tolstoy, Author, Philosopher (1828) -
"If there be, in nature, no such **principle as justice**, there is no **moral** standard, and never can be any moral standard, by which any controversy whatever, between two or more human beings, can be settled in a manner to be obligatory upon either; and the inevitable doom of the human race must consequently be to be forever at war; forever striving to plunder, enslave, and murder each other; with no instrumentalities but fraud and force to end the conflict."

Mark Passio, De-Occultist, Philosopher (1974) -
"**Natural Law** gets boiled down to two words, **'don't steal.'** That's it. You want the key out of the prison? You've got to understand property. You ought to understand all rights or **property rights**. Stop taking the property of other beings. Stop condoning the taking of the property of other beings. The end."

Frederick Douglass, Former Slave, Abolitionist (1817) -
"I have never placed my opposition to slavery on a basis so narrow as my own enslavement, but rather upon the indestructible and unchangeable **laws of human nature**, every one of which is perpetually and flagrantly violated by the slave system."
"It is the nature of slavery to beget a state of things all around it favorable to its own continuance. This fact, connected with the system of bondage, is **beginning** to be more fully realized."

Joseph Dejacque, Abolitionist (1821) -
"Who has been *moralised* by a slave has slave thoughts in
the brain. Who is betrothed to a slave, who is the owner of
a slave, is betrothed to slavery, is possessed of slavery. If
we want for man new destinies, let us engrave the right, this
morality of nature, in the heart of his companion; let's make
the oak crown for the girl instead of the orange crown, let's
give, let's give a new mold to the human embryo."

Jean-Jacques Rousseau, Philosopher (1712) -
"However we might view things, the **right of slavery** is null
and void, not only because it is illegitimate, but because it is
absurd and meaningless. These words, slavery and right,
are contradictory and mutually exclusive."

Bryan J. Butts, Abolitionist (approx. 1826) -
"Just so long as the individual **depends** on the government,
or the church, to settle the **moral** law, so long will slavery of
every hue exist."

Are We Justifying Any Evils In The Modern Day?
This is the question we must continually ask ourselves as
humanity, if we want to put an end to practices that are not
serving humanity, even if that means learning from
thousands of years of experience. As an example,
Democide, *the top cause of unnatural death*, is known as
"death by government." Professor R.J. Rummel from *the
University of Hawaii* estimates 133+ million deaths pre-20th
century and 262 million deaths in the 20th century, for a
total of 395 million deaths, not including the combatants
killed in the 350+ wars between governments since 1800 or
the 40+ million international and civil war combatant deaths
in the 20th century. Other statistics thereof may be included
within *War and Peace In Islam* which was compiled by
many different professors, detailing 318 events in history

where religions used the *authority* of governments for their ability to coerce and compel non-believers or infidels, totaling around 577+ million deaths. Does the use of government justify breaking the moral codes of religions, such as *the golden rule*, which is often said as the most commonly shared teaching among them? Democide is responsible for deaths carried out in the name of "following orders," often for the "greater good," with *World War 2* provided as a good example. Notice the adoration in crowds of people for the *authority*-figures like Hitler, Stalin or Mao and the millions of people willing to follow the few, *willing* to suppress their *Own* moral compass or conscience questioning if the individual action should actually be committed or condoned. This may be related to the concept known as **Menticide**, or mind control, among many other traits regarding the empowerment of *toxic narcissism*. Additionally, notice the abdication of responsibility, for the order-follower blaming the person who gives the order, when they were the ones who committed the actions. This type of behavior is shockingly documented well among the *Stanley Milgram psychology experiments*, as well as the *Stanford Prison experiments*, yet the scientists of these studies and the world at large in modern times, is unaware of Democide and it's corresponding root cause which has *everything* to do with slavery, as it does *morality without contradiction*. If we want a sustainable future, if we want to act on principle and according to what we deem as truth, *wrong is always wrong*, and *right is always right*, even if nobody agrees, even if the majority says otherwise, even if it takes centuries to fully find this out and align our actions toward it. While we may not able to get rid of all wrong in the world, we can prevent it's manifestation, or it's permissibility. Chaos will ultimately ensue in our ignorance, to teach us our wrongs, this is humanity receiving their own doing. Then, knowing *why and how* exactly such wrongs have manifested, we can prevent the chaos from happening again. **Slavery can be gone, for actual good.**

Miles Davis, Musician (1926) -
"**Knowledge** is freedom and **ignorance** is slavery."

Larken Rose, Philosopher, Author -
(Story-Book) "Edmund Burke proclaimed that all that is necessary for evil to triumph is for good people to do nothing. You've probably even heard that one, but you still didn't listen. Albert Einstein put it another way, saying that the world is a dangerous place to live, not because of the evil people, but because of the people who don't do anything about it. But you weren't listening."

Leo Tolstoy, Author, Philosopher (1828) -
"Slavery exists in full vigor, but we do not **perceive** it, just as in Europe at the end of the Eighteenth Century the slavery of serfdom was *not perceived*."

Why Do We Make Claims About Others And Reality?
It may be easy for us to think we know what we know. It is where we get stuck, that it is known as **cognitive dissonance**, defined as the "psychological conflict resulting from incongruous beliefs and attitudes held simultaneously." The slave-master holds claim over another being's life and self-ownership, and they may even claim that such condition is truthful. When faced with the criticism that their "truth" is not *actually* truth, especially if they long-held their worldview, they may fiercely and insecurely resist. To make a claim is to make an imposition, declaration or demand based either upon belief or knowledge. An individual may *believe* something to be true, but do they truly *know*? An individual may *declare or demand* something to be true, but is it really true? Just because an

action *can* be committed, does that make it right? To claim over property that belongs to you is *not only* just, it is correct. Morality for the 19th century Abolitionists is not mere matter of empathy and feeling for others, it is the matter of truth and god's jurisdiction. In their eyes, perhaps we may ask the question: why fear ending a long-held practice when you know you stand with the truth of god, for whom you love and trust? Despite knowing this, why were prominent Abolitionists like William Lloyd Garrison refusing to use law and government to their benefit? Abolitionist Adin Ballou in his text *The Superiority of Moral over Political Power* from 1845, argues that god's kingdom cannot be enforced through human jurisdiction which is backed by violence and cannot truly change hearts and minds, but rather through the mechanisms which god implanted inside us, the conscience and reason which is backed by and similarly touted as the "law of love." Not the *love of law*, but the *law of love*. Not *authority as truth*, but *truth as authority*. In other words, **the 19th century Abolitionists recognized god as their true and only master and ruler.**

Lucretia Mott, Abolitionist (1793) -
"Truth for authority, not authority for truth."

Larken Rose, Philosopher, Author -
"Whether the issue is math, morality, or anything else, there is a huge difference between trying to **determine** what is true and trying to **dictate** what is true. The former is useful; the latter is insane."

What Is Equality?
If we don't see any one individual as qualified to be the slave-master over another or a slave under another, where does that put every individual? Equality is the condition in which everyone has the same rights, ie. it is the condition of

which no slavery is present. Rights are sometimes said as birth-rights, referring to the fact that people are born equal by their base-nature of everyone *sharing humanity*. This would mean *everybody* should be respected as such, and not as slaves or slave-masters. In other words, no one person can have any more or less rights than anyone else. People can only be kept away from exercising their *Own* rights and freedom, by others doing wrong to them or by their own belief that they need *permission* from an "authority" in order to exercise a right. Many slaves had to obtain *permission* from their slave-masters just to leave the plantation, go from plantation to plantation, or let alone do anything. With our understanding of Equality, any action that is *right*, is an action that promotes equality, for which *the golden rule* more obviously helps to portray in it's reciprocal nature of application.

In contrast with Equality, **Inequality** is known as the condition in which some people *claim* to have more rights than others. It is therefore a condition of which slavery *is* present. This would mean that rights are not respected as birth-rights, and are instead treated as privileges, assuming that some people have the right to "grant" and "revoke" other's rights, and assuming that those with this "authority" are more-human or a special-kind of human in order to do so. This creates a dynamic where those of less rights are not *allowed* to conduct actions that those of more rights could exercise. In other words, you *require permission* to be free from the master, and the most freedom is for the master. For chattel slavery in the past, the "granting" of freedom for the slaves was known as manumission or enfranchisement.

William Lloyd Garrison, Journalist, Abolitionist (1805) -
"**Everyone** should be treated fairly no matter what they look like"

Frederick Douglass, Former Slave, Abolitionist (1817) -
"No man can put a chain about the ankle of his fellow man without at last finding the other end fastened about his own neck."

Mahatma Gandhi, Indian Independence (1869) -
"A slave holder cannot hold a slave without putting himself or his deputy in the cage for holding the slave"

Josiah Warren, Abolitionist (1798) -
"I hardly know which of the two classes is most enslaved, or most to be pitied, slaves or masters."

Auberon Herbert, Philosopher (1838) -
"From the moment you possess power, you are but its slave, fast bound by its many tyrant necessities. The slave-owner has no freedom; he can never be anything but a slave himself, and share in the slavery that he makes for others. It is, I think, plain it must be so. **Power once gained, you must anxiously day by day watch over its security, whatever its security costs**, to prevent the slippery thing escaping from your hands."

Rose Wilder Lane, Philosopher (1886) -
"The slavery-owners were in process of destroying their own economy by maintaining slavery. That's why they could not win a military victory over the northerners. 'Natural resources' were more abundant in the south than in the north, but wealth was progressively less in comparison because slavery inhibited the use of human energy in the south. So **the southerner was hampering the use of his**

own liberty by suppressing the slave's use of his. The increasingly indebted slave-owner on his increasingly mortgaged property was unable to do much that he wanted to do, and the reason for his diminishing area of freedom was his denial of freedom to his slaves... More and more southerners were seeing this fact and trying to get rid of their slaves; there were all kinds of plans for doing this. So many simply freed their slaves that most, if not all, southern legislatures passed Acts forbidding this—Acts intended to compel slave-owners to continue to bear their responsibility for their slave-property, and to prevent an increase of the numbers of untrained, uncontrolled, unfed and unsheltered person at large in those states. To evade these laws slave-owners moved temporarily into 'free' territory, freed their salves there, and returned. So laws were passed forbidding this. And laws forbidding such freed slaves to return to the slave States, on penalty arrest, punishment and sale."

Jackie Robinson, Baseball Player (1919) -
"I'm not concerned with your liking or disliking me... All I ask is that you **respect** me as a **human being.**"

Ralph Waldo Emerson, Abolitionist, Author (1803) -
"A man in debt is so far a slave."

Wordsworth Donisthorpe, Philosopher (1847) -
"Equality in slavery is not liberty"

JJ Dewey, Philosopher, Author -
"He who seeks freedom at the **expense of another** is only building prison walls that will enslave him"

George Wallace, Activist (1919) -
"If nature has made any thing a man's **own**, his mind and body are so. At least it is evident, that whatever right one

man has in his mind and body, another man must have the same right in his; that is, as far as we can judge from any appearance in nature, each man has an **equal right** in his own mind and body respectively. But no man's mind and body can be his own, unless the faculties of both, that is, his judgment, his will, and his powers of acting are so. Now he, who has a right in his faculties of judging of choosing and of acting, is no slave. And since nature, which gave every man a right in his own mind and body, gave him a right likewise to these faculties; the consequence is, that nature has not placed any man in a state of slavery."

Larken Rose, Philosopher, Author -
"The reason that the belief in 'authority' can drive people to commit evil, but in the end cannot limit the evil they commit, is simple. Aside from whatever 'technical' limitations there are supposed to be on an agent of 'authority,' the primary concept that the enforcer is taught, and the primary concept that he must accept in order to do his job, is that, as a representative of 'authority,' he is above the common folk and has the **moral right** to forcibly control them. In short, he is taught that his badge and his position make him the rightful master of all the 'average' people. Once he is convinced of that lie, it should be expected that he will despise the average citizen and treat him with contempt, in the same way – and for the same reason – that a slave owner will treat his slaves not as human beings, but as **property**, whose feelings and opinions matter no more than the feelings and opinions of the master's *cattle* or his furniture. It is very telling that many modern **'law enforcers'** quickly become angry, even violent, when an average citizen simply speaks to the 'officer' as an equal, instead of assuming the tone and demeanor of a subjugated underling. Again, this reaction is precisely the same- and

has the same cause – as the reaction a slave master would
have to an 'uppity' slave speaking to him as an equal."

Etienne de La Boetie, Philosopher (1530) -
"It should not enter the mind of anyone that nature has
placed some of us in slavery, since she has actually
created us all in **one likeness**."

Jean-Jacques Rousseau, Philosopher (1712) -
"One thinks himself the master of others, and yet he is a
greater slave than they."

Herbert Spencer, Psychologist, Polymath (1820) -
"The tyrant is nothing but a slave turned inside out."

Sarah E. Holmes (1847, from Liberty newspaper) -
"The slavery of each is my slavery."

William Batchelder Greene, Abolitionist (1819) -
"**Equality** is the condition that obtains in every society
where no special or artificial privilege is granted to any one,
or to any set, of its members."

What Is Freedom?

That which is the direct opposite of slavery may be said as
liberty, otherwise known as freedom. It is not where one
merely is given permission (hence "permits") to be free only
in certain aspects of their life. It is not where you are
dependent upon another individual's whim, in the case of
the slave-master or a legislative "authority." Freedom
means being able to live as you please, so long as you do
not hinder other's freedoms, otherwise known as "live and
let live" and that which allows Equality. Exercising freedom
may be said as exercising rights. Is freedom *really*
embraced by the mere declaration of the slave-master

telling the slave that they are "now free"? Is freedom not their *natural* condition or birth-right, so to *require* permission? Is freedom or equality created by citing it on fancy pieces of paper with writing? Why *must* an "authority" *provide* someone their *Own* freedom, if it belongs with them? Would a thief *become moral* if they gave back what they stole? Frederick Douglas, a former slave and Abolitionist, tells us how, by *freeing himself*, he is merely taking what what was always his to begin with. He, among others, recognized that *true* freedom requires the acquisition of **sovereignty**, otherwise known as recognizing your *Own* freedom, or *being able to bypass mental slavery beyond also physical slavery*. **The condition of freedom is the absence of slavery.** Freedom may also be said as *infinite possibility*, for which includes the possibility of wrong that may attempt to limit freedom. The fear of chaos, then, may correlate to **the fear of freedom**, as would be the case of the pro-slavery advocate who asks "who will pick the cotton?" Additionally, if the slave rebels against their master, the pro-slavery advocate may use such "chaotic" acts to reinforce the idea that the slave should remain in their state of *limited freedom*. The justification may even be that the slave is too ignorant, unable to practice self-ownership, even pointing to any mistaken or immoral action. Does *one wrong doing* by an individual, justify their slavery for *continual wrong doing*? Does the wrong actions of one individual, justify the punishment upon many? Does the wrong actions of one individual, reflect that of everyone else who "looks" or *seems like* the same? Are human beings merely beasts that need to be caged and kept away from the rest of the world? To reiterate, freedom is the ability to live your life as you so choose since it belongs to you, however, *freedom is not free*. Freedom requires self-ownership, for if you don't *Own* you, who does? Freedom being your birth-right property, means that you are *responsible* for it therein understanding and practicing self-ownership. In seeing freedom as necessary for our very concepts of individuality, or self, or ownership, or conscience and choice, we may see it then as natural and destined for mankind, as another reinforcing argument of the 19th century Abolitionists. They saw hypocrisy in the U.S. government's founding documents claiming that "all men are created equal" despite claiming that slaves, being men that are also capable of being men like any other men, are *not* equal. William Lloyd Garrison would publicly burn the *U.S. Constitution* in the streets due to this, as he called it "a covenant with death" and "an agreement with hell." Lawyer and Abolitionist Lysander Spooner claimed that the U.S. Constitution was actually anti-slavery in his writing *The Unconstitutionality of Slavery* in 1845, but he later wrote extensively about how such documents have no legitimate authority over anyone, detailing many moral and philosophical problems, while considering how nobody gave their explicit consent to it's usage in his text *No Treason: The Constitution of No Authority* in 1867. Therefore, although these two individuals differed on the U.S. Constitution, especially in the beginning, they both agreed that slavery was wrong and that freedom is *not* determined by the slave-master, the government, or their materials. In summary, **you must Own up to your Own freedom.**

Mortimer Adler, Philosopher, Author (1902) -
"**Freedom** is the emancipation from the **arbitrary rule** of other men"

Wayne Dyer, Author (1940) -
"**Freedom** means you are unobstructed in living your life as you choose. **Anything less is a form of slavery.**"

William Lloyd Garrison, Journalist, Abolitionist (1805) -
"**Liberty** for each, for all, and forever."
"There is much declamation about the sacredness of the compact which was formed between the free and slave states on the adoption of the Constitution. A sacred compact, forsooth! We pronounce it the most bloody and heaven-daring arrangement ever made by men for the continuance and protection of a system of the most atrocious villany ever exhibited on earth. Yes – we recognize the compact, but with feelings of shame and indignation; and it will be held in everlasting infamy by the friends of justice and humanity throughout the world. It was compact formed at the sacrifice of the bodies and souls of millions of our race, for the sake of achieving a political object — an unblushing and monstrous coalition to do evil that good might come. Such a compact was, in the nature of things and according to the **law of God**, null and void from the beginning. No body of men ever had the right to guarantee the holding of human beings in bondage. Who or what were the framers of our government, that they should dare confirm and authorize such high-handed villany – such a flagrant violation of all the precepts and injunctions of the gospel — such a savage war upon a sixth of our whole population? —They were men, like ourselves – as fallible, as sinful, as weak, as ourselves. By the infamous bargain which they made between themselves, they virtually dethroned the Most High God, and trampled beneath their feet their own solemn and heaven-attested Declaration, that all men are created equal, and endowed by their Creator with certain inalienable rights – among which are life, **liberty**, and the pursuit of happiness. They had no awful power to bind themselves, or their posterity, for one hour – for one moment – by such an unholy alliance. It was not valid then – it is not valid now."

Henry Clarke Wright, Abolitionist (1797) -
"I abjure allegiance to a constitution that sanctions slavery or war. It has *no authority* over me, and I shall embrace every opportunity to make it and the government that is based upon it, the scorn of mankind."
"Those who have the might have regarded the weak as lawful prey; they act as if might was right. It is an unnatural and unrighteous *principle*, and is the foundation of all tyranny and slavery. This is the basis of all individual and governmental oppression."

Anna Julia Cooper, Sociologist, Activist (1858) -
"The **cause of freedom** is not the cause of a race or a sect, a party or a class – it is the cause of humankind, the very **birthright** of humanity"

Deepak Chopra, Author, Doctor (1946) -
"I experience true freedom when I **accept, understand, and move on** from the conditioning of the past."

Stefan Molyneux, Philosopher, Author (1966) -
"The **only freedom** is freedom from **illusion**"

Epictetus, Former Slave, Philosopher (50 AD) -
"Is freedom anything else than the **right to live** as we wish? Nothing else."
"A free man is only master of what he can master without impediment. And the only thing we are entirely free to master without impediment is ourselves. Therefore, if you see a person wishing to control not himself but others, you know that he is not free: he has become a slave of his desire to dominate people."
"No man is free who is not master of himself"
"**Freedom is the name of virtue: Slavery, of vice.** None is a slave whose acts are free."

Rose Wilder Lane, Philosopher (1886) -
"Freedom is not a **permission** granted by any *Authority*.
Freedom is a fact. Whether or not this fact is known,
freedom is in the nature of every living person, as
gravitation is in the nature of this planet. Life is energy;
liberty is the individual control of human life-energy. It can
not be separated from life. Liberty is inalienable; as I can
not transfer my life to anyone else, I can not transfer my
liberty, my control of my life-energy, to anyone else."

Victoria Woodhull, Activist (1838) -
"That **the basis of order is freedom from bondage**; not,
indeed, of such 'order' as resigned in Warsaw, which grew
out of the bondage; but of such order as reigns in Heaven,
which grows out of that developed manhood and
womanhood in which each becomes **'a law unto himself.'**
That **freedom is a principle**, and that as such it may be
trusted to ultimate in harmonious social results. That the
evils, sufferings and disabilities of women, as well as of
men, are social still more than they are political, and that a
statement of woman's rights which ignores the rights of
self-ownership as the first of all rights is insufficient to
meet the demand, and is ceasing to enlist the enthusiasm
and even the common interest of the most intelligent portion
of the community. That the principle of freedom is one
principle, and not a collection of many different and
unrelated principles; that there is not at bottom one principle
of freedom of **conscience** as in Protestantism, and another
principle of freedom from slavery as in Abolitionism, another
of freedom of locomotion as in our dispensing in America
with the passport system of Europe, another of the freedom
of the press as in Great Britain and America, and still
another of social freedom at large; but that freedom is on
and indivisible; and that slavery is so also; that freedom and
bondage or restriction is the alternative and the issue, alike,

in every case; and that if freedom is good in one case it is good in all... the individual is either self-owned and self possessed or is not so self-possessed. If he be self-owned, he is so because he has an **inherent right** to self, which right cannot be delegated to any second person."

William Batchelder Greene, Abolitionist (1819) - "**Liberty** is the power which every human being ought to possess of acting according to the dictates of his own private **conscience**"

Thomas Hodgskin, Philosopher (1787) - "Wherever the right of **property** is placed on a proper foundation, slavery, with all its hateful consequences, is unknown:—wherever this foundation is rotten, freedom cannot exist, nor justice be administered."

Josiah Warren, Abolitionist (1798) - "Liberty defined and limited by others is slavery."

How Do We Exercise Freedom?
In a simpler way of understanding the exercise of rights and Equality in relation to freedom and slavery, **any voluntary interaction is a freedom-based interaction, and any involuntary interaction is a slavery-based interaction.** A voluntary action is that which is consensual, where nobody is being coerced against their will and choice, and therefore where individuals can operate with equal freedom among each other. An involuntary action is coercing someone in telling them what to do with their *Own* property, committing theft upon their right to choose how to live their *Own* life, otherwise known as the act of violating somebody's rights, or simply violence. If we are *forcing* an individual in telling them what to do with their *Own* life, we are making a *claim* upon the property of another as if it is our *Own*, and

therefore creating slavery. **Voluntaryism** is said to be the philosophical term based on this idea, though associated with *philosophical anarchism*. 19th century Abolitionists like Charles Lane recognized the importance in voluntary interaction, among many others, much like the reasons they did not participate in politics due to it's connection with violence. Individuals like him are titled as "voluntaryists," while the *New England Non-Resistant Society* founded by William Lloyd Garrison is said to be of "philosophical anarchism" and Lysander Spooner is said to be an "individualist anarchist." However, these individuals never explicitly used these titles themselves, they merely emphasized how society should be based on voluntary or non-violent action. In fact, they despised the media using the word "anarchist" at the time, as an attack against their Abolitionist ideals, since they never said we should *not* have any government or rules at all, they said that we owe allegiance *only* to the "government of god," or "natural law." These ideas continue to arise, especially heading into the 20th and 21st century, where the title of "anarchist" and "voluntaryist" become more established. Leo Tolstoy, who is known as "one of the greatest authors of all time" studied upon the 19th century Abolitionists after their time, even speaking with some of them, for which greatly influenced his Christian, non-resistant and anarchist positions. The works of 19th century Abolitionists Henry David Thoreau and Ralph Waldo Emerson would also emerge in sharing these positions. Mahatma Gandhi would then be raised on "Tolstoy's Farm" and learn about the value in nonviolent resistance or "civil disobedience" as a form of protest, to help India achieve independence. Eventually, it would also reach the liking of Martin Luther King Jr. Now, it reaches you. You have the freedom to choose what to do with this knowledge. The Abolitionists extensively taught others about this **moral suasion**, because if people are to act, they are to do as they see necessary in their *Own* life, given what they know. People can bring order to a world of chaos, simply by teaching the world what they *need* to know in order to act, rather than telling people that they need to act or in a certain way. In other words, we can give individuals the freedom to exercise their *Own* judgment, alongside the greater freedom of options at their disposal, much like how a holistic or supportive practitioner would go about in helping the health of their patients or clients. One may say that the Abolitionists exercised their freedom in merely being willing to question not just one institution and long-practice, but many.

Ayn Rand, Philosopher, Author (1905) -
"What is the basic, the essential, the crucial **principle** that differentiates freedom from slavery? It is the principle of **voluntary** action versus physical **coercion** or compulsion."

William Lloyd Garrison, Journalist, Abolitionist (1805) -
"**No** man shall ruler over me without my **consent**. I will rule over no man"
"We purpose, in a moral and spiritual sense, to assail iniquity in high places and in low places, to apply our **principles** to all existing evil, political, legal, and ecclesiastical **institutions**, and to hasten the time when the kingdoms of this world will have become the kingdom of our Lord Jesus Christ."

Henry Clarke Wright, Abolitionist (1797) -
"God has a government & Man has a government. These two are at perpetual War… Man is trying to subject his fellow man to himself… God gave to man dominion over all beasts & fowls & fish. But this does not satisfy. Man is not content to rule over the animal creation. He would get dominion over man. He tries all **arts** to obtain this end. I

regard all Human Governments as usurpations of God's power over Man."

"Politics has held such a ungovernable sway of the land for the last five or six years, that it seems to have well nigh absorbed the **moral and intellectual** faculties of the nation in its devouring element. **Principles** new and old are pushed forward on the stream of party influence, and are sacrificed at its shrine."

"We hope now that the elections are generally over, the public mind will again become settled, and that the great questions of **moral**, duties will again receive their due attention."

"Withdraw your mind from the abstraction that there is a tangible something called human government... a human being with the ignorance, the selfishness, the revenge, the prejudice, the avarice, the self-esteem, the approbativeness, the competitiveness, the destructiveness, and all the other lusts and passions of a human being. Look on this human being, invested with the war-making power, the right to declare war and to do all that is essential to conduct war, with a 'sovereign, irresistible, absolute, uncontrolled *authority* ' over the persons and lives of men; then arm that human being with the **brute force** of fifteen millions of men, and leave him to say, on his **responsibility** to God if you wish, when, how, and to what extent this force shall be used; then set him, thus clothed with powers and armed with deadly weapons, upon the watch-tower of the nation, to watch the approach of danger from within and without; to protect *our* property, liberty, and lives; to redress *our* wrongs,' suppress insurrections and repel invasion; 'to exercise an *absolute dominion* over our persons and lives; and you have a human government, as defined by the Constitution of the United States, and by the theory and practice of *all* human governments. It matters not whether the government consists of one, ten, a hundred, fifteen million, or a billion; it is a human being empowered and armed as above described. Could you be this being, this government? Could any man, professing to follow Him who forbade his followers to exercise *authority* and dominion over men, consent to becoming that being? But every man who consents to become a member of Congress or to become a part of the sovereign power of *any* human government does so to become the being that I have delineated. Every man who consents to become a part of any human government on earth and to be recognized as invested in the powers or rights claimed by all such governments is that human being or government described above. That human government *looks* far more comely and kindly, wears a far milder and more benign *attire*, and has far less of the eagle, the lion, the bear, the tiger, the alligator, and the rattlesnake (emblems by which human governments are, at this moment, proudly and not inappropriately represented) when viewed as an *abstraction* than when viewed as a being, I am aware. An idea, invested with the war power and with absolute dominion over the persons and lives of men, especially when arrayed in robes of royalty and decorated with titles of honor, is rather a magnificent and not an unpleasing object. Deadly weapons in the hands of a non-entity do not seem very formidable, palled, and with unbundled cheeks. But to see these weapons in the firm grasp of a man, or body of men; to know that that human being is invested with the war power, *the right of absolute dominion* over the persons and lives of men; and to see that being excited to wrath by supposed or real insults and injuries; to hear him declare war, and to see him paving his way with the bodies of men, crushing out their hearts, and bestriding the earth 'with garments rolled in blood;' this is another affair. From this, your soul shrinks with horror. Yet this is human government as it is. It is human government, as described in the

Constitution of the United States. - It is human government, as embodied in those men who compose Congress. Could you consent to be one of those men, a member of that body, or a part of that government? If not, can you elect another to that fearful station? Even to free the slave? The case would be different: could I enter Congress and have it understood that the gospel rather than the constitution was to be my directory; **my own conscience** rather than the conscience of the body political; the will of God rather than the will of the people? Could I be allowed to take **the will of God as my constitution**, the gospel as my code of laws, and my own conscience, illuminated from above, as my interpreter of duty as a public man or agent of the people? I should find no difficulty in consenting to become a member of Congress or in voting for others to do the same, but this I could not do... No man, therefore, who thinks war is wrong, can be a Congressman and not be faithless to his conscience and disloyal to his God. Nor can he consent to be considered a part of the sovereignty of any human government on earth, consistent with his allegiance to the **government of God**, for he must be invested with the power to make war if he does."

John Smith (from The Non-Resistant), Abolitionist -
"Our fathers were once under the direct government of God. He *alone* was their King. But the experiment failed."
"I owe allegiance to no one but the Prince of Peace. I belong to no worldly kingdom, or government, no more than my master did, who said his kingdom was not of this world: and I see plainly that those who profess to be disciples of Jesus Christ, and voluntarily uphold or receive support from civil, military or ecclesiastical governments, are traitors."
"My motto respecting human governments is, 'Let the dead bury their dead.'"

"If God has given to man the right of self-government, surely our non-resistance brethren have a right, and act safely and wisely in placing themselves under the **government of God**, acknowledging no allegiance to any rebellious, blood-stained human government."

"**The golden rule** this. Do as you would be done by. Rulers who act under the ordinance of Heaven dare not act by any other rule; and those who do act by any other rule, are worse than the Scribes and Pharisees of old, with all their hypocrisy, gospel rejection and bloodshed, and are commissioned by the devil. If judges, sheriffs and constables were to be governed by this rule of our Saviour, there would be a wonderful accession to those who are reproached as *no-government men*."

"The will of God can never be done on earth as in heaven, while a vestige of **brute government** continues to be exercised by man over man. There is but one law in heaven, and that is, **the law of love**."

"It is the spirit of retaliation, revenge, litigation, military honor, pride, ambition, that destroy the peace of society, and fill the nation with direful calamity. This is the spirit that is fed and fostered, and made fat by human governments. Whether a wicked world can be peaceable, or even tolerable, without human government, is not the question. At any rate, nation after nation, and century after century, have demonstrated the fact, that **there cannot be peace with human governments**."

"Our only weapon will be *TRUTH*."

"We do not present ourselves as reformers, or inventors of any new or improved system of government; nor do we give preference to any particular form, or advocate any man's 'party.'"

Samuel May, Abolitionist (1797) -
"Those rulers are not such as God approves, and we should respect, who aim merely to exact from their subjects a *blind obedience* to their own *authority*; instead of encouraging and assisting them to discern the things that are **right**, and to do them because they are right. Much less are those rulers ordained of God, who prescribe what they know to be not right, but only, as they think profitable or expedient for the time being, or accordant with an iniquitous compact,—and then set about to **compel** their subjects to obey such laws, however they may violate their **consciences**, and outrage their feelings. To compel any man to do wrong, is to compel him to set his own **moral** nature at naught, which is to do himself the greatest harm. If the subject consents to this, he sins—nay—he sets God at defiance; and chooses to serve Baal, or Moloch, or Mammon instead."

Percy Shelley, Author (1792) -
"Shake your chains to earth like dew, Which in sleep had fallen on you— Ye are many—they are few. 'What is Freedom?—ye can tell, That which slavery is, too well— For its very name has grown, To an echo of your own, Let a vast assembly be, And with great solemnity, Declare with measured words, that ye, Are, as God has made ye, free... 'Paper coin—that forgery, Of the title-deeds, which ye, Hold to something of the worth, Of the inheritance of Earth. 'Tis to be a slave in soul, And to hold no strong control, Over your own wills, but be, All that others make of ye... 'What art thou Freedom? O! could slaves, Answer from their living graves, This demand—tyrants would flee"

Thomas Paine, American Independence (1737) -
"It is to the great and fundamental **principles** of society and civilization — to the common usage *universally consented*

to, and *mutually and reciprocally maintained* — to the unceasing circulation of interest, which, passing through its million channels, invigorates the whole mass of civilized man — it is to these things, infinitely more than to anything which even the best instituted government can perform, that the safety and prosperity of the individual and of the whole depends."

Stefan Molyneux, Philosopher, Author (1966) -
"We can all understand that it would be completely irrational to say that slaves cannot be freed, because they lack initiative and education. We all perfectly understand that slaves are barred from **education**, and punished for taking initiative." *(The latter contributes to the former)*

Arthur Schopenhauer, Philosopher (1788) -
"That the Negroes were enslaved more than other races, and on a large scale, is evidently a result of their being, in contrast to other races, inferior in **intelligence** - which, however, does *not justify* such slavery"
"The *mind* is by its nature free, not a slave"
"While *illusion* distorts reality for a moment, error can reign for a millennia in abstractions, throw its iron yoke over whole peoples and stifle the noblest impulses of humanity; those it cannot *deceive* are left in chains by those it has, by its slaves."

Frederick Douglass, Former Slave, Abolitionist (1817) -
"We must get character for ourselves, as a people... With character, we shall be powerful. Nothing can **harm** us long when we get character... Industry, sobriety, honesty, combined with intelligence and a due **self-respect**, find them where you will, among black or white, must be looked up to ~ can never be looked down upon."
"Abolition of slavery had been the deepest desire and the

great labor of my life"

"To make a contented slave, you must make a **thoughtless** one. It is necessary to **darken his moral and mental** vision, and, as far as possible, to **annihilate his power of reason.** He must be able to detect no inconsistencies in slavery. The man that takes his earnings, must be able to convince him that he has a perfect **right** to do so. It must not depend upon mere force; the slave must **know no Higher Law than his master's will.** The whole relationship must not only demonstrate, to his mind, its **necessity**, but its **absolute rightfulness."**

"I expose slavery in this country, because **to expose it is to kill it.** Slavery is one of those monsters of **darkness** to whom the light of truth is death."

Josiah Warren, Abolitionist (1798) -
"Public influence is the *real government* of the world."

John Stuart Mill, Philosopher (1806) -
"It remains certain that slavery is incompatible with any high state of the arts of life, and any great efficiency of labor... hopeless **slavery effectually brutifies the intellect**."

Josephine (from Liberty newspaper, approx. 1881) -
"Contentment means stagnation. Contentment kept the savage a savage. Contentment made slaves of men. Contentment kept men in ignorance and poverty. Contentment of the many made rulers of the few... Ambition is a tool. Put in the hands of a few men, it makes all others slaves to them; put in the hands of all men, it gives plenty and happiness to all, and makes humanity constantly greater and grander."

Larken Rose, Philosopher, Author -
"If a slave can be convinced that he should be a slave, that his enslavement is both proper and legitimate, that he is the **rightful property** of his master and that he has an obligation to produce as much as possible for his master, then he does not need to be physically oppressed. In other words, **enslaving the mind** makes enslaving the body unnecessary. And that is exactly what the belief in 'authority' does: it teaches people that it is morally virtuous that they surrender their time, effort and **property**, as well as their freedom and control over their own lives, to a ruling class."

Isabel Paterson, Philosopher, Author (1886) -
"Before the Civil War, some of the Southern states passed laws making it **a crime to teach a slave to read or write.** Then the desire to learn, and the readiness to impart knowledge, are so spontaneous and universal that they can be restrained *only by legal penalties*, even when the social gulf is that between master and bondsman."

Mortimer Adler, Philosopher, Author (1902) -
"True freedom is impossible without a **mind** made free by **discipline**"

Abby Kelley Foster, Abolitionist (1811) -
"Our own **moral destruction** is consequent upon our leaving slavery to go on."
"All the great family of mankind are bound up in one bundle. When we aim a blow at our neighbor's rights our own are by the same blow destroyed. Can we look upon the **wrongs of millions** - can we see their flow of tears and grief and blood, and not feel our hearts drawn out in sympathy?"

Maria Weston Chapman, Abolitionist (1806) -
"We believe that it is practicable, by appeals to the **consciences**, hearts, and interests of the people, to awaken a public sentiment throughout the nation that will be opposed to the continuance of slavery."

Bryant McGill, Author, Activist (1969) -
"True freedom is where an **individual's thoughts and actions** are in alignment with that which is **true, correct**, and of honor – no matter the personal price"

William Sloane Coffin Jr., Activist (1924) -
"The one true freedom in life is to come to terms with death, and as early as possible, for death is an event that embraces all our lives. And the only way to have a good death is to lead a good life. The more we do **God's will**, the less unfinished business we leave behind when we die."

Lysander Spooner, Abolitionist, Lawyer (1808) -
"This science of justice, or **natural law**, is the only science that tells us what are, and what are not, each man's natural, inherent, inalienable, individual **rights**, as against any and all other men. And to say that any, or all, other men may rightfully compel him to obey any or all such other laws as they may see fit to make, is to say that he has no rights of his own, but is their subject, their **property**, and their slave."

In contrast to the Abolitionists who argued for the government of god in disregard to human governments whilst promoting an end to slavery, many pro-slavery advocates emphasized the need for human governments as necessary for the government of god. Pro-slavery advocates felt that the Abolitionists were encroaching on everything civilization stood upon. The pro-slavery advocate

Thornton Stringfellow *(1788)* states "What is Slavery in the United States? It is a system of personal servitude, under a form of government adopted for the African race, the leading principle of which belongs to every form of government among men. What is that leading principle? It is submission to, and control by the will of another. This is the essential principle of all forms of government; and without it there an be no government... What is government? And what is its origin? Government is control; it is the opposite of freedom, or a right to do as we please. It is power to compel obedience to the will of a superior. Where did it originate? It originated in the will of God... Government must begin in absolute despotism, instead of absolute freedom... The principle of subordination sought to be overthrown, is vital in church and state. The infidel principle of 'freedom and equality' sought to be established on its ruins, is unknown to the Bible, contradicted by all experience, and subversive of all government among men... One teaches 'freedom and equality;' the other teaches inequality and subordination. One leads to anarchy—the other to order. One leads to love—the other to hatred. One leads to war—the other to peace. Either liberty, or civilization, or both, must die when the world is subjected to the control of their leading principle of 'freedom and equality' among men. It is self destroying when adopted, and seeks to destroy all governments which do not recognize it." Arguments aside from god, government, economy and natural inequality, would also include the idea that we are slaves to many things within our lives, and that slavery is alike the family and business structure. Even on the *Wayback Machine Website Archive*, a modern website called "SlaveryAdvocate" as "the only pro-slavery website on the internet" collects anti-abolitionist literature, and it states as it's motto, "slavery, hierarchy, virtue" and that "absolute liberty is the death of morality." The website features hundreds of materials, even some modern sources, and it explains that "humanity has embraced a doctrine of freedom, individual autonomy, and the goal of mass emancipation from fixed hierarchy. We oppose these pursuits." This becomes even more apparent upon reading leading pro-slavery advocates such as George Fitzhugh, among others usually engaged in politics in the 19th century. We may use many sources to argue our points, but the question must be regardless, who is speaking the truth?

What Is Order And Chaos?
The opposite condition of order is chaos. Order is often associated with balance, harmony and following "the way" or "Li" as said in Taoism, or "*the* law" as said in Natural Law or Christianity. In other words, chaos may be seen as the misalignment or misapplication of truth. Often similar to the concept of "tyranny," chaos is the condition of which slavery and violence is systemic, since individuals are not able to live among each other peacefully and cordially. How could there be order, if two people refuse to cooperate with one another? If there is inequality or the lack of freedom, would the likelihood of rebellion and violence increase? If an individual is often not treated kindly, are they are likely to treat others kindly? The cycle of chaos can continue if we don't understand *why* people *feel the need* to act wrongly, but it can aggregate to even greater forms of chaos if we don't recognize the chaos to begin with. This makes chaos a potential teacher for *apophasis*, or *what not to do*, on a collective or societal level. Chaos is manifested evil, it is injustice as opposed to justice. By keeping ourselves in *order* or having **sovereignty**, we have freedom. What happens when we try to order the lives of *others*? If we correlate freedom with chaos, will we ever be free?

How Do We Prevent Slavery?

In preventing violence and chaos, historically people have applied the use of **self-defense** in order to retaliate against an active aggressor. It may be seen as the *final* ability to defend self-ownership, the defense of freedom. Throughout history, many tyrants and slave-masters kept populations and slaves disarmed or limited in ability, keeping arms and powerful weapons only for the few and chosen, as a means of preventing dissent and rebellion. Though methods have been disputed among 19th century Abolitionists, the different forms of self-defense may include martial arts or firearms, as done by slaves of the past in order to free themselves. Abolitionists would help free slaves by helping them run away, arming them directly, teaching them in what to do, appealing to slave-masters and doing trades, if not by directly partaking in the self-defense of the slave they are trying to free. Again, the actions of the slave in trying to free themselves *against their slavery*, might be used *against them* as a justification *for their slavery*. In any case, Frederick Douglas also encouraged that the slaves learn how to read and write, since a mind that is made free, will make physical slavery *impossible*. This also becomes apparent when you notice how the slaves *always* outnumber the slave-masters. These same dynamics take place with citizens and their government *authority*, affirming the statement that "knowledge is power." Many people, constantly in history, have felt a sense of being *stuck* under the *authority* of whoever is "in charge" and perhaps this is just one sign that an individual isn't *really* free or living in a voluntary world. Some may learn to live with their condition, but others will realize there is a whole world beyond that is *destined* for them. Why stifle our imagination, our freedom and creativity? **If the slave recognizes that they are indeed a slave, and that they are not meant to be a slave, then slavery is gone for good.** Douglas had a *moral obligation* to do what he *knew* was *right*, and it would be hard to erase such duty and revelation once known. A slave may even do *anything in their power* just to achieve the freedom and life they know rightfully belongs to them. If convinced otherwise, comfortable in their security, slavery can *feel* acceptable, not that it actually *is* acceptable or secure, or that it will *always* be and for others. To reiterate, you can help other's achieve their *Own* freedom, but *only you* can *truly* free yourself. If someone refuses to be free or never embraces their freedom, they will never *truly* be free. However, you can *voluntarily choose* to help defend other's freedom against those who seek to do violence against them. This is also said as "the self-defense principle." To choose not to commit violence, is known as "the non-aggression principle."

Frederick Douglass, Former Slave, Abolitionist (1817) - "**Knowledge** makes a man unfit to be a slave."

12 Years a Slave (2013 Movie) -
(Three slaves are in dialogue with one another) "If you want to survive do and say as little as possible, tell no one who you really are and tell no one you can read and write unless you want to be a dead negro" "I say we fight" "Crew is fairly small" "I believe they could be strong armed" "Three can't go against a whole crew, the rest here are Negros, born and bread slaves, Negros ain't got no stomach for a fight, not a damn one." "Survival is not about certain death, it's about keeping your head down." "**Well I don't want to survive, I want to live**"

J. Wm. Lloyd (from Liberty newspaper, approx. 1881) - "Brothers, do ye not see, That wise men will be free, But we are slaves? 'Tis **knowledge** that we need; Truth's voice we do not heed; With folly, fear, and greed, We dig our graves."

Huey Newton, Activist (1942) -
"Any **unarmed people** are slaves, or are subject to slavery at any given moment."

Zygmunt Bauman, Philosopher, Sociologist (1925) -
"**Security** without freedom means slavery."

The Liberator, Abolitionist Newspaper (1831) -
"**Knowledge** is power. A people generally enlightened cannot be enslaved."
"We will not lay down our arms until liberty is proclaimed throughout all the land, to all the inhabitants thereof."

Auberon Herbert, Philosopher (1838) -
"The only true use of **force** is for the destruction, the annihilation of itself, to rid the world of its own mischief-making existence. Even when used **defensively**, it still remains an evil, only to be tolerated in order to get rid of the greater evil. It is the one thing in the world to be bound down with chains, to be treated as a slave, and only as a slave, that must always act under command of something better and higher than itself."

John F. Kelly (from Liberty newspaper, approx. 1881) -
"The people can be freed only by **themselves**... and those who seek to **force** them to be free but doom themselves to disappointment" In the same edition, Victor Yarros tells us "To say that the people will never have liberty till they are worthy of it is tantamount to saying that they are doomed to eternal slavery, for in slavery they can never become self-free and self-wise enough to be worthy of liberty. If you want to elevate a slave, you must first set him free. **Liberty fits men for the proper fulfillment of the duties and functions which a liberty-conditioned life exacts from them**, while slavery kills in them every manly impulse and

makes cowards and sycophants of them." An integrative approach may thus be seen, in *moral suasion* for freedom, and freedom for *moral suasion*. He even tells us "physically we are all slaves, and our bodily chains can never be broken till we gain **spiritual** freedom. When a sufficient number of people have, like us, liberated their souls, slavery in *all* its forms will be abolished."

How Does Slavery Manifest?
As evident from studying the words of Frederick Douglas, other former-slaves and 19th century Abolitionists, as well as those who have followed them, *all* slavery is said to consist in mainly two forms, starting in the mind (internal), and ending with the physical reality (external).
From *Mental Slavery* → To *Physical Slavery*
Slavery additionally manifests when it is committed and condoned, the same way we may recognize wrong-doing turning into chaos, or a lesser chaos turning into a greater chaos.

As taught among Ancient teachings like Hermeticism with the **principle of mentalism**, the universe is mental as thoughts lead to the manifestation of things and events, they also create the quality of our experiences. The mental or "why" is the *plane of causation*, where *all power to affect change* lives with, and therefore we *must* be responsible for everything we create by *first* being responsible for everything we think. Additionally, the mind we have, or figurative heart and soul, is something nobody can take from us, but we may *attempt* to take away from ourselves. Many philosophies teach us to discipline the mind and learn of it's power for this reason. As an example, the Taoist practice of "fasting the heart" or "xin" (heart-*mind*) for "the uncarved block" is meant to help create freedom past societal conditioning and attachments.

What Is Mental Slavery And Physical Slavery?
The condition of unquestionable or self-induced servitude, not being able to reason and think for yourself, is known as **Mental Slavery** or *internal slavery*. It is the condition of mind control or *Menticide*, leading to and maintaining *Physical Slavery* or external slavery, and therefore it is the root cause to all "slavery," which then may also be referred to as *the most dangerous form*. Many slaves are trained into thinking they are meant to be slaves, as it would be unquestionable for them having a reality without it. Similarly, those who are pro-slavery convince themselves that slavery for others is a necessity, creating *cognitive dissonance* and embracing *inequality*. Therefore, Mental Slavery is where *freedom is feared* and *security-dependence* is embraced. It would be normal for the slave to have a lack of *responsibility* over their *Own* property, as it wasn't recognized and embraced as their *Own*, it instead belonged to their "master." Visible violence or *Physical Slavery* isn't necessary if the slave complies on their own and becomes convinced of their own slavery and *lack of need* in freedom. In other words, **the individual assumes their property, their life, their freedom, their ownership, their responsibility, simply is being a slave.**

The condition of visible violence-based compliance for servitude is known as **Physical Slavery** or external slavery. Whether the slave is a *mentally* a slave or not, violence will ensure that the slave becomes mentally enslaved through the *trauma of fear*. However, this *trauma and fear* does not need to occur or persist, and thus Physical Slavery *always* depends on *Mental Slavery*. Therefore, Physical Slavery is the outward expression and manifestation of *Mental Slavery*. Simply so, **the Abolitionists recognized that by empowering slaves both mentally and physically, but mainly mentally, they no longer can be a slave.**

Mahatma Gandhi, Indian Independence (1869) -
"Freedom and slavery are **mental** states"
"The moment the slave resolves that he will no longer be a slave, his fetters fall. He **frees himself** and **shows the way** to others."

Martin Luther King Jr, Activist, Author (1929) -
"As long as the **mind is enslaved**, the body can never be free. Psychological freedom and a firm sense of self-esteem is the most powerful weapon against the long night of **physical slavery**. No Lincolnian Emancipation Proclamation or Kennedyan or Johnsonian civil rights bill can totally bring this kind of freedom."
"With the ending of **physical slavery** after the Civil War, new devices were found to 'keep the Negro in his place.'... Where, in the days of slavery, social *license* and custom placed the unbridled power of the whip in the hands of overseers and masters, today... armies of officials are clothed in uniform, invested with *authority*, armed with the instruments of violence and death and conditioned to believe that they can intimidate, maim or kill... with the same recklessness that once motivated the slaveowner... the question is not whether we will be extremists, but what kind of extremists we will be. Will we be extremists for hate or for love?... The old order ends, no matter what Bastilles remain, when the enslaved, within themselves, bury the psychology of *servitude*... a painful reminder of the capacity of society to remain complacent in the midst of **injustice**... The **imposition** of inferiority, externally and internally, are the slave chains of today... every Negro knows a thousand examples in which law and government do not protect him... if people who are enslaved sit around and feel that freedom is some kind of lavish dish that will be passed out on a silver platter by the federal government... he will never get his freedom... whenever Pharaoh wanted to prolong the

period of slavery in Egypt, he had a favorite, favorite formula for doing it. What was that? He kept the slaves fighting among themselves... When the slaves get together, that's the beginning of getting out of slavery."

"They prefer to remain oppressed. When Moses led the children of Israel from the slavery of Egypt to the freedom of the Promised Land, he discovered that slaves do not always welcome their deliverers. They would rather bear those ills they have, as Shakespeare pointed out, than flee to others that they know not of. They prefer the 'fleshpots of Egypt' to the ordeals of emancipation. But this is not the way out. Softminded acquiescence is cowardly... Passively to accept an unjust system is to cooperate with that system, and thereby to become a participant in its evil... Slavery, racial segregation, war, and economic exploitation is testimony to the fact that the church has hearkened more to the *authority* of the world than to the authority of God... We so often ask, 'What will happen to my job, my prestige, or my status if I take a stand on this issue? Will my home be bombed, will my life be threatened, or will I be jailed?' The good man always reverses the question... **Slavery in America was perpetuated not merely by human badness but also by human blindness**... [based on the psychological indoctrination of slaves detailed by Kenneth Stampp in *The Peculiar Institution*] The way to produce a perfect slave. Accustom him to rigid discipline, demand from him **unconditional submission**, impress upon him a sense of his **innate inferiority**, develop in him a paralyzing **fear**... train him to adopt the **master's code of good behavior**, and instill in him a sense of complete **dependence**... He who lives with untruth lives in spiritual slavery... This degradation was sanctioned and protected by institutions of *government*... human beings cannot continue to do wrong without eventually reaching out for some rationalization to **clothe their acts** in the garments of righteousness. And so, with the growth of slavery... The haunting ambivalence, the **intellectual and moral** recognition that slavery is wrong, but the emotional tie to the system so deep and pervasive that it imposes an **inflexible unwillingness** to root it out"

Bob Marley, Rastafari Freedom, Musician (1945) -
"Emancipate yourself from **mental slavery**, none but ourselves can free our minds"

Marcus Aurelius, Philosopher (121 AD) -
"Stop allowing your **mind** to be a slave, to be jerked by selfish impulses, to kick against fate and the present, and to mistrust the future"

Robert A. Heinlein, Author (1907) -
"Mighty little force is needed to control a man whose **mind** has been *hoodwinked*; contrariwise, no amount of **force** can control a free man, a man whose mind is free. No, not the rack, not fission bombs, not anything – **you can't conquer a free man**; the most you can do is kill him."

Seneca, Philosopher (4 BC) -
"Slavery takes hold of few, but **many take hold of slavery.**"

Wade Horn, Psychologist-
"If we are going to abolish modern-day slavery, then we have to put the traffickers out of business. That's going to demand, unfortunately, the **cooperation of the victims.**"

Dresden James, Author (1931) -
"The ideal tyranny is that which is **ignorantly** self-administered by its victims. The most perfect slaves are, therefore, those which blissfully and **unawaredly enslave themselves.**"

Rudolph Steiner, Philosopher (1861) -
"Only when they enslave my *mind* and spirit and drive my own impulses to action from my head and want to replace them with theirs, do they then intend my *inner unfreedom*."
"Whoever wants to eradicate the pleasure of satisfying human desires must first make the human being into a slave who does not act because he wants to, but only because he *ought*."

Luc de Clapiers, Philosopher (1715) -
"*Servitude debases* men to the point where they end up liking it."

Clarence Lee Swartz, Philosopher (1868) -
"Habits of **unthinking obedience** may be trained in the individuals that will bring their social behavior close to slavery - a slavery in one sense *voluntary*, because the spirit of self-determination will have been crushed out or 'conditioned.'"

H.L. Mencken, Author (1880) -
"I believe that it is better to be free than to be not free, even when the former is dangerous and the latter safe. I believe that the finest qualities of man can flourish only in free air — that progress made under the shadow of the policeman's club is *false progress*, and of *no permanent value*. I believe that any man who takes the liberty of another into his keeping is bound to become a tyrant, and that **any man who yields up his liberty, in however slight the measure, is bound to become a slave.**"

Herbert Spencer, Psychologist, Polymath (1820) -
"If men use their liberty in such a way as to **surrender their liberty**, are they thereafter any the less slaves?"

"All the barbarisms of the past have their types in the present. All the barbarisms of the past grew out of certain dispositions: those dispositions may be weakened, but they are not extinct; and so long as they exist there must be manifestations of them. What we commonly understand by command and obedience, are the modern forms of bygone despotism and slavery... To whatever extent the will of the one is overborne by the will of the other, to that extent the parties are tyrant and slave."

John Stuart Mill, Philosopher (1806) -
"There have been, and may be again, great individual thinkers, in a general atmosphere of **mental slavery.**"
"By selling himself for a slave, he abdicates his liberty; he foregoes any future use of it, beyond that single act. He therefore defeats, in his own case, the very purpose which is the *justification* of allowing him to dispose of himself. He is no longer free; but is thenceforth in a position which has no longer the presumption in its favor, that would be afforded by his voluntarily remaining in it. **The principle of freedom cannot require that he should be free not to be free.**"

Johann Wolfgang von Goethe, Polymath (1749) -
"None are more hopelessly enslaved than those who falsely **believe** they are free."

Ezra Heywood, Abolitionist (1829) -
"Slavery is voluntary or involuntary; voluntary when one sells or yields his or her **own** person to the **irresponsible** will of another; involuntary when placed under the absolute power of another without one's own **consent**."
"For seventy years one-eightieth part of the American people ruled our States with the iron rod of **property** in man; that form of *political robbery* is now broken, but,

through *subtler methods*, slaveholders survive... the sad fact that 'the **contentment of slaves** renders objection to liberty possible,' makes it a more imperative duty to bestir ourselves to see *justice* done. Living in a world of petty details engenders narrow habits of *mind*, and the bounding aspirations of youth are killed out in the dull round of restricted life. 'It might have been' is written over the tomb of many buried hopes. To think slavery liberty and **dependence** an honor; to be satisfied 'with what we have rather than with what we want,' that is the calamity... Those who would send the fugitives back, tighten the laws and double the guards, are little aware of what a **moral** earthquake they are reading the riot act to. The old notion that slavery was the corner-stone of the republic was not more absurd and monstrous than the idea that woman's *legal suppression* is the corner-stone of the family. The question is not whether reform will disturb existing relations, but whether any system should continue if that system invades **essential right** and public interest."

Auberon Herbert, Philosopher (1838) -
"It must be borne in mind that the unfailing distinction between direct and indirect compulsion, as I have employed the words, is that in one case *(indirect compulsion)* the person in question gives his consent, in the other case *(direct compulsion)* his consent is not required from him. It is no answer to say that the weakness of men is such that their own consent is a mere form. Our effort in all cases must be to build up sufficient strength in the man so as to **make his consent a real thing.**"

Angelina Grimke, Abolitionist (1805) -
"The doctrine of **blind obedience** and unqualified **submission** to any human power, whether civil or ecclesiastical, is the doctrine of despotism"

Samuel Taylor Coleridge, Philosopher (1772) -
"Slaves by **their own compulsion!** In mad game, They burst their manacles and wear the name, Of Freedom, graven on a *heavier chain*."
"A willing slave is the *worst* of Slaves - His Soul is a Slave."

Lizzie M. Holmes, Philosopher (1850) -
"He *realized* that he was practically a slave, but he *felt* that his bondage was achieved through some hold his masters had over his **mind**. He felt a sort of dog like **attachment** to his masters and if for a moment he ever dreamed of deserting them a *feeling* of shame at his disloyalty came over him. He found that a *faith* dwelt somewhere in his bosom that he would go to a place of ineffable bliss when he died if he remained true to his masters and kept his honor with them. While these *feelings and beliefs* ruled his *mind* there was no need of bonds and shackles—his master always found him at hand and **eagerly obedient**."

Mary Wollstonecraft, Philosopher (1759) -
"Strengthen the female **mind** by enlarging it, and there will be an end to **blind obedience**; but, as blind obedience is ever sought for by power, tyrants and sensualists are in the right when they endeavour to keep women in the dark, because the former only want slaves, and the latter a play-thing. The sensualist, indeed, has been *the most dangerous* of tyrants, and women have been *duped* by their lovers, as princes by their ministers, whilst dreaming that they reigned over them."

Larken Rose, Philosopher, Author -
"Though slavery is no longer practiced openly, the **mentality** of loyal subservience **remains**."

Charles Lenox Remond, Abolitionist (1810) -
"When the world shall learn that '**mind** makes the man'- that goodness; **moral** worth, and integrity of soul, are the true tests of Character, then prejudice against caste and color, will cease to be."
"**I have only to speak for myself**; to speak for freedom for myself; to determine for freedom for myself; and in doing so, I speak and determine for the freedom of every slave on every plantation, and for the fugitives on my right hand."

Etienne de La Boetie, Philosopher (1530) -
"I am of the opinion that one should pity those who, at *birth*, arrive with the yoke upon their necks. We should exonerate and forgive them, since they have not seen even the shadow of liberty, and, being quite *unaware* of it, **cannot perceive** the evil endured through **their own slavery**."

Manly Palmer Hall, Author (1901) -
"It is demonstrated that to capture a man **it is not sufficient to enslave his body** – it is necessary to enlist his **reason**; that to free a man it is not enough to strike the shackles from his limbs—his **mind** must be liberated from bondage to **his own ignorance**."

Benjamin Tucker, Philosopher (1854) -
"No man can **make himself so much a slave** as to forfeit the right to issue **his own emancipation proclamation**."
"Slavery so dwarfs men **mentally** that they will patiently suffer under bonds because **ignorant of the blessings of freedom**."

William Godwin, Philosopher (1756) -
"If in any instance I am made the mechanical instrument of absolute violence, in that instance I fall under a pure state of **external slavery**. If on the other hand, not being under

the influence of absolute **compulsion**, I am wholly prompted by something that is frequently called by that name, and act from the hope of reward or the **fear** of punishment, the **subjection** I suffer is doubtless less aggravated, but the effect upon my **moral** habits may be in a still *higher degree injurious*."

"If there be any man who, in suffering punishment, is not conscious of injury, he must have had his **mind** previously debased by slavery, and his sense of **moral right** and wrong blunted by a series of oppressions."

"Having always been accustomed to the slaves of necessity or the slaves of choice, **he does not understand even the meaning of the word freedom.**"

What Is Fear And Trauma?

The condition of an individual who can not be aware or be in a position of courage and love, as these have been suppressed, is known as **Fear**. The individual in fear becomes vulnerable to those who take advantage of their lack of awareness and sense of self. In manifestation on an individual and collective basis, we may observe that from fear comes ignorance, then confusion, then control and *chaos*. In relation to fear, is the notion of trauma, for which fear itself may consist thereof. **Trauma** can be defined as an overwhelming experience that exceeds an individual's capacity to cope. It can be caused by a variety of events, including physical or emotional abuse, neglect, loss, or violence. Psychologist Gabor Mate argues that cultural trauma, such as colonization, war, discrimination, or socioeconomic inequalities, can permeate generations, shaping the collective psyche. Unresolved trauma can be transmitted from one generation to the next, leading to cycles of dysfunction, addiction, and violence. He calls for a shift from punitive approaches to addiction, crime, and mental illness to ones that emphasize understanding, support, and healing. It is often said that the escape from fear is courage or bravery, and the opposite of fear is love and care. This "shadow work" as Dr. Carl Jung calls it, is one that everybody goes through in some regards of their life. For a slave, we may imagine that work can be quite tough, which is why the 19th century Abolitionists, being outsiders, were able to share the burden in a sense for helping the slaves become free. Perhaps this, among making it hard for the media to attack them, is another reason why they emphasized their "law of love" and non-resistance to *never* add fuel to the fire of the already-existent violence. In studying psychology, it would be interesting to also observe the mind of the slave-owner, for which Larken Rose deeply details in his talk *The Nature Of The Beast,* identifying it as **toxic narcissism**. A slave owner doesn't truly *love* a human being that they consider less than human, or adequate for slavery, other than as a means for their own power and suppressing their own shadows or insecurities. The slave owner is in fear of losing their slave-control, remaining ignorant of their *Own* responsibilities and their slave's *Own* property. A slave may never know real love, as obedience to *authority* is the only virtue, the only reward. Notice the cruel hardships endured by slaves, the harsh punishments created by slave owners and the revolution attempts by slaves throughout history, which could all be detailed as their own works. It does not matter which slave was punished *more* than another, if slavery is *inherently wrong*. Slavery should not be committed or condoned at all, hence it is why the 19th century Abolitionists were called "immediatists" as opposed to "gradualists." They saw the lesser problem as still a problem, for within sight, was also the solution that does not need to be a problem *at all*. In other words, they saw better-conditioned slavery as still slavery, for within sight, was the solution of freedom that does not need to be slavery *at all*.

While *Mental Slavery* may be a more *covert* form of *overt* Physical Slavery, it *must* be addressed if it *always* leads to the condition of Physical Slavery. Similarly, While better-conditioned slavery may be a more covert form of overt violent slavery, it *must* be addressed if it *always* leads to the condition of violent slavery. Trauma resurfaces if it's unaddressed, our fears never faced will lead us nowhere, and power gets abused, as history is evident of examples. **Perhaps nobody is supposed to be in that position of power as "slave-master" or "slave" to begin with?** Asking this question was needed for too long, for it came at the expense of many millions of people. *All the death in the world just from one lie.* Dr. Carl Jung states that **Mass Psychosis**, or mass deception, is the greatest form of catastrophe in the world. What does this wisdom share with us in light of *Democide*, the top cause of death? The act contributes to the condition and vice versa, but any action *first* requires a *mindset*, or mental state, that permits it.

Carl Jung, Psychoanalyst (1875) -
"It is not famine, not earthquakes, not microbes, nor cancer, but man himself who is man's greatest danger to man, for the simple reason that there is no adequate protection against **psychic epidemics, which are infinitely more devastating than the worst of natural catastrophes.**"

Seneca, Philosopher (4 BC) -
"Show me a man who is not a slave… one is a slave to lust, another to greed, another to ambition, and all men are slaves to **fear**." It is important to note that slavery to things or emotions may be found in ourselves, since it may contribute to our external condition and our most-affecting forms of slavery. As Oscar Wilde states, "Pity he has, of course, for the poor, for those who are shut up in prisons, for the lowly, for the wretched; but he has far more pity for

the rich, for the hard hedonists, for those who waste their freedom in becoming *slaves to things*." In any case, the same dynamics of freedom and dependence, or lack of self-ownership and autonomy are at stake.

Jean-Jacques Rousseau, Philosopher (1712) -
"You care more for profit than for liberty, and you **fear** slavery far less than you do poverty."

Marcus Aurelius, Philosopher (121 AD) -
"Alexander and Caesar and Pompey. Compared with Diogenes, Heraclitus, Socrates? The philosophers knew the what, the why, the how. Their minds were their **own**. The others? Nothing but anxiety and enslavement"

Thomas Jefferson, American Independence (1743) -
"When the people **fear** the government, there is tyranny; when the government fears the people, there is liberty."

Mark Twain, Abolitionist, Author (1835) -
"**Courage** is resistance to **fear**, mastery of fear, not absence of fear."
"In many countries we have taken the savage's land from him, and made him our slave, and lashed him every day, and broken his pride, and made death his only friend, and overworked him till he dropped in his tracks; and this we do not **care** for, because *custom* has inured us to it... I knew the man had a right to kill his slave if he wanted to, and yet it seemed a pitiful thing and somehow wrong, though why wrong I was not deep enough to explain if I had been asked to do it. Nobody in the village *approved of that murder*, but of course no one said much about it."
"The **conscience**--the unerring monitor--can be trained to approve any wild thing you want it to approve if you begin its education early & stick to it."

"In my schoolboy days I had no aversion to slavery. I was not **aware** that there was anything wrong about it. No one arraigned it in my hearing; the local papers *said nothing against it*; the local pulpit taught us that *God approved it*"

Robert Anton Wilson, Psychologist (1932) -
"The **fear** of death is the beginning of slavery."

Butler Shaffer, Philosopher (1935) -
"Because we **fear** the **responsibility** for our actions, we have allowed ourselves to develop the **mentality of slaves.** Contrary to the stirring sentiments of the Declaration of Independence, we now pledge 'our Lives, our Fortunes and our sacred Honor' not to one another for our mutual protection, but to *the state*, whose actions *continue* to exploit, despoil, and destroy us."

Larken Rose, Philosopher, Author -
"Even slaves can exhibit a **dread of being freed.** This is because the life of a prisoner or a slave, though not likely fulfilling, is predictable, and imagining a new, drastically changed life, in a strange place, among strangers, with all of the related uncertainties- how will I eat? where will I live? what will it be like? Will I be safe? — *scares* almost everyone. So it is when most people contemplate human society without a ruling class. The concept is so foreign to everything they have ever known and ever thought about, and everything they were taught is *necessary and good*, that they hardly know how to begin to *imagine* it. Even our very language illustrates our **fear** of living in society as **free equals**, because such a state is defined as '**anarchy**'- a term also used to describe chaos and destruction. We have grown so accustomed to the **mental** cage which the myth of '*authority*' has formed around each of us that most of us are

terrified of the idea of life without that cage. We are literally **scared** of our own freedom."

Thomas Paine, American Independence (1737) - "**Reason** was considered as rebellion; and the slavery of **fear** had made men afraid to think."

William Godwin, Philosopher (1756) - "The most wretched of all slaveries is that which I **endure** alone; the whole weight of which falls upon my own shoulders, and in which I have no fellow-sufferer to share with me a particle of my burthen. Under this slavery the mind pusillanimously shrinks. I am left alone with my tyrant, and am utterly hopeless and forlorn."

Frederick Douglass, Former Slave, Abolitionist (1817) - "It is the duty of a master occasionally to whip a slave, to remind him of his master's *authority*. Such was his theory, and such his practice. Mr. Hopkins was even worse than Mr. Weeden. His chief boast was his ability to manage slaves. The peculiar feature of his *government* was that of whipping slaves in advance of deserving it. He always managed to have one or more of his slaves to whip every Monday morning. He did this to alarm their **fears**, and strike **terror** into those who escaped. His plan was to whip for the smallest offences, to prevent the commission of large ones. Mr. Hopkins could always find some excuse for whipping a slave. It would astonish one, unaccustomed to a slaveholding life, to see with what wonderful ease a slaveholder can find things, of which to make occasion to whip a slave. A mere look, word, or motion,—a mistake, accident, or want of power,—are all matters for which a slave may be whipped at any time. Does a slave look dissatisfied? It is said, he has the devil in him, and it must be whipped out. Does he speak loudly when spoken to by his master? Then he is getting high-minded, and should be taken down a button-hole lower. Does he forget to pull off his hat at the approach of a white person? Then he is wanting in reverence, and should be whipped for it. Does he ever venture to vindicate his conduct, when censured for it? Then he is guilty of impudence,—one of the greatest crimes of which a slave can be guilty. Does he ever venture to suggest a different mode of doing things from that pointed out by his master? He is indeed presumptuous, and getting above himself; and nothing less than a flogging will do for him. Does he, while ploughing, break a plough,—or, while hoeing, break a hoe? It is owing to his carelessness, and for it a slave must always be whipped... I will give Mr. Freeland the credit of being the best master I ever had, till I **became my own master**... For my part, I should prefer death to hopeless bondage."

Han Ryner, Stoic Philosopher (1861) -
"It is only through contempt for pain and **fear**, by contempt for *all* authority and **obedience** that I liberate my being."

How Do We Base Our Concepts Against Slavery?
When we posit the idea that there is such a concept of ownership, property or rights, and we ask of the basis or foundation for which these are understood, we are often looking for an objective, universal, timeless and unchanging source. That **source** is often said to be nature, in one way or another (god, universe, reality, honesty, truth, etc.), another word for birth. Without which, the concepts of freedom, equality and slavery become much harder to discuss and dispute. Additionally, if we did not have this foundation, everything would merely be based upon whims and opinions (illusion, unreality, dishonesty, lies, falsity, etc.), regardless of real-world consequences, such as the condition of *chaos* as opposed to order. If we want a *better*

world, one of *more-right*, it would help to know what *is right*, learning from our behavior overtime, in the same way we may learn from history so *not* to repeat it. Our projections of reality will not be perfect, and hence it is why we must realize they are indeed projections on reality. Therefore, we may strive to work with truth in attaining virtue accordingly, but we can't get *stuck* or involuntarily impose what we think is the truth upon others, for this *will* disrespect their conscience in also breaking the golden rule, as people *will* disagree and we even need their help. **At the basis of ending slavery or basic injustice anyways, is just learning how to leave people alone**, the mere question of what *not to do*, not what *to do*. The Taoist concept for wu-wei represents this non-action (effortless action), which allows "the way," truth or source to express itself.

Lao Tzu (Laozi), Philosopher (500 BC) -
"Do not conquer the world with **force**, for *force only causes resistance*. Thorns spring up when an army passes. Years of misery follow a great victory. Do only what needs to be done *without using violence*."
"Good leaders reach solutions, and then stop. They do not dare to rely on **force**."
"Water does not force its way"

Frederick Douglass, Former Slave, Abolitionist (1817) -
"**I prefer to be true to myself**, even at the hazard of incurring the ridicule of others, rather than to be false, and to incur *my own abhorrence*."

Maxim Gorky, Philosopher (1868) -
"**Lies are the religion of slaves** and bosses. Truth is the god of the free man."

Richard W. Wetherill, Author, Philosopher -
"The person who chooses to be **right** is free, and any other *so-called freedom* actually is a form of unsuspected slavery"
"No matter how successful he appears to be, the **wrong** thinker is a slave to his wrongness."

Elizabeth Cady Stanton, Abolitionist (1815) -
"Truth is the only **safe** ground to stand on."
"The most enlarged freedom of thought and action; a complete emancipation from all forms of bondage, of custom, dependence, superstition; from all the crippling influences of **fear**—is the solitude and personal **responsibility** of her own individual life... Who, I ask you, can take, dare take on himself the **rights**, the duties, the responsibilities of another human soul?"

How Does Someone Become A Slave?
Taking someone out of their natural or *source* condition, chaining and indoctrinating them, employing fear and trauma, will result in someone who we may deem as "disconnected from source," in need of a *"return to nature"* for they never had *themselves to themselves*. To reiterate, an individual becomes a slave *mentally or physically*. Either they are convinced to be a slave, *mentally*, or they are *violently complied* into being a slave, *physically*. **People have historically become slaves as the result of government wars or government jailing systems, and the children of slaves become automatic slaves**. In other words, *Physical Slavery* through captivity instills *Mental Slavery*, dependent upon the captive's mental fortitude, that then continues the *Physical Slavery*.

Etienne de La Boetie, Philosopher (1530) -
"Let us imagine some newborn individuals, neither acquainted with slavery nor desirous of liberty, ignorant indeed of the very words. If they were **permitted** to **choose** between being slaves and free men, to which would they give their vote? There can be no doubt that they would much prefer to be guided by **reason** itself than to be ordered about by the **whims** of a single man."
"All men, as long as they remain men, before **letting themselves become enslaved** must either be driven by **force** or led into it by **deception**; *conquered* by foreign armies, as were Sparta and Athens by the forces of Alexander or by political factions, as when at an earlier period the control of Athens had passed into the hands of Pisistrates. When they lose their liberty through deceit they are not so often betrayed by others as **misled by themselves**."
"Plays, farces, spectacles, gladiators, strange beasts, medals, pictures, and other such opiates, these were for ancient peoples the **bait toward slavery**, the price of their liberty, the instruments of tyranny. By these practices and enticements the ancient dictators so successfully lulled their subjects under the yoke, that the stupefied peoples, fascinated by the pastimes and vain pleasures flashed before their eyes, learned **subservience as naively**, but not so creditably, as little children learn to read by looking at bright picture books."
"They always fooled their victims so easily that while mocking them they enslaved them the more."

From Liberty newspaper (1881) -
"Glory is hers and high honor of those that oppress and enslave; Shelter she gives to the poor in the *sheltering* mouth of the grave."

William Godwin, Philosopher (1756) -
"Another idea which has suggested itself with regard to the removal of offenders from the community they have injured is that of reducing them to a state of slavery or hard labor... To the *safety* of the community it is unnecessary. As a means to the reformation of the offender it is inexpressibly illconceived. Man is an intellectual being. **There is no way to make him virtuous but in calling forth his intellectual powers. There is no way to make him virtuous but by making him independent.** He must study the **laws of nature**, and the necessary consequence of actions, not the arbitrary caprice of his superior. Do volt desire that I should work? Do not drive me to it with the whip; for, if, before, I thought it better to be idle, this will but increase my alienation. Persuade my understanding, and render it the subject of my choice. It can only be by the most deplorable **perversion of reason** that we can be induced to believe *any species of slavery*, from the slavery of the school boy to that of the most unfortunate Negro in our West India plantations, favourable to **virtue**."

Is Slavery Natural?
Slavery is not the reality or *natural, source* condition of the human captive. If it were, we would not be able to live without it, as nature and truth is much unavoidable. Slavery being natural is based upon *belief* or man-made whim, for the condition itself *is* man-made. Therefore, we may attempt to justify the man-made condition of slavery due to what other man-made conditions and beliefs we have, and in not recognizing what truth is possible *beyond* it (known in *Naturosophy* as the "appeal to denature"). Nobody is *born a slave* by nature, even if we *claim* they are, they don't start with chains on them, and they are given a mind and conscience of their *Own*. They *only* become a "slave" due to man-made imposition. As we understand basic morality,

equality and ownership, a right action doesn't violate the nature of another, and *the nature of people are to simply be people*, not cattle for *other people* who are just as much human as they are. The fact that chattel slavery was long *believed* as simply *the way* of life, with individuals even being born into a slave-family in order to become automatic slaves, this makes the practice *appear* legitimate. All that came with slavery may then be seen as "natural," as a result. From mass long-endured unpaid labor, to severe punishment, to prisoners of war, to obedience to *"authority,"* it was seen as necessary and natural for the growth of society, even if it was at the cost of others' freedoms or others' lives. Many writers and thinkers, though they may not have been mainstream during their time, were challenging such presumptions throughout history, leading up to the "enlightenment era" in the 18th and 19th century, with the invent of the printing press and the ability to further educate oneself and spread word. Abolitionist Josiah Warren was known to invent the first rotary press in the 1830s, though he didn't patent it and the business titled *Hoe and Company* made an identical product which would garner large sums of money and revolutionize printing. Incidentally, these eras are where we start to see frequent usage of "natural rights" and "natural law" typically used as a means for freedom or rebellion, in the name of nature and god or simply a higher *authority* than man. Josiah Warren's newspaper in 1833 was even titled *The Peaceful Revolutionist* known to be "the first anarchist paradoxical." The abolitionists standing on their principles, were considered "radical" for merely challenging the norm, and questioning if something considered natural and necessary, is in fact not natural or necessary *at all*. One might say *cognitive dissonance* and *controversy* could be expected, and therefore necessary and natural within itself. From a more personal point of view, we are working out the problems in our life, having to face them, in order to become stronger and move on. From the Taoist point of view, we are like water moving down a river, learning how to get past the hurdles in our way. From an enlightenment point of view, doing the "shadow work" can be painful and may involve hardship, though worth it in the end. **Humanity is evolving, we are collectively growing up, and we often find that we must.**

Etienne de La Boetie, Philosopher (1530) -
"It is fruitless to argue whether or not liberty is **natural**, since none can be held in slavery without being **wronged**, and in a world governed by a **nature**, which is reasonable, there is nothing so contrary as an **injustice**. Since **freedom is our natural state**, we are not only in **possession** of it but have the urge to **defend** it."
"If we led our lives according to the ways **intended by nature** and the **lessons taught by her**, we should be intuitively obedient to our **parents**; later we should adopt **reason** as our **guide** and become *slaves to nobody*."
"It is true that in the beginning men submit under constraint and by **force**; but those who come after them *obey without regret and perform willingly* what their predecessors had done because they had to. This is why men born under the yoke and then nourished and reared in slavery are *content*, without further effort, to live in their native circumstance, unaware of **any other state or right**, and considering as quite **natural the condition** into which they were born."

Alfred Marshall, Philosopher (1842) -
"Slavery was regarded by Aristotle as an **ordinance of nature**, and so probably was it by the slaves themselves in olden time."

Nelson Mandela, Philanthropist, Activist (1918) -
"Like slavery and apartheid, poverty is **not natural**. It is **man-made** and it can be overcome and eradicated by the **actions** of human beings"

Hannah Arendt, Philosopher (1906) -
"Slavery's crime against humanity did not begin when one people **defeated and enslaved its enemies** (though of course this was bad enough), but when slavery became an **institution** in which **some men were 'born' free and others slave**, when it was forgotten that it was man who had deprived his fellow-men of freedom, and when **the sanction for the crime was attributed to nature**."

From Liberty newspaper (1881) -
"When I was a boy, most people thought **slavery to be right.** Humanity is advancing continually... *Perfect freedom is not, yet.* The great mass of mankind are **mentally servile.** That degree of freedom enjoyed by any people is the outward manifestation of what exists in the brains of said people. Well, some few see a truth before the many. And, as Emerson says, the truth rests with the minority, and for a time with a minority of one."

Ralph Waldo Emerson, Abolitionist, Author (1803) -
"I conceive that thus to detach a man and make him feel that he is to owe all to himself, is the way to make him strong and rich; and here the optimist must find, if anywhere, the benefit of Slavery. We have many teachers; we are in this world for culture, to be instructed in realities, in the **laws of moral and intelligent nature**; and our **education** is not conducted by toys and luxuries, but by austere and rugged masters, by poverty, solitude, passions, War, Slavery; to know that Paradise is under the shadow of swords; that divine sentiments which are always soliciting

us are breathed into us from on high, and are an offset to a Universe of suffering and **crime**"

William Godwin, Philosopher (1756) -
"Men long inured to slavery, for example, undoubtedly have a less exquisite sense of its hatefulness; perhaps instances may be found where it is borne without a murmur. But this is by no means a proof that it is the fit and *genuine* state of the beings who suffer it. To such men we ought to say, 'You are satisfied with an oblivion of all that is eminent in man; but we will *awake* you. You are contented with **ignorance**; but we will **enlighten** you. **You are not brutes**: you are not stones. You sleep away existence in a miserable neglect of your most valuable privileges: but you are capable of exquisite delights; you are formed to glow with benevolence, to expatiate in the fields of knowledge, to thrill with disinterested transport, to enlarge your thoughts, so as to take in the wonders of the material universe, and the principles that bound and ascertain the general happiness.'"

Angelina Grimke, Abolitionist (1805) -
"Slavery always has, and always will produce insurrections wherever it exists, because **it is a violation of the natural order of things**"
"Slavery is an insurmountable barrier to the increase of **knowledge** in every community where it exists"
"Not placed under his *authority* as a subject, but by his side, on the same platform of **human rights, under the government of God only.**"

Herbert Spencer, Psychologist, Polymath (1820) -
"When he is under the impersonal coercion of **Nature**, we say that he is free; and when he is under the personal coercion of some one above him, we call him, according to the degree of his **dependence**, a slave, a serf, or a *vassal.*"

"It was once also universally supposed that slavery was a **natural** and quite legitimate **institution**—a condition into which some were born, and to which they **ought to submit** as to a **Divine ordination**; nay, indeed, **a great proportion of mankind hold this opinion still.**"

Stephen Symonds Foster, Abolitionist (1809) -
The *U.S government* is "a wicked and nefarious conspiracy against the **liberty** of more than two million of our countrymen." Northerners who supported the government were "the basest of slaves, the vilest of hypocrites and the most execrable of man-stealers, inasmuch as they voluntarily consent to be the watch-dogs of the plantation."

Jean-Jacques Rousseau, Philosopher (1712) -
"Just as to establish slavery it was necessary to do **violence to nature**, so it was necessary to **alter nature** to perpetuate such a **right**"
"If, then, there are slaves **by nature**, it is because there have been slaves contrary to nature. **The first slaves were made by force; their cowardice kept them in bondage.**"
"Slaves lose everything in their chains, even the *desire* of escaping from them: **they love their servitude**, as the comrades of Ulysses loved their brutish condition."

What we *believe* or *claim* may not be true, and this differentiates it from *knowledge*. In other words, the more knowledge we have, the less we may say it's just a "belief." It is belief that makes us say slavery is natural because "it's always existed," but it is knowledge that makes us say slavery is not natural because "nobody has ownership over other people." If one doesn't *know* their self-ownership, they won't say "no" where it is due in order to exercise it. Be*lief*, also said as "blind belief," can often be a *lie*. It is belief systems that are often associated with limited thought, contributing to the close-mindedness of individuals. Historically, beliefs have been held about religion, money, politics, sexuality, race and more. Similarly, a myth or *superstition* is a long held false belief. People will always hold beliefs, but the question is what they do with it, as we come to evaluate *voluntary* action and it's importance. To reiterate, every individual already has the freedom to live their life as they please. The slave master is only able to impose their will upon the willing slave as much as they please, because the slave was not able to say "no" or they have been kept from the *know to say "no."* If somebody is in a toxic, abusive or unhealthy relationship, would it be important to *learn* how to say "no"? If somebody is consuming a food or partaking in an act they *know* they should not do, would it be important to *learn* how to say "no"? The slave may beg their master for change, *believing* that they need permission to be free, but that merely reinforces their slavery, because *we know* freedom by definition, does not *require permission*. In this scenario, the slave does not have the *knowledge* that the situation they are in is *inherently immoral* and *cannot be changed*, it *must* be *abolished*. In other words, **to say "no" is no, you are either a slave or you are free, you either Own yourself or you don't.** Let us not mistake evil for good or giving people more rights than others, **slavery is not a way of life, slavery is a way of death.**

Mahatma Gandhi, Indian Independence (1869) -
"Nobody can hurt me without my **permission**"

What Are The Historic Origins Of Slavery? (as of 2024)
The following information is mainstream, and not a theory. Let us start with our understanding of **human history**. BC (Before Christ) and BCE (Before Common Era) are the same, counting down before the year "1." AD (Anno

Domini) and CE (Common Era) are the same, counting up after the year "1." BP (Before Present) counts before the year 1950 AD/CE. Humans supposedly first appeared on earth around 300,000 years ago in the Middle Paleolithic Stone Age, which was from 300,000 BP to 50,000 BP. The first and oldest formal government was known as the Sumerian Empire or Ancient Mesopotamia, first settled between around 4500-4000 BC. This is also when systemic slavery was officially first established. Slavery has historically been known as an "established institution," most often *claimed* to be *necessary* for the economy, morality and an overall productive world. **Is the foundation of slavery and government being together, a strange coincidence or is there an important connection we aren't seeing?** It is worth noting that Sumerian ancient religious texts reveal the figures Enlil and Enki talking about creating a slave-species with disputes between the two brothers. It also details how they went about purposefully weakening intellect or strength, in order to maintain a slave species that would make perfect workers who would not rebel, not too stupid and not too intelligent. This is controversially detailed in texts such as *Slave Species of God: The Story of Humankind from the Cradle of Humankind* by Michael Tellinger. However, if we do the math, it has been about 6000+ years since the first form of government and the invention of chattel slavery. It has been about 200 years since the Abolitionist movement for ending chattel slavery, and it has been about 300 years since the "founding fathers" of America challenged the "authority" of Monarchies (kings and queens). For about 294,000- years, human beings lived without any form of government or systemic slavery that we can account for. In Sumeria, the authority of "rulers" or "masters" was seen as legitimate as they had the supposed "divine right to rule" as a "priest class" above others who were not. **How does someone**

obtain the "right to rule" and does that fit how we view "rights" and voluntaryism or morality? From our own analysis of these concepts, nobody can be born into this world as a "master" or vested "authority" unless they are able to *convince* others *physically and mentally* that they are a special kind of human, as done in Sumeria. This "authority" isn't a right they are born with, it is a right that never can and never will exist, it is entirely of *belief*. There is little to no evidence to be found of systemic slavery occurring until the founding of the Sumerian Empire, as slavery was practiced in *every* ancient civilization known thereafter. **How can the "established institution" of chattel slavery be created without a system of mass violence in place that allows it? How can it be systemic without a system, especially as an unnatural condition?** These may be the questions that daunt us now. The oldest law codes of these ancient empires often convince their populous about the legitimacy of their system, the *need* for masters and slaves, proclaiming to be of "equity" and "truth" as it says in the *law code of Ur-Nammu*, or "to prevent the strong from oppressing the weak" as it says in the *law code of Hammurabi.* **How can these law codes claim to enforce good in the world, while they are actively partaking in evil? What if this type of deception is intentional?** You can look up any hierarchical chart of these ancient empires, and the structure is one and the same, kings and slaves, with the most freedom at the top, and the least freedom at the bottom. **Is having less freedom or more freedom, actually freedom?** A slave could feel grateful and content in what they are given, but that doesn't mean they are living the life they are meant to live, for what makes the "master" special? These same ancient empires would tell their slaves what their rights are and deciding upon their own whims, what their punishments are to be. To reiterate, they even had systems in place where the slave can work for their freedom, which would be granted to them by their master, known as *manumission* or *enfranchisement*. Let us remember, it did not matter what the slave-masters decided to title themselves, whether they were Priests or Kings, or Priest-Kings, or what they tried to *make sound* just and *make better*, as they were still engaging in the slavery of others. **Simply leaving other people alone is no option for the slave-master.**

From a historic view, people may correlate slavery with the growth in population, however this disregards our study on the nature of slavery, including why people are willing to put up with it despite knowing how immoral it is or how they wouldn't want it done to themself. When we are able to look at the amassed reasons —the disregard and lack of morality, the idea that *might makes right*, the focus on centralization and collectivism *(justifications and deceptions made to violate individual rights)*, the result of war or the monopoly on violence, the obedience to presumed and claimed *"authority"* or even the growth of mass agriculture and industry, our "detachment" from *source*, with all these reasons contributing to malnourishment, poverty and disease— we can come to understand why the slave felt powerless or needing to accept their condition, or why the master felt powerful and doing everything to keep their condition. Such imbalances keep crashing down, but quickly become imbalanced again since as 16th century writer Etienne de la Boetie says, "people tend to enslave themselves."

From Liberty newspaper (1881) -
"'You must not disturb my *authority*, because it was **ordained by God** that I should rule,' said the king. 'Slavery is a **divine institution**,' protested the Southern planter."

Larken Rose, Philosopher, Author -
"The notion that people, by virtue of their mere existence, are **entitled** to all sorts of things – things which come into being only as the result of human **knowledge** and effort – is delusional. The logical result of this supposedly loving and compassionate viewpoint is **violence** and slavery, because if one's 'need' entitles him to something, that means that it must be **forcibly** taken from anyone else who has it or can produce it, if he will not supply it **willingly**."

Thomas Clarkson, Abolitionist (1760) -
"Africa was a country divided into many kingdoms, which had different *governments and laws*. In many parts the princes were despotic. In others they had a limited rule. But in all of them, whatever the nature of the government was, **men were considered as goods and property**, and, as such, subject to plunder in the same manner as property in other countries. The persons in power there were naturally fond of our commodities; and to obtain them, (which could only be done by the sale of their countrymen) they waged **war** on one another, or even **ravaged their own country**, when they could find no pretence for quarrelling with their neighbours: in their courts of law many poor wretches, who were *innocent*, were condemned; and to obtain these commodities in greater abundance, thousands were kidnapped and torn from their families, and sent into slavery. Such transactions, he said, were recorded in *every history of Africa*"
"**That one set of men should be slaves to another.** This truth was as old as it was universal. It was recognized in *every history*, under **every government**"
"It was received in some of the islands with a declaration, 'that they possibly might, in some instances, endeavour to *improve the condition* of their slaves; but they should do this, *not with any view to the abolition* of the Slave Trade;

for they considered that trade as their *birth-right*, which could not be taken from them; and that we should *deceive ourselves* by supposing, that they would agree to such a measure.'"

"I never heard whether Mr. Fox, when he came into power, made any stipulations with His Majesty on the subject of the Slave Trade: but this I know, that he determined upon the abolition of it, if it were practicable, as the highest glory of his administration, and as the greatest earthly blessing which *it was in the power of the Government* to **bestow**; and that he took considerable pains to *convince* some of his colleagues in the cabinet of the propriety of the measure."

"For evil, when once **sanctioned by governments**, spreads in a tenfold degree... In no instance has this been verified more than in the case of the Slave Trade... While they acknowledged the necessity of removing one evil, they were terrified by the prospect of introducing another; and were, therefore, only able to relieve their feelings by, lamenting, in the bitterness of their hearts, that this traffic had ever been begun at all."

"Wallis, in his System of the Laws of Scotland, maintains, that 'neither men nor governments have a **right** to sell those of their own species. Men and their **liberty** are neither purchaseable nor saleable.' And, after arguing the case, he says, 'This is the *law of nature*, which is obligatory on all men, at all times, and in all places. — Would not any of us, who should be snatched by pirates from his native land, think himself cruelly abused, and at all times *entitled to be free*? Have not these unfortunate Africans, who meet with the same cruel fate, the same right? Are they not men as well as we? And have they not the same sensibility? Let us not, therefore, defend or support an usage, which is contrary to all the *laws of humanity*.'" *(This may relate to how people are traded as property by governments through birth certification and citizenship)*

Jeremey Locke, Author -
"Collectivism teaches that good things can come from compulsion. It teaches that people can be forced to accomplish things **'for their own good.'** It *pirates* the love people have for their neighbors and twists it into *authority's* demands. Slavery is the result. If an individual will not choose a thing, then it is not good for him. **Force** crushes the human spirit. **Choice enables life.**"
"As in every instance in history, the *pattern of tyranny* repeats itself by *reinventing lies* to hide **the same slavery**." **The Tytler cycle** represents this idea that "history repeats," however there are new inventions and ideas, including technology and the progression in our moral development to end *chattel slavery*. The perceived order takes place as the following: Faith, courage, liberty, abundance, selfishness, complacency, apathy, dependence, bondage, and back to faith. These are eight steps, four steps on each side, separated by *selfishness*, which may be seen as the bridge from good to evil. With a deep understanding of slavery, as by the victims realizing their freedom, selfishness does not need to manifest into complacency, since the master's claim over the slave will *not persist*. In other words, the slave will *not* allow selfishness in the slave master claiming *ownership* over them. If they did, but were transported to another plantation, we may say this cycle will repeat. This is due to the fact selfishness represents *entitlement* and self-absorption, whilst complacency represents a lack of personal *responsibility* and *conscience*. In ending the deadly cycle of slavery for good, the slave with their *knowledge* would say about their master, "what entitlement?" and *take control of their own life*.

Etienne de La Boetie, Philosopher (1530) -
"The fundamental political question is why do people obey a government. The answer is that they tend to **enslave**

themselves, to let themselves be governed by tyrants. Freedom from servitude comes not from violent action, but from the **refusal** to serve. Tyrants fall when the people withdraw their support."

Thomas Hodgskin, Philosopher (1787) -
"These **conquerors were the first legislators**. By an almost uninterrupted succession, the power of legislation has continued in the hands of their descendants *to the present day*. If other conquerors have on some occasions overcome them, it has only been to succeed to their places... 'Almost **all governments**,' Hume correctly observes, 'which exist at present, or of which there remains any record, have been **founded originally on usurpation or conquest**, or both.' 'The laws,' says a writer in the Quarterly Review, 'in relation to the inferior classes of society, were throughout *all* European governments, made by **the strong against the weak**, the natural consequence of **government founded on oppression**.' 'The first materials,' it is stated in the Edinburgh Review, 'of the laws of England, were little more than the schemes of avarice and aggrandizement, or the ebullitions of revenge. The text, though written often upon sand, was **written with the sword.** The practice, indeed, afforded an evil commentary, but the **law itself was the parent crime**.' And this law, founded on oppression, upheld by *force* and *fraud*, intended solely to preserve **ill-gotten power**, or ill-gotten wealth, to maintain the dominion of an aristocracy, and the supremacy of a **priesthood**, to perpetuate the slavery, ignorance, and poverty of the great body of the people, the political writers of our day, call on *all mankind to obey*, as the only means of social salvation. *Obedience to such law is the master-folly of mankind*; and this folly is inculcated with as much pertinacity by those who have apparently no interest in making men fools and slaves, as if their own bread, and

their own breath, hung on the doctrine... The great and important fact, which it is necessary to promulgate far and wide then is, that *all European legislation was originally founded on oppression*. But the oppressors and their descendants have never ceased to be in possession of the power of legislation... Seeing that *conquerors have always been the legislators*, and knowing that they have always endeavoured to preserve their own power, I cannot avoid concluding, that the law has always been made with a view to preserve, as much as possible, that appropriation of the soil, that **artificial right of property**, and that system of government... They were free themselves, but they reduced other men to slavery. **Being the masters, they were of course the legislators.** Their great object was, as far as that could be effected by legislation, to preserve their power over their slaves... That one great object of the law was, in the first instance, to *keep the slaves obedient* to their masters, and after they became emancipated, to keep them, as labourers, poor and **dependant**, is an admitted fact... Europe, in spite of the legislator, personal slavery has been *abolished*. The claim of some men to possess others as their property is now universally scouted. This great and beneficial change in the right of property has not been effected by the lawgiver, who has always endeavoured, and is now endeavouring, to keep the slave-descended labourer poor and dependant... The chief cause of alterations in its condition, is the increase of population leading to inventions in the arts, discoveries in science, and to the creation of new wealth... discoveries in science, and improvements in art, have wrought the greatest changes in our political condition... Though we may not be able to foresee the **moral** effects of the splendid mechanical inventions of modern times, yet we may be sure that they are the harbingers of a more extensive change in the moral condition of society, than was *ever* effected by political institutions... In those parts of the United States where slavery has been abolished, the negroes as they are called, are now as badly treated, as much domineered over,—their society is as much scorned as before they were emancipated... The *custom of obedience* was of course far more influential than the words of the lawgiver, and those who had declared they should be free, continued, under its influence, to *treat them like slaves*."

Wordsworth Donisthorpe, Philosopher (1847) -
"In the **dawn of civilisation**, we find the bulk of the people in a state of **absolute bondage**, and even those who supposed themselves to be the independent classes, subject to a most rigorous despotism."

Mark Twain, Abolitionist, Author (1835) -
"Slaves to its priests, and **through the priests to the king.** It was the best friend a king could have, and the most dependable... They *rob the natives* of their cattle under the *pretext* that all the cattle in the country belonged to the king whom they have tricked and assassinated. They issue 'regulations' requiring the incensed and harassed natives to work for the white settlers, and neglect their own affairs to do it. This is slavery"
"The blunting effects of slavery upon the slaveholder's *moral perceptions* are known and conceded the world over; and a priveleged class, an aristocracy, is but a band of slaveholders under another name."
"Nobody but a parcel of *usurping little monarchs and nobilities* who despise you; would feel defiled if you touched them; would shut the door in your face if you proposed to call; whom you slave for, fight for, die for, and are not ashamed of it, but proud; whose existence is a *perpetual* insult to you and you are **afraid** to *resent it*; who are mendicants supported by your alms, yet assume toward

you the airs of benefactor toward beggar; who address you in *the language of master to slave*, and are answered in the language of slave to master; who are *worshiped by you* with your mouth, while in your heart--if you have one--you despise yourselves for it. The first man was hypocrite and a coward, qualities which have not yet failed in his line; it is *the foundation upon which all civilizations have been built.*"

"Look at the tyranny of party-- at what is called party allegiance, **party loyalty-- a snare invented** by designing men for *selfish* purposes-- and which *turns voters into chattels, slaves*, rabbits; and all the while, their masters, and they themselves are *shouting rubbish about liberty*, independence, freedom of opinion, freedom of speech, honestly unconscious of the fantastic *contradiction*; and forgetting or ignoring that their fathers and the churches shouted the same blasphemies a generation earlier when they were closing their doors against the hunted slave, beating his handful of humane defenders with Bible-texts and billies, and pocketing the insults nad licking the shoes of his Southern master."

"There you have the just measure of that freedom of **conscience**, freedom of opinion, freedom of speech and action which we hear so much inflated foolishness about as being the precious possession of the republic. Whereas, in truth, the surest way for a man to make of himself a target for almost universal scorn, obloquy, slander, and insult is to stop twaddling about these priceless independencies and attempt to *exercise* one of them... I repeat that the new party-member who supposed himself independent will presently find that the party have somehow got a mortgage on his soul, and that within a year he will recognize the mortgage, **deliver up his liberty**, and actually believe he cannot retire from that party from any motive howsoever high and right in his own eyes without shame and dishonor. Is it possible for human wickedness to invent a doctrine

more infernal and poisonous than this? Is there imaginable
a baser servitude than it imposes? **What slave is so
degraded as the slave that is proud that he is a slave?**
What is the essential difference between a lifelong
democrat and any other kind of lifelong slave? Is it less
humiliating to dance to the lash of one master than
another?"

"The truth was, the nation as a body was in the world for
one object, and one only: to grovel before king and Church
and noble; *to slave for them*, sweat blood for them, starve
that they might be fed, work that they might play, drink
misery to the dregs that they might be happy, go naked that
they might wear silks and jewels, pay taxes that they might
be spared from paying them, be familiar all their lives with
the degrading language and postures of adulation that they
might walk in pride and think themselves the gods of this
world. And for all this, the thanks they got were cuffs and
contempt; and so poor-spirited were they that they took
even this sort of attention as an honor."

"Monarchies, aristocracies, and religions are all based upon
that *large defect* in your race — the individual's *distrust* of
his neighbor, and his desire, for *safety's or comfort's sake*,
to stand well in his neighbor's eye. These *institutions* will
always remain, and always flourish, and *always oppress
you, affront you, and degrade you*, because you will always
be and remain *slaves of minorities*. There was *never* a
country where the majority of the people were in their secret
hearts loyal to *any* of these institutions."

"The 'poor whites' of our South who were always despised
and frequently insulted by the slave-lords around them, and
who owed their base condition simply to the presence of
slavery in their midst, were yet pusillanimously ready to side
with the slave-lords in all political moves for the upholding
and perpetuating of slavery, and did also finally shoulder
their muskets and pour out their lives in an effort *to prevent*

*the destruction of that very institution which degraded
them."*
*(May include story quotes) Twain additionally details how
mankind is "the sole animal that robs, persecutes,
oppresses and kills members of his own tribe, the sole
animal that steals and enslaves the members of any tribe."*

Clarence Lee Swartz, Philosopher (1868) -
"From the simple effort of one individual to overcome and
rob another, there soon developed the attempt of one clan,
tribe, or group to **conquer** and subjugate another group,
thus not merely taking the occasional accumulation of
property of a person or persons, but also carrying off and
enslaving the persons themselves. From that first primitive
act of conquest and subjugation - that first act of 'governing'
as it is known today - came **what we now call the State.**
And through all the ages the State has retained the same
old characteristic: **it started in conquest, and that
characteristic still dominates**; it started, by plundering,
and that *(compulsory taxation)* continues to be one of its
chief activities."

Jean-Jacques Rousseau, Philosopher (1712) -
"The **origin of society and law**, which bound new fetters
on the poor, and gave new powers to the rich; which
irretrievably **destroyed natural liberty**, eternally fixed the
law of **property and inequality**, converted clever
usurpation into unalterable right, and, for the advantage of a
few ambitious individuals, subjected *all* mankind to
perpetual labour, slavery and wretchedness... till hardly a
corner of the world was left in which a man could escape
the yoke, and withdraw his head from beneath the sword
which he saw perpetually hanging over him by a thread...
Ambitious chiefs profited by these circumstances *[divisions]*
to perpetuate their offices in their own families: at the same

time the people, already used to **dependence, ease**, and the conveniences of life, and already incapable of breaking its fetters, **agreed to an increase of its slavery**, in order to secure its tranquillity. Thus magistrates, having become hereditary, contracted the habit of considering their offices as a family estate, and themselves as proprietors of the communities of which they were at first only the officers, of regarding **their fellow-citizens as their slaves**, and numbering them, like cattle, among their belongings, and of **calling themselves the equals of the gods and kings of kings**... Tyrants, the enemies of the very people it was their duty to make happy, maintained regular troops, apparently to withstand the foreigner, but *really to enslave their countrymen*... This first disorder gave rise to murmurs among the people; in order to suppress them, the number of troops had to be increased, and consequently the misery of the people also got worse."

Henry Clarke Wright, Abolitionist (1797) -
"Men, as a government over men, in the legitimate use of their governmental powers, have, trampled under foot the **moral government of God**. Shall I refer you to Sparta? Athens? Rome? To the Romish Hierarchy, with the Pope at its head, reputed God's earthly vicegerent? Look at the **history** of the British government; at the empire of Napoleon; see their treatment of their own subjects and of foreign nations; see human governments in their connection with the Africans and Aborigines of this continent."
"The following points have been established: 1. *All* human governments have been invested with the war-making power. 2. *All* human governments have considered war power essential to their existence. The proof of this is found in the theory and practice of *every* government that is or has been. If there be an exception, it is thine to present it for I never heard or read of one. The universal sentiment

and experience of mankind, from the day when Cain claimed and exercised this power over the life of his brother, to this hour, declare that *no human government can exist without it.*"

"Human government has made the earth a slaughter house of the human race for **six thousand years**."

"As there defined, Congressmen and the President are men invested, by the nation, with power to make war. Take away this power, and the offices cease to exist. The Constitution is all changed. The government is *abolished*... **A bullet is in every ballot**; and when the ballot is cast into the box, the bullet goes in with it... Slave-holders claim discretionary power over human liberty — warriors the same power over human life; and **without the war power, slavery could not exist**... Humanity, in the person of the slave, during the whole time of our national existence— defying God, hunting, hanging, buying and selling his image. The government has butchered over one million in war, *unaccused, and unconvicted of any crime*... May a man consent to be invested with power to do an evil, and swear to do it, *even for the purpose of abolishing that evil?* With power to lie, in order to abolish lying?... Of the eighteen millions in the United States, only two millions and a half are voters. These constitute the sovereignty or governing power of the nation, and hold absolute, uncontrolled, discretionary power over the **property, liberty** and lives of the rest. **Their will is law, and to it all must yield, or die**... I did feel as a child, and have always felt since, though of course I could not give expression to the feeling then as I can now, that I was competent to be a church, a priesthood, a government, an empire, in myself, and I never could see good reason why any created being should exercise *authority* over me. This feeling may be **natural** to all children. It was certainly deep and strong in me, and had it been **encouraged** and properly directed, I had been spared many bitter **mental conflicts** in after life... The great fault of this kingdom, and of *all governments, is, they govern the people to death.* They throw *obstacles* in the way of the improvement of the people. **To make criminals, and then punish them, is the real, practical result of all governments, even those called most civilized.** Nine-tenths of all the criminals of this kingdom are made so, more or less, by the influence of government... Let men think, speak and act *unregulated* by the arm of violence, and only guided by **social sympathy, by mutual interest, and by justice**, and wars would cease."

"It is as absurd and irrational to authorize a government to kill men, to prevent men from being enslaved; or to empower them to make war, to abolish slavery." *This speaks as to how governments cannot "abolish slavery" in the totality, since by it's nature, it is founded upon slavery.*

C.F. Volney, Abolitionist (1757) -
"From **ignorance** and cupidity, man has armed against man, family against family, tribe against tribe; and the earth is become a theatre of blood, of discord, and of rapine. By ignorance and cupidity, *a secret war*, fermenting in the bosom of **every state**, has separated citizen from citizen; and the same society has **divided itself** into oppressors and oppressed, into masters and slaves; by these, the heads of a nation, sometimes insolent and audacious, have **forged its chains within its own bowels**; and mercenary avarice has founded political despotism."

"The oppressors being less numerous than the oppressed it was necessary to **perfect the science of oppression**, in order to support this false equilibrium. *The art of governing became the art of subjecting the many to the few.*"

In a written dialogue by Volney about the coming "new age" between "people" and "civil governors" and "priests," the people challenge both groups, and among the

conversation, the priests ask "would you live without gods or kings?" The people respond saying "we would live without oppressors." The priests state "you must have mediators, intercessors." The people respond saying "Mediators with God and with the king! courtiers and priests, your services are too expensive: we will henceforth manage our own affairs." Both the priest and governor groups give up saying, "We are lost! The multitude are **enlightened**." The people answer them saying "You are safe; since we are enlightened we will commit no violence; **we only claim our rights.** We feel resentments, but we will forget them. We were slaves, we might command; but we only wish to be free, and **liberty is but justice.**"
"Every individual being absolute master of his own person, it follows that a **full and free consent is a condition indispensable to all contracts and all engagements.**" Volney additionally details how governments will look at the idea of freedom as needing to be co-opted in order to maintain their control. In speaking for what they would say, Volney states, "if all men are **equal**, where is our exclusive right to honors and to power? If all men are to be free, what becomes of our slaves, our vassals, our **property**? If all are equal in the civil state, where is our prerogative of birth, of inheritance? and what becomes of nobility? If they are all equal in the sight of God, what need of mediators?—where is the priesthood? Let us hasten, then, to destroy a germ so prolific, and so contagious. We must *employ all our cunning against this innovation.* We must *frighten the kings*, that they may join us in the cause. We must **divide the people** by national jealousies, and occupy them with commotions, **wars, and conquests.** They must be alarmed at the power of this free nation. Let us form a league against the common enemy, demolish that sacrilegious standard, *overturn that throne of rebellion*, and stifle in its birth the flame of revolution... True believers and loyal subjects! can

you suppose that truth has been first discovered to-day, and that hitherto you have been walking in error? that those men, more fortunate than you, have the sole privilege of wisdom? And you, rebel and misguided nation, perceive you not that your new leaders are misleading you? that they destroy the **principles** of your faith, and overturn the religion of your ancestors?... But, inaccessible to seduction as well as to **fear**, the free nation kept silence, and rising universally in arms." In concluding, Volney forms a unity among the free peoples with the "natural law" speaking as to the *universal morality and equality* we are to follow, beyond different systems of religion and state.

John Stuart Mill, Philosopher (1806) -
"Was there ever any domination which did *not* appear natural to those who possessed it? There was a time when the division of mankind into two classes, a small one of masters and a numerous one of slaves, appeared, *even to the most cultivated minds*, to be a **natural**, and the *only* natural, condition of the human race. No less an intellect, and one which contributed no less to the progress of human thought, than Aristotle, held this opinion without doubt or misgiving; and rested it on the same premises on which the same assertion in regard to the dominion of men over women is usually based, namely that there are different natures among mankind, *free natures, and slave natures*; that the Greeks were of a free nature, the barbarian races of Thracians and Asiatics of a slave nature. But why need I go back to Aristotle? Did not the slaveowners of the Southern United States maintain the same *doctrine*, with all the fanaticism with which men cling to the theories that justify their passions and legitimate their *personal interests*? Did they not call heaven and earth to witness that the dominion of the white man over the black is *natural*, that the black race is by nature **incapable of freedom**, and marked

out for slavery? Some even going so far as to say that the freedom of manual labourers is an *unnatural order* of things anywhere. Again, the theorists of absolute monarchy have always affirmed it to be *the only natural form of government*: issuing from the patriarchal, which was the primitive and spontaneous form of society, framed on the model of the paternal, which is anterior to society itself, and, as they contend, the most *natural authority* of all. Nay, for that matter, **the law of force** itself, to those who could not plead any other, has always seemed the most natural of all grounds for the exercise of *authority*."
"For the governors are as much the slaves of their organization and discipline, as the governed are of the governors."

John Wesley, Abolitionist (1703) -
"'The Commander of the vessel sent to acquaint the king, that he wanted a cargo of slaves. The king, promised to furnish him, and in order to it, set out, designing to surprize some town, and make all the people prisoners. Some time after, the king sent him word, he had not yet met with the desired success: Having attempted to break up two towns, but having been twice repulsed: But that he still hoped to procure the number of slaves. In this design he persisted, till he met his enemies in the field. A battle was fought, which lasted three days. And the engagement was so bloody, that four thousand five hundred men were slain upon the spot.' Such is the manner wherein the Negroes are procured!... It is alleged by the planters in excuse for these **unnatural**, these monstrous cruelties, that the greatest severity, the most cruel punishments, are absolutely necessary for the management of slaves, on account of those train of vices which slavery necessarily introduces. A late author remarks how shocking it is to think that those unhappy victims must from the nature of the

thing become dangerous and refractory, in proportion to the greatness and generosity of their minds." *(Wesley also details several examples of laws which actively backed the slave-trade or claims to tell slave-masters what they can or can not do; Wesley even mentions "if the most natural act of 'running away' from intolerable tyranny, deserves such relentless severity, what punishment have these law-makers to expect hereafter, on account* **of their own enormous offences?***")* Wesley shares quotes from judge Blackstone, showing us how there cannot be a right to or justification for slavery, as it is thought "1. Slavery is said to arise from **captivity in war**... Secondly, slavery may begin, by one man's selling himself to another... Third, that men may be **born slaves**, by being the children of slaves." "**Liberty** is the **right** of every human creature, as soon as he breathes the vital air. And **no human law can deprive him of that right**, which he derives from the **law of nature**... Let none serve you but by his own act and deed, by his own **voluntary choice.--Away with all whips, all chains, all compulsion!** Be gentle towards men. And see that you invariably do unto every one, as you would he should do unto you." Wesley goes on, like many other writers, to speak of how the "slaves" are like anybody else, whom deserve respect and to be simply treated as people. He defines slavery as the "execrable sum of all villainies."

Thomas Lediard, Writer, Surveyor (1685) -
"That Sir John Hawkins in his several voyages to the Canary Islands, understanding that negroes were a very good **commodity** in Hispaniola, (then settling by the Spaniards) and that they were easy to be had in great numbers on the coast of Guinea. Having opened his mind to his friends, he soon found adventurers for his undertaking; amongst whom were Sir Lionel Docket, Sir Thomas Lodge, and others: and having fitted out three

small vessels, manned only with 100 men, he departed from the coast of England in October 1562, and sailed first to Teneriffe, where he took in several refreshments; from thence to the coast of Guinea, where he got in possession, **partly by the sword, and by other means**, upwards of three hundred of the natives, besides several commodities which that country afforded: with this booty he set sail for the island of Hispaniola in the West-Indies; where he *disposed of his negroes*. Two years after, he went another voyage on the coast of Guinea; there he staid several days at the island Sabula, where every day they took some of the inhabitants; *burning and ravaging their towns*: when having compleated their number of negroes, they set sail for the West-Indies." *(The enormous cruelties also described by individuals like Thomas Phillips, Sir Hans Sloan, and others including John Wesley are excluded here, but needless to say, the practice of slavery was horrifying and yet almost entirely unquestioned for thousands of years)*

Francis Dashwood Tandy, Philosopher (1867) -
"The difficulty of being able to make use of a very large number of slaves in countries which were beginning to be relatively thickly settled, gradually led the victors to permit the **conquered people** to continue to occupy their lands, on condition that they *paid an annual tribute*. It was thus that the Romans spread their dominion over the ancient world and sowed the seeds of the Feudal System."

Edward Carpenter, Philosopher (1844) -
"Governments and Laws are Instituted with primary reference to its creation, *protection* and enjoyment. **It introduced human slavery** as an instrument in its production."
"The slavery thus outwardly appearing in society being the symbol of the **inward enslavement** of the man."

Thomas Paine, American Independence (1737) -
"Under how many subtilties or absurdities has the **divine right** to govern been imposed on the credulity of mankind?"
"It is by **distortedly exalting some men** that *others are distortedly debased*, till the whole is out of **nature.** A vast mass of mankind are degradedly thrown into the background of the human picture, to bring forward with greater glare **the puppet-show of state and aristocracy**... To reason with governments, as they have existed for ages, is to **argue with brutes.**"

John Gurney quoting Gerrard Winstanley (1609) -
"Man had been given dominion over the birds, beasts and fishes, but 'not one word was spoken in the beginning, that one branch of mankind should rule over another'. As 'human fleshe (that King of Beasts)' fell to delighting in the objects of the creation, *selfish* imagination took possession of the five senses and, along with covetousness, 'did set up one man to teach and rule over another': 'and thereby the Spirit was killed, and man was brought into bondage, and became *a greater slave to such of his owne kind*, then the Beasts of the field were to him'. The earth was then hedged into inclosures by teachers and rulers, 'and the others were made servants and slaves'; and what had first been made as a 'common Store-house for all' was now 'bought and sold, and kept in the hands of a few'. The great Creator was thus 'mightily dishonoured, as if he were a respecter of persons, delighting in the comfortable livelihood of some, and rejoicing in the miserable poverty and straights of others. *From the beginning it was not so.*' Covetousness had led people to accept **outward teachers and rulers** and to neglect the **Law of Righteousness in their hearts**"

Gustave de Molinari, Philosopher (1819) -
"The **conqueror** now became interested in protecting his sources of supply, and began to **devise systems** for the better exploitation of territories and of the populations which were enslaved. These systems are *the first Political States*"

Amos Bronson Alcott, Abolitionist, Philosopher (1799) -
"We take too much notice of states and masses, if we think them more mighty than individuals."

Wendell Phillips, Abolitionist (1811) -
"**Government began in tyranny and force**, began in the feudalism of the soldier and bigotry of the priest; and the ideas of justice and humanity have been fighting their way, like a thunderstorm, against the organized *selfishness* of human nature."
"**Every government is always growing corrupt**... By the necessity of his position, an apostate... An enemy of the people"

Auberon Herbert, Philosopher (1838) -
"Those who bid you use **force** are merely using language of the same kind as **every blood-stained ruler** has used in the past, the language of those who paid their troops by pillage, the language of the war-loving German general, who in old days looked down from the heights surrounding Paris, and whispered with a gentle sigh 'What a city to sack!' It is the language of those who through *all the past history of the world* have believed in *the right of conquering*, in **the right of making slaves**, who have set up *force as their god*, who have tried to do by the violent hand whatever smiled to **their own desires**, and who only brought *curses upon themselves*, and a deluge of blood and tears upon the world. Force--whatever forms it takes --can do nothing for you. It can redeem nothing; it can give you nothing that is

worth the having, *nothing that will endure*; it cannot even give you material prosperity. There is no salvation for you or for any living man to be won by the force that narrows rights, and always leaves men lower and more brutal in character than it found them. It is, and ever has been the *evil genius of our race*. It calls out the reckless, violent, cruel part of our nature, it *wastes precious human effort* in setting men to strive one against the other; it turns us into mere fighting animals; and ends, when men at last become sick of the *useless strife and universal confusion*."

Frederick Bastiat, Author, Philosopher (1801) -
"Actually, it is not strange that during the seventeenth and eighteenth centuries the human race was regarded as inert matter, ready to receive everything — form, face, energy, movement, life — from a great prince or a great legislator or a great genius. These centuries were nourished on the study of antiquity. And antiquity presents everywhere — in Egypt, Persia, Greece, Rome — the spectacle of a few men molding mankind **according to their whims**, thanks to the prestige of **force and of fraud**. But this does not prove that this situation is desirable. It proves only that since men and society are capable of improvement, it is naturally to be expected that error, **ignorance**, despotism, slavery, and **superstition** should be greatest towards the origins of **history**… They did not understand that **knowledge** appears and grows with the passage of time; and that in proportion to this growth of knowledge, might takes the side of **right**, and society regains **possession of itself**."

Lysander Spooner, Abolitionist, Lawyer (1808) -
"In 1787, 1788, and 1789, all the great governments of Europe, except England, claimed to exist by what was called "**Divine Right.**" That is, they claimed to have received *authority* from God Himself, to rule over their

people. And they taught, and a servile and corrupt *priesthood taught*, that it was a religious duty of the people to obey them. And they kept great standing armies, and hordes of pimps, spies, and ruffians, to keep the people in subjection... the Supreme Court of the United States virtually says that our constitution intended to give to our government the same 'sovereignty' — the same absolutism — the same supremacy over all the **natural rights** of the people — as was claimed and exercised by those 'Divine Right' governments of Europe, a hundred years ago."
*(It may be worth noting that the word "citizen" is often used interchangeably with "subject" which from The Online Etymology Dictionary, the early 14th century subget means "person under control or dominion of another" or "submissive, compliant, obedient," related to subjection meaning "servitude, bondage, captivity, inferior," subduing and subordination, subjeccioun, subiectus, subicere, subiicere, etc.; also from the late 14th century, subjecten, "make a person or nation subject to another by **force**")*

Joseph Dejacque, Abolitionist (1821) -
"If the sword of the soldier makes the multitude **physical slaves**, the catechism of the **priest**,—a weapon far more dangerous,—makes them **moral slaves.**"

Mikhail Bakunin, Philosopher (1814) -
"The natural and real process by which the first States in history were founded, without any intervention of legislators or divine prophets. The **brutal fact of brigandage, conquest**, and slavery, the material and real base of **all States, past and present**, has always preceded the idealization of this fact by some sort of religion and legislation. First the conqueror, the fortunate brigand, the hero of history, founds the new State; then, and often directly with him, come priests, prophets, and legislators at

the same time, who consecrate in the name of their God, and establish as legal foundations, the very consequences of this accomplished fact."

William Godwin, Philosopher (1756) -
"**War** has hitherto been found the inseparable ally of **political institution**. The earliest records of time are the annals of **conquerors** and heroes, a Bacchus, a Sesostris, a Semiramis and a Cyrus. These princes led millions of men under their standard, and ravaged innumerable provinces. A small number only of their forces ever returned to their native homes, the rest having perished by diseases, hardship and misery. The evils they inflicted, and the mortality introduced in the countries against which their expeditions were directed, were certainly not less severe than those which their countrymen suffered."
"If a prince sends forces into a nation where the people are poor and ignorant, he may *lawfully* put the half of them to death, and **make slaves** of the rest, in order to *civilize* and reduce them from their barbarous way of living."
"**The feudal spirit still survives** that reduced the great mass of mankind to the rank of slaves and cattle for the service of a few."

What Is A Bully?

When we speak of domination and slavery, something more relatable to everyday people in the modern world would be the concept of Bullies. A **Bully** is someone who dominates or pressures over another, with aggression often on a consistent basis as a means of *coercion* to get someone to do something. This is a concept related to that of peer pressure, and in the 21st century, it makes a common conversation regarding morals among the youth. It is taught so that the student can properly identify what *is* Bullying, so that they will know how to avoid and handle it. It is to prevent being bullied or being the bully themselves. Bullying involves an *abuse* and of *power*, whether it be of a *mental* or *physical* expression. It is important to remember that the dominator could be *more* luring if you are trained to see them *not* as a bully, or you are raised into the condition. Furthermore, we could identify bullies in one area of our life, but we may fail to identify bullies going by another name. **The slave-master is no different from a bully.** If you don't know who *is* the slave-master and what *is* slavery, you may be more likely to be enslaved. We must understand the *mental* lure used among all these dominators, seeing the *actions* for what they are, regardless of who they are or *claim* to be. It is the *action* that makes something slavery, abuse or bullying, for it is the *action* of giving away your self-ownership or violently imposing your will on another, that makes it so. Therefore, if it took *action* to create, we can equally take *action* to *abolish*. The most potent strategies against Bullies, is to walk away if possible or find a way to stand up to them. The goal is to be where a bully becomes someone who cannot bully you or anyone else, anymore. **Bullies don't need to be bullies and victims don't need to be victims, in the same way slave-masters don't need to be slave-masters and slaves don't need to be slaves.** All these people can heal, when the disease is not fed. When the Bully becomes *devalued* in this way, so to promote equality and compassion, they are not any more or less special than their victims to ever dominate over them again. In other words, since the dominator *depends* upon the victim, without the victim, they are deduced to *nothing*. To reiterate, the best way to prevent bullies, is to turn the *powerless victim* into an empowered individual who exercises their self-ownership, which may also mean utilizing *the principle of self-defense*. On a societal level, the people who do wrong are *almost always* outnumbered, and therefore they have little to no power when *many* who do *right* stand for what they know to be *right*. When treating bullying, the victim is *never* told to *just* ask for the Bully to be nicer, and it would be *absurd* for many of the victims to confront the Bully in demanding that they are simply Bullied *less*. As if Bullying was not already a projection of ego, this *(acknowledgment, permission)* only often makes the situation worse and points to more mental manipulation occurring. We can have compassion, but *not* if it's being used against us because we tolerate too much. Bullying, like slavery, is something we don't want in our lives *at all*, if we truly claim that we *Own* ourselves.

Bullying, being related to the concept of abuse, may help us understand how slavery acts as an unhealthy or toxic relationship. As an anonymous writer wrote for the *modern abolitionist The Liberator 2 News*, "**boundary-setting** is a vital skill that ensures healthy relationships with others. Without healthy boundaries, we can either have such rigid boundaries that we don't allow people to get close, or such non-existent boundaries that we give too much of ourselves to others. Without effective boundaries, unhealthy, or even toxic, relationships can develop leading to severely impacted mental health and well-being." He goes on to tell us that we often don't learn how to set our *Own* boundaries, then sharing the benefits thereof when we *do*, informing us that it is "linked to happier relationships with others, better self-esteem, reduced symptoms of mental health issues such as depression and anxiety, as well as a happier, more fulfilled life." He then warns us about how the systems of our world may be contributing to the problem. "School, religion and government *(intentionally or not)* were *(subtly or not)* giving us this toxic trait of being **afraid** of other peoples individuality and to drop all boundaries." That which helps us recognize these boundaries, he deems as *care* which then fulfills *truth*. We may similarly understand, that if a slave or slave-master *cares* about who they are versus who they are *not*, then they will fulfill the truth as to their **self-ownership**, which is why anonymous tells us "it can be attained by continuously learning and knowing who you are." As a main point of reference, he teaches us about boundaries to help us realize that we must apply them in *all* relationships within our life, so that we don't live with contradiction and create harm that otherwise could be prevented. "We as individuals have every right to set boundaries with every single relationship we have, and that includes government. Government is *not* god, no matter how much anyone *believes* that. We need to remind people that they have the ability to set boundaries. Ask them or yourself: Have you ever set a boundary with any relationship in your life? A parent, child, spouse, coworker, boss, relative, friend? What do you do if that person *violates* your boundaries? Do you no longer associate with them? How many chances do you give them? How long until you leave that relationship altogether? Even at your job, do you have boundaries that if violated, you would be willing to quit? Why is it not okay for your friends and family to violate your boundaries but it is okay for government to do it? The more people that we can get to understand this dynamic, the more we can wake people up to the reality that government *consistently violates* our boundaries." On why slavery is closely correlated with this concept, or why large populations would be enslaved, he shares with us the role of *trauma*. "Trauma has been used on us all large scale. Why? Because it scares people into dropping their boundaries. Why are we being scared into dropping our boundaries? So that we are easier to control. Perhaps the 'abuse of power' is really *just* power, which is abusive by it's nature. **The science of creating a slave - remove individuality and remove boundaries."**

A related danger of psychological obedience we may observe, is how slavery and tyrannical governments throughout history can become like an **addiction**. Nikola Pavkovic whom has wrote for the *modern abolitionist The Liberator 2 News*, tells us that slavery "makes victims of innocent people, and turns them into servants for an irrational power over their will. It grows larger over time, as the victim is *deceived* that they 'need' more to be happy or *secure*. As it grows, it becomes harder to stop, the victim creates ingrained patterns of behavior and *justifications* for their addiction, they will often fight like their life *depends* on it in order to satisfy the addiction. Most sinister, it makes the victim dependent, creating a **painful withdrawal** should the victim ever decide to escape, and feeding into delusions and *justifications* that the person 'needs' the addiction." This may be related to the concept of **Stockholm Syndrome**, or the condition in which hostages develop a psychological bond with their captors. In seeing this similar dynamic within governmental structures, Nikola tells us "just as 'the *right* of the people to keep and bear arms shall not be infringed,' so too 'I will only smoke once a day.' We have heard both lines before, shortly before it was proven false. *All* states hurt their population, even if they purport to *protect* them, so too are all addicts harmed by their addiction. Either *directly*, through physically harming the body of the victim, or *indirectly*, through destroying their well-being and prosperity, it is a harm. The longer the victim is addicted, the greater the damage, and the greater the withdrawal. And *all* states turn their victims into dependents. 'State welfare,' a vicious oxymoron like much of the state's vocabulary, creates the illusion of satisfaction, but in reality only tightens its grip on the victim, making them view the state not as a violent attacker, but a paternal provider. To some greater or lesser extent, the state makes everyone in its borders a 'beneficiary' of its works, and so convinces them that they 'need' the state. The smoker feels irritable, and so he smokes and feels better– not realizing he is irritable because he is a smoker. So too, 'citizens' are poor, and so when the state 'gifts' them goods such as shelter or police, they feel their needs are somehow alleviated, not realizing it is the state which destroys wealth and promotes poverty. This substance, *the state*, has fascinating properties and effects on the society which is its victim. At once, it is a stimulant, causing activity where there otherwise shouldn't be, like the rapid heartbeat of an economic boom and the seizure that is an economic bust. It is also a depressant, crushing activity and response where there otherwise would be, like the hampered breath of a centralized healthcare system, or the incontinence of a state environmental agency. As well, it is a hallucinogen, with the profound effect that the subject imagines a heartbeat of 300 beats per minute and gasping breaths to be a normal state of affairs, no matter how it harms or hampers them." In facing our withdrawal, he concludes that "for a time, those who depended on the state for healthcare will go without healthcare. For a time, those who depended on the state for protection will go unprotected. But a free society will reassert itself in good health, if given time to heal. As said previously, **the longer the addiction goes on, the more painful the withdrawal is, as dependence has grown.** Therefore, for the good of our society, the best course of action is that we release ourselves from this addiction *immediately*, and heal as soon as possible."

Aristotle, Philosopher (384 BC) -
"The **worst** thing about slavery is that the slaves eventually get to like it."

Larken Rose, Philosopher, Author -
"It should be stressed that 'authority' is *always* in the eye of the beholder. If the one being controlled believes that the one controlling him has the **right** to do so, then the one being controlled sees the controller as 'authority.' If the one being controlled does not perceive the control to be legitimate, then the controller is not viewed as 'authority' but is seen simply as a **bully** or a thug."
(Story-Book) "Someone who acts like a slave will be treated like a slave. Someone who acts like a bulldog, well, the best a tyrant can do is kill him. Ayn Rand called it **'the sanction of the victim.'** If you give the impression to your oppressor that you accept, or even approve of, his oppression of you, things *will only get worse*. Whatever else happens, never tell someone that you accept that he has the **right** to rule you. Never. You will make him into a monster, and you will **make yourself into a slave**."

Gustav Landauer, Philosopher (1870) -
"The worker is not a free man entering the market of life and exchanging goods, but that he is a slave whose subsistence must be **granted by his master** and *guaranteed by society*."
"Some enslave, and others take away the most basic necessities or leave only the barest necessity, or serve the enslaving lords as agents and supervisers. **Not from the spirit of revenge, anger or destructiveness will the new be created.**"

Jeremey Locke, Author -
"For all who wish to feed the poor of the world, there is only one solution. *End authority.* **Freedom** solves the world's ills. The reason the earth has widespread poverty is simply because people are not free to pursue prosperity. **A free people are a prosperous people.**"

What Should We Teach Our Children?

The world that awaits the current world, relies on our children. Do we teach them about *bullying, addiction, trauma* or *boundary-setting*? Do we teach them how to think for themselves, practice *self-ownership* or have **self-reliance** as taught by Abolitionist Ralph Waldo Emerson? Do we remain of our authentic self or "uncarved block," as taught by many ancient traditions, including the non-conformist Ancient Chinese philosopher Zhuangzi, what scholar Burton Watson deems as for "the spiritual elite"? It may even be that if parents are to teach their children, they need to *teach themselves first*. Additionally, if parents want the best for them, to help them through their growth and decision-making, then parents will likely uphold what they see as most important for the child to *know*, including the exercise of *self-ownership*. Without self-ownership, will *you* ever be *you*? If the child does not learn to be *responsible* over-time, we may say that they will never become an "adult" or learn to use their *Own* mind, thus they will be taken advantage of by others. To have healthy relationships, to love oneself but also to love others in respecting who they are among you, what could be more important? Many people may *want* truth, equality, love, justice, order and freedom, but how many actually teach it or practice it? Perhaps the greater question is, do we actually know it? This is why we can inquire upon the *opposite* condition, thereof slavery. Perhaps we should want our children to know how to recognize evil and not partake in it's growth in any fashion. To live with and practice principles, without contradiction. To see *why* chattel slavery was *abolished* in the 19th century. In other words, if people *truly care* for their children, they want them to make the right actions in life, to achieve a happy and healthy condition, *not* the wrong actions in life that lead to a slavish condition. It's the difference between what we say "everybody deserves" as opposed to what we say "nobody deserves." Therefore, the parental figure is responsible for the ones they bring into this world, until they can be responsible for themselves. Perhaps even later in time, those children will become responsible for their parents, if they are in need of help. However, in each case, the *responsibility* of the individual shall be encouraged, for how could you live the life of another? We can only *help guide* each other, but we foremost can only help guide ourselves, especially if we want to *continue* to help guide others. There is wisdom throughout history we may find in every culture, that families pass down from generation to generation, to do the hard-staking mental work, the trial and error, the hardships of labor, for the continual preservation of their family and for those after their time to *not* have to experience what they experienced, and in preventing *traumatic* or *chaotic* history that does not *need* to repeat. Examples of this wisdom may be to "do no harm, but take no harm." "Do not tread on me, but do not tread on anyone." "Don't put people on pedestals." We may see these as simple principles to live by, despite how sometimes there may have been hardship involved in reaching such conclusions. In the condition of slavery, the relationship is authoritative and *not* supportive, and there are no *self-ownership* principles. The only time it *is* supportive, is to *maintain the authoritative*, and the only time there are "self-ownership" principles, is for the slave to still be at the behest of the master. It's worth noting that the dominator may cave into the desires of the victim, including their lack of a mother-like or father-like figure, as Dr. Carl Jung notes, in order to increase the victim's dependence. Should truth be twisted into something we think is truth, but it's not? Should we teach morality or authority? Can you *Own* yourself but still be under the ownership of others? If we try to do both, there inevitably will come a time of contradiction, and we then may *feel* the need to complicate morality through complex systems in order to *attempt* to embrace it but never face it. Observe the complex legal and slavery codes throughout history, in how the arbitrary rules often become more and more complex overtime because they are not simple truths based in nature, they are humans confused and trying to justify and adapt to their confusion. Was it fair for slavery to be considered right, having very many people suffer, for the next moment, it being considered wrong? Chaos can be expected in a child who knows no principles, or who lives with contradictions, and the same goes for the world.

Carl Jung, Psychoanalyst (1875) -
"All mass movements, as one might expect, slip with the greatest ease down an inclined plane represented by large numbers. Where the many are, there is *security*; what the many believe must of course be true; what the many want must be worth striving for, and necessary, and therefore good. In the clamor of the many, there lies the power to snatch wish-fulfillments by **force**; sweetest of all, however, is that gentle and painless slipping back into the kingdom of childhood, into the paradise of parental care, into happy-go-luckiness and **irresponsibility**. All the thinking and looking after are done from the top; to all questions there is an answer; and for all needs, the necessary provision is made. The infantile dream state of the mass man is so unrealistic that **he never thinks to ask who is paying for this paradise.** The balancing of accounts is left to a higher political or social *authority*, which welcomes the task, for its power is thereby increased; and the more power it has, the weaker and more helpless the individual becomes. Wherever social conditions of this type develop on a large scale the road to tyranny lies open and the freedom of the individual turns into **spiritual and physical slavery.**"

Lysander Spooner, Abolitionist, Lawyer (1808) -
"Children learn the **fundamental principles of natural law**
at a very early age. Thus they very early understand that
one child must not, without just cause, strike, or otherwise
hurt, another; that one child must not assume any **arbitrary
control or domination** over another; that one child must
not, either by **force, deceit**, or stealth, obtain possession of
anything that belongs to another; that if one child commits
any of these wrongs against another, it is not only the right
of the injured child to resist, and, if 'need be, punish the
wrongdoer, and compel him to make reparation, but that it
is also the **right**, and the **moral duty**, of all other children,
and all other persons, to assist the injured party in
defending his rights, and redressing his wrongs. These are
fundamental principles of natural law, which govern *the
most important transactions* of man with man. Yet children
learn them earlier than they learn that three and three are
six, or five and five ten. Their childish plays, even, could not
be carried on without a constant regard to them; and it is
equally *impossible* for persons of any age to live together in
peace on any other conditions."

Larken Rose, Philosopher, Author -
"Children learn by example. If a child sees his parents
always acting as *unquestioning subjects* of a ruling class,
the child will **learn to be a slave.** If, instead, the parents
demonstrate in their daily lives how to use and to follow
one's *own* heart and mind, the child will learn to do likewise.
The child must understand that it is his duty, not merely to
follow the rules of being a good person, but to figure out for
himself what *the rules* of being a good person are. The
standards which a 'self-owner' lives by may still be
described as 'rules,' but the worth of such 'rules' does not
come from the fact that an 'authority' issued them, but
because the individual believes that such 'rules' describe

inherently moral behavior. This is not to say that everyone agrees upon what is **moral**, though there is wide consensus on some basic **principles.** But even with each person's behavior guided by his own imperfect, incomplete understanding of right and wrong, the overall results would be drastically improved compared to the authoritarian alternative, in which basically good people do things they know to be **wrong**, because they feel **compelled** to do whatever 'authority' tells them to do."

Josiah Warren, Abolitionist (1798) -
"Children are **principally** the creatures of example. Whatever surrounding adults will do, they will do."
"Where parents are obliged to bear the consequences of the child's acts, the parent must have deciding power. But in things in which the child can alone assume the cost of his acts, he may safely be intrusted to the **natural government** of consequences."

What Does It Mean To Be A Leader?
Similar to that of a parental figure, may be someone who guides and inspires another to be a better person, that we may simply call a **leader**. We may observe many individuals fulfilling this role, such as a doctor, teacher, boss or coach. People are willing to follow them, perhaps seeing them as a source of wisdom or inspiration which we deem as *leadership skills*, therefore *voluntarily* following their insights. When people don't *want* to follow them, they may *choose* another leadership figure in their life, if they don't also *choose* to partake in the desired roles themself. Freedom and self-ownership is being exercised here since the whole relationship is *voluntary*, even if an individual is willingly having others be responsible for them. Whereas, if an individual were to tell *other* individuals that they *must* use a certain leadership figure, by the threat of *violence*,

then it would *not* be *voluntary*, they would be creating an "authority." Even if this was a whole group of individuals forcing one individual in what to do, or even if they gave a whole list of options which they have *no choice but to choose from*, the scenario would *still* be *involuntary*. Even children wouldn't want to be *violently coerced* by their own parents, because if they were in a happy and healthy relationship, they'd *voluntarily* follow. Similarly, animals in nature want to have autonomy over their *Own* lives, which is why they try to escape when captured. If however, a child or animal was raised in captivity, *only knowing* or *conditioning* to what we would consider to be an *abusive* or *unhealthy relationship*, their lack of autonomy would be more likely accepted. Though, with total dependence as such, the victim would have a difficult time or not be able to survive when they become *abandoned*. Additionally, outsiders of that relationship, who will be the ones that *know* if it's unhealthy, may engage in *leadership* to try to help the victim, in helping them in their necessary escapes. If we look at an example in the case of World War 2, if the outsider sees the action of bringing others to a gulag or concentration camp as *wrong*, they could defend or help the victims. However, the main reason why that action was committed by *order-followers*, was because they perceived their "authority" or *order-giver* as legitimate in disregard to morality or what they would do on their own. If outsiders also perceived that "authority" as legitimate, they would not engage in their *leadership skills* to disrupt these order-followers and help their victims, they would instead *become* the *order-followers*. This is why an outsider may focus on changing or attacking the *order-giver* or *slave-master*, although these aren't the *many* followers who are *actually* taking the *action* and the "authority" is *dependent* on *them*. In other words, the outsider may *not* want to look at the possibility of *themselves* being *the problem*, because the *"authority," their order-followers* or *slavery advocates* are actually among *them*. We are all human, and the identities we give ourselves make us *no different*. You can't end slavery by changing the master or the master's identity or placing the slaves on a "new" or "better" plantation, if slavery is *wrong to begin with*. Thus, the position of "authority" must be challenged to begin with, *not* what is done *with* that "authority." Order-followers don't question "authority" because **order-following**, by definition, means suppressing your own exercise of self-ownership or your own conscience and decision making, because you are simply "doing what you are told" from a perceived "authority." If you are *always* thinking for yourself and upholding what you *know* to be right, you are *not* an order-follower. Does thinking for yourself make you a leader? It is no coincidence that new and emerging leaders or products, are those who challenge the current *status quo*, because that is the nature of leadership and innovation. However, by merely leading yourself, you challenge societal norms and conditions *naturally*. Thus, *leaders can be leaders without intending to be*. When we consider leading others, knowing about the nature of slavery, we can't stop leading ourselves even if we get *voluntary help*, but we *must know* our own *boundaries* in *not* violently imposing our will on *anybody*.

In other words, **it takes leadership of everyday people not claiming to be "authority" in order to dismantle "authority" and leadership is not "authority."** It takes *Abolitionist* leaders to abolish slavery with the help of everyone else who is merely a fellow *Abolitionist*; the morality remains the same among all the *Abolitionists*, as it would be hypocritical for someone to claim they have more rights than another while claiming they want to end slavery. Understanding the belief in "authority" is called *The Most Dangerous Superstition* by screen-writer Larken Rose, *The*

One True Divide by lecturer Mark Passio and *The End Of All Evil* by author Jeremey Locke. Therefore, we may see a leader as someone who empowers those they influence, who helps to create other leaders, who respects the freedoms and self-ownership of those they want to help, and sees themself as an *equal* among them. Would we say a ruler or slave-master, is the same as a leader by this definition? In other words, would we see the institution of slavery or government, as the same as organizations, businesses and schools? The difference lives between the *voluntary* and the *involuntary*, the freedom-based interaction and the slavery-based interaction. This is similarly differentiated as the *real* or *true* leader, versus the fake leader or "authority." In other words, would you rather someone *helps* show you your options to have you choose for yourself, or would you rather someone *forces* you to go with the option they think is best for you whether you like it or not? The individual with mastery who we may call a "master" does *not need* to be a "slave-master." If an idea is so good, it does *not* need to be mandated, it can be taught and that takes work, but that *is* what creates a real leader. Can we inspire others to be the change and find the inner leader within themselves? Do we not all have something to uniquely provide, being our unique self or having our own unique talents and gifts? Rather than suppressing who could be better leaders than us or what the best product is to buy, let us allow leaders and products to rise among each other, by allowing everyone to *voluntarily* decide how to live their *Own* lives. It is their *Own* after all, is it *not*?

In understanding this, for what may seem to be a complex relationship involved, between those who partake in slavery, those who actively promote slavery, those who rebel against slavery and those who are complacent in allowing slavery, we can observe a simple three-tier dynamic. Notice that those who *claim* any special rights above everyday people, *depend* upon them. Therefore, change relies in the everyday people and slaves realizing that everyone is no more or less special than anyone else. An "authority" or order-follower will be less likely to change their ways, since they made it their occupation and identity to be in their position. **Real leaders need no 'authority.'**

William Godwin, Philosopher (1756) -
"It is a violation of political justice to confound the *authority* which depends upon force, with the *authority* which arises from reverence and esteem; the modification of my conduct which might be due in the case of a wild beast, with the modification which is due to superior **wisdom**... The consequence which has flowed from confounding them has been **a greater debasement of the human character than could easily have followed upon direct and unqualified slavery.**"

From Liberty newspaper (1881) -
"The little sergeant was not pleased with his office; he condemned sometimes, often, always, in his inner **conscience**, the severity which his commanders or the **laws** obliged him to apply; and yet, a slave of passive **obedience**, he executed his orders, with death in his soul and tears filling his throat, but promptly nevertheless."
"Adopting a principle for our guide and keeping straight on through calm and storm, we are sure to reach our destination sooner or later. **The man of principle is the true leader**, the mover and saviour of the blind and unhappy masses, while the time-server, though called a leader and enjoying for a time popular favor, is actually a slave to the prejudices and passions of the multitude and is led and used by them."

Tiers of the Slavery Identity (Ego-centric):

- ❖ Authority, Order-Giver, Slave-Master
  - ➢ Quasi-Authority, Order-Followers, Slave-Drivers
    - ▪ Everyday People, Outsiders Or Slaves

Tiers of the Freedom Identity (Eco-centric):

- ❖ Everyday People

Jason Gregory, Author -
Excerpt from "The Natural Human Being" (Recommended)
"We can only leave people alone to live their own lives if we
are sincere in our own **introspection** and willing to discard
the **conditioning** that clouds our **unity** with our brothers
and sisters. Where we are sincerely humble and **free from
agendas**, we nourish and secretly transform the world—
again, **through not seeking to transform it.** A sage has
no agenda, and this brings spiritual oxygen into the world.
We all have undergone various sorts of conditioning and we
all have the same physical and emotional states, so we can
sympathize with the rest of the world, which suffers as a
result of the same *hypnosis* as ours. On the other hand, if
we are all inherently the same, we also possess the same
qualities that a sage lives by. Ziran *(naturalness, self-so)*
can only come to fruition when we trust that everything the
universe has produced is fundamentally right and could be
no other way. The systems of government, politics,
banking, religion and commerce are **unnatural**, but they
have gotten us to a certain point, and we have **learned**
many lessons from them. It is just that they are no longer
needed. If we cannot trust the world and the people in it, we
stand no chance for survival, because a **species at war
with itself is doomed.** People often say that they trust the
universe, but then they consistently condemn life according
to their conditioned perspectives."

In realizing that the change relies in our own minds, or that we may be under *Mental Slavery* without realizing it, we may evaluate our own morals and worldview to simply notice if there are any contradictions, to see if we may be contributing to a system of slavery, chaos or confusion. Answers are provided based on our contextual understanding of *Mental* and *Physical Slavery*.

The Seven Moral Questions by Brian Young:
1) Do you have the moral right to rule or dominate another individual against their will? **NO**
2) Does anyone have the moral right to rule or dominate you, if you don't want them to rule or dominate you? **NO**
3) Does anyone have a legitimately higher claim over your life and property than you? **NO**
4) Do you have a legitimately higher claim over the life and property of another? **NO**
5) Do you have a legitimate right to steal your neighbors stuff? **NO**
6) Does anyone have the legitimate right to steal your stuff? **NO**
7) If you don't have the right to steal from or harm another person, can you confer that right (that you don't have) onto another person or group? **NO**

The Five Moral Questions by Larken Rose:
1) Is there any means by which any number of individuals can delegate to someone else the moral right to do something which none of the individuals have the moral right to do themselves? **NO**
2) Do those who wield political power (presidents, legislators, etc.) have the moral right to do things which other people do not have the moral right to do? If so, from whom and how did they acquire such a right? **NO**

3) Is there any process (e.g., constitutions, elections, legislation) by which human beings can transform an immoral act into a moral act (without changing the act itself)? **NO**

4) When law-makers and law-enforcers use coercion and force in the name of law and government, do they bear the same responsibility for their actions that any-one else would who did the same thing on his own? **In reality, we are all responsible for our own actions, YES**

5) When there is a conflict between an individual's own moral conscience, and the commands of a political authority, is the individual morally obligated to do what he personally views as wrong in order to "obey the law"? **NO**

Henry David Thoreau, Abolitionist, Philosopher (1817) - "Must the citizen ever for a moment, or in the least degree, resign his **conscience** to the legislator? Why has every man a conscience, then?"
"The *only obligation* which I have a right to assume is to do at any time what I think right."
"Is it a freedom to be slaves, or a freedom to be free, of which *we boast*?"

What Need Is There For Modern Abolitionism?

We have reached the moral crux. With asking ourselves questions and getting clear on all our definitions explored regarding ownership and morality, **are the parallels between slavery and government coincidental?** We see these two "institutions" as separate from one another, but what makes them different? Explore any of the past definitions within this text, or the quotes said by 19th century Abolitionists and observe what happens if we correlate our concepts in regards to the government systems of today. The goal of **Modern Abolitionism**, is to determine any of the systems of slavery still present within the world after the abolition of *chattel slavery*, and work toward creating the freedom that the whole world deserves. As great 19th century abolitionist William Lloyd Garrison tells us, "our country is the world and our countrymen are all mankind." Many people break this simple wisdom in cheering on their nation and condemning other nations, unable to see the philosophical undertones of all the world's people. Many people will even acknowledge that the whole world is in a disturbed place, or that there are many divisions keeping people from their own humanity. Many people will also engage and look for different methods to help fix these conditions *(ie. elections, petitions, changing laws, paperwork, violence)*, arguing that others are not doing enough. To be outright, as the *Modern Abolitionist* I am, many of these same people are simultaneously *willingly* supporting slavery. *People support slavery for both themselves and their neighbors.* These people don't *know* it, and when they are given signs or warnings, they don't inquire upon it. Since I am the Abolitionist saying that you are the slave, though I must admit I was once among you, allow me to help you see it, if you will allow yourself to listen. It could be tempting for an Abolitionist like me to yell or get frustrated, seeing evil and it's ignorant supporters, yet this resistance can be expected in regards to any significant change through history. Thus, I will patiently plea for your attention, in hopes that you may *care* for this world as much as any voluntaryist does. To reiterate, I encourage you go back if you must, to learn about the nature of slavery, but let us come to understand that **the nature of slavery is merely that of government.** To be clear, when I say "government," what is referred to is the concept of "authority," the "right to rule", *involuntary* hierarchy. *The ruler of subjects is no different from the master of slaves.*

If claiming 100% ownership of someone's property is slavery, what percentage isn't? If taking 100% of someone's property is theft, what percentage isn't? **Taxation** is simply a euphemism for theft, written on fancy pieces of paper and covered with *justification*. *Physical slavery* is having someone work for you *involuntarily*, whereas theft is having someone pay you *involuntarily*. What makes one moral and the other *not*? Both situations are *involuntary*, and therefore both involve a lack of *freedom*, and the *need* for violence for compliance. Both situations involve a *claim* over ownership that does not belong to the *claimant*. Yet, where are the anti-slavery advocates abhorring this obvious problem that almost the entire world engages in? In the same way vegans abhor animals being mistreated, when they are also still being mistreated. In the same way spiritual gurus and religious individuals abhor violence and fear, when they are still allowing this practice to go on without question. In the same way atheists abhor dogmatic beliefs, when they are still believing in euphemisms creating exceptions to morality. In the same way social justice warriors attack others for being oppressive and racist, when they are allowing oppression and separation between peoples and nations. In the same way any activist can argue that we need to create better laws or attain grants for certain projects, when they disregard how those laws or grants are carried out. Now we may know why it is said that **lies mixed with truth makes the lies more dangerous.** We may argue that nobody is able to be *perfectly* moral, looking across all their actions, but that does not give us an excuse to ignore outright violence or slavery, *most especially* when we see it as the *exact opposite*, since most will argue taxation is "necessary" if not even "moral" or "good." Then as for those who say it's a "necessary evil," they devalue the word "evil" as if making such a clarification has no effect, since "evil" would automatically insinuate it is *not* necessary as we acknowledge there *is* a good. If someone claims ownership over the property of your life, you open yourself up for them to obtain ownership over the property of everything else within your life. What is yours *is* yours unless you *voluntarily* give it away, but if it's *involuntary*, someone is trying to hold you captive. As it must be reiterated, **you are not beholden to any person, group or system, you own you.**

William Lloyd Garrison, Journalist, Abolitionist (1805) -
"I will be as harsh as truth and as uncompromising as justice. I am in earnest, I will not equivocate, I will not excuse, I will not retreat a single inch, and I will be heard."

Mark Passio, De-Occultist, Philosopher (1974) -
"Freedom comes before everything including life. It isn't life, freedom, property, it's freedom, life, property; that's the correct order. Life without freedom isn't worth living because life without freedom is slavery. Most people are so **fearful** and attached to life that they would give up freedom to have **safety**. No amount of safety is worth the loss of freedom, no amount of even health is worth the loss of freedom. Dangerous unhealthy freedom is still more important than a life where you are perfectly safe and perfectly healthy and enslaved. As soon as some crisis comes down that threatens their safety or health, they're immediately willing to sacrifice their freedom in the name of safety or health. You have to be willing to die. **Liberty or death means liberty or death."**

Charles Bukowski, Author (1920) -
"Slavery was never abolished, it was only extended to include all the colors."

Voltaire, Philosopher (1694) -
"It is forbidden to kill; therefore all murderers are punished *unless* they kill in large numbers and to the sound of trumpets."
"In general, the **art of government** consists in taking as much money as possible from one party of the citizens to give to the other."
"The best government is a benevolent tyranny tempered by an occasional assassination."
"Imagine all contradictions, all possible incompatibilities-- you will find them in the government, in the law-courts, in the churches, in the public shows of this droll nation."
"It is dangerous to be right, when the government is wrong."

Benjamin Tucker, Philosopher (1854) -
"Customs absolutely necessary to the very existence of society are *skilfully mingled* with practices imposed by the tyrants, and the masses are expected to respect both alike. 'Do not, kill!' says the Code, and, 'Pay the priest his tithe!' it hastens to add. 'Do not steal!' says the Code, and immediately after, 'He who will not pay his tax shall have his arm cut off.' Such is the **Law**, and this double character it has retained up to the present time. Its origin is the desire of tyrants to perpetuate the customs which they have imposed for their own advantage. Its character is the cunning mixture of customs useful to society,— *customs which have no need of the law* to make them respected,— with those other customs which present no advantages except for the tyrants, are harmful to the masses, and are maintained only by **fear** of punishment."
"So-called governments are established and maintained for the sole purpose of robbing the people. So-called governments are **mobs**, conspiracies, usurpations. The people have practically no voice in their constitution and administration. But the **people tolerate them**, fight for

them, and pay taxes to support them. The people are the ignorant victims of **superstition**, fraud, and consequent slavery."

"The slave is the victim, not necessarily of passion and error, but of oppression. Slavery, as Colonel Greene so well puts it, is the confiscation of individuality by an extraneous *usurping will*. **My direct battle is for freedom as the opposite of slavery**; only indirectly am I fighting, though the more powerfully and effectively, for freedom as the opposite of weakness and deformity."

"'You shall not learn to read,' said the slaveholder to his slaves. 'You shall read nothing but lies,' says capital and government to their victims. But their efforts are in vain. Light has a penetrating power that is irresistible, and is bound to make its way. **Liberty will be seen and read and understood more and more as time goes on**, and will eventually force its way to a place of honor on the shelves of libraries everywhere"

"**The very purpose of the State** is to make the mass of the people the slaves of the privileged classes. The State, in its very nature, cannot be of the people and by the people. It is of the few and by the few by virtue of its organic structure."

From Liberty newspaper (1881) -
"You apologize for your government with its majority tyranny. You patronize it as a necessary evil. Where, you ask, are your individuals with free minds to seek the truth, find the truth, and live the truth? **A far greater tyranny is that which enslaves the mind than any that enslaves the body.** To have free men capable of self-government, we must have the right of private judgment on all matters pertaining to all the concerns of life freely and persistently *exercised*."

Mahatma Gandhi, Indian Independence (1869) -
"How can one be **compelled** to accept slavery? I simply
refuse to do the master's bidding. He may torture me,
break my bones to atoms and even kill me. He will then
have my dead body, not my **obedience.** Ultimately,
therefore, it is I who am the victor and not he, for he has
failed in getting me to do what he wanted done."

Samuel May, Abolitionist (1797) -
"They cannot make us slaves. Our legalized persecutors
may take from us our money; but they cannot rob us of our
respect for the **rights of man**, and our consciousness of
good intention. They may incarcerate our bodies, but they
cannot imprison our souls. They cannot confine our
thoughts or the expression of them within a dungeon. They
cannot build walls so high, that our prayers shall not
overleap them, and go up to the God of the oppressed.
They may (though it is too monstrous to be apprehended in
this age and country) perhaps inflict death upon us, but that
would only set our spirits free a little sooner, and send them
into the more immediate presence of Him, who has filled
our hearts with this **Love of Liberty**."

Lysander Spooner, Abolitionist, Lawyer (1808) -
"The principle that the majority have a **right to rule** the
minority, practically resolves **all government** into a mere
contest between two bodies of men, as to which of them
shall be masters, and which of them slaves."
"Here was a government that had **never had any
legitimate existence.** It professedly rested all its authority
on a certain paper called a constitution; a paper, I repeat,
that, *nobody had ever signed, that few persons had ever
read, that the great body of the people had never seen.*
This government had been **imposed**, by a few **property**
holders, upon a people too poor, too scattered, and many of

them too ignorant, to resist. It had been carried on, for some seventy years, by a mere cabal of **irresponsible** men, called **lawmakers.** In this cabal, the several local bands of robbers — the slaveholders of the South, the iron monopolists, the woollen monopolists, and the money monopolists, of the North — were represented. **The whole purpose of its laws was to rob and enslave the many —** both North and South — for the benefit of a few. But these robbers and tyrants quarreled — as lesser bands of robbers have done — over the division of their spoils. And hence the **war.** No such **principle** as justice to anybody — black or white — was the ruling motive on either side."

Frederick Douglass, Former Slave, Abolitionist (1817) -
"I was now getting, as I have said, one dollar and fifty cents per day. I contracted for it; I earned it; it was paid to me; it was rightfully my own; yet, upon each returning Saturday night, I was compelled to deliver every cent of that money to Master Hugh. And why? Not because he earned it,—not because he had any hand in earning it,—not because I owed it to him,—nor because he possessed the slightest shadow of a **right** to it; but solely because **he had the power to compel me to give it up**... This is the same man who gave me the roots to prevent my being whipped by Mr. Covey. He was 'a clever soul.' We used frequently to talk about the fight with Covey, and as often as we did so, he would claim my success as the result of the roots which he gave me. **This superstition is very common among the more ignorant slaves.**"

Auberon Herbert, Philosopher (1838) -
"If being a slave and owning a slave are both wrong relations, what difference does it make whether there are a million slave-owners and one slave, or one slave-owner and

a million slaves? Do robbery and murder cease to be what they are if done by ninety-nine per cent of the population?” **"You may say, as a friend of mine says -- 'I feel neither like a slave-owner, nor like a slave'** -- but his feelings, however admirable in themselves, do not alter the system, in which he consents to take part, of trying to **obtain control over his fellow men**; and, if he fails, in acquiescing in their control over himself.”
“You can collect three men on one side, and only two on the other side, that can offer no reason--no shadow of a reason--why the three men should dispose of the lives and **property** of the two men, should settle for them what they are to do, and what they are to be: that mere rule of numbers can never justify the turning of the two men into slaves, and the three men into slave-owners. There is one and only one **principle**, on which you can build a true, rightful, enduring and progressive civilization, which can give peace and friendliness and contentment to all differing groups and sects into which we are divided and that principle is that **every man and woman should be held by us all sacredly and religiously to be the one true owner of his or her faculties, of his or her body and mind, and of all property, inherited or--honestly acquired.**”

Larken Rose, Philosopher, Author -
“The only purpose of the rhetoric is to obfuscate the fact that the relationship between **every 'government' and its subjects is the same as the relationship between a master and a slave.** One master may whip his slaves less severely than another; one master may allow his slaves to keep more of what they produce; one master may take better care of his slaves – but none of that changes the basic, underlying nature of the master-slave relationship. **The one with the right to rule is the master; the one with the obligation to obey is the slave.** And that is true

even when people choose to describe the situation using inaccurate rhetoric and deceptive euphemisms, such as 'representative government,' 'consent of the governed,' and 'will of the people.'"

Rose Wilder Lane, Philosopher (1886) -
"Representative government cannot express the will of the mass of the people, because there is no mass of the people; The People is a **fiction**, like The State. You cannot get a Will of the Mass, even among a dozen persons who all want to go on a picnic. The only human mass with a common will is a mob, and that will is a temporary insanity. In actual fact, the population of a country is a multitude of **diverse human beings with an infinite variety of purposes and desires and fluctuating wills.**"

P. J. O'Rourke, Author (1947) -
"It's not an endlessly expanding list of **rights** – the 'right' to education, the 'right' to health care, the 'right' to food and housing. That's not freedom, that's **dependency**. Those aren't rights, those are the rations of slavery — hay and a barn for human cattle."

Henry Clarke Wright, Abolitionist (1797) -
"States and nations are to be regarded as we regard combinations of men to pick pockets, so steal sheep, to rob on the road, to steal men, to range over the sea as pirates—only on a larger and more imposing scale. **When men steal, rob and murder as states and nations, it gives respectability to crime**—the enormity of their crimes is lost sight of, amid the imposing number that commit them, and amid the glitter and pomp of equipage. The little band of thieves is scorned and hunted down as a felon; the great, or governmental band of thieves, is *made respectable by numbers*, and their crimes cease to be

criminal and hateful in proportion to the number combined to do them."

"Have men, acting as individuals or as a state or kingdom, a right to prescribe the rule of action to themselves or others, and to punish all violations of the rule to prescribe the penalty and execute it? **None will pretend that men possess this governing power over men as inherent, underived, inalienable.**"

"Use a little reason, and present some show of argument that *men are invested with a governing power over men.* If they will not, but continue to blackguard without decency and rail without reason, we must suppose they can bring no arguments, and that they maintain civil government as a **divine institution**, *as slaveholders do slavery* i. e. because their interest, ambition and lust of power wish to have it so."

"If slavery be the 'creature of law,' it is necessary that the law be abolished to insure its destruction. The moral influence of slavery is so debasing, that the seat of its disease can only be reached by the prosecution of high **moral principles.** It is quite common to hear men condemn the course of the government on this question, and they are equally severe in their condemnation of the 'course pursued by those that are termed 'no-government men' for abstaining from the polls. We have neither the ability or wish to grapple with this question. We maintain that the **rights of conscience should be held sacred.** Let every man inform himself, and so let him act"

"You admit that slavery is sin on this ground. *Why not human government?*"

"But I forget I am speaking of human government What else can be expected of it than theft, robbery and *injustice*? And yet, **it is declared to be approvingly ordained of God!**"

"Commit to human government 'unlimited, uncontrolled, absolute' power over the persons and lives of men, and then talk of their abusing it. **As though it were possible**

for a man, or any body of men, to be invested with it and not abuse it. The fact that man cannot hold this power over man without being corrupted by it, and without abusing it, shows that it is wrong. Thus we reason on the slave power. It tends to corrupt the possessor; and to horrible *abuses*. Therefore it is a sin. *So of human government.* The *assumption* of the power constitutes the wrong and the abuse. The greatest wrong man can do to man is to claim a right to kill him for any cause."

"The authority of human government! It has none but the point of the sword; since all moral obligation originates with God."

"Are you, am I, is any one, obliged to live in rebellion and be a partaker in the blood and carnage of the human government? We cannot, without treason against God."

"I look at human government as it is; I analyze it, as it is; I denounce it as it is; and as it is I pronounce it a system of **legalized warfare**"

"We call, then, for an **immediate abolition of dominion of man over man, of all government** of human will and human slaughter, as in itself wrong and only wrong"

"Man to hold dominion over beasts and things. *GOD TO RULE OVER MAN. In this there is found the last hope of bleeding humanity.*"

"Necessity.' By whom created? By human guilt. **Sin always creates a necessity for sin; then the necessity, created by the first sin, is offered as an apology for the second.** So, by sinning, men create a necessity for human government. Then offer that necessity as an apology. If the necessity is wrong, the government is wrong."

Ellen Craft on William Craft, Former Slave (1824) -
"He had not been urged away by abolitionists. He needed no information they could give him about slavery to stimulate his desire for **freedom**. He looked at his hands,

and remembered that they were once in irons. What **security** had he that they would not be so again? Mr. Sands was kind to him; but he might indefinitely postpone the *promise* he had made to give him his freedom. He might come under pecuniary embarrassments, and his property be seized by creditors; or he might die, without making any arrangements in his favor. He had too often known such accidents to happen to slaves who had *kind masters*, and he wisely resolved to make sure of the present opportunity to **own himself**. He was scrupulous about taking any money from his master on *false pretences*; so he sold his best clothes to pay for his passage to Boston. The slaveholders pronounced him a base, ungrateful wretch, for thus requiting his master's indulgence. *What would they have done under similar circumstances?*"

On the great state of "dependence" taking place between citizens and newly freed chattel slaves toward the government after the U.S. Civil War, Booker T. Washington, a former slave, shares about the state of Washington, "among a large class there seemed to be a **dependence upon the Government** for every conceivable thing. The members of this class had little ambition to create a position for themselves, but wanted the Federal officials to create one for them. How many times I wished then, and have often wished since, that by some power of magic I might remove the great bulk of these people into the county districts and plant them upon the soil, upon the solid and never deceptive foundation of **Mother Nature**, where all nations and races that have ever succeeded have gotten their start, — a start that at first may be slow and toilsome, but one that nevertheless is **real**." Slaves also often sought out going to other countries, such as Canada or England. As former slave William Still stated, "Washington, D.C., the seat of Government, where, if Slavery was not seen in its worst aspects, the Government in its support of Slavery appeared in a most revolting light." In a letter to William, from N.R. Johnston, he states "I only add that every case of this kind only tends to make me abhor my *(no!) this* country more and more. **It is the Devil's Government**, and God will destroy it." Many slaves expected life to be easy and free when their chattel slavery ended, but it evidently had it's own evils, due to the political (government dependency), social (racial prejudices) and economic (poverty) slavery as Lysander Spooner deemed it. Gustave de Molinari, before his death in 1912, would state how the American Civil War had *not* been simply a humanitarian crusade to free the slaves. Oscar Wilde tells us that "slaves themselves they received, not merely very little assistance, but hardly any sympathy even; and when at the close of the war the slaves found themselves free, found themselves indeed so absolutely free that they were free to starve, many of them bitterly regretted the new state of things." It must be noted that the rough conditions for the freed slave cannot *justify* their re-enslavement, as William Graham Sumner shares with us, "the Negroes, once slaves in the United States, used to be assured care, medicine, and support; but they spent their efforts, and other men took the products. They have been set free. That means only just this: they now work and hold their own products, and are assured of nothing but what they earn. In escaping from subjection they have lost claims. Care, medicine, and support they get, if they *earn* it. Will any one say that the black men have not gained? Will any one deny that individual black men may seem worse off? Will any one allow such observations to blind them to the *true significance* of the change? If any one thinks that there are or ought to be somewhere in society *guarantees* that no man shall suffer hardship, let him understand that *there can be no such guarantees*, unless other men give them—that is, unless we go back to slavery, and make one man's effort conduce to another man's welfare." Francis Dashwood Tandy helps further clarify, "no doubt the abolition of slavery was very hard on a number of slave owners, but that was as nothing when compared with the misery the slaves had endured. So with the modern form of slavery, it must be *abolished*, even if it prove inconsistent to those who are accustomed to live off the toil of others. Every change involves hardship on some class. We are fortunate indeed if that hardship falls solely upon those who have reaped the benefit of the previous *injustice*."

What is the worst form of slavery?
Just ask yourself, why in many people's view, can chattel slavery only be "abolished" by the government that claims to have a higher "authority" than the slave-master? Does that mean their "authority" is any more legitimate? The 19th century *Abolitionists* referenced did not appeal to the government, they only appealed to the individual conscience of everyday people and god. Yet, *here we go again*, many Christians *claim* to be following *the golden rule* and morality, yet they wouldn't personally go to their neighbors house and steal their money, they'd rather hire someone else to do it for them, and they wouldn't go to jail and disobey the governments like the *Abolitionists* were willing, to stand for what they see as "higher law." In not thinking through the scenario, the justification may be that it is for the "greater good," yet this then gives a free-pass for the individual to be violated. Another justification may be that anyone could steal their money anyways without the law to "protect" them, but taxation creates the *guaranteed* theft of property to prevent the *possible* theft of property. Whereas, if someone steals someone else's property, that act is seen by everyone as immoral, and therefore it is *not* continued or guaranteed. In other words, the perception of

"authority" or rulership is the continual or allowed violation of individual rights, because it holds individuals under duress and slavery. **Abolitionism is needed now just as much as it was in the 19th century.** A truth so obvious, it is inevitable. The question becomes, how much harm will incur until we learn it? By teaching it, we may prevent the harm in such lesson, as with lessening the time it takes to grasp. As we understand the nature of *Physical Slavery*, we realize it is the *direct* form of slavery. As we understand the nature of *Mental Slavery*, we realize it is the *indirect* form of slavery. However, what differentiates chattel slavery from the slavery that we correlate to the government? The 19th century *Abolitionist* and lawyer Lysander Spooner coined this type of slavery as "**Political Slavery**," for which he directly tells us that it is what ever created or maintained other forms of slavery to begin with. To obtain an even greater differentiation however, we may see *Political Slavery* as the *covert* form of slavery, and *chattel slavery* as the *overt* form of slavery. Both involve *physical* and *mental* slavery, however we may argue that *Political Slavery* being the *covert* form, involves an even greater *Mental Slavery* due to it living at the very roots to slavery, historically as an "organized institution." This is why individuals may say that the form of slavery we are under now, is *more* dangerous than it were back then, especially as the tools by which governments can employ to enslave it's citizens, has increased in effect. However, let us also know that the tools by which we can be free, such as the ability to use technology for good, as is making and printing this text, has simultaneously increased in effect. It must be known that what can make the slavery we have now *even more* dangerous, is when we can't tell it *is* slavery, as with accepting a perceived "limited government" otherwise known as *minarchism*, although many people may claim to desire this condition, because it is when we give it permission to grow and dominate in a way even worse than before. Our future is our choice, and quite literally, we won't have a future if we don't have a choice. **Liberty is life, slavery is death.**

Stephen A. Douglas, Activist (1813) -
"Slavery *cannot* exist a day or an hour anywhere, unless it is supported by local **police** regulations."

Isabel Paterson, Philosopher, Author (1886) -
"Slavery and class privilege were **legal institutions**; they *cannot* obtain otherwise."
"With **state ownership**, nothing can be done except by command or permission, A slave is under command and permission. He is not free."

From The Herald of Freedom newspaper (1835) -
"If people were governed by the **principles of peace** and benevolence, they would never need, and could scarcely have, *any other government*. But so long as **war and oppression are the leading objects of mankind**, they must unite in wicked combinations. Three millions of slaves never could be holden in bondage by fifteen millions of freemen, if the fifteen millions were not combined for *the purpose* of enslaving them. The three millions would easily throw off the yoke and emancipate themselves; *if there were no combination among their enslaves to prevent it.*"

Henry Bibb, Former Slave, Abolitionist (1815) -
"*The state* of Georgia, by an act of 1770, declared 'that it shall not be *lawful* for any number of free negroes, molattoes or mestinos, or even slaves in company with white persons, to meet together for the purpose of **mental instruction**, either before the rising of the sun or after the going down of the same.' Similar laws exist in most of the

slave States, and *patrols* are sent out after night and on the Sabbath day to enforce them. They go through their respective towns to prevent slaves from meeting for religious worship or mental instruction. This is the regulation and law of American Slavery, as **sanctioned** by the Government of the United States, and *without which it could not exist.* And almost **the whole moral, political, and religious power of the nation are in favor of slavery** and aggression, and against liberty and justice. I only judge by their actions, which speak louder than words. **Slaveholders are put into the highest offices** in the gift of the people in both Church and State, thereby making slaveholding popular and reputable... The laws of Kentucky, my native State, with Maryland and Virginia, which are said to be the mildest slave States in the Union, noted for their humanity, Christianity and democracy, declare that 'Any slave, for rambling in the night, or riding horseback without leave, or running away, may be punished by whipping, cropping and branding in the cheek, or otherwise, not rendering him unfit for labor.' 'Any slave convicted of petty larceny, murder, or wilfully burning of dwelling houses, may be sentenced to have his right hand cut off; to be hanged in the usual manner, or the head severed from the body, the body divided into four quarters, and head and quarters stuck up in the most public place in the county, where such act was committed.'" Bibb, among other former slaves would recount in detail how dreadful "slave prison" was, in only further degrading their character, giving an *excuse* so as to their slave condition. Among "modern" Abolitionists against *modern slavery*, many individuals protest against **prisons** due to their continuation of chattel slavery and other horrid practices. Abolitionist Jeremiah Hacker, having direct experience with the prison systems, talking with many prisoners, tells us that "brotherly counsel and assistance are better than prisons." "Wo too the nation, whose laws will throw such a child into prison, and try him in court, to disgrace, harden and ruin him, when by a little kindness, he might be reclaimed." Oscar Wilde who went to jail despite being victimless, states that "prison life with its endless privations and restrictions makes one rebellious. The most terrible thing about it is not that it breaks one's heart—hearts are made to be broken—but that it turns one's heart to stone." However, *prison abolition at the root would be state abolition*, for just as the state relies on the existence of taxation or prisons, the state relies on violence and slavery for their continuance.

Stefan Molyneux, Philosopher, Author (1966) -
"When we look at an **institution** such as slavery, we can see that it survived, fundamentally, on two central pillars – patronizing and fear-mongering mythologies, and the shifting of the costs of enforcement to others... Slavery as an institution could not conceivably survive economically if the slave owners had to pay for the actual expense of slavery themselves. **Shifting the costs of the capture, imprisonment and return of slaves to the general taxpayer** was the only way that slavery could remain profitable. The use of the **political coercion** required to make slavery profitable, of course, generates a great demand for mythological 'cover-ups,' or ideological distractions from the violence at the core of the institution. Thus **violence always requires intellectualization**, which is why governments always want to fund higher education and subsidize intellectuals."

Stephen Symonds Foster, Abolitionist (1809) -
"Slaveholding was, necessarily, **a social crime**; that it was only by means of a **social organization**, by which the power of a whole community could be combined and concentrated on a given point, at a given time, that the

liberty of an individual could be crushed. **The federal and state governments, linked together as they now are, constitute such an organization."**

"The army, the navy, and the militia, of the whole country, are placed at the bidding of the slave power; and every officer in them, from the highest to the lowest, is put under oath to fight the battles of slavery at the master's call."

"They preach and practice **allegiance to a government** which is based upon the bones and sinews, and cemented with the blood, of millions of their countrymen, and hold themselves in readiness to execute its every decree, at the point of the bayonet. *Thus emphatically are they the holders of the slaves* — the bulwarks of the bloody slave system"

Jeremiah Hacker, Abolitionist (1801) -
"This nation, at the present time, appears to be a nation of bondholders and bond-slaves, with *a government instituted to protect the one and subjugate the other* to incessant toil for their support in idleness and vice. For the *purpose* of subjugating the toilers, and **making them slaves**, the priests and politicians have instituted a large standing army, who are riding down, with whip and spur, all opposition to their *authority*, and flashing their flaming swords and bayonets in our faces to **intimidate us into submission."**

Gustave de Molinari, Philosopher (1819) -
"In the United States, for example, **the government guarantees the southern planters the ownership of their slaves.** There are, however, in the United States, abolitionists who rightly consider slavery to be a *theft*. It counts for nothing! The communal mechanism obliges them to contribute out of their wealth to the maintenance of this sort of theft. If the slaves were to try one day to *free themselves* of this wicked and odious yoke, the abolitionists

would be *required* to go and defend, by force of arms, the property of the planters. That is the **law of majorities.**"

Salmon Chase, Activist, Abolitionist (1808) -
"Slavery is the complete and absolute *subjection* of one person to the control and disposal of another person, by **legalized force**. We need not argue that *no person can be, rightfully, compelled to submit* to such control and disposal. **All such subjection must originate in force**; and, *private force not being strong enough to accomplish the purpose*, public force, in the form of **law**, *must* lend its aid. The government comes to the help of the individual slaveholder, and punishes resistance to his will, and *compels submission*. **The government, therefore, in the case of every individual slave, is the real enslaver**, depriving each person enslaved of all liberty and all **property**, and all that makes life dear... For slavery cannot subsist a moment after the support of the public force has been withdrawn."

Herbert Spencer, Psychologist, Polymath (1820) -
"Those sins of responsible **legislators** seen in the long list of laws made in the interests of dominant classes—a list coming down in our own country to those under which there were long maintained slavery and the slave-trade"

Parker Pillsbury, Abolitionist (1809) -
"Slavery was the sin and crime of north as well as south. It was **sustained by the government**, it was *sanctified* by almost the whole religion of the nation."
"The clergy to-day would have the world believe they were always opposed to slavery, and sought its overthrow. They were opposed to slavery just as was the government. No more; no less. **And if the church and government were against slavery, why did they not put it out of existence?** How could it have stood against them? If they

were opposed to slavery why were Louisiana and Florida bought for its extension? Why was Mexico robbed of Texas after a four years' bloody and cruel, and fearfully unjust war on our part, only to reinstate slavery where Roman Catholicism a few years before had abolished it, as it hoped, forever? Whatever of slave-breeding, or slave-holding, or slave-trading abroad, or slave-hunting at home the **government authorized and supported**, the church sanctioned and sanctified. So also of slavery extension."

The Liberator, Abolitionist Newspaper (1831) -
"Slave Power, which now rules **the government** of this nation with a rod of iron."

Oscar Wilde, Poet, Playwright (1854) -
"Just as the worst slave-owners were those who were *kind to their slaves*, and so **prevented the horror of the system being realised** by those who suffered from it, and understood by those who contemplated it, so, in the present state of things in England, **the people who do most harm are the people who try to do most good."**
"Slavery was put down in America, not in consequence of any action on the part of the slaves, or even any express desire on their part that they should be free. It was put down entirely through the **grossly illegal conduct of certain agitators in Boston and elsewhere**, who were not slaves themselves, nor owners of slaves, nor had anything to do with the question really. It was, undoubtedly, **the Abolitionists who set the torch alight, who began the whole thing."**

Richard Price, Philosopher (1723) -
"For it is self-evident, that if there are any men whom they have a **right** to hold in slavery, there may be *others* who have had a right to hold *them* in slavery"

"The things that he would he does not, and the things that he would not, those he does. He is, therefore, a slave in the properest sense."
"The quiet which prevails under **slavish governments** and which may seem to be a recommendation of them, proceeds from an ignominious tameness, and **stagnation of the human faculties.**"

Tak Kak (from Liberty newspaper, approx. 1881) -
"One form of slavery is abolished to give place to *another* so long as men **consent** to be held **subject**... When, however, it comes to his consciousness that he is naturally a subject till he **refuses**, and realizes that power and will are the essential matters, he **makes himself free** so far as he can... **There is more virtue in the criminal classes than in the tame slaves.**"

Benjamin Tucker, Philosopher (1854) -
"The government's first crime *(if we except the crime of it existing at all)* was in persistently **protecting African slavery with the Federal bayonet.** To this, and to this *alone*, was the perpetuation of chattel slavery due. When Garrison cried to the American government to take the bayonet from the breast of the slave and leave the master to take his chances with the victim, he was answered by the educated mob of Boston with the halter and *scouted by politicians* of every stripe as an *outlaw and madman*. To refuse to furnish slavery with its *only sure protection*, the bayonet, was arch treason to the 'law and order' upon which this government stood. The government having forcibly protected slavery and sanctified it with the mantle of *constitutionality*, **the slave power naturally counted upon its governmental guarantees**... The volume of men set to work by this slavery-protecting government to kill their fellow-men aggregates a number equal to the combined

populations of Maine, New Hampshire, Vermont, Connecticut, and Rhode Island, with nearly half the population of Massachusetts thrown in."

Francis Dashwood Tandy, Philosopher (1867) -
"The invasive acts of **individual transgressors are comparatively insignificant beside those of the State.** The power of the individual for harm is at worst limited to a short term of years. His acts are isolated and temporary. But those of the State are organized, systematic, universal and well nigh eternal."

Parker Pillsbury, Abolitionist (1809) -
"*Imprisonments* at that period were frequent of abolitionists, some of whom being *non-resistants*, were committed for refusing to take lessons in **the art of human slaughter, under the milder name of 'military duty.'** Most of the victims from our ranks were for the crime of a too liberal interpretation and **exercise of the rights** of speech and worship, in a country whose *government* and religion were incorrigibly committed to breeding, trafficking in and holding slaves."

Larken Rose, Philosopher, Author -
"The truth is that **any form** of authoritarian control – any type of 'government,' whether constitutional, democratic, socialist, fascist, or anything else – will result in a set of masters forcibly oppressing a group of slaves."
(Story-Book) "Some of us realize the self-evident truth that no election, no constitution, no legislation, and no other pseudo-religious political ritual can bestow upon anyone the **right** to rule another. Nothing can make a man into a rightful master; nothing can make a man into a rightful slave."

"The evils of slavery, for example, are often blamed on racism and greed, but 'authority' played a huge role in making slavery economically feasible. If there was *not* a huge, organized network of 'law enforcers' to capture escaped slaves, and any who helped them escape, how long would slavery have continued? If freeing slaves was *not* 'illegal,' and thus immoral in the eyes of authoritarians, how much larger and more effective would the 'underground railroad' have been? (It probably would not have been known as an 'underground' anything, if it was not 'illegal.')"

"The '**abolitionist**' movement consisted of people who thought slavery was **immoral**, and who wanted the **'laws'** changed to officially declare slavery to be immoral and 'illegal.' If, instead of petitioning for a change in 'laws,' the abolitionists were actively freeing slaves, the slave trade most likely would have collapsed decades earlier, if it ever happened at all. Shipping slaves halfway around the world would be a very risky business indeed if, the moment you landed, your 'cargo' might be forcibly liberated. The problem is that **most people believe that even immoral, unjust 'laws' should be obeyed** until the 'law' is changed. Clearly this means that such people's loyalty to the myth of 'authority' is stronger than their *loyalty to morality*, and doing what the masters tell them is more important to them than doing what they know is **right.** And mankind has suffered greatly because of it."

"Whether slavery could have existed had it not been 'legally' enforced (as mentioned above), similar questions could be asked about the treatment of the American Indians. If not for the authoritarian 'government' edicts and the state mercenaries to enforce them, would there have been such a large-scale, concerted effort to exterminate or forcibly evict the natives from the lands they had inhabited for generations? No doubt there would still have been smaller conflicts due to the clash of cultures and demands for farming and hunting lands, but would it have been in anyone's personal interest to engage in large-scale **violent** combat?"

The **underground railroad** was a secret effort created by the Abolitionists in the 19th century, as a network of towns, churches and meeting points that provided safety away from governments and away from slavery. Abolitionists were willing to break *the fugitive slave act* in order to uphold *morality*, maintain freedom and help runaway slaves, and that is exactly why the underground railroad is considered "underground," much like the concept of *black markets*. In the new printing age of the 19th century, among the need for secrecy, not many people were aware of all their town experiments and struggles, yet here we are now, able to study their efforts and realize how we can make an impact that wasn't able to be fully made before in shared sympathy for *voluntary community*. One town experiment was known as the "Hopedale Community" by Adin Ballou, founded in 1843. It stood for temperance, abolitionism, women's rights, spiritualism and education. Fourteen years after the purchase of the land however, the town went bankrupt and was sold off to the Draper corporation. The town did what it had to do at the time, welcoming individuals who were in need of help. Many stories from this town have surfaced since, even with community gatherings about it occurring in the modern day, sharing how many of the residents loved their stay and safety away from the rest of the world, many passionate about the *principles of non-violence*. Another town was called "Fruitlands" by Charles Lane among other transcendentalists, which now serves as a museum today. The town was to promote principles mostly of self-sufficiency. They broke away from trade or any connection whatsoever to slavery, including the clothes they wear.

Though efforts became extreme to such an extent, the land was found not able to be used for crops, causing the town to no longer continue, though it still played a role in the efforts of abolitionism nonetheless. Lane would continue to experiment joining with other communities. This passion we see in these freedom fighters breeds the search of excellence. Not every engagement based on principle is successful, but that does not mean one should abandon principle. Among towns, reform schools for boys in Maine were created by Jeremiah Hacker. Through his educative efforts, both him and his readers were able to start up projects that went on for more than 100 years after his death, also having created one of the top reform schools in the country. The governor of his town would go on to take credit, and Jeremiah criticized it, since the idea originated with his work. His advocacy efforts for land reform also was able to provide land for those without, as estimated for about *two million people* over the next century. This is the power of influence and education done by everyday people. Among one the most accredited abolitionists, Josiah Warren created several towns, one called Modern Times, emphasizing the *sovereignty* of individuals. No money, no laws, no government, yet there was very little crime and commotion throughout all 13 years of it's history. He was able to provide homes for families without. The reason why this town could not continue was due to the 1857 Panic and the Civil War; among the fact as resident Charles Codman stated, the ideas of Modern Times were not spreading to the rest of the world. As the name of the town began to get criticized, the civil war preoccupied the era, the name was changed and the ideals died out. Still, inspiring and may be considered successful at times none the less. Therefore, with the successes by these communities, often only with failure due to an outside world not ready for it, why do historians call them "utopian"? Simply because there were voluntary ideals contrary to the involuntary government? Should we disband ourselves from the rest of the world and create our own community? Perhaps the world is in need of knowledge, of the concepts of authority and the nature of governments, among the questions challenging *political slavery* we may propose for all to inquire, before we can ever voluntarily create whatever society we choose to live in for ourselves. The domino effect can occur from just one community stopping their support for slavery and showing the reasoning behind their actions to the rest of the world. **We cannot just run away from our problems, otherwise they will come back to get us.** We must face them, and therefore help our fellow man who is enslaved, come to freedom. That is, **freedom for all**. Upon however observing the Abolitionist towns, we cannot have strict plans of community among individuals, whose individualism we must respect, as Josiah Warren concludes upon his many experiments, stating "it seemed that the difference of opinion, tastes and purposes increased just in proportion to the demand for conformity... it appeared that it was nature's own inherent law of diversity that had conquered us... our 'united interests' were directly at war with the individualities of persons and circumstances and the instinct of self-preservation."

Joseph Sobran, Journalist (1946) -
"Since **outright slavery** has been discredited, 'democracy' is the only remaining rationale for **state compulsion** that most people will **accept**."

The Liberator, Abolitionist Newspaper (1831) -
"O what crimes are perpetrated under the *mask* of democratic liberty!"

Theodore Dwight Weld, Abolitionist (1803) -
"The Spartans boasted of their *kindness to their slaves*, while they whipped them to death by thousands at the altars of their gods. The Romans lauded their own *mild treatment of their bondmen*, while they branded their names on their flesh with hot irons, and when old, threw them into their fish ponds, or like Cato 'the Just,' starved them to death. It is the boast of the Turks that they *treat their slaves as though they were their children*, yet their common name for them is 'dogs,' and for the merest trifles, their feet are bastinadoed to a jelly, or their heads clipped off with the scimetar. The Portuguese pride themselves on their *gentle bearing toward their slaves*, yet the streets of Rio Janeiro are filled with naked men and women yoked in pairs to carts and wagons, and whipped by drivers like beasts of burden."
"It was **public opinion** that made him a slave."

Jeremey Locke, Author -
"What we consider as real 'slavery' is indeed **only one form of slavery.** The African slaves in the United States were *compelled* to work and toil for other people's benefit. Their lives were mostly controlled for the benefit of the master, but they had some very **limited freedoms.** Some were able to create distinct traditions and maintain families. They did their best to build joy into their lives despite the tyranny wrought upon them. **Because they were in control of portions of their lives, were they free? How much freedom does a person deserve?** How much freedom can be destroyed before we recognize that it is evil? Slavery is not a concept of totality. *Slavery exists wherever the freedom of man is destroyed.* **Theft** and **bullying** are slavery. In history, African natives, Jews and many others have experienced lifelong slavery. *The ultimate slavery* is **murder.** Slavery stops people from being able to make *choices* for their own lives. Everything that restricts your

mind, your movements and your speech is evil. Slavery is found in *both the partial and complete* destruction of freedom."

"Authority is not designed to destroy the enemy; it is **designed to enslave you**."

"If authority is not questioned, if it is accepted as the proper ruler over man, slavery is the result."

"Political correctness is **engineered slavery**."

"When culture teaches that working for money is greed, it also teaches that **labor** without money is noble. Laboring by **rule of law** for the collective 'we' is taught as the proper form of ambition. If you cannot choose to give or to keep, then you are not 'we;' you are a slave"

"Culture teaches that the only **security** to be found in life is in **government.** Only they can secure your water, your air and your food. *Yield authority to them.* The strength of environmentalism is that it can be used to regulate every aspect of your life. Transportation, food, housing, energy and communication; they all fall under this umbrella of regulation and control. Environmentalism is just one more *excuse* to implement slavery."

"Make no mistake – **you are a slave and government is your master.** The brilliance of your masters as opposed to **'conventional' slavery'** is that they allow you to believe that you earn what you work for, and that you own what you buy. It keeps you complacent and agreeable."

"The cultures of earth teach you to accept, to yield and to obey. The end of evil is found in *refusing* this slavery of the **mind**."

"The government is a group of politicians and bureaucrats who are gradually **conquering** the country. Have you ever heard this side of the story before? It is rather startling, isn't it? And it explains why governments have been wrecking economies, creating poverty, and **murdering and**

enslaving people for thousands of years. It's what they were invented to do. It's the nature of the beast."

Etienne de La Boetie, Philosopher (1530) -
"For although the means of coming into power differ, still the **method of ruling** is practically the same; those who are elected act as if they were breaking in bullocks; those who are **conquerors** make the people their prey; those who are heirs plan to treat them as if they were their **natural** slaves."

Edmund Burke, Philosopher (1729) -
"We have given our Necks to the Yoke of **political and theological Slavery.**"
"Parties in religion and politics make sufficient discoveries concerning each other, to give a sober man proper caution against them all. The monarchist, and aristocratical, and popular partisans have been jointly laying their axes to the **root** of *all* government, and have in their turns proved each other absurd and inconvenient. In vain you tell me that **artificial government** is good, but that I fall out only with the abuse. The thing! **The thing itself is the abuse!**"
"What slave so passive, what bigot, so blind, what enthusiast so headlong, what politician so hardened, as to stand up in *defence of a system calculated for a curse to mankind?* — a curse under which they smart and groan to this hour, without thoroughly knowing the **nature** of the disease, and wanting understanding or courage, to supply the remedy."
"The **government** is, one day, **arbitrary** power in a single person; another, a juggling confederacy of a few to cheat the prince and *enslave the people*; and the third, a frantic and unmanageable democracy. The great instrument of all these changes, and what infuses a peculiar venom into all of them, is party. It is of no consequence what the **principles** of any party, or what their pretensions, are; the

spirit which actuates *all parties is the same,*— the spirit of ambition, of self-interest, of oppression, and treachery. This spirit entirely *reverses all* the principles which a benevolent **nature** has erected within us; all honesty, all **equal justice**, and even the ties of natural society, the natural affections." "They have **enlisted reason to fight against itself** and employ its whole force to prove that it is an insufficient guide to them in the conduct of their lives. But, unhappily for us, in proportion as we have deviated from the plain rule of our nature, and turned our reason against itself, in that proportion have we increased the follies and miseries of mankind. The more deeply we penetrate into the labyrinth of art, the further we find ourselves from those ends for which we entered it. This has happened in almost every species of **artificial society** and in all times. We found, or *we thought we found*, an inconvenience in having every man the judge of his own cause; therefore, judges were set up, at first with discretionary powers. But it was soon found a miserable slavery to have our lives and properties precarious, and hanging upon the arbitrary determination of *any one man or set of men.* We fled to **laws** as a remedy for this evil. By these we persuaded ourselves we might know with some certainty upon what ground we stood. But lo! differences arose upon the sense, and interpretation of these laws. Thus we were brought back to our old incertitude. New laws were made to expound the old; and new difficulties arose upon the new laws; as words multiplied, opportunities of caviling upon them also. Then recourse was had to notes, comments, glosses, reports, *responsa prudentum*, learned readings: eagle stood against eagle; **authority was set up against authority.** Some were *allured* by the modern, others reverenced the ancient. The new were more **enlightened**, the old were more venerable. Some adopted the comment, others stuck to the text. The confusion increased, the mist thickened, until it could be discovered no longer what was allowed or forbidden, what things were in property, and what common. In this uncertainty (*uncertain even to the professors*, an Egyptian darkness to the rest of mankind) the contending parties felt themselves more effectually ruined by the delay than they could have been by the injustice of any decision. Our inheritances have become a prize for disputation; and disputes and litigations have become an inheritance."

"The blindness of one part of mankind, **co-operating with the frenzy and villainy of the other**, has been the real builder of this respectable fabric of **political society**: and as the **blindness of mankind has caused their slavery**, in return their state of slavery is made a *pretence* for continuing them in a state of blindness"

"The poor by their excessive labor, and the rich by their enormous luxury, are set upon a level, and rendered equally ignorant of any **knowledge**, which might conduce to their happiness. A dismal view of the interior of all civil society! The lower part broken and ground down by the most cruel oppression; and the rich by their *artificial* method of life bringing worse evils on themselves than their tyranny could possibly indict on those below them. Very different is the prospect of the *natural state*. Here there are no wants which nature gives (and in this state men can be sensible of no other wants) which are not to be supplied by a very moderate degree of labor; therefore *there is no slavery*."

"We have shown that **political society**, on a moderate calculation, has been the means of murdering several times the number of inhabitants now upon the earth, during its short existence, not upwards of four thousand years in any accounts to be depended on. But we have said nothing of the other, and perhaps as bad, consequences of these wars, which have spilled such *seas of blood and reduced so many millions to a merciless slavery*."

"For the *free governments*, for the point of their space, and the moment of their duration, have felt more confusion, and committed more flagrant acts of tyranny, than the most perfect despotic governments which we have ever known."
"If *pretended* revelations have caused wars where they were opposed, and slavery where they were received, the pretended wise **inventions of politicians** have done the same. But the **slavery has been much heavier, the wars far more bloody, and both more universal by many degrees.**"
"Pursuing the same plan of punishing by the denial of the exercise of government to still greater lengths, we wholly abrogated the ancient government of Massachusetts. We were confident that the first feeling, if not the very prospect, of anarchy would instantly enforce a complete submission. The experiment was tried. A new, strange, unexpected face of things appeared. **Anarchy is found tolerable.** A vast province has now subsisted, and subsisted in a considerable degree of health and vigor for near a twelvemonth, without Governor, without public Council, without judges, without executive magistrates."

P. W. Grayson, Philosopher (approx. 1830) -
"Age rolled on after age, and **generation after generation**, with tyranny still riding at the head of human affairs, directing and controlling them with the **pretexts of patriotism**, but with the *purposes* of oppression."
"If mankind were as wise, not as one could easily imagine them to be, but only as wise as an **enlightened self love** could make them, there were **no need for either government or law**... Feeling this truth so intensely, I have steadily, for some time, been engaged in considering and unravelling to myself, for the ease and satisfaction of my own mind, the various causes which might, in my apprehension of their nature, have *conspired*, through all

time, to doom mankind to the vexation and incumbrance of government and laws; as also to shut out from their understandings the light of **principles** which appeared to me inherent in their **nature**, and so, wholly, to prevent their beautiful dominion over the face of the earth... The bearing of this, in the end, is to bring every one to consider **obedience** as even a part of his very nature, so as never to look beyond the duties which are assigned him. A people thus trained and disciplined to **conformity to their superiors**, make, indeed, very *convenient subjects*; and are no other than the identical sort of *machines*, that *unrighteous power* demands for the successful execution of its ends... *What has authority, which has been at work these thousands of years, done for the condition of human nature? Absolutely nothing...* It is certain that the **subjects of the British government are slaves.** How, indeed, can a subject, anywhere, be anything but a slave? *The first word, to my mind, is entirely synonimous with the last.* To be sure, the slavery of this people I allude to here is a very *mitigated* one; so much so, that they are all **even proud of it**."

"By no art can nature be *defrauded* of the *omnipotent rule* which she has carefully diffused through all her works"

"The repeal of **all law**, as far as it has been treated on in this essay as matter of evil, I have brought myself to believe, would be at once *the beginning of human prosperity...* It would be that of the wickedest men seriously mourning the absence of law, which themselves took delight in eluding!... That which must be done, is to clear from his mind the horrible mists and fogs of prejudice—to bid him no longer worship the cold prescriptions of policy, for the warm **principles of justice**—to free his soul from the fetters of *authority*—to remit and exalt him to himself— to let him seek, by the light of his **conscience** alone, in the joyous, genial climate of his own free spirit, for all the **rules**

of his conduct. *Then, and not till then, will he be virtuous and happy."*
(Grayson also explains how a voluntary subject will be happy and a subject by necessity will develop resentment and be spiritless, which he calls the "shadow of slavery")

William Godwin, Philosopher (1756) -
"Such is man in himself considered; so simple his **nature**; so few his wants. How different from the man of **artificial society!** Palaces are built for his reception, a thousand vehicles provided for his exercise, provinces are ransacked for the gratification of his appetite, and the whole world traversed to supply him with apparel and furniture. Thus vast is his expenditure, and the purchase slavery. He is *dependent* on a thousand accidents for tranquillity and health, and his body and soul are at the devotion of whoever will satisfy his imperious cravings."
"**Which was most meritorious, the unresisting and dastardly submission of a slave, or the enterprise and gallantry of the man who dared to assert his claims?** Since, by the partial administration of our laws, innocence, when power was armed against it, had nothing better to hope for than guilt, what man of true courage would fail to set these laws at defiance, and, if he must suffer by their **injustice**, at least take care that he had first shown his contempt of their yoke?"
"**We were slaves, and we deserved to be so.** In almost every country there now appeared a king, that puppet pageant, that monster in creation, miserable itself, a combination of every vice, and **invented for the curse of human kind.**"
"There is a constant struggle between the genuine sentiments of the understanding, which tell us that all this is an imposition, and the imperious voice of government, which bids us, **Reverence and obey.** In this unequal

contest, alarm and apprehension will perpetually haunt the **minds** of those who exercise usurped power. In this **artificial state** of man, powerful engines must be employed to **prevent him from rising to his true level.** *It is the business of the governors to persuade the governed that it is their interest to be slaves.* They have no other means by which to create this fictitious interest but those which they derive from the *perverted understandings*, and **burdened property**, of the public, to be returned in titles and bribes." "The plebeian must be the maker of his own fortune; the lord finds his already made. The plebeian must expect to find himself neglected and despised in proportion as he is remiss in cultivating the objects of esteem; **the lord will always be surrounded with sycophants and slaves.**"

Lysander Spooner, Abolitionist, Lawyer (1808) -
"The result of all this is that the little wealth there is in the world is all in the hands of a few,— that is, in the hands of **the law-making, slave-holding class**, who are now as much slave-holders in spirit as they ever were, but who accomplish *their purposes* by means of the **laws** they make for keeping the laborers in **subjection and dependence**, instead of each one's owning his individual slaves as so many **chattels**."
"The slaveholders bargained for, and secured, protection for slavery and the slave trade"

Thomas Hodgskin, Philosopher (1787) -
"To point out the inevitable consequences of erring systems of policy, whether they be intended to secure the dominion of the whites over the blacks, or of the landlords of England over their former slaves, whether they be intended to preserve superstition erect, and men groveling in **political slavery**, is, or ought to be, as far as society is concerned, *the one great and only duty of observers*"

Gertrude B. Kelly (from Liberty newspaper, approx. 1881) -
"Governments were *not* instituted to promote **justice**, but to maintain and to foster injustice. **There were no governments, until one tribe conquered another, and appropriated its persons and properties.** It then set up a machine to keep itself in power, and to aid it in extorting from its subjects all that it could possibly take... As was its birth, so has its life been; it lives, acts, and grows *only* on extortion and injustice... **If it had not protected the slave-holders in their property, the slavery question could have been settled without bloodshed.**"
"O sorrowing hearts of slaves, We heard you beat from far! We bring the light that saves, We bring the morning star; Freedom's good things we bring you, whence all good things are."

Karl Heinzen, Abolitionist (1809) -
"Where there is *authority*, there must also be servants. But *a free people know neither the one nor the other*... The popular conception of **the State** is still tainted by the dominating influence of the examples of the past, the historical models, and therefore most men cannot conceive of even the freest State without a *dualism of the people* and a special power which is called *authority and government.*"

David Andrade (from Liberty newspaper, approx. 1881) -
"**The natural function of government is to perpetuate slavery**; for the more *reverence* there is in the people, the more they are law-abiding and cowardly, the more humility and loyalty they show, the easier it is for the few adventurers called "the State" to rule over them. No State can make much progress where the individual members of the community are brave, independent, and **self-reliant**... People are already beginning to learn that **to be a soldier**

is to be a slave, and to pay taxes to support the army is to be a worse slave still."

"The history of all government; Fools have built powerful institution for self-protection, and rogues have taken the management of them. *Anarchy, knowing this, strikes direct at this greatest of all tyrannies,—* **the "State"**. Society is just in that stage of its evolution where *brute force* (of which government is the concentrated *embodiment*) is giving way before the **force of intellect**,— the force which promises to govern the future. Government is one of the last semblages of the old force. **Anarchy the force of the new.** Men are realizing that the perpetual spoilation and exploitation of each other is not conducive tot he general welfare; that nothing is gained by each man holding down the hands of every other man; that social improvement is dependent upon the improvement of each individual part and that there is scope for improvement only where there is **liberty.**"

William Graham Sumner, Social Scientist (1840) -
"The notion of a free state is *entirely modern*. It has been developed with the development of the middle class, and with the growth of a commercial and industrial civilization. **Horror at human slavery is not a century old as a common sentiment in a civilized state.** The idea of the 'free man,' as we understand it, is the product of a revolt against mediaeval and feudal ideas."

Regarding the notion of the touted form of "modern slavery" known as "wage slavery," Benjamin Tucker shares with us "there is no such thing. A man's true wages are fixed and paid by nature, and consist of what he produces or its equivalent. No man is a slave because he gets his wages, though many men are slaves because they do *not* get their wages. As far as **freedom** is concerned, there is no difference between the man who produces for unknown parties on problematical terms, working with his **own** tools at his **own** risk, and the man who produces for known parties on specified terms, working with their tools at their risk. Both of these are wage systems, and there is no other system. Where there is *monopoly*, both are slave systems; where there is no monopoly, neither is a slave system. The one condition essential to the rightfulness of both is the absence of the *usurer*, whose sole function is to secrete for his own benefit a portion of the laborer's wages." It may be noted that rulers may prevent education to people whom could be self-employed or entrepreneurs, just as chattel slaves were, as their potential may be *in all ways* suppressed for the sake of maintaining authoritative power. Regardless, whether an individual philosophically regards private property as null or not, or wage slavery as a valid form, or egoism as the primary argument for freedom, morality as objective or relative, property or free-will being social constructs or not, or socialism, collectivism or individualism, capitalism and communism relevant in this talk, all these differing opinions only further strengthens the need for voluntary interaction and self-ownership, a care for humankind and Anarchy, for which many of the people concerned with these topics may be able to unite with in true equality or tolerance *(hence anarcho-capitalism, anarcho-communism, anarcho-egoism, anarcho-primitivism, anarcho-syndicalism, anarcho-pacifism, agorism etc., though these terms may have us wear labels ignorant of reality beyond labels)*. Tucker tells us "governments set men against men and classes against classes by their favoritism, system of privileges, and special opportunities. This **artificial inequality** gives rise to class prejudices, jealousy, hatred, and discord. It *tempts and forces* some to commit crimes, while it reduces others to abject slavery. Thus it gradually undermines society. Soon comes revolution, and a civilization is in ruins. The modern conflict between the rich and the poor could not exist but for **the State**, which feeds on strife and strengthened in war. A solution of the labor problem would involve a dissolution of the State. For all that is required to such solution is State *non-interference*. Labor would reap its full reward, if the States did not furnish a *special class* of people with weapons and means whereby the latter is enabled to enslave and plunder the former. **The State produces nothing and possesses nothing.** If it is seen to give something to anybody, that must have been taken *forcibly or fraudulently* from somebody else." 20th century Abolitionist Voltairine de Cleyre in speaking of the unity between ideas, as with the concept of "anarchism without adjectives," tells us about her relationship with Emma Goldman, "Miss Goldman is a communist; I am an individualist. She wishes to destroy the *right of property*, I wish to assert it. I make my war upon *privilege and authority*, whereby the right of property, the true right in that which is proper to the individual, is annihilated. She believes that co-operation would entirely supplant competition; I hold that competition in one form or another will always exist, and that it is highly desirable it should. But whether she or I be right, or both of us be wrong, of one thing I am sure; the spirit which animates Emma Goldman is the only one which will emancipate the slave from his slavery, the tyrant from his tyranny — the spirit which is willing to dare and suffer." The different schools of thought, if anything, teach us that our work is never done toward optimization and encouraging freedom from *all* forms of slavery. Similarly, they all help to show how a world without slavery is absolutely possible, and can be worked out in numerous ways, whilst dispelling superstition and myths regarding "anarchy." As reflected among the many differences with 19th century Abolitionists, here is what Parker Pillsbury had to say in concluding the movement in

1883: "Abolitionists did think, and deeply too. And they felt as intensely as they thought. And so how could they but differ? And there were disagreements that were not all reconciled before death sundered the parties to meet on earth no more. But they lived and died with their faces ever towards freedom, justice and love. A little more toleration, a very little more remembrance of our difference of temperament, of power of perception, of inherited tendencies, of possible material, mental or moral infirmity in ourselves, for which we should be scarcely responsible in the least degree, might have preserved from many a discordant note that seemed to ring on down to the gates of the grave. It was not anger, it was not hate. It was rather the result of *intensity of love*. At least it was so among some of our very truest, bravest, best, whose natures could but love, could never hate." He admits there was still work to be done, and that there was debate on ending their anti-slavery societies, however, a general contentedness was formed around the aggregate end of *chattel slavery*. It is our reflections now, with their help, which help us see where slavery *must* be further addressed. Herbert Spencer's explanation may give us examples by looking at the bigger picture when he tells us "what is essential to the idea of a slave? We primarily think of him as one who is owned by another. To be more than nominal, however, the ownership must be shown by control of the slave's actions—a control which is habitually for the benefit of the controller. That which fundamentally distinguishes the slave is that he labours under *coercion* to satisfy another's desires. The relation admits of *sundry gradations*. Remembering that originally the slave is a prisoner whose life is at the mercy of his captor, it suffices here to note that there is a harsh *form of slavery* in which, treated as an animal, he has to expend his entire effort for his owner's advantage. Under a system less harsh, though occupied chiefly in working for his owner, he is allowed a short time in which to work for himself, and some ground on which to grow extra food. A further amelioration gives him power to sell the produce of his plot and keep the proceeds. Then we come to the still more moderated form which commonly arises where, having been a free man working on his own land, *conquest* turns him into what we distinguish as a serf; and he has to give to his owner each year a fixed amount of labour or produce, or both: retaining the rest himself. Finally, in some cases... he is allowed to leave his owner's estate and work or trade for himself elsewhere, under the condition that he shall pay an annual sum. What is it which, in these cases, leads us to qualify our conception of the slavery as more or less severe? Evidently the greater or smaller extent to which effort is *compulsorily* expended for the benefit of another instead of for self-benefit. If all the slave's labour is for his owner the slavery is heavy, and if but little it is light. Take now a further step. Suppose an owner dies, and his estate with its slaves comes into the hands of trustees; or suppose the estate and everything on it to be bought by a company; is the condition of the slave any the better if the amount of his compulsory labour remains the same? Suppose that for a company we substitute the community; does it make any difference to the slave if the time he has to work for others is as great, and the time left for himself is as small, as before? The essential question is—How much is he compelled to labour for other benefit than his own, and how much can he labour for his own benefit? The degree of his slavery varies according to the ratio between that which he is forced to yield up and that which he is allowed to retain; and it matters not whether his master is a single person or a society. If, without option, he *has* to labour for the society, and receives from the general stock such portion as the society awards him, he becomes a slave to the society."

Simply notice how manipulative *Political Slavery* can really be, in the following scenario: You tell your goon to steal other people's money, because the goon believes in your "authority" and you convinced him of it's "necessity." You then pay your goon some of the money they stole, and give some money back to "the people" so they think you "serve them," but you also give yourself some of the money as well because it's "necessary" since you "work for them." In truth, this whole scenario is only made possible due to the belief in "authority," and the use of violence. It creates a never-ending loop of financial security for yourself, at the disposal of another, but nobody can tell it's theft since it is all done under the name of "authority" and "necessity." Everyone is then left dependent upon you, who has most of the money and resources, including the ability to do violence and put pressures upon them, and thus they comply. You then teach them more about the "necessity" and learn how to manipulate them through other means but mostly psychologically, and they soon become willing slaves.

Lysander Spooner, Abolitionist, Lawyer (1808) -
"If any man's money can be taken by a so-called government, without his own personal **consent**, all his other rights are **taken** with it; for with his money the government can, and will, hire soldiers to stand over him, compel him to **submit** to it's **arbitrary will**, and kill him if he resists"

Murray Rothbard, Philosopher (1926) -
"For centuries the State has committed mass murder and called it 'war'; then ennobled the mass slaughter that 'war' involves. For centuries **the State has enslaved people** into armed battalions and called it 'conscription' in the 'national service.' For centuries the State has robbed people at bayonet point and called it 'taxation.'"

Rod Taylor (From "Mad As Hell" With Aaron Russo 1996) - "In virtually **every culture** from ancient Egypt to Babylon to Greece and Rome, Africa, Asia, Europe and the United States, Germany and Japan openly practiced widespread slavery only fifty years ago, in the soviet union until less than a decade ago, China even today. **It's a disease of our human nature** and yet people are under the impression that it no longer exists. I say to you that **in a subtle form it exists in America today** and it's becoming less subtle and more manifest. Madison avenue has just cleaned it up a little bit dressed it up in new words. **The slave master is now big brother, someone to protect you**, someone to confide in but it's all the same, he **owns your life**. This may sound far-fetched but i think I can prove it. When the IRS allows you a tax deduction, they and their congressional collaborators and the media call it a tax subsidy, in other words they designate it as a gift to you; a subsidy, the only way they could conceive this terminology is by presupposing that they i.e the government own all the money. Their view is that they're entitled to it all that which they **allow** you to keep, is their compassionate and generous gift, to you. How can this be? You create the money by your efforts, your sacrifice, your creativity, your risk taking, so how can it belong to them? It's very simple, they own you, they **own everything you produce**, your money, your house, your thoughts and ideas, your children. If you go to a foreign country to work you still have to pay the *U.S. income tax*. You could dig a hole in the middle of Siberia and they'd be entitled to a cut of your wages because in their minds, **under their law, they own you.** They create arcane and esoteric laws to criminalize you. You can't even understand them without a lot of professional help, you have to run around *slavishly* collecting little pieces of paper receipts, seven years of detailed financial records because you might be called on to give an account of yourself to the big boss man; and if you've made a mistake, he can take everything you have, he loves it that way, that's total power over you, slavery. In this modern age, the information age, getting your money is not enough, even though money, don't let anyone deceive you, is the material source of your **freedom**. They want your **mind**. If you deviate in your thinking, if you commit one of the ten thousand taboos and they perceive your actions as a threat, they'll come out and kill you. It was the thought police who killed the children at Waco and Ruby Ridge. **We're not free, we belong to the government.** Who else holds a counterfeit license to kill, incarcerate and confiscate for **non-crimes**. Remember, America is about liberty first and last, not **obedience** to bureaucrats. The Washington power-click wants you to shut up, get in line, do what you're told to do and most outrageously, think what you've been told to think. We have hundreds of politicians and thousands of lobbyists crawling all over Washington thinking of ways to control you, to extend **their will over you**, to subvert your freedom and replace it with their will to capture, that is to **steal**, your life force and so we should all be very angry, because anger is the engine that drives our will to resist and without resistance, without awareness, they will take it all. It's not just politically perverse, it's a sin against mankind because *freedom is actually sacred.* Drop an ant into a jar and seal the lid, it will spend the rest of its life trying to get out, it has nowhere to go, but it wants to be free, that is its **nature**. It's the way every living thing is made, once a long time ago, I saw something at the zoo, a wolf lying in its cage i thought about how this magnificent animal was the end product of millions of years of evolutionary design, a nose that could detect the faintest scent, ultrasonic hearing, eyes that could see in the dark, teeth and jaws capable of crushing thick bone, heart and lungs that could run him for hours in a sub-zero blizzard and yet there he was, lying forlorn and full of despair. He was well fed he had a clean habitat and water and medical care, so what was the problem? He was sick with the **knowledge** that his wonderful powers would never be **exercised** again, and so he lay there, his head on his paws, staring blankly ahead at perhaps some imaginary forest that he could never reach because there were bars around him, they had not killed his body but they were destroying his soul. God gave Adam and Eve freedom even though he knew they would invite death into the world, that's how important freedom is in the divine scheme of things and that's why we urge you to **defend** it."

From *The Liberator 2 News:* "Abolitionism" from *The Online Etymology Dictionary* is defined as "belief in the **principle of abolishing (something)**," originally purely in an anti-slavery sense (sourced from 1790). From abolitionist William Lloyd Garrison as "the denial of the right to make man the property of man." From an 1846 alphabet book, "'a' is for *Abolitionist*, a man who wants to free the wretched slave and give to all an **equal liberty**." *"Abolitionist"* is defined as a "person who favors doing away with some **law, custom, or institution**" or originally in reference to abolishing the institution of *chattel slavery* (sourced from 1792-1825). *"Modern Abolitionism"* can therefore be defined as "the revival and continuance of the original *abolitionism*, in ending *all* forms of slavery, particularly in reference to *political slavery*." The first *abolitionism* was focused on ending *chattel slavery*, with many *abolitionists* noting problems with the closely associated *political slavery*. Our work, as *modern abolitionists*, is bringing their influential and powerful voices back to life. The *American abolitionists* were considered among *the first voluntaryists* in helping the world in it's evolution towards realizing their freedom. Living shortly thereafter the foundation of America, they noticed many problems concerning the government and it's *false claims of liberty, equality, peace or security.* Their cause for freedom from slavery, constantly disregards *political action (voting, elections, law-changing)*, instead emphasizing the constant need for *"moral suasion."* They were successful in shifting the moral conscience of the nation, having a ripple effect onto the rest of the world, after being attacked relentlessly by the media. We intend to further the moral education of slavery, in finishing the work they have started, for ending *political slavery* with *voluntaryism.*

Notable Outspoken 19th Century
Voluntaryist Chattel Slavery Abolitionists:
William Lloyd Garrison, Lysander Spooner, Adin Ballou, Henry Clarke Wright, Ezra Heywood, Josiah Warren, Charles Lane, Henry David Thoreau, Ralph Waldo Emerson, Jeremiah Hacker, William Batchelder Greene, Stephen Pearl Andrews, etc. *(more individuals from quotes)*

Into the 20th century, *abolitionist* works were being revisited by many individuals, including notably Leo Tolstoy and Benjamin Tucker, with the introduction of the term "anarchism" (from Greek *an-archon* "no rulers," *not* no rules, just as *mon-archon* or "monarchy" means "one ruler") otherwise known as *voluntaryism*, becoming prominent.

William Lloyd Garrison, Journalist, Abolitionist (1805) - "The **Abolitionism** which I advocate is as absolute as the **law of God**, and as unyielding as His throne. It admits of no compromise. **Every slave is a stolen man; every slaveholder is a man stealer.** By no precedent, no example, no law, no compact, no purchase, no bequest, no inheritance, no combination of circumstances, is slave holding **right** or **justifiable**."

"'That all men are created **equal**; that they are endowed by their Creator with certain inalienable **rights**; that among these are life, liberty, and the pursuit of happiness.' Hence, I am an **Abolitionist**. Hence, I cannot but regard oppression in every form—and most of all, that which turns a man into a thing—with indignation and abhorrence. Not to cherish these feelings would be recreancy to **principle**. They who desire me to be dumb on the subject of Slavery, unless I will open my mouth in its defence, ask me to give the lie to my professions, to degrade my manhood, and to stain my soul. I will not be a liar, a poltroon, or a hypocrite, to accommodate any party, to gratify any sect, to escape any odium or peril, to save any interest, to preserve **any institution**, or to promote any object."

"Act as **free moral agents**, not as tools of *party*."

"We have appealed to Christians, philanthropists, and patriots, for their assistance to accomplish the **great work** of national redemption through the agency of **moral power**—of public opinion—of individual duty. How have we been received? We have been threatened, proscribed, vilified, and imprisoned—a laughing-stock and a reproach. Do we falter, in view of these things? Let time answer. If we have been hitherto urgent, and bold, and denunciatory in our efforts,—hereafter *we shall grow vehement and active with the increase of danger.*"

"Liberty for each, for all, forever! Man above **all institutions!**"

Ralph Waldo Emerson, Abolitionist, Author (1803) - "Representative Government is *really* misrepresentative; Union is a conspiracy against the Northern States which the Northern States are to have the privilege of paying for; the adding of Cuba and Central America to the slave marts is enlarging the area of Freedom. **Manifest Destiny, Democracy, Freedom, fine names for an ugly thing.**

They call it otto of rose and lavender,—I call it bilge-water. They call it Chivalry and Freedom; I call it the stealing all the earnings of a poor man and the earnings of his little girl and boy, and the earnings of all that shall come from him, his children's children forever. But this is Union, and this is Democracy; and our poor people, led by the nose by these fine words, dance and sing, ring bells and fire cannon, with *every new link of the chain which is forged for their limbs by the plotters in the Capitol*... **Massachusetts, in its heroic day, had no government – was an anarchy. Every man stood on his own feet, was his own governor**; and there was no breach of peace from Cape Cod to Mount Hoosac. California, a few years ago, by the testimony of all people at that time in the country, had the best government that ever existed. Pans of gold lay drying outside of every man's tent, in perfect security. The land was measured into little strips of a few feet wide, all side by side. A bit of ground that your hand could cover was worth one or two hundred dollars, on the edge of your strip; and there was no dispute. Every man throughout the country was armed with knife and revolver, and it was known that instant *justice* would be administered to each offence, and perfect peace reigned. "

"There *never* was in any man sufficient faith in the power of rectitude, to inspire him with the broad design of renovating the State on the principle of right and love. All those who have *pretended* this design, have been partial reformers, and have admitted in some manner the supremacy of the bad State. **I do not call to mind a single human being who has steadily denied the authority of the laws, on the simple ground of his own moral nature.** Such designs, *full of genius and full of fate as they are*, are not entertained except avowedly as air-pictures. If the individual who exhibits them, dare to think them practicable, he disgusts scholars and churchmen; and men of talent, and women of superior sentiments, cannot hide their contempt.

Not the less does **nature continue to fill the heart of youth with suggestions of this enthusiasm**, and there are now men, — if indeed I can speak in the plural number, — more exactly, I will say, I have just been conversing with one man, to whom no weight of adverse experience will make it for a moment appear impossible, impossible, that thousands of human beings might exercise towards each other the grandest and simplest sentiments"

Charles Lane, Abolitionist (1800) -
"Why should we have all this complicated and costly machinery of **government**?"
"What are we to do? *Do nothing.* Like all our enemies, State oppression will die of itself if we meddle not with it."

Thomas Paine, American Independence (1737) -
"For upwards of two years from the commencement of the American War, and to a longer period in several of the American States, there were **no established forms of government.** The old governments had been *abolished*, and the country was too much occupied in defence to employ its attention in establishing new governments; yet during this interval order and harmony were preserved as inviolate as in any country in Europe. There is a *natural aptness* in man, and more so in society, because it embraces a greater variety of abilities and resource, to accommodate itself to whatever situation it is in. The instant formal government is abolished, society begins to act: a general association takes place, and *common interest produces common security.*"

Mary Wollstonecraft, Philosopher (1759) -
"**Slavery to monarchs and ministers**, which the world will be long in freeing itself from, and whose deadly grasp stops

the progress of the human mind, is not yet *abolished*... I call women slaves, I mean in a **political and civil** sense."

Victoria Woodhull, Activist (1838) -
"In the sixteenth century, was begun the battle for *Individual freedom.* The claim that **rulers had no right to control the consciences** of the people was boldly made... It may seem to be a strange proposition to make, that there is no such thing yet existent in the world as **self-government**, in its political aspects. But such is the fact. If self-government be the rule, every self must be its subject. *If a person govern, not only himself but others, that is despotic government*, and it matters not if that control be over one or over a thousand individuals, or over a nation; in each case it, would be the same principle of power exerted outside of self and over others, and this is despotism, whether it is exercised by one person over his subjects, or by twenty persons over a nation, or by one-half the people of a nation over the other half thereof."

S. Mitchell (letter to William Lloyd Garrison) -
"The moment we begin to have any **faith or trust in political action**, all is lost. Can Satan cast out Satan? Will slavery ever be destroyed in this country, so long as *government exists*? *Never!* Slavery is part and parcel of it. When we *lay the axe at the root of the tree, (government)*, then will *all wrong* cease, and not till then... Our business is to preach truth, to show that man is governed by the principles of Christianity, which are **Love, Liberty, Justice, Right and Truth.**"

Albert Tarn, Philosopher (1862) -
"Having obtained the 'liberty to vote' they naturally think to use it to get **the State** to cure all the evils to which human flesh is heir. Have they long hours? Call on the state to

shorten them. Have they low wages? Call on the state to raise them. Are they uneducated? Call on the state to educate them. And all the while they are **ignorant** of the final outcome of all this state intervention. They do not know that they are thereby perpetuating **the very institution which enslaves them**, that by subjecting themselves to the State they are shutting the door of Liberty in their own faces, and they do not know how many Acts of Parliament have been utter failures, defeating their own ends, and what **imperfect instruments even the best Acts are**, ever calling for more legislation to make up their defects... Again the state, by military and police coercion, maintains such monstrous **inequalities** of Wealth, and such **monopolies** of possessions, that many have no choice between slavery, starvation and thieving. Naturally they choose the latter as the most lucrative and enterprising occupation, and the State, which is itself **the biggest of thieves**, and which *protects thieving* on the largest scale, seizes the pickpocket and locks him up, to be maintained at the public expense for a while, and then turned adrift again upon society with no better chance of earning a livelihood than before."

As documented on *TheLiberatorFiles* website, Alvan Stewart, a presidential candidate, was angered with Abolitionists like William Lloyd Garrison. "Stewart claims that in a discussion with Garrison 'in my own house,' Garrison had said that he would not vote or petition for the end of slavery even if it would accomplish that. When he asked Garrison for his reason, he reports Garrison's response was 'Because that would be using our corrupt *human government*.' According to Stewart, Garrison further said that he had no doubt the time would come when voting would be regarded as infamous, and 'the same as visiting the gambling-table or the brothel.' Confusion was amplified for many when Garrison declared that it would be for him a 'sin' to vote." The website goes on to detail that "some abolitionists felt that Garrison included so many extraneous issues in his concern that it actually 'dis-organized' the movement. The blame fell often on Garrison. An example of that strong view comes from the *New England (Catholic) Reporter*, in an 1842 article titled, 'The Liberator, alias, the Disorganizer.' It calls *the Liberator* 'that mighty advocate for the slave, whose puissant editor should be immediately transported to Ethiopia, there to dwell in all love and harmony with the wild negroes – the Liberator is the most factious and disorganizing journal that aims at the severance of the federal Union, the stake-burning of religion's ministers, all of whom it stigmatizes.'" The Quincy Patriot criticizes Garrison saying "the Society is no long an Anti-Slavery Society simply, but in its principles and modes of action, has become a woman's rights, *non-government* Anti-Slavery Society." Oh, how wrong and misguided the people may have thought about Garrison, and yet how right he may have been all along. Hannah Webb tells us that "Garrison was working for a world in which there would be no slavery, no king, no beggars, no lawyers, no doctors, no soldiers, no palaces, no prisons, no creeds, no sects, no weary and grinding labor, no luxurious idleness, no particular Sabbath or temple.. no restraint but moral restraint, no containing power but love. Shall we judge such a man because he may go a little further than we are prepared to follow? Let us first consult our consciences and our testaments." One of the most absurd attacks, based on our study of slavery, is that which claims Henry Clarke Wright and William Lloyd Garrion's view on the government as being essentially worthless, stating "the vagaries of William Lloyd Garrison, and H.C. Wright, relative to *political action*, and *allegiance to civil government*, have nothing to do with the discussion of the great question of Abolition of Slavery." *TheLiberatorFiles* states, "At the occasion when

John Stuart Mill and John Bright called Garrison the preeminent agitator of the century, it was said of Garrison … 'he emancipated not only slaves, but the American mind. The whole intellect of the country has been set thinking about *the fundamental question about society and government.*'" Charles Lenox Remond stated, "whether you believe it or not, that if the cause of **universal liberty** shall ever be established in our country, within our day and generation, it can only be by the promulgation to the country of **the most radical type of Anti-Slavery**, known as *the 'Garrison doctrine.'*" Many like Garrison, including Nathaniel P. Rogers and Abby Kelley may deserve the same credit as Garrison, since they also supported non-resistance, moral suasion and the questioning of *authority*. Stacey Robertson, biographer of abolitionist Parker Pillsbury, states "Rogers distrusted anyone in a position of authority, including ministers and priests, politicians and bureaucrats." Pillsbury in his own work from 1883 states about Rogers that he is "becoming convinced that **all legislation was force**, and that as anti-slavery, in our opinion, was a strictly moral and religious movement, a work of repentance and reformation, we could not resort to physical force. He contended that without the life-taking power, or the power and right, usurped or *assumed right*, to enforce its decrees, government would be powerless; a mere exhortation. That if slave-holding were forbidden by congress, it must be with penalties and power to enforce them at whatever cost, otherwise all such legislation must be null and void. If the penalty were resisted by force, it must be repelled by force to the extent, if need be, of cutting off the head of every offender by the sword. And so, **to enforce a law, would be as the march of an army.** Or if the penalty were not death, but only imprisonment, and the culprits refused to enter the dungeon doors, the sword of the marshal must enforce the penalty even at cost of life.

Or if fine only be the penalty, it must be collected though at point of bayonet or sword. If law be penal, it is capital; and if not penal it is no law. 'Finally,' said Rogers, 'legal abolition of slavery would be abolition at the point of the sword, and as decidedly military in spirit, and as far from being moral as would be an invasion of the slave plantations by an anti-slavery army.'"

Parker Pillsbury, Abolitionist (1809) -
"How much we need a host of independent, free, noble minded men, pledged to *no party*, no religious affiliation, no mere human ties of any kind-model men, in every high and divine sense of the word." Pillsbury was additionally skeptical about even if "Emancipation" were to occur, with Samuel May, Jr. giving an account, "he said he dreaded to give way to any rejoicing, for he had noticed that **any good thing in the government was quite sure to be followed by some extraordinary baseness!**"

Jeremiah Hacker, Abolitionist (1801) -
"Bound to *no party*, to no sect confined, the World our Church, **our brethren all mankind.**"
"The [Pleasure] Boat owns no distinction of sect nor party, and recognizes no national bounds but claims **the whole universe as its nation**; and would rejoice to see *every party division, political and religious, swept from the earth.*"
"Truth against error, victory or death."
"We had much rather be all alone in the **right** than with the whole world in the wrong."
"That we are **right** in denouncing **all wars as unnecessary** and wicked, we daily have the witness of peace and a clear **conscience**."
As a promoter of the popular 19th century movement of Temperance, restraining from alcohol usage, among other Abolitionists, he would criticize those who would want to

use the law to their aid, saying that their "moral suasion" should not be using "the strong arm of the law." Furthermore, he states "men will not *permit* others to say what they shall or shall not eat or drink. They are willing to be reasoned with in these matters, but are not willing to be **forced.** What folly, then, for any man or set of men to enact penal laws by which to govern the appetites of others. Such a course ever has and ever **will increase the evil it aims to cure."**

He stated that the *only* government people would need would be **"the government of truth in their own minds."** "As for voting, I do not believe in it for either sex." "What do I care which party a man belongs to? If people will dabble in filth they will find no lack of it in either party." He commonly stated that government was making people "robbed of the earth."

"When I look upon the two great political parties, I see only a couple of wolves, nearly alike in size and ferocity, fighting over the fat carcass of a foolish sheep that has run headlong into their den. Sometimes one is rather fatter, sometimes the other, and when I witness their quarrels... I rejoice in the distant prospect of that day, when **both parties will be destroyed by the spread of the gospel of peace and humanity."**

"There are two kingdoms or principles which are directory opposite to each other, in spirit and in practice. One is the kingdom or **principle of love, and rules its subjects by convincement and persuasion**. It teaches us what is evil and what is good, and saves the erring. The other is the **kingdom of force, and labors to overcome evil by evil, and destroys, crushes, and ruins.** No man can belong to both these kingdoms at the same time... If he is a peace man, he cannot willingly move a finger to aid the government of force, *he can neither vote for nor hold office under such a government"*

"My object has not been to reform the leaders – they are at present too intent on unrighteous gain – too earnest after the loaves and the fishes, to listen; they would only regard my testimony as the rattle of a pleasure boat. **My work is with the people.**"

Booker T. Washington, Former Slave (1856) -
"The reputation that I made as a speaker during this campaign induced a number of persons to make an earnest effort to get me to enter **political life, but I refused**, still believing that I could find *other service which would prove of more permanent value to my race.* Even then I had a strong feeling that what our people most needed was to get a foundation in **education, industry, and property**, and for this I felt that they could better afford to strive than for political preferment. As for my individual self, it appeared to me to be reasonably certain that I could succeed in political life, but I had a feeling that it would be a rather *selfish* kind of success — individual success at the cost of failing to do my duty in assisting in laying a foundation for the masses."

Dyer Lum, Philosopher (1839) -
"**Anarchism, in place of abolitionism**, was the secret of peace."

The Non-Resistant newspaper (1839) -
"Our object in noticing the rival claims of **human governments, civil, and ecclesiastical**, is to show that the whole of them are based upon impious *assumptions are without any just foundation whatever*, and, as such, should be discountenanced and opposed by every friend of God and man."
"*God is the only independent sovereign in the universe and the only rightful legislator* among men or angels, while all created beings are but dependent subjects of his righteous

government. His laws recognize every possible case of criminality; hence, the enactment of other or additional laws by men are, to say the least, *unnecessary* if they are not an implied impeachment of the divine wisdom and goodness."
"When men take the government of themselves into their own hands, they thereby declare themselves independent of their lawful and only sovereign, the Lord Almighty. It is the very thing which makes men rebels against the laws and government of God, it is putting self upon the throne in man instead of the king of all the earth, it is the creature endeavoring to wrench the reins of the **governmental chariot out of the hands of the Creator**, and is the very essence of that carnal mind which is enmity against God."
"It is said, both by politicians and priests, that *the government of this country may properly be denominated an experiment*, designed to prove the sufficiency of man to govern himself; and the failure of this experiment is equally deprecated by both, inasmuch as it will extinguish the last hope of the world, in regard to this momentous question. To both these classes of men we can say with the most undoubting confidence, *your experiment will fail* -as has every similar one to invent a self-moving machine, or to detect a universal specific among medicines."
"If man has no such **right**, as an individual, he has none as a member of a family as the inhabitant of a town, county, state, or nations hence, cannot delegate any such rights to others, called legislators, magistrates, judges, sheriffs."

Benjamin Tucker, Philosopher (1854) -
"**We Anarchists are political abolitionists**. We earnestly desire the abolition of the State. Our position on this question is parallel in most respects to those of... *the slavery abolitionists.*"
"I would say that it would be foolish for slaves, *as we are*, to build up a system for the coming free generation. Our duty

ought to be only to *remove the obstacles to order*, set men free, and create Liberty, and this will create order, because **'Liberty is the mother, not the daughter, of order.'"**
"When **human slavery in all its forms** shall have disappeared, I fancy that the credit of the victory will be given quite as exclusively to the *Anarchists*"
"Surely **no government can be based on consent** which does not take the trouble to learn the people's wishes; and surely no government can be more despicable, unprincipled, and cowardly than that which drowns the cries of anguish and of suffering of the slaves whom it crushes beneath its iron heel in loud boasts of popular choice and noisy celebrations of independence."

Joseph Labadie, Philosopher (1850) -
"You must become an Anarchist before Anarchism can be; that **you must have an intelligent desire to be free** before timid freedom ventures within your reach—that freedom is only for those who want it; that you must **realise your slavish conditions before slavery can be abolished**; that you must comprehend your own degradation and servility before human dignity and self-respect can be yours; that you must know that you are being despoiled of the greater share of the results of your honest efforts before the despoilers will cease their spoliation; that you must have the knowledge, *the will and the courage* to **take your own and leave what belongs to others** before you will be fit to associate with those who love justice and hate wrong, who are wise enough to know their own rights, and strong enough to refrain from aggressing another's security."

Pierre-Joseph Proudhon, Philosopher (1809) -
"As man seeks justice in **equality**, so society seeks **order in anarchy.**"

Victor Yarros, Lawyer, Philosopher (1865) -
"No sincere and thinking person can live long in the
atmosphere of **State slavery**"
"Tyranny is a two-edged sword. The strong are brutalized
and degraded in the exercise of their tyranny, while the
weak become slaves, cowards, and nobodies under its
yoke. **Only free individuals can live in harmony**, and only
under *diseased* conditions can their interests be
antagonistic."

J. Wm. Lloyd (1857, from Liberty newspaper) -
"The Government is Master and *we are Slaves*."

"Voluntaryism" from *The Online Etymology Dictionary* is
defined as the "principal of using *voluntary* action rather
than coercion (in politics, religion, etc.)" (sourced 1838).
"Voluntary" from Latin *voluntarius* "willing, of one's free will,"
related to "consent," which means to "agree, give assent;
yield when one has the right, power, or will to oppose"
(sourced 1300). From *voluntaryist.com*, "*voluntaryism* is the
doctrine that relations among people should be by *mutual
consent*, or not at all... *voluntaryists* are advocates of non-
political, non-violent strategies to achieve a free society. We
reject electoral politics, in theory and in practice, as
incompatible with *moral principles*... governments *must*
cloak their actions in an aura of *moral legitimacy* in order to
sustain their power, and *political methods invariably
strengthen that legitimacy*."

The Liberator, Abolitionist Newspaper (1831) -
"The triumphant progress of the cause of **Temperance and
Abolition** in our land, through the instrumentality of
benevolent and **voluntary** associations, encourages us to
combine our own means and efforts for the promotion of a
still *greater cause*."

"**Authority and compulsion are out of the question.** All association must be quite voluntary. It is *only* in **voluntary associations** that man is fine."

"*Every man* must be left quite free to choose his own work. **No form of compulsion** *must* be exercised over him. If there is, his work will not be good for him, will not be good in itself, and will not be good for others. And by work I simply mean activity of *any* kind."

"**Every Law**, That men have made for Man, Since first Man took his brother's life, And the sad world began, But straws the wheat and saves the chaff, With **a most evil fan.** This too I know—and wise it were, If each could know the same—That **every prison** that men build, Is built with bricks of shame, And bound with bars lest Christ should see, How men *their brothers* maim."

"**The State must give up all idea of government.** It must give it up because, as *a wise man once said many centuries before Christ*, there is such a thing as leaving mankind alone; there is no such thing as governing mankind. **All modes of government are failures.** Despotism is unjust to everybody, including the despot, who was probably made for better things. Oligarchies are unjust to the many, and ochlocracies are unjust to the few. High hopes were once formed of democracy; but democracy means simply the bludgeoning of the people by the people for the people... **The form of government that is most suitable to the artist is no government at all.**" *(Wilde is referring to Zhuangzi from Ancient Taoism, as the man before Christ. When Wilde went to jail after sharing these views and his homosexuality, Benjamin Tucker in his newspaper Liberty would defend him)*

"One is absolutely sickened, not by the crimes that the wicked have committed, but by the **punishments that the good have inflicted**; and a community is infinitely more brutalized by the *habitual employment of punishment*, than it is by the occasional occurrence of crime."

Auberon Herbert, Philosopher (1838) -
"Life divided between **rulers and ruled, between slave-owners and slaves**; or on the side of Liberty, that is, of self-dependence and self-responsibility, of free thought, free religion, free enterprise, free trade, of **every free moral influence that grows where force is not**, of all those countless individual energies and countless individual differences that arise where men are not constrained to live in imitation of each other, and of that natural selection that eventually preserves every improved form in either *mental or material things*, where these individual energies and individual differences are allowed to clash freely together. In other words every man has to decide for himself, as his creed in life, whether men are to be made happier by a system that rests on and believes in coercion, or a system of self-directed agencies and moral influences; whether their continual co-operation throughout life is to be **voluntary or to be imposed.**"
"For a nation whose units are willing to place **their bodies and their minds in the keeping of others**, there are no hopes of growth and movement. It is only reserved to them to fall from one depth to another depth of **State slavery**, whilst they live in the mocking dream that they are moving onwards and upwards."
"We, who call ourselves **Voluntaryists**, appeal to you to **free yourselves** from these many systems of **State force**, which are rendering impossible the true and the happy life of the nations of to-day. This ceaseless effort to compel each other, in turn for each new object that is clamored for by this or that set of politicians, this ceaseless effort to **bind chains round the hands of each other**, is preventing progress of the real kind, is preventing peace and friendship

and brotherhood, and is turning the men of the same nation, who ought to labour happily together for common ends, in their own groups, in their own free unfettered fashion, into enemies, who live conspiring against and dreading, often hating each other."

William Lloyd Garrison, Journalist, Abolitionist (1805) - "As **every human government is upheld by physical strength**, and its laws are enforced virtually at the point of the bayonet, **we cannot hold any office** which imposes upon its incumbent the obligation to **compel** men to do right, on pain of imprisonment or death. We therefore **voluntarily** exclude ourselves from every legislative and judicial body, and repudiate *all* human politics, worldly honors, and stations of *authority*."
"We do not acknowledge allegiance to *any* **human government**."
"We are bound by the laws of a kingdom which is not of this world; the subjects of which are forbidden to fight; in which Mercy and Truth are met together, and Righteousness and Peace have kissed each other; which has *no state lines, no national partitions, no geographical boundaries*; in which there is no distinction of rank, or division of caste, or **inequality** of sex; the officers of which are Peace, its exactors Righteousness, its walls Salvation, and its gates Praise; and which is destined to *break in pieces and consume all other kingdoms.* Our country is the world, our countrymen are all mankind. We love the land of our nativity only as we love all other lands. The interests, **rights**, **liberties** of American citizens are no more dear to us than are those of the *whole human race.* Hence, we can allow *no appeal to patriotism*, to revenge any national insult or injury."
"Our mission is, to regenerate **public opinion.** We are *not* concerned for the loaves and fishes of office, we are *not*

seeking the elevation of any particular man, *nor* the success of *any* particular party."

On **"patriotism,"** this notion may be simply be seen as a form of admitting one's own *Mental Slavery.* As Richard Price tells us, "what has the love of their country hitherto been among mankind? What has it been but a love of domination; a desire of **conquest**, and a thirst for grandeur and glory, by extending territory, and enslaving surrounding countries? What has it been but a blind and narrow *principle*, producing in every country a contempt of other countries, and forming men into combinations and factions against their common **rights** and **liberties**?... What was the love of their country among the Jews, but a wretched partiality to themselves, and a proud contempt of all other nations? What was the love of their country among the old Romans? We have heard much of it; but I cannot hesitate in saying that, however great it appeared in some of its exertions, it was in general no better than a principle *holding together a band of robbers* in their attempts to **crush all liberty but their own."** Leo Tolstoy shares with us, "patriotism in its simplest, clearest, and most indubitable meaning is nothing but an instrument for the attainment of the government's ambitious and mercenary aims, and a renunciation of human dignity, common sense, and **conscience** by the governed, and a **slavish submission** to those who hold power. That is what is really preached wherever patriotism is championed. Patriotism is slavery."

Aldous Huxley, Philosopher (1894) -
"Men are persons, *not pawns or slaves*, and their **freedom to reject must never be overborne by force** whether or violence or of bribery or of the supernatural... Military efficiency demands extreme concentration of power, a high degree of centralization, the training of the masses in

passive obedience to their superiors, the imposition of some form of conscription or **slavery to the state**, and the creation of a local idolatry with the nation or a semi-deified **tyrant as the object of worship**... In any future war there will be, not merely military conscription, but also *industrial, intellectual and moral conscription*: and the whole population, women, children and the aged, as well as men, will be subjected to this *State-imposed slavery*."
He notes that "war is incompatible with liberty," further detailing what he called "military slavery" through the act of conscription.

Abbe Defourny, Philosopher -
"What characterizes the slave is this, that he is in the hands of his master like a **chattel**, a tool, and *no longer a man*. **Just so it is with a soldier, an officer, a general**, who march to murder and to death without any care as to justice, by the **arbitrary will** of ministers... Thus *military slavery* exists, and it is *the worst of slaveries*, particularly now, when by means of enforced military service it **puts the chain about the necks of all free and strong men of the nations**, in order to make of them tools of murder, *killers by profession*, butchers of human flesh"

Anselme Bellegarrigue, Philosopher (1813) -
"You thought to this day that there were tyrants? Well! You were in error, as there only are slaves: **where no one obeys, no one commands.**"
"**The people has thanked those responsible for its enslavement; by means of its votes**, it has awarded them the right to hunt it down with snare and bait, to stalk and harry, snipe and trap, with **the law for a weapon** and its neighbours for hunting hounds."

Epictetus, Former Slave, Philosopher (50 AD) -
"He is free who lives as he wishes to live; who is **neither subject to compulsion nor to hindrance, nor to force**; whose movements are not impeded, and whose desires attain their purpose."

Charles Dickens, Author, Philosopher (1812) -
"**Public opinion in the slave States is slavery, is it not?** Public opinion, in the slave States, has delivered the slaves over, to the gentle mercies of their masters... Public opinion has knotted the lash, heated the branding-iron, loaded the rifle, and shielded the murderer. *Public opinion threatens the abolitionist with death*, if he venture to the South; and drags him with a rope about his middle, in broad unblushing noon, through the first city in the East."

The Liberator, Abolitionist Newspaper (1831) -
"It is **wrong to hold an office** in which we must consent to be *vested with life-taking or war-making powers* or to come under an *obligation* to use it... It is **wrong to vote** for others to office which it is wrong for us to hold. We must look to the *character of the office itself* and not to the candidate or measures he proposes, *however good these may be*. **To exercise the franchise even to effect the abolition of slavery would be wrong, would be to vote for murder to prevent theft.**"

Josiah Warren, Abolitionist (1798) -
"**Government, and its function is to use force**, to prevent him from using force against me and mine; it interferes, with my **consent**, to prevent interference with my **sovereign right** to control my **own**. Its mission is 'intervention for the sake of non-intervention.'"

Lysander Spooner, Abolitionist, Lawyer (1808) -
"**Government is in reality established by the few**; and
these few **assume the consent** of all the rest, *without any
such consent being actually given.*"
"**The number of slaves, instead of having been
diminished by the war, has been greatly increased**; for a
man, thus *subjected to a government* that he does not
want, is a slave."
"A man is *none the less a slave* because he is **allowed** to
choose a new master once in a term of years. Neither are a
people any the less slaves because **permitted** periodically
to choose new masters. What makes them slaves is the
fact that they now are, and are always hereafter to be, in
the hands of men whose power over them is, and always is
to be, absolute and **irresponsible**."
"It cannot be said that men put all their **rights** into the
hands of the government, in order to have them *protected*;
because there can be no such thing as a man's being
protected in his rights, any longer than he is allowed to
retain them in his own possession. The *only* possible way,
in which any man can be protected in his rights, is to protect
him in his own actual possession and *exercise* of them. And
yet **our government is absurd enough to assume that a
man can be protected in his rights, after he has
surrendered them altogether into other hands than his
own.** This is just as absurd as it would be to assume that a
man had given himself away as a slave, in order to be
protected in the enjoyment of his liberty."
"These tyrants, living solely on plunder, and on the **labor** of
their slaves, and applying all their energies to the seizure of
still more plunder, and the enslavement of still other
defenseless persons; increasing, too, their numbers,
perfecting their organizations, and multiplying their
weapons of war, they extend their conquests until, in order
to hold what they have already got, it becomes necessary

Slavery Gone For Good

for them to act **systematically**, and co-operate with each other in holding their slaves in subjection. **But all this they can do only by establishing what they call a government, and making what they call laws.** *All* the great governments of the world- those now existing, as well as those that have passed away- have been of this character. They have been mere bands of robbers, who have **associated for purposes of plunder, conquest, and the enslavement of their fellow men.** And their laws, as they have called them, have been only such agreements as they have found it necessary to enter into, in order to maintain their organizations, and act together in plundering and enslaving others, and in *securing to each his agreed share of the spoils.* All these laws have had no more *real obligation* than have the agreements which brigands, bandits, and pirates find it necessary to enter into with each other, for the more successful accomplishment of their crimes, and the more peaceable division of their spoils. Thus substantially *all the legislation of the world has had its origin* in the desires of one class of persons to plunder and enslave others, and hold them as **property**."

"The result – and a natural one – has been that we have had governments, State and national, *devoted to nearly every grade and species of crime* that governments have *ever* practised upon their victims; and these crimes have culminated in a war that has cost a million of lives; **a war carried on, upon one side, for chattel slavery, and on the other for political slavery**; upon neither for liberty, justice, or truth. And these crimes have been committed, and this war waged, by men, and the descendants of men, who, less than a hundred years ago, said that all men were equal, and could owe neither service to individuals, nor allegiance to governments, except with their *own consent.*"

Patsy Mitchner, Former Slave -
"Slavery was a bad thing, and **freedom**, of the kind we got, with nothing to live on, was bad. Two snakes full of poison. One lying with his head pointing north, the other with his head pointing south. Their names was slavery and freedom."

Jonathan Swift, Author (1667) -
"For in reason, **all government** without the **consent** of the governed is *the very definition of slavery*"

Mahatma Gandhi, Indian Independence (1869) -
"Freedom is like birth. Till we are **fully free**, we are slaves"

Eric Williams, Activist (1911) -
"Slavery was not born of racism; rather, **racism was the consequence of slavery.**"

Mikhail Bakunin, Philosopher (1814) -
"If there is a **State**, there *must* be **domination** of one class by another and, as a result, slavery; **the State without slavery is unthinkable** – and this is why we the enemies of the State."

Karl Marx, Philosopher (1818) -
"The **existence of the state** is *inseparable* from the existence of slavery."

Henry David Thoreau, Abolitionist, Philosopher (1817) -
"Disobedience is the true foundation of liberty. **The obedient must be slaves.**"
"**Law never made men a whit more just**; and, by means of their respect for it, *even the well-disposed are daily made the agents of injustice.*"

"If it is of such a **nature** that it requires you to be the agent of **injustice** to another, then I say, *break the law*."

"When I meet a **government** which says to me, 'Your money or your life,' why should I be in haste to give it my money?"

"The progress from an absolute to a limited monarchy, from a limited monarchy to a democracy, is a **progress toward a true respect for the individual.**"

"**Is a democracy, such as we know it, the last improvement possible in government?** Is it not possible to take a step further towards recognizing and organizing the rights of man? There will never be a really free and enlightened State until the State comes to recognize *the individual as a higher and independent power*, from which *all its own power and authority are derived*, and treats him accordingly. I please myself with imagining a State at least which can afford to be just to all men, and to treat the individual with respect as a neighbor; which even would not think it inconsistent with its own repose if a few were to live aloof from it, not meddling with it, nor embraced by it, who fulfilled all the duties of neighbors and fellow-men. A State which bore this kind of fruit, and suffered it to drop off as fast as it ripened, would prepare the way for a still more perfect and glorious State, which also I have imagined, but **not yet anywhere seen.**"

"**Even voting for the right is doing nothing for it.** It is only expressing to men feebly your desire that it should prevail. A wise man will not leave the right to the mercy of chance, nor wish it to prevail through the power of the majority. There is but little virtue in the action of masses of men. When the majority shall at length vote for the abolition of slavery, it will be because they are indifferent to slavery, or because there is but little slavery left to be *abolished* by their vote. *They* will then be the only slaves. Only *his* vote can hasten the abolition of slavery who asserts his own freedom by his vote."

"**I have no designs on society, or nature, or God.** I am simply what I am, or I begin to be that. I live in the present. I only remember the past, and anticipate the future. I love to live."

"In my short experience of human life, the outward obstacles, if there were any such, have not been living men, but *the institutions of the dead*... Its officer, as a living man, may have human virtues and a thought in his brain, but as the **tool of an institution**, a jailer or constable it may be, he is not a whit superior to his prison key or his staff. Herein is the tragedy; that men doing outrage to their *proper natures*, even those called wise and good, lend themselves to perform the *office of inferior and brutal ones*. Hence come war and slavery in; and what else may not come in by this opening? But certainly there are modes by which a man may put bread into his mouth which will not *prejudice* him as a companion and neighbor."

"To one who *habitually endeavors* to contemplate the *true state* of things, the **political state** can hardly be said to have *any existence* whatever. "

"What is called **politics** is comparatively something so **superficial and inhuman**, that, practically, I have never fairly recognized that it concerns me at all."

"I doubt if there is a judge in Massachusetts who is prepared to **resign his office, and get his living innocently**, whenever it is required of him to pass sentence under a law which is merely contrary to the **law of God**. I am compelled to see that they put themselves, or rather are by character, in this respect, exactly on a level with the marine who discharges his musket in any direction he is *ordered to*. They are just as much *tools*, and as little men. Certainly, they are not the more to be respected, because their master **enslaves their understandings and**

consciences, instead of their bodies... Slavery, there are so many keen and *subtle masters* that enslave *both North and South*. It is hard to have a Southern overseer; it is worse to have a Northern one; but worst of all when you are the **slave-driver of yourself.**"

Larken Rose, Philosopher, Author -
"It is the enslavement of mankind, the subjugation of free will, and the destruction of **morality**, masquerading as 'civilization' and 'society.' The problem is not just that 'authority' can be used for evil; the problem is that, at its most basic essence, *it is evil*. In everything it does, it defeats the free will of human beings controlling them through **coercion** and **fear.** It supersedes and destroys moral **consciences**, replacing them with unthinking **blind obedience**."

Jeremey Locke, Author -
"Understand that choices made of your own free will are *not* evil. There is nothing wrong with sacrifice, if it is made **willingly**. But sacrifice without choice is not sacrifice, it is slavery. Authority always places demands on people by force. Authority never asks **permission**."

Herbert Spencer, Psychologist, Polymath (1820) -
"As a corollary to the proposition that **all institutions** must be subordinated to the **law of equal freedom**, we cannot choose but admit the right of the citizen to adopt a condition of **voluntary outlawry**. If every man has freedom to do all that he wills, provided he infringes not the equal freedom of any other man, then he is free to drop connection with **the State**,—to relinquish its **protection** and to refuse paying towards its support. It is self-evident that in so behaving he in no way trenches upon the liberty of others; for his position is a passive one, and, *whilst passive, he cannot*

become an aggressor... **Not only does magisterial power exist because of evil, but it exists by evil.** Violence is employed to maintain it; and all violence involves criminality. Soldiers, policemen, and gaolers; swords, batons, and fetters,—are instruments for inflicting pain; and all infliction of pain is, in the abstract, wrong. **The State employs evil weapons** to subjugate evil, and is alike contaminated by the objects with which it deals and the means by which it works... So that, however insignificant the minority, and however trifling the proposed trespass against their **rights**, no such trespass is permissible... That **moral sense** whose supremacy will make society harmonious and **government unnecessary** is the same moral sense which will then make each man assert his freedom even to the extent of ignoring the State—is the same moral sense which, by deterring the majority from coercing the minority, will eventually render *government impossible*. And, as what are merely different manifestations of the same sentiment must bear a constant ratio to each other, **the tendency to repudiate governments will increase only at the same rate that governments become needless."**

"From Shoa (Abyssinia), where 'of their persons and worldly substance he **[the King] is absolute master'**; or from Dahome, where '**all men are slaves to the king.**'... So alien to the truth, indeed, is the alleged creation of rights by government, that, contrariwise, rights having been established more or less clearly before government arises, become obscured as government develops along with that militant activity which, both by the *taking of slaves and the establishment of ranks*, produces status; and **the recognition of rights begins again to get definiteness only as fast as militancy ceases** to be chronic and governmental power declines."

"He feels that a fellow-man may be enslaved by imperious words and manners as well as by tyrannical deeds; and hence he avoids a dictatorial style of speech to those below him. Even paid domestics, to whose services he has obtained a right by contract, he does not like to address in a tone of authority. He seeks rather to **disguise his character of master.**"

Henry Seymour, Philosopher (1860) -
"We affirm that anything short of **individual liberty** is only a conventional restriction of liberty, that is to say, **slavery is disguise**, the worst of all slaveries... **Government and slavery are the same in purpose and effect.** Grotius denied that human power was ever established for the benefit of the governed; but he cited slavery as proof... Law, to be sure, is the generic term for all the various factors of politic administration which enable the few to *secure* those **special privileges and artificially fostered advantages that enslave the many.**"

Josiah Warren, Abolitionist (1798) -
"Theorists have told us that **laws and governments** are made for the **security** of person and **property**; but it must be evident to most minds, that they *never have, never will accomplish this professed object*; although they have had the world at their control for thousands of years, they have brought it to a worse condition than that in which they found it, in spite of immense improvements in mechanism, division of **labor**, and other elements of civilization to aid them. On the contrary, under the plausible pretext of securing person and property, they have spread *wholesale destruction, famine, and wretchedness* in *every* frightful form over all parts of the earth, where peace and security might otherwise have prevailed. They have shed more blood, committed more murders, tortures, and other frightful

crimes in the struggles against each other for the *privilege of governing*, than society ever would or could have suffered in the *total absence of all governments whatever*. It is *impossible* for any one who can read the history of governments, and the operations of laws, to feel secure in person and property under *any form of government* or any code of laws whatever. They invade the private household, they impertinently meddle with, and in their blind and besotted wantonness, presume to regulate the most sacred individual feelings. **No feelings of security, no happiness can exist under such circumstances.**"

"The more business there is thus committed to governmental management, the more must each of the governed **surrender his liberty** or control over his *own*, and the greater must be the amount of power delegated to the government." *(How government is a jack-of-all-trades in destroying freedom and productivity is detailed in "The Thirty-Six Trades of the State" by Ausene Alexandre)*

"Experience has proved, that power cannot be delegated to rulers of states and nations, in sufficient quantities for the management of business, without its *becoming an indefinite quantity*, and in this indefiniteness have mankind been cheated out of their **legitimate liberty.**"

"Government, strictly and scientifically speaking, is a **coercive force**; a man, while governed with his **own consent**, is not governed at all. Deliberative bodies, such as legislatures, congresses, conventions, courts, etc., scientifically speaking, are *not* government, which is simply coercive force."

"The right of secession or **self-sovereignty**... The right of secession being included in, and settled by, the admission of this great *universal right*, **political slavery** of all colors is logically at an end."

"There is nothing in **voluntary subordination** that violates the **natural liberty** of the individual, and the **fear** that

natural liberty would uproot all order is as groundless and as futile as the idea that *coercive subordination* has benefited mankind."
"Governments commit more crimes upon persons and **property** and contribute more to their **insecurity** *than all criminals put together.*"

Samuel May, Abolitionist (1797) -
"We are told that our government is what it is—not perfect, though the best that exists upon the face of the earth—and that while we live under this government, enjoying its protection, we are bound to *obey its laws.* I reply, in the first place, as to **protection**, we are very much less indebted for that to our government, than we are to a correct **moral** and humane sentiment, prevalent throughout the community—and, that if our law makers, expounders and administrators are doing what tends to corrupt that public sentiment, to obscure the people's vision, and blunt their sense of **right**, they are doing the worst they can, to undermine our security, and expose our **property**, reputation and life, to *unprincipled* men... Then, say some, leave the country and escape from your obligation, by going beyond the reach of the power which oppresses you. But, I reply, we shall not be likely to better our condition. Other forms of wrong and tyranny might meet us, wheresoever we may go, that we should be equally bound to withstand. Besides we owe our country, which, with all her faults, we dearly love, we owe our country something more and better than desertion, in this hour of her utmost trial." In quoting a popular pamphlet at the time called "The Higher Law" to prove the point of disobedience rather than reform, it states "Their reasoning is this: Because an unjust law is enacted we **must obey** it as a law, and do all we can to repeal it, because it is unjust. Seeing that iniquity is established by statute, we must keep the statute till we can destroy it; uphold it, till it can be

overthrown! Such beetle logic may safely be left to confute itself. Because the majority have resolved to sin, we must go with them, and keep on sinning to the end of the chapter, and then turn right about and sin no more, because we have at length succeeded in convincing the majority that we are all miserable sinners, especially we who knew better, and so have added the guilt of **hypocrisy** to the guilt of cruelty." May concludes saying "tell me not, then, that we are setting up our individual **consciences** against the conscience of the nation. A vast majority abhor the law—though there may be a majority, that for certain reasons of state have concluded it is expedient to enforce the law, bad though it be. **We have the heart of the nation with us—though the head may be against us.**"

Benjamin Tucker, Philosopher (1854) -
"We make war upon **the State as the chief invader of person and property**, as the cause of substantially all the crime and misery that exist, as itself **the most gigantic criminal extant**. It manufactures criminals much faster than it punishes them. It exists to create and sustain the privileges which produce economic and social **chaos**. It is the sole support of the **monopolies** which concentrate wealth and learning in the hands of a few and disperse poverty and ignorance among the masses, to the increase of which **inequality** the increase of crime is directly proportional. It **protects** a minority in plundering the majority by methods too subtle to be understood by the victims, and then punishes such unruly members of the majority as attempt to plunder others by methods too simple and straightforward to be recognized by the State as legitimate, crowning its outrages by **deluding scholars and philosophers**... into pleading, as an *excuse for its infamous existence*, the necessity of repressing the crime which it *steadily creates*."

"The only pretext on which the defender of **political government** can make existing usurpations float upon **consent** is to assert that going to the polls and voting, bearing arms, paying taxes, serving on juries, etc., are *presumptive* evidences that those who do so consent to the *institutions* under which they live. As well might it be argued that, in accepting the offer of a highwayman to toss one's last penny to see whether the robber should take it or leave it, the victim thereby consents to the highwayman's occupation. As the only alternative against extortion, a man may go to the *polls and vote* against the proposed levy of a corrupt ring of political jobbers, recognizing the ballot-box only on grounds of expediency, as a sinking man might hug a filthy pile in the dock."

A justification for *political slavery* is made when people say "if you don't exercise your *right to vote*, then you don't have a right to complain." If someone has the right to vote, shouldn't they also have the right to *not* vote? Mandatory compliance would be the antithesis of freedom. Additionally, someone may say "if you don't like it, then leave." If you recognize freedom of speech or freedom to travel, or voluntary interaction in every aspect of life, seeing that we are all humankind on the same earth, we should be able to freely live and criticize as we please so long as we are not infringing on the life of others. Both menticidal justifications shadow the *involuntary nature of the state*.

William Godwin, Philosopher (1756) -
"The vote by ballot, in its obvious construction, is not the symbol of liberty, but of slavery. What is it, that presents to every eye the image of liberty, and compels every heart to confess. This is the temple where she resides? An open front, a steady and assured look, a habitual and uninterrupted commerce between the heart and the tongue. The free man communicates with his

neighbour, not in corners and concealed places, but in market-places and scenes of public resort; and it is thus that the sacred spark is caught from man to man, till all are inspired with a common flame. **Communication and publicity are of the essence of liberty; it is the air they breathe; and without it they die.**"

"When we look at the **political history** of man, the case is infinitely worse. This too often seems one tissue of misery and vice. **War, conquest**, oppression, tyranny, slavery, insurrections, massacres, cruel punishments, degrading corporal infliction, and the extinction of life *under the forms of law*, are to be found in *almost every page.* It is as if an evil demon were let loose upon us, and whole nations, from one decade of years to another, were struck with the most pernicious *madness*."

Dr. J. H. Swain (from Liberty newspaper, approx. 1881) - "We are not combating order or organization so long as it is **not compulsory**, so long as no one's liberty is abridged. Under Liberty all that wish to be governed, or such as desire to be enslaved, will not be interfered with, but they must not force others to join in such action. It is not supposable that sane men would do either of these with society around them in a state of **freedom**. How long could the slaves have been held in bondage without the use of brute force. No longer can men be held in **subjection to the State** except by compulsion. Maintaining public order is one thing. Maintaining the State is another and very different thing. The first is not only possible under Anarchy, it is *impossible* without it, as is shown under government every day and more emphatically when riots occur. Under Liberty a mob, which is one party striving for the power held by another, would be *impossible*. To deny this is to show **ignorance** of the whole matter. **All government is pure usurpation**, since it began and has continued through all its changes by one part of the people compelling the other part to submit to their *authority*. To determine which party shall control the other we have recourse to the *ballot*,— a game of chance *dishonestly* played, but behind whichever party wins, by whatever fraud, is the army to awe and, if need be, murder the others into submission. We hold that no party has a **right** to fight or gamble with Liberty for a stake. They may fight or gamble for power over each other so long as they do it at their own expense, but not at the cost of others or of one other, or, as Mill states it, they may do whatsoever seems to them best so long as they do not interfere with others doing the same. So, **when each does what seems to him best, no one is compelled to act as another or others think best.** This is Liberty, or Anarchy, from which by necessity will grow the highest form of society, a public **order** as perfect as the times will admit of and in comparison with which all so called public order is organized disorder and society a menagerie in which personal conduct is moral when the brutes submit to bars and chains because compelled to do so by a stronger and more intelligent brute. Because of this, *submission to authority* is the test and standard of morality of Church and State and all their adherents. I have declared that *morality is a mental drug with which authority stupefies its subjects* that it may the more safely plunder them. Morality is then an **invisible weapon**, but the most potent of all wielded by robbers and murderers."

Maria Weston Chapman, Abolitionist (1806) -
"Save yourself the trouble of calling caucuses, printing party journals, distributing ballots, and the like. Let men who are fit for nothing of more consequence do this *little work,* which is best done by mere nobodies."

The word "government" has been associated with the Latin verb *gubernare* (guverno, guvernare): "to control" and the Latin noun *mens* (mentis): "the mind." If this is true, then *self-government* or self-mind-control would make sense, since *only we can control our Own minds*. However, this source may be disputed. Some scholars would prefer to use the word "state" as opposed to "government," as they may argue that "government" simply refers to people coming together to engage in governing as leadership which can be *totally voluntary*. In any case, the word "government" has been used interchangeably with the word "state" for thousands of years, *all* of which have *never* been voluntary, thus it may continue to be used in the connotation that it *is* based in violence and slavery. To reiterate, 19th century abolitionist Charles Lane when he argued for a *voluntary government*, found many critics among fellow *abolitionists* because they saw this as a contradiction of terms, much like how an individual may call themselves a *"sovereign citizen."*

What Must We Do To End Slavery?

Whilst *The Liberator* newspaper was created to help end *chattel slavery* with *Abolitionism*, the founding of *The Liberator 2* news was created to help end *political slavery* with *Modern Abolitionism*. The methods used among both these projects are to encourage **moral suasion**, the appeal to *morality* in order to change or influence behavior. In each case of application, we must be able to recognize moral contradictions, as with the case of asking ourselves questions, in grounding ourselves with logical consistency or *principles*. If we *say* we are against slavery, do our *actions* match our words or intentions? The goal may be said to create *order* within ourselves, in *order* to to create *order* within the world. This has been deemed by some as "the one great work" since the collective condition of *freedom* for all of humankind is beyond the duty of mere individual pursuits, and it *requires* an *amass of individuals* in the exercise of *self-ownership*, though many revolutions throughout history may have taken place with as little as 1-3% of the population. Even 19th century abolitionist William Lloyd Garrison tells us that "the success of any great moral enterprise does *not* depend upon numbers." As we come to understand that *true* freedom is *not* the result of *political action (ie. elections, legislation, paperwork)* but of this *moral suasion*, and in fact, *political action reinforces political slavery* due to legitimizing the concept of "authority," *modern abolitionism* emphasizes the necessity in *voluntaryism*. This in turn, emphasizes *any voluntary* solution available, such as mass education through the many tools we have, unique products and businesses, spiritual practices, music and culture, permaculture food forestry, or homeschooling co-ops. We may deem these as the *actual* determinants of our world condition, due to how influential they are upon us on a *daily basis*. Just observe the impact of the music we listen to or the products we use, alone. The 19th century *Abolitionists* chose to boycott certain products, such as those made with cotton due to it's connection to slavery, and they may have even created their own products. Similarly, many chattel slaves would sing songs talking about the life of freedom and happiness that awaits them or could be achieved, not just as a means of coping with their condition, but also as a means of inspiration for getting out of their condition. Notice the many songs and movies about the good rising above evil, about people being able to coexist in a world based on love. We may argue that their undying passion and curiosity may be answered among understanding and embracing who they are *meant* to be or *truly* would want to be. Many *Abolitionists* would quite literally "be the change you wish to see in the world" when they would set up their own towns away from the government for **the underground railroad**, some also utilizing it's own currency systems to show the better systems by example. Many people nowadays would deem these to be "parallel institutions" or "constructive programs." One may even imitate political action in campaigning around an idea, rather than an election. They may put up signs, knock on doors or even raise funds to continue, and at least the message would last the test of time as opposed to politics, but it would also help usher in direct change to "the people" without begging, without dishonesty, without attacking some "side," without legitimizing "authority" and without using euphemisms of violence. In addition, *nonviolent resistance* strategies as taught by the efforts of Mahatma Gandhi or Martin Luther King Jr. could be implemented. Dr. Erica Chenoweth has determined and demonstrated that strategies such as civil resistance, civil disobedience and overwhelming the state not only works, but it has more effect than any other form of resistance – including revolutionary violence, within her address *The Success of Nonviolent Civil Resistance*. In other words, we may exercise what is deemed as the **law of freedom**, which helps us understand that "as morality increases, freedom increases" and "as morality declines, freedom declines," or the more we encourage people to just treat others as people, the more equality and the less slavery takes place. Talking with others and sharing that which goes against an individual's current *belief system* may take care, patience, willpower and practice. It is merely the *recognition* that we are born *free by nature* and of a shared humanity, that sovereignty *(moral rules, an internal ruler)* is required for freedom *(no external rulers)*. We shall assist each other in this work, so that our *fear* of "chaos" regarding *true* freedom no longer has us fear the freedom that we deserve in *abolishing* slavery. The slave-master or governments of the world would like for us to abide to what may be called the **law of slavery**, to believe that "as slavery increases, order increases" and "as slavery declines, order declines." We will *never* be free or who we are *meant* to be if we fear our *self-ownership* or our own nature. As this fear, and all slavery depends upon *Mental Slavery*, and the teachings of philosophy and psychology warn us about our unnecessary identities and attachments, highlighting the importance of our thoughts creating our reality, our work lives mostly with the *mind*. It is a process in which we break our own *cognitive dissonance* to sympathize with our fellow man, being willing to make an apology and to say "no" where it is due. Many writers have said that freedom and slavery *are really* mental conditions, and therefore let us *imagine* and start to embrace the reality that *is* possible. **When we start to see ourselves as free peoples, we can start to act as free peoples.**

Theodore Dwight Weld, Abolitionist (1803) -
"Slaves sometimes sing, and so do convicts in jails under sentence, and both for the same reason. Their singing proves that they want to be happy *not* that they are so. It is the means that they use to make themselves happy, not the evidence that they are so already. Sometimes, doubtless, the excitement of song whelms their misery in momentary oblivion. He who argues from this that they have no conscious misery to forget, knows as little of **human nature** as of slavery."

Gertrude B. Kelly (from Liberty newspaper, approx. 1881) -
"If some women have had courage enough to dare **public opinion**, and insist on **thinking for themselves**, they have been so beaten by that most powerful weapon in society's arsenal, ridicule, that it has effectually prevented the great majority from *making any attempt to come out of slavery*."

Leo Tolstoy, Author, Philosopher (1828) -
"Men are thrown into slavery, into the most terrible slavery, *worse than has ever before existed*; but **Political Science** tries to persuade men that it is *necessary and unavoidable*."
"Wherever **violence becomes law**, there is slavery."
"The answer is very definite, applicable, and practicable, for it demands the activity of that one person over whom each of us has **real, rightful**, and unquestionable power, namely, oneself; and it consists in this, that if a man -- whether slave or slave owner -- really wishes to better not his position alone, but the position of people in general, he must not himself do those **wrong** things which enslave him and his brothers. And in order not to do the evil which produces misery for himself and for his brothers, **he should, first of all, neither willingly nor under compulsion take any part in Governmental activity**, and should, therefore, be neither a soldier, nor a Field-Marshal, nor a Minister-of-

State, nor a tax-collector, nor a witness, nor an alderman, nor a juryman, nor a governor, nor a Member of Parliament, nor, in fact, hold *any* office connected with **violence**."
"But slavery of all kinds has been going on so long, so many **artificial** wants have grown about it, so many people with different degrees of familiarity with these wants are interwoven with one another, through so *many generations* men have been spoiled and made effeminate, such complicated temptations and **justifications** of luxury and idleness have been invented by men, that for one who stands on the top of the pyramid of idle men, it is not at all so easy to understand his sin as it is for the peasant"
"In order to **free oneself** from the evil one should not fight with its consequences: the *abuses of Governments, the seizures and plunders of neighboring nations*, — but with the root of the evil; with the relations in which the people have placed themselves towards **human authority**. If the people recognize human power as higher than the power of God, higher than the law (Tao), then the **people will always be slaves** and the more so the more complex their organization of Power (such as a *constitutional* one) which they institute and to which they submit. Only those people can be free for whom the law of God (Tao) is the *sole supreme law* to which all others should be subordinated."
"A member of a *constitutional State* is always a slave because, imagining that he has participated or can participate in his Government, he recognizes the **legality of all violence** perpetrated upon him; he **obeys all the orders of the authorities.** So that people in constitutional States **imagining that they are free**, owing to this very imagination lose the idea itself of what **true freedom** is, and more and more *surrender themselves* into increasing slavery to their Governments."
"This error is that men of our times imagine that the servile subjection to violence in which they stand, in relation to the

Government, is a **natural** position and that the *authorization* by governmental power of certain actions defined by this power, is freedom; somewhat as if slaves were to regard as freedom the power, is freedom; somewhat as if slaves were to regard as freedom the **permission** to go to church on Sundays, or to bathe in hot weather, or in their leisure time to mend their clothes, and so forth... This man, in some States (the majority), as he comes of age, is ordered to enter for several years the military service, *the most cruel servitude*, and to go and fight, and in other States (Britain and America), he must hire other people for this same purpose. Yet **people placed in this position not only fail to see their own slavery but are proud of it, regarding themselves as free citizens** of the great States of Britain, France or Germany; they are proud of this... *Every* recognition of a **truth** by man, or rather, every deliverance from an error, as in the case of slavery before our eyes, is always attained through a conflict between the awakening **conscience** and the inertia of the old condition. At first the inertia is so powerful, the conscience so weak, that the first attempt to escape from error is met only with astonishment. The **new truth seems madness.** *Is it proposed to live without slavery? Then who will work?* Is it proposed to live without fighting? Then everybody will come and conquer us... Conscience continues to grow and to become clear; the number increases of those who recognize the new truth, and sneer and contempt give place to *subterfuge and trickery.* Those who support the error make slow to understand and admit the *incongruity* and cruelty of the practice they defend, but *think its abolition impossible just now, so delaying its abolition indefinitely.* 'Who does not know that slavery is an evil? But men are not yet ripe for freedom, and liberation will produce horrible disasters'— men used to say concerning slavery... Nevertheless, the idea is doing its work; it grows, it burns the falsehood; and

the time has come when the madness, the uselessness, the harmfulness, and wickedness of the error are so clear (as it happened in the sixties with slavery in Russia and America) that even now it is *impossible to justify* it."
"The only means to destroy Governments is *not force*, but it is the **exposure** of this fraud."
"The age of veneration for governments, notwithstanding all the hypnotic influence they employ to maintain their position, is more and more passing away. And it is time for people to understand that **Governments not only are not necessary, but are harmful and most highly immoral institutions**, in which a **self-respecting**, honest man cannot and must not take part, and the advantages of which he cannot and should not enjoy. And as soon as people clearly understand that, they will naturally cease to take part in such deeds, i.e. cease to give the Governments soldiers and money. And as soon as a majority of people ceases to do this, *the fraud* which enslaves people will be **abolished**. *Only in this way can people be freed from slavery.*"
"Therefore, the means of escape from slavery, if such means exist, must be found, *not in setting up fresh violence*, but in **abolishing whatever renders governmental violence possible.** And the possibility of governmental violence, like every other violence perpetrated by a small number of people upon a larger number, has *always* depended, and still depends, simply on the fact that the small number are **armed** while the large number are unarmed, or that the small number are better armed than the large number."
"In regards to those few people who oppress the rest, you do not need to win them over, do not need to protect yourselves from them - they are always defeated, **if only people would not agree to be slaves.**"
"The working people are also so **perverted by their compulsory slavery** that it seems to most of them that if

their position is a bad one, it is the fault of the masters, who pay them too little and who own the means of production. It does not enter their heads that *their bad position depends entirely on themselves*, and that if only they wish to improve their own and their brothers' positions, and not merely each to do the best he can for himself, the great thing for them to do is themselves to *cease to do evil.* And the evil that they do is that, desiring to improve their material position by the same means which have brought them into bondage, -- the workers (for the sake of satisfying the habits they have adopted), sacrificing their human dignity and freedom, accept humiliating and *immoral employment* or produce unnecessary and harmful articles, and, above all, **they maintain Governments, -- taking part in them by paying taxes and by direct service -- and thus they enslave themselves.**"

"The cause of the bad conditions and of the **existing slavery lies in the violence used by Governments.** There is only one way to **abolish** Governmental violence: that people should abstain from participating in violence."

"One hundred years ago, the illiterate masses, who had *no conception* as to who composed their government and as to what nations surrounded them, **blindly obeyed** those local officials and gentry, whose slaves they were. And it sufficed for the g*overnment by means of bribes and rewards to keep these officials and this gentry in their power*, in order that the masses might obediently do what was *demanded* of them. But now, when the masses for the most part can read and more or less know of whom their government is composed, and what nations surround them; when the men of the masses constantly move about with ease from one place to another, bringing to the masses information about what is going on in the world, a mere demand to carry out the commands of the government no longer suffices: **it becomes necessary to obscure the true conceptions**

which the masses have concerning life, and to impress
them with improper ideas concerning the conditions of their
life and concerning the relation of other nations toward
them. And so, thanks to the diffusion of *the press*, of the
rudiments, and of the means of communication, the
governments, having their agents everywhere, by means of
decrees, church sermons, the schools, the newspapers
inculcate on the masses the wildest and most **perverse
conceptions** about their advantages, about the relation of
the peoples among themselves, about their properties and
intentions; and the masses, which are so crushed by labour
that they have no time and no chance to understand the
significance and verify the correctness of those conceptions
which are inculcated upon them, and of those demands
which are made on them in the name of their good, *submit
to them without a murmur.*"
"Educated in these traditions they were **not only
unashamed of their slavery**, but were proud of the power
of their Governments as slaves are always proud of the
greatness of their masters."

Richard Price, Philosopher (1723) -
"Ignorance is the parent of bigotry, intolerance, persecution
and slavery. **Inform and instruct mankind; and these
evils will be excluded.** Happy is the person who, himself
raised above vulgar errors, is conscious of having aimed at
giving mankind this instruction. Happy is the scholar or
philosopher who at the close of life can reflect that he has
made this use of his learning and abilities, but happier far
must he be if, at the same time, he has reason to believe he
has been successful and actually contributed by his
instructions to disseminate among his fellow-creatures just
notions of themselves, of their **rights**, of religion, and the
nature and end of civil government. Such were Milton,
Locke, Sidney, Hoadly, etc. in this country, such were

Montesquieu, Fenelon, Turgot, etc. in France. *They sowed a seed which has since taken root and is now growing up to a glorious harvest.* To the information they conveyed by their writings we owe those revolutions in which every friend to mankind is now exulting. What an encouragement is this to us all in our endeavours to **enlighten the world**? Every degree of illumination which we can communicate must do the greatest good. It helps to prepare the minds of men for the recovery of their rights, and hastens **the overthrow of priestcraft and tyranny.** In short, we may, in this instance, learn our duty from the conduct of the oppressors of the world. They know that light is hostile to them, and therefore they labour to keep men in the dark. With this intention they have appointed licensers of the press, and, in Popish countries, prohibited the reading of the Bible. Remove the darkness in which they envelope the world and their usurpations will be exposed, *their power will be subverted, and the world emancipated."*

"I have lived to see a diffusion of **knowledge**, which has undermined **superstition** and error—I have lived to see the **rights of men** better understood than ever; and nations panting for **liberty**, which seemed to have lost the idea of it.—I have lived to see Thirty Millions of people, indignant and resolute, spurning at slavery, and demanding liberty with an irresistible voice; their king led in triumph, and an *arbitrary* monarch surrendering himself to his subjects.— After sharing in the benefits of one Revolution, I have been spared to be a witness to two other Revolutions, both glorious.—And now, methinks, I see the ardor for liberty catching and spreading; a general amendment beginning in human affairs; the dominion of kings changed for the dominion of laws, and the dominion of priests giving way to **the dominion of reason and conscience."**

"Tremble all ye oppressors of the world! **Take warning all ye supporters of slavish governments**, and slavish hierarchies! Call no more (absurdly and wickedly) reformation, innovation. You cannot now hold the world in darkness. Struggle no longer against increasing light and liberality. Restore to mankind their **rights**; and consent to the correction of abuses"

"Civil liberty (it should be remembered) must be enjoyed as a **right** derived from the Author of nature only or it cannot be the blessing which merits this name. If there is any human power which is considered as giving it, on which it depends, and which can invade or recall it at pleasure, it changes its **nature** and *becomes a species of slavery*... The master of slaves working on a plantation, though he may keep them down to prevent their becoming strong enough to *emancipate themselves*, yet is led by interest, as well as humanity, to govern them with such moderations as to *preserve their use*. But these causes will produce more of this good effect when the slaves are under the eye of their proprietor and form a part of his family than when they are settled on a distant plantation where he can know little of them and is obliged to trust them to the management of rapacious servants. It is particularly observable here that *free governments, though happier in themselves, are more oppressive to their provinces than despotic governments.* Or, in other words, that the subjects of free states are worse slaves than the objects of slaves not free... The regulations *necessary* to the support of civil society laid the foundation of oppression. *Government degenerated into tyranny, and subjection to legal authority into slavery*... If they are free they are subject to *intestine broils* which keep them in a constant ferment and sometimes end in insurrections and civil wars. If they are slavish they may be indeed more quiet, but that quiet is founded on a **depression of the human mind**, which is *the greatest of all calamities.*"

"There is danger that a state of society so happy will not be of long duration, that simplicity and virtue will give way to

depravity, that **equality** will in time be lost, *the cursed lust of domineering shew itself*, liberty languish, and civil government gradually degenerate into an instrument in the hands of the few to oppress and plunder the many. Such has hitherto been the progress of evil in human affairs."
"Men in power (unless better disposed than is common) are *always* endeavouring to extend their power. They hate the doctrine that it is a trust derived from the people and not a **right** vested in themselves. For this reason **the tendency of every government is to despotism.**"

In regards to the idea of **going off-grid or leaving society**, Maria Weston Chapman shares with us an analogy, "hide from tyranny, instead of defying it: whisper a testimony; form a bad **habit of mind** in regard to despotism; try to keep out the sea with a mop, when you ought to build a dike... What I would discourage is, not mercy and compassion in an individual case, but a disgraceful mistake in the economy of well doing; spending in salving a sore finger what would buy the elixir vitae; preferring the less, which excludes the greater, to the greater, which includes the less."

Etienne de La Boetie, Philosopher (1530) -
"Which men do you think would march more gallantly to combat—those who anticipate as a reward for their suffering the maintenance of their **freedom**, or those who cannot expect any other prize for the blows exchanged than the enslavement of others?"
"Obviously **there is no need of fighting** to overcome this single tyrant, for he is automatically defeated if the country **refuses consent to its own enslavement**: it is not necessary to deprive him of anything, but simply to give him nothing"

Mary Wollstonecraft, Philosopher (1759) -
"Why do men halt between two opinions, and expect impossibilities? Why do they expect virtue from a slave, from a being whom the constitution of civil society has rendered weak, if not vicious?"

Larken Rose, Philosopher, Author -
"If you love death and destruction, oppression and suffering, **injustice** and violence, repression and torture, helplessness and despair, perpetual conflict and bloodshed, then teach your children to respect 'authority:' and teach them that **obedience is a virtue**. If, on the other hand, you value peaceful coexistence, compassion and cooperation, **freedom** and justice, then teach your children the **principles of self-ownership**, teach them to respect the **rights** of every human being, and teach them to recognize and reject the belief in 'authority' for what it is: the most irrational, self contradictory, anti-human, evil, destructive and dangerous **superstition** the world has ever known."

Max Nettlau, Historian (1865) -
"May all the anarchists, all the libertarians, all freedom-loving human beings become a united force, which, while preserving the autonomy of each of its members, will practise mutual aid among all of them. May this force, by **overthrowing authority** in one place, weakening it in another, through **our own genuine progress**, develop in innumerable ways in order to advance liberty on a small scale and a large one, **within ourselves and around us, anywhere and everywhere.** Let us have hope. *For authority, powerful as it may be, can bring forth nothing but evil.* All the good in the world has come, is now coming and will always come only with liberty and from liberty."

Jeremey Locke, Author -
"**Personal sovereignty is the end of evil.** When every person on earth will **defend** themselves and those they love. When evil cannot gain even a foothold because all people are watching for it, and recognize that it seeks to destroy their value. This is the exact opposite of perfect evil, in which every person is a slave and a master of slaves. **Perfect liberty is life, and in it there are no slaves and no masters of slaves.** Perfect liberty is life."

Frederick Douglass, Former Slave, Abolitionist (1817) -
"I prayed for freedom for twenty years, but received no answer *until I prayed with my legs*"
"Those who profess to favor **freedom**, and yet depreciate agitation, are men who want crops without plowing up the ground."
"Without a struggle, there can be *no progress*."

William Lloyd Garrison, Journalist, Abolitionist (1805) -
"What an idiotic absurdity it is to say that earnest, persistent, uncompromising **moral opposition** to a **system of boundless immorality** is the way to strengthen it; and that the way to **abolish** such a system is to say nothing about it!"

Ezra Pound, Author (1885) -
"A slave is one *who waits for someone to come* and free him."

Thomas Jefferson, American Independence (1743) -
"**Educate** and inform the **whole** mass of the people. They are the **only** sure reliance for the preservation of our liberty."

Mary Harris Jones, Teacher, Activist (1837) -
"And who is **responsible** for this appalling child slavery? *Everyone*"

Edward Carpenter, Philosopher (1844) -
"Neither man nor woman will be tied in slavery to the lodge which they inhabit; and in becoming once more a part of **nature**, the human habitation will at length cease to be what it is now for at least half the human race — a prison."
"As to **External Government and Law, they will disappear**; for they are only the travesties and transitory substitutes of Inward Government and Order."

Mahatma Gandhi, Indian Independence (1869) -
"To end slavery, you must overcome the **mental** and physical inertia of the masses and quicken their **intelligence and creative** faculty."

Walt Whitman, Philosopher (1819) -
"You are either to **abolish slavery or it will abolish you**"
"Oh while I live, to **be the ruler of life, not a slave**, to meet life as a powerful conqueror, and nothing exterior to me will ever take command of me."

Sojourner Truth, Former Slave, Abolitionist (1797) -
"Life is a hard battle anyway. If we laugh and sing a little as we fight the good fight of **freedom**, it makes it all go easier. I will not allow my life's light to be **determined by the darkness** around me."
"I feel safe in the midst of my enemies, for the **truth is all powerful and will prevail**."

Booker T. Washington, Former Slave (1856) -
"If you want to lift yourself up, *lift up someone else.*"

Lysander Spooner, Abolitionist, Lawyer (1808) -
"It is only those who have a **false and superstitious** reverence for the **authority of governments**, and have contracted the *habit of thinking* that the most tyrannical and iniquitous laws have the power **to make that right which is naturally wrong, or that wrong which is naturally right**, who will have any doubt as to the right of the Slaves (and those who would assist them) to make **war**, to all possible extent, upon the **property** of the Slaveholders and their abettors."

Adin Ballou, Abolitionist (1803) -
"**Moral power is putting forth mighty energies to abolish slavery,** and elevate four millions of degraded beings to the rank of manhood. It is exerting its multiform influence to regenerate a corrupt public sentiment, and to super-induce a will in the people of the United States to let the oppressed go free. **Political power hinders and obstructs the progress of this reform by every possible means. It is wedded to slavery**, and will uphold it till a new public opinion compels it to stand off... Political power operates through a complex and cumbrous machine, with immense internal friction, and very awkwardly *accomplishes a small amount of good at an enormous expense*... Moral power educates the people, intellectually, religiously, morally, socially and, industrially. Political power tickles their ambition, uses up their faculties, consumes their substance, and punishes a few of their grosser crimes. Moral power is busy in the nursery, in the schoolhouse, academy and college, in the laboratory, the library, the study, the hall of science, the meetinghouse, the conference room, and the sick chamber. Political power is busy managing caucuses,

overseeing elections, legislating, holding courts, guarding prisoners, hanging murderers, punishing criminals, and executing all manner of legal processes... Think of the authors, editors and publishers; of their works, from the alphabetical primer to the huge folio; textbooks, histories, biographies, scientific repositories, encyclopedias, fiction, romance and sentiment in every variety of prose and verse; all that a man knows, thinks, imagines or suspects, written and printed in countless volumes, annuals, quarterlies, monthlies, weeklies and dailies! If one of former times could say with truth, '**Let me write the ballads of the nation, and I care not who writes it laws**,' what shall we think of the concurrent influence of education and literature, acting upon the people of this country, though all these appliances? What has political power to compare with it?... **voluntary associations**: charitable, humane, philanthropic and moral reform societies of every description. All these are instrumentalities developed and employed by moral power. And who can estimate the good they have done, or the evil they have prevented?" *(Recommended text: "The Superiority of Moral over Political Power" by Adin Ballou)*

Lucretia Mott, Abolitionist (1793) -
"Man is not by **nature** a tyrant, but **becomes a tyrant by power conferred on him.**"

Benjamin Tucker, Philosopher (1854) -
"If the individual has a **right to govern himself**, *all* external government is tyranny. Hence the necessity of **abolishing the State.**"

Maria Weston Chapman, Abolitionist (1806) -
"**Slavery can only be abolished by raising the character of the people** who compose the nation; and that can be done only by *showing them a higher one.*"

William Goodell, Abolitionist (1792) -
"The conversion of the world must *be nothing less* than the conversion of the masses of its inhabitants, and this would involve the **moral renovation** of society, as well as of the individuals of whom society is composed."

How Do We Know When Slavery Is Occurring?

As with looking at any problem in the world, there will be symptoms or signs that come as a result. These **symptoms** tell us that there is an underlying problem needing to be addressed. When we go about ending *Mental Slavery*, we may approach the slave as would a supportive practitioner, learning from them, asking questions and working from where they are currently at, because we are to merely facilitate self-healing or *self-realization* as to their *self-ownership*. We will notice patterns or recurring symptoms among them and obtain a better approach overtime, as we help free one mind to the next. Slavery, from our analysis, is a problem for which exhibits the symptoms of order-following, conflict *(war)*, trauma, fear *(including the fear of freedom)*, unnatural or violent death *(Democide)*, having few possessions, and the *lack* of health, movement, love, knowledge, sovereignty *(self-ownership)*, freedom, conscience and order. As we understand the *necessity* of the *shadow work* or internal work on part of the individual recognizing their freedom, we may say that these symptoms manifest and are reflective in the micro and macro, otherwise known as the individual and collective. Additionally, by raising children with a sense of self-ownership, this process of healing may be drastically increased within them, or they may never be *mentally enslaved* to begin with. Then, as generations teach this basic lesson, the superstition of "authority" will die out much like how it is *perfectly acceptable* in many parts of the modern world for nobody to engage in *chattel slavery*. We can't just want ourselves to not be a slave, especially as *abolitionists* or practitioners or leaders, we must empathize and help those enslaved become free, and therefore to some degree, share the pain and suffering to help relieve the slave of their condition and eventually bring them to the healing truth of freedom. In other words, we have suffered the disease of slavery but we have conquered it ourselves, and therefore we may be better equipped to now help others do the same, if we learn from our own process. The *abolition* of what is wrong is the *integration* of what is right. It is wrong to say the slaves are in charge of their slave-master, just as it is wrong to say the citizens are in charge of their government, since by definition, they give others the "authority" over their *Own* lives and property, and in simply seeing these justifications, we bring awareness to what *is* right. We may start to *realize* how embarrassingly simple the truth is, in a world of growingly complicated evils.

Former Slave (from online audio) -
"Now I couldn't go from here across the street, or I couldn't go through nobody's house 'out I have a note, or something from my master. And if I had that pass, that was what we call a **pass**, if I had that pass, I could go wherever he sent me. And I'd have to be back, you know, whoever he sent me to, they, they'd give me another pass. And I'd bring that back so as to show how long I'd been gone."

William Lloyd Garrison, Journalist, Abolitionist (1805) -
"While a slave remains in his fetters, the land must have no rest."
"Whether permitted to live to witness the abolition of slavery or not, I felt assured that, as I demanded nothing that was not clearly in accordance with **justice** and humanity, **some time or other, if remembered at all, I should stand vindicated in the eyes of my countrymen.**"

How does the law relate to slavery?
You may grow curious as to the many more complications
we concern ourselves with, that may be used as means to
justify our slavery, or aggregate our confusion in keeping
our *fear* against our *Own* freedom. Therefore, let us
observe the nature of the term "law" as an example, since it
is what constitutes the government or "authority" by which
political slavery operates. An "*author*ity" is an *author* of
man-made "law." If we observe "law" as merely a principle
or recommendation that people should follow, rules that
constitute moral behavior or rules that an individual has
regarding their own business or property, we are *not*
observing man-made law or "authority." Similarly, if we
observe "law" as "natural law" which is said to be immutable
(non-man-made), universal and eternal conditions, like
inertia or thermodynamics, which we must learn to live with,
we are *not* observing man-made law or "authority." Man-
made law, as it is like saying man-made government as
opposed to "god's government" or "god's law," is dictates
based upon *dogmatic beliefs*. In other words, "law" is
merely "authority" scribbling on a piece of paper their
opinion and imposing it on others. If it weren't their opinion
and it were truth, they need not "declare" it to be true since
it is already present. To reiterate, saying something *is* right
is *very different* from claiming that because *you* said it, that
makes it right. **The dictates of "law" simply deduces to
"obey or die." Is not the slave-master of chattel slavery
making the same statement, when they claim that the
slave must follow their "authority"?** Man-made law is
always complied with due to the *fear* of punishment, or
violence. It is *never* universal or timeless, it differs with
location and changes with time. We may ask ourselves,
even if 99% of people agree with something, should their
worldview be imposed upon the 1%? If 99% of people get
to be free, and 1% have to be slaves, is that *right*? 19th

century *abolitionist* William Lloyd Garrison even asked, "are right and wrong convertible terms, dependent upon popular opinion?" As well as saying "surely, nothing can be more dangerous than the doctrine that *moral obligations* of men change with the latitude and longitude of a place." This affirms the warnings by C.S. Lewis and Richard Wetheril regarding *moral relativism*, or the idea that we can disregard basic morality and *claim* that *might is right*. A right can't be turned into a wrong, and nobody deserves to be a slave. Slavery can never be freedom, they are exact opposites. If all slavery and all government, is *tyranny*, then no slavery and no government, is *liberty*. **There is no balance on a wrong that can never be right, so why hold onto and attach to what will never work?** Those who continue to presume that freedom is chaos, will disregard how the perception of "authority" operates in giving permission for people to do evil, and even be seen as *good* for it. Those who presume we need "authority" for the few nasty people in the world, make a justification for the individual to be violated as the means for an end. We may simply ask, as an *abolitionist*, "what would *you* want done with *me* if I do not comply or consent to the government that *you* want?" Find out how willing they are to say that you *should* be coerced against your will, and let that demonstrate their *character*. Those who presume we need "authority" because people generally cannot be trusted, contradict themselves in saying that among them we can trust some, as how could we trust those who can make this possible, and how are we sure we know what's best for everyone else? How would we be sure *not* to be tricked by psychopaths or narcissists who would gravitate toward taking the position of "authority"? People will always make rules for their own property, but if there is no violence for compliance, if it is *voluntary*, if it's of their *ownership*, it is not slavery, it is just people working together. The idea that we must *justify* violence and slavery by all means due to our *mental slavery*, not working toward *voluntary* solutions instead that *are* possible, is ignorance begging for evil that will inevitably grow as the result. Endless bloodshed is *always* the result of slavery, and it is similarly used as a *justification* for it's continuance. It isn't the "law" that made slavery wrong, instead it made it "illegal" but did not change the hearts and minds of people; it also reinforced *political slavery* just as the *abolitionists* wrote about, especially since it was all done under the pretense of the "civil war" which *many of them did not want*, which is why the movement continued well-after into the "civil rights" era, where the hearts and minds would begin to shift even more. **Let us remind ourselves that as of 2024, it hasn't been more than 80 years since millions of people fought for the commands of "authority" unleashing massive bloodshed, not more than 100 years since different races have been recognized as equal to one another, not more than 200 years since we recognized chattel slavery as wrong and not more than 300 years since we recognized monarchy as fallacious.** There is still work to be done, but it's to happen inevitably nonetheless, sooner than we think as we dispel age-old superstitions with simple logic. This may also explain why rulers may employ the use of AI (artificial intelligence) or technological and medicinal attacks, in fear of losing their power, which we may say *falsely secures* their own insecurities just as much as their "services" *falsely secures and protects* "the people."

Here are just some examples of restrictions by law created by the position of 'authority' that makes it so you require **permission to be free and live voluntarily**: collecting rainwater, going fishing, owning a property, starting a business, building a home, getting married, going hunting, owning a weapon, cutting hair, selling a product, doing a protest, selling food, feeding the homeless, exposing secrets *(ex. Edward Snowden)*, having a newborn baby, living without needing to go to war, using different forms of money, being able to travel, using different schooling options, living without needing to keep bills and receipts, growing plants *(ex. marijuana)*, being able to keep your own money, being able to live without vaccination, drinking raw milk, saying what you want. If you break any of these rules, you get locked up in a cage. Is this how we treat humankind? What gives people the *authority* to do this?

Thomas Jefferson, American Independence (1743) -
"I prefer **dangerous freedom** over peaceful slavery"

Benjamin Franklin, American Independence (1706) -
"**Any** society that will give up a little liberty to gain a little **security** will *deserve neither and lose both*."

Thomas Moore, Author (1779) -
"Better to **dwell in freedom's hall**, With a cold damp floor and mouldering wall, Than bow the head and bend the knee, In the proudest palace of slaverie."

Mahatma Gandhi, Indian Independence (1869) -
"Freedom is not worth having if it does not include the **freedom to make mistakes**"

Plato, Philosopher (427 BC) -
"Good people don't need laws to tell them to act **responsibly** – and *bad people will find a way around the laws*."

William Molyneux, Philosopher (1656) -
"I have *no other notion of slavery*, but being bound by a **law to which I do not consent**."

Samuel Seabury, Philosopher (1729) -
"Will you submit to this **slavish regulation**? – You must. – Our sovereign Lords and Masters, the High and Mighty Delegates, in Grand Continental Congress assembled, have ordered and directed it. Will you be instrumental in bringing the most abject **slavery on yourselves**? Will you choose such Committees? Will you submit to them, should they be chosen by the weak, foolish, turbulent part of the country people? – Do as you please: but, *by him that made me, I will not. – No, if I must be enslaved, *let it be by a king at least*, and not by a parcel of upstart lawless Committeemen. If I must be devoured, let me be devoured by the jaws of a lion, and not gnawed to death by rats and vermin... Are our supervisors our masters? ... You ought, my friends, to **assert your own freedom.** Should such another attempt be made upon you, assemble yourselves together: tell your supervisor, that he has exceeded his commission: – That you will have no such Committees... But however, as I said before, do as you please: If you like it better, choose your Committee, or suffer it to be chosen by half a dozen Fools in your neighbourhood, – open your doors to them, – let them examine your tea cannisters, and molasses-jugs, and your wives' and daughters' petty-coats, – bow, and cringe, and tremble, and quake, – fall down and worship our *sovereign Lord the Mob*. – But I repeat it, *I will not. –* No, my house is my castle: as such I will consider it, as such I will defend it, while I have breath... **Before I submit, I will die: live you, and be slaves**... It is vile, *abject* slavery, and I will have none of it." *(this relates to recognizing slavery, yet accepting the lesser form of slavery)*

Richard J. Maybury, Philosopher (1946) -
"In our **government-controlled schools** we are taught that Lincoln was our greatest president because his **war** ended

slavery and saved the Union. As usual, the other side of the story – the side that reflects poorly on the **government** – somehow gets lost." Many abolitionist works, including from Garrison, speak as to the distrust concerning Lincoln, and his sometimes pro-slavery positions, or his lack of care for the anti-slavery positions.

Granville Sharp, Abolitionist (1735) -
"I know it has been said, that questions, concerning the states of persons ought to be determined by the *Law of the country*, to which they belong; and that, therefore, one, who would be declared to be a slave in America, ought, in case he should happen to be imported into Britain, to be adjudged, according to the Law of America, to be a slave: A *doctrine*, than which nothing can be more barbarous. Ought the judges of any country, out of the respect to the Law of another, show no **respect** to their kind and to humanity? Out of respect to a law, which is in no sort obligatory upon them, ought they to disregard the **Law of Nature**, which is *obligatory on all men at all times, and in all places*? Are any laws so binding as the eternal **laws of justice**?"

Ezra Heywood, Abolitionist (1829) -
"Our **laws and customs** to-day actually destroy more girls and women than slave codes murdered Negroes then!"

Jeremey Locke, Author -
"A **principle** is a truth that creates **freedom**. A **law** is a lie that creates slavery."
"When **law** challenges its competition, it labels them criminals and racketeers. The definition of racketeering is the creation of a threat, and then charging for **protection** against it. Such racketeering is *institutionalized slavery*. **Mafias and governments** follow the same pattern. History

shows us that the names given to each are a matter of who is the more successful extortionist."

James Russell Lowell, Abolitionist (1819) -
"Six slave States added at a breath! One flourish of a pen, And fetters shall be rivetted on millions more of men! **One drop of ink to sign a name, and slavery shall find**, For all her surplus flesh and blood a market to her mind!... Is't not enough that we must bow to all that they decree,— These cotton and tobacco lords, these pimps of slavery? That we must yield our **conscience** up to glut Oppression's maw, And break our faith with God to keep the letter of **Man's law**?... They're coming but to speak one word, they're coming but to say,— 'Poor minions of the tyrant's cause, **your grovelling hearts obey**! But, hear it, North, and hear it, South, and hear it, East and West, We will not help you bind your slaves! In God's name, we protest!'"
"Against the bestial and the false, The Kingdom of Unreason, All **Nature** gathers force and falls, At once to plotting treason; Hush every voice you start at now, **Bring Slavery to perfection**, And every leaf upon the bough, Would whisper insurrection."
"They are slaves who **fear** to speak, For the fallen and the weak; *They are slaves who will not choose*, Hatred, scoffing, and abuse, Rather than in silence shrink, From the truth they needs **must think**; They are slaves who dare not be, In the **right** with two or three."
"Truth forever on the scaffold, **Wrong forever on the throne**,— Yet that scaffold sways the future."

Hector Morel, Philosopher (approx. 1862) -
"Scan the **history of the entire world**, among the ancient peoples as among the moderns,—and **no matter the form of government**,—the nation *always* presents to you this terrible and ominous tableau: **tyrants and subjects,**

masters and slaves, exploiters and exploited; *which is to say, authority, rights, and privileges on one side*; on the other, servitude, duties, charges. Consult the social contracts, past and present constitutions,—*whatever their spirit and origin,*—monarchist or republican, liberal or democratic, that have been voted in by the representatives or granted by the despots; they all can be summarized thus: *Art. I. The people MUST obey, suffer and labor. Art. 2. The possessor MUST command, enjoy and do nothing."*
"Liberty is impossible, where *authority* becomes necessary!"

Thomas Hodgskin, Philosopher (1787) -
"When we inquire, *casting aside all theories and suppositions*, into the end kept in view by legislators, or examine *any* existing laws, we find that the first and chief object proposed is to preserve the **unconstrained dominion of the law over the minds and bodies of mankind.** It may be simplicity in me, but I protest that I see no anxiety to preserve the **natural right of property** but a great deal to enforce **obedience to the legislator.** No misery indeed is deemed too high a price to pay for his supremacy, and for the **quiet submission** of the people. To attain this end many individuals, and even nations, have been extirpated. **Perish the people, but let the law live, has ever been the maxim of the masters of mankind.** Cost what it may, we are continually told, the dominion of the law, not the natural right of property, must be upheld. Every writer, in our newspapers, whether he writes about a rebellion in Ireland, or killing partridges, loudly and continually repeats this maxim of our masters... I have shown you that the legal right of property is undergoing subversion, and that no earthly power can stop it. I have now remarked, that this **legal right, and the laws made to uphold it, are the sources of almost all crimes**; and, therefore, when fearful, timid, mistrustful politicians tell me,

that society would fall into **anarchy** if their hold of it were to be relaxed, and if the incubus of their regulations were removed, I answer them, and I answer all such schemes, and all such apprehensions, by pointing to these facts, and calling on them to believe that the **God of nature** has appointed a means, not merely for the repression, but for the extinction of crime."

Leo Tolstoy, Author, Philosopher (1828) -
"*The slavery of our times* results from three sets of **laws**: those about land, taxes, and **property**."
"The fundamental cause of slavery is legislation: the fact that there are *people who have the power* to make **laws**."
"**The cause of slavery is legislation.** Legislation rests on *organized violence*."
"Slavery results from laws, laws are made by governments, and, therefore, **people can only be freed from slavery by the abolition of Governments.**"
"If there be no such **science as justice**, there can be no science of government; and all the rapacity and violence, by which, in all ages and nations, a few confederated villains have obtained the mastery over the rest of mankind, reduced them to poverty and slavery, and established what they called governments to keep them in subjection, have been as legitimate examples of government as any that the world is ever to see."
"Talk about abolishing slavery—**we have not abolished slavery**; we have only abolished one rude form of it, *chattel slavery*."
"Of old, human sacrifices, the worship of idols, divinations tortures, slavery, and many other things, were instituted. But they were all abolished when people were so far **enlightened** that these **institutions** became *superfluous* burdens and evils. *So also with Governments*."

"Man has no choice; he must be the slave of the most unscrupulous and insolent amongst slaves, or else the servant of God."

"**The state, which makes every individual a slave** in the name of the will of all... People generally think that the armies are increased by the governments for the purpose of **defending** the states against other states, forgetting the fact that armies are needed by the governments for the *purpose* of protecting themselves *against their own crushed and enslaved subjects*... **Every government needs armies, first of all, in order to keep its subjects in submission, and to exploit their labors.** But the government is not alone; side by side with it there is another government, which exploits its subjects by means of *the same violence*, and which is always ready to take away from another government the labors of its already enslaved subjects. And so every government needs an army, not only for internal use, but also for the protection of its booty against neighboring *ravishers*. Every government is in consequence of this involuntarily led to the necessity of increasing its army in emulation with the other governments; but the increasing of armies is contagious, as Montesquieu remarked 150 years ago. *Every increase of an army in a state, directed against its subjects, becomes dangerous even for its neighbors, and evokes an increase in the neighboring states...* Beginning with the end of the last century, almost every forward step of humanity has not only *not* been encouraged by the government, but has always been retarded by it. Thus it was with the abolition of corporal punishment, of torture, of slavery, and with the establishment of the freedom of the press and of assemblies. In our time the power of the state and the governments not only fail to cooperate with, but are distinctly opposed to, all that activity by means of which men work out *new forms* of life. **The solutions of laboring,**

agronomic, political, religious questions are not only not encouraged, but directly interfered with by the power of the state... Intimidation, bribery, hypnotization, make men desirous to become soldiers; but it is the soldiers who give the power and the possibility for punishing people, and picking them clean (and bribing the officials with the money thus obtained), and for hypnotizing and enlisting them again as soldiers, who in turn afford the possibility for doing all this. The circle is closed, and *there is no way of tearing oneself away from it by means of force*... Can we imagine a more striking example of how men flog themselves than the humbleness with which the men of our time carry out the very obligations which are imposed upon them and which lead them into servitude, especially the military service? **Men obviously enslave themselves**, suffer from this slavery, and believe that it must be so, that it is all right and does not interfere with the liberation of men, which is being prepared somewhere and somehow, in spite of the ever increasing and increasing slavery... A man of our time lives, doing his work or enjoying himself, employing the fruits of his own labor or those of others for his own sake or for the sake of those who are near to him, like any other man, despising all kinds of oppressions and privations, hostility, and sufferings. The man lives peacefully; suddenly people come to him, who say: 'In the first place, promise and swear to us that you will slavishly obey us in everything which we shall prescribe to you, and that everything we shall invent, determine, and call a law you will consider an indubitable truth and will submit to; in the second place, give part of your earnings into our keeping: we shall use this money for keeping you in slavery and preventing you from forcibly opposing our decrees; in the third place, choose yourself and others as **imaginary participants in the government**, knowing full well that the government will take place entirely independently of those stupid speeches which you will utter to your like, and that it will take place according to our will, in whose hands is the army; in the fourth place, appear at a set time in court and take part in all those senseless cruelties which we commit against the erring men, whom we ourselves have corrupted, in the shape of imprisonments, exiles, solitary confinements, and capital punishments. And finally, in the fifth place, besides all this, though you may be in the most friendly relations with people belonging to other nations, be prepared at once, when we command you, to consider such of these men as we shall point out to you your enemies, and to cooperate personally or by hiring others in the ruin, pillage, and murder of their men, women, children, old people, and, perhaps, your own countrymen, even your parents, if we want it.'... What importance can there be in such phenomena as the refusals of a few dozens of madmen, as they are called, who do not wish to swear to the government, or pay taxes, or take part in courts and military service? These men are punished and removed, and life continues as of old. It would seem that there is nothing important in these phenomena, and yet it is these very phenomena that more than anything else undermine the power of the state and prepare *the emancipation of men*. They are those individual bees which begin to separate from the swarm and fly about, awaiting what cannot be delayed — the rising of the whole swarm after them. The governments know this, and are afraid of these phenomena more than of all socialists, communists, anarchists, and their plots with their dynamite bombs... **The public leaders preach that it is not only unnecessary, but even harmful and immoral, for every individual to try and free himself from slavery.** It is as though some people, to free a dammed up river, should have all but cut through a ditch, when nothing but an opening is necessary for the water to flow into this ditch and do the rest, and there should appear some people who would persuade them that, rather than let off the water, they should construct above the river a machine with buckets, which, drawing the water up on one side, would drop it into the same river from the other side... The judge of everything, the *fundamental force* which moves men and nations, has always been the one invisible, impalpable force — the resultant of all the spiritual forces of a certain aggregate of men and of all humanity, which is expressed in **public opinion.**"

Frederick Bastiat, Author, Philosopher (1801) -
"It is easy to understand how **law**, instead of checking **injustice**, becomes **the invincible weapon** of injustice. It is easy to understand why the law is used by the legislator to destroy in varying degrees among the rest of the people, their personal **independence** by slavery, their liberty by oppression, and their **property** by plunder. This is done for the benefit of the person who makes the law, and in proportion to the power that he holds."
"There is in all of us a strong disposition to **believe that anything lawful is also legitimate.** This belief is so widespread that many persons have erroneously held that things are 'just' because law makes them so. Thus, in order to make plunder appear just and sacred to many **consciences**, it is only necessary for the law to *decree and sanction* it. Slavery, restrictions, and monopoly find defenders not only among those who profit from them but *also among those who suffer from them.*"

Oscar Wilde, Poet, Playwright (1854) -
"It is indeed a burning shame that there should be one law for men and another law for women. I think that **there should be no law for anybody.**"

Hugh O. Pentecost, Philosopher, Lawyer (1848) -
"Most people think they can **rob one another by law**, by
methods that have nice business names, and then prevent
the robbery that goes by the name of pick-pocketing,
burglary, and the like. *But they can't.* Most people think that
men can be made to pay their debts or their taxes by law.
But they can't. Most people think that sobriety and morality
can be enforced by law. *But they can't.* Most people think
that when you bring an injustice into this world by law, you
can prevent it from being followed to its natural
consequences by another law. *But you can't.*"

Lysander Spooner, Abolitionist, Lawyer (1808) -
"I cannot delegate to another man any **right** to *make* **laws**
— that is, *laws of his own invention* — and **compel me to
obey them.** Such a contract, on my part, would be a
contract to part with my **natural liberty**; to give myself, or
sell myself, to him as a slave."

On talking about the laws against **women's rights**, Sarah
Grimke states, "such laws approximate too nearly to the
laws enacted by slaveholders for **the government** of their
slaves, and must tend to **debase and depress the mind** of
that being." Seeing the end of chattel slavery as *not* just *the*
end of slavery, is seen reflected upon such works. Sarah
goes on to say "where confidence and love exist, a wife will
naturally converse with her husband as with her dearest
friend, on all that interests her heart, and there will be a
perfectly free interchange of sentiment; but *she is no more
bound to be governed by his judgment, than he is by hers.*
They are standing on **the same platform of human rights**,
are equally under the *government of God*, and accountable
to him, and **him alone**." Individuals as she, had to further
the cause of *Abolitionism*, to prove *slavery still exists* in
other forms and that there are *intrinsic natures* or *natural*

rights needing to be upheld past the concept of "sex" or "gender" in order for *true equality* and *freedom*.

What Really Creates Slavery?

As we may come to realize the importance in *Mental Slavery* and *Political Slavery*, as being the roots to *all* slavery, the internal and covert, for the more external and overt, we may need to clarify the link between the two. Can we identify what exactly it is, if we wanted to? *Mental Slavery* and *Political Slavery* is actually known as **statism**. It is *statism* that creates the government *state*. *Statism* is the *belief* that there is such a thing as "authority" vested in certain human beings, magically giving them the "right to rule" over other people. This "authority" means that certain people, who we call "government," have the "moral right" to issue commands to those whom they rule (those under their jurisdiction: "to say what the law is"), and that their "subjects" (slaves, slave-drivers) have a "moral obligation" to obey the arbitrary dictates ("laws") set by the government (slave-masters). Most simply put, *statism* is the *belief* in the legitimacy of slavery. **Without statism present in the minds of individuals, there can be no slaves of masters, and therefore there can be no masters of slaves.** The slaves must free themselves or with free people's help, hence the cause for *abolitionism*. Breaking statism is the realization that those called "government" or "police" are *no different (do not have more rights)* from everyday people, and therefore their "authority" is illegitimate, otherwise such would be of the nature of *inequality*. It is even that government policing has it's roots based on the *continuation of slavery*, as we may see the American government's policing is based on the 19th century "slave patrol" or slave-driver which would recapture runaway slaves or re-enslave those slaves considered "free." In other words, anyone who promotes or believes in government or slavery, is engaging in *statism*. People mentally *believe* in slavery, so that they can physically *try* to *create* slavery, despite freedom being our evident reality. When the *Mental Slavery* or *statism* of a slave is breaking, they may become in constant conflict with that of the slave master, as they ultimately desire to be free because they realize they are *meant* to be free. They also may become in conflict with themselves, since their mind becomes averted to their physical condition. The slave-master and slave-driver may even have psychological problems within themselves or shadows they have not addressed, projecting their problems to their slaves, or developing psychopathic traits. Yet, throughout the whole slave and master relationship, we may observe that freedom is desired in both of them, and it is simply that the slave thinks their freedom is dependent on the slave-master, and the slave-master thinks their freedom is provided by having a slave they can rely upon. In fearing change and the unknown or finding justifications, both succumb to their condition and promote *statism*. However, we may come from the position of love, exercising our *self-defense* and *non-aggression* in the known *self-ownership* we have over ourselves, and in returning the self-ownership the slave-master also has over themselves, to promote *voluntaryism*. To reiterate, in disregarding the concept of "authority" and *statism* for *no external rulers*, we regard *the rules* for ourselves, our internal ruler, and we *must know* them, we must *know ourselves*, to become a master of self or exercise self-mastery, *self-ownership*, self-government or *self-responsibility*. **We are to bring truth to action, the mental freedom to physical freedom, for ourselves and for others, this is Abolitionism.**

Larken Rose, Philosopher, Author -
"Even the nicest, most friendly slave owner, if he continues to believe in the **legitimacy of slavery** and continues to practice it, will be committing evil and will inflict **harm** upon the people he imagines to be his **rightful property.** And he will *naturally develop a degree of contempt* toward the victims of his aggression, and will behave contemptuously toward them."

"Why would a master ever put his own interests below the interests of his slaves?"

"Even when a slave master fights to prevent some other slave master from stealing his slaves, he is *still* no friend of the slaves themselves."

"If he hands over money only because some 'law' or other 'authority' *compelled* him to, and then expresses pride in having done so, he is in essence boasting about having been **forcibly dominated**, precisely the way **a thoroughly indoctrinated slave might take pride in serving his master well.**"

"Maligning a fellow victim of **coercion** for complaining about it is a sure sign that a person actually takes **pride in his own enslavement.**"

"To delight in a 'tax cheat' being punished, for example, as many Americans do, is akin to a slave taking **pleasure in the whipping of a fellow slave** who tried to escape."

"What statists actually want is equality among the slaves, but enormous inequality between the slaves and the masters. This again shows that they view 'government' as being *superhuman*, because it never occurs to them, as they push 'equality for all,' that the **equality should also include the politicians and the police.**"

"There is a big difference between striving for a new, wiser, nobler master, and striving for a world of **equals**, where there are **no masters and no slaves.** Likewise, there is a big difference between a slave who believes in the

principle of freedom, and a slave whose ultimate goal is to become the *new master*."

Jean-Jacques Rousseau, Philosopher (1712) -
"Since no man has any **natural authority** over his fellow men, and since **might is not the source of right**, *conventions* remain as the basis of all lawful authority among men. If an individual, says Grotius, can alienate his freedom and become the slave of a master, why should a whole people not be able to alienate theirs, and become **subject to a king**?"
"To alienate is to give or sell. Now, a man who becomes another's slave does not give himself; he sells himself at the very least for his subsistence. But **why does a nation sell itself?** So far from a king providing his subjects with their subsistence, he draws his from them; and, according to Rabelais, a king does not live on a little. Do subjects, then, give up their persons on condition that their property also shall be taken? *I do not see what is left for them to keep*"
"As for you, modern nations, **you have no slaves, but you are slaves.**"
"Every man being **born free and his own master**, no-one, under any pretext whatsoever, can make any man subject without his **consent**... So long as **government and law** provide for the **security** and well-being of men in their common life, the arts, literature and the sciences, less despotic though perhaps more powerful, *fling garlands of flowers over the chains which weigh them down*. They stifle in men's breasts that sense of **original liberty**, for which they seem to have been born; cause them to **love their own slavery**... individuals *only* allow themselves to be oppressed so far as they are hurried on by **blind ambition**, and, looking rather below than above them, come **to love authority more than independence, and submit to**

slavery, that they may in turn enslave others. It is no easy matter to reduce to obedience a man who has no ambition to command; *nor would the most adroit politician find it possible to enslave a people whose only desire was to be independent.*"

Why Don't We Teach Our Children About Slavery?

For many years, people have taught their children about the horrors of *chattel slavery* and *the civil war* which "ended" it, yet the words of Abolitionists and slaves, or the nature of slavery was left unchecked. We don't ponder about other forms, or if we ourselves may be enslaved. Perhaps this is due to the very fact that the schools in which we bring our children, are owned or supported by the government, the very systems which embody *political slavery* or statism. Johann Fichte (1806) is a philosopher who helped create the Prussian school system, which would be imported into the U.S. by *politician* Horace Mann in 1852. He tells us that "education should aim at destroying free will so that after pupils are thus schooled they will be incapable throughout the rest of their lives of thinking or acting otherwise than as their *schoolmasters* would have wished. When the technique has been perfected, *every government* that has been in charge of education for more than one generation will be able *to control its subjects securely without the need of armies or policemen.*" Frederick T. Gates, (1913) a business adviser to John D. Rockefeller Sr., who created the *General Education Board*, tells us "we shall *not* try to make these people or any of their children into *philosophers* or men of learning or of science. We are *not* to raise up among them authors, orators, poets, or men of letters. We shall *not* search for embryo great artists, painters, musicians. Nor will we cherish even the humbler ambition to raise up from among them lawyers, doctors, preachers, statesmen, of whom *we now have ample supply.*" Is learning supposed to be natural, *voluntary* and fun, or is it supposed to be forced? **We may observe that the increase of homeschooling, unschooling, and voluntary schools can be attributed to the desire for self-directed learning, which empowers every student.**

David Rodriguez, School Principal, Author - **"Self-directed learning is the height of education**, wherein the learner directs himself and pursues knowledge and skills for his own personal self-interest, **not for the state.** You learned to walk and talk *without coercive curriculum* because you naturally desired to learn these skills. This natural tendency to pursue **self-growth is innate** and will continually encouraged in all relevant learning organizations." David shares strategies to resolve the problem of government compulsory schools, urging us to "see your child as a born genius who loves learning and **developing his/her own mind.** Distinguish the different meanings of "education" and "schooling." Empower your child with **voluntary learning opportunities, not mandatory assignments.** Encourage curiosity and *question asking.* Accept the mystery of the universe and keep your wonder alive. Understand that learning is always happening. Begin and complete your own learning projects. Demonstrate respectful manners to and with your child. Co-create adventures with your child. Inspire explorations of your local surroundings, especially streets and neighborhoods. Invite your child to observe and participate in your activities, like cooking, cleaning, dancing, conversing, thinking, and analyzing, as you deem fit. Visit museums, grocery stores, book stores, hardware stores, groceries etc. with questions and intentions. Learn about the history and intentions of government schools."

John Holt, Educator, Author (1923) -
"Education... now seems to me perhaps *the most authoritarian and dangerous of all the social inventions of mankind.* It is **the deepest foundation of the modern slave state**, in which most people feel themselves to be nothing but producers, consumers, spectators, and 'fans,' driven more and more, in all parts of their lives, by greed, envy, and fear. My concern is not to improve 'education' but *to do away with it*, to end the ugly and anti-human business of people-shaping and to **allow and help people to shape themselves.**"
"If we take from someone his **right** to decide what he will be curious about, we destroy his **freedom of thought.** We say, in effect, you must think not about what interests and concerns you, but about what interests and concerns us."
"What is essential is to realize that **children learn independently**, they learn out of interest and curiosity, not to please or appease the adults in power; and that they ought to be in control of their own learning, **deciding for themselves what they want to learn and how they want to learn it.**"

Dayna Martin, Educator, Author -
"I cannot imagine needing to ask **permission** for time with my children or having to live our lives around a school's agenda. The school's needs always come before family needs. This to me is madness, and I choose not to have that be a part of our lives at all."
"*Care* what your children think of you more than what strangers think of you."
"**Our kids are mirrors of who we are and what we do.** When you really understand this, everything changes in your interactions. You let go of being punitive and authoritarian and become kind, patient, understanding, loving, and joyful. These qualities make people feel good.

Isn't feeling good and being happy what life is all about?... **Children learn what they live. Being raised in an authoritarian paradigm, children learn that forcing others to meet their needs is what life is all about.** This creates a cycle of *narcissism* that our culture actually blames on a parent not being controlling enough!... I do not look at myself as my children's teacher. I am not standing in front of them pouring knowledge into them as the *all-knowing authority*. My job is to give them as much of the world as possible to learn and grow from. **I look at myself as a facilitator of my children's interests and desires in life.** I do not have to know all the answers. I do, however, need to know how to find answers through the resources that the world offers. Through the internet, television, books, video games, day trips, vacations, community resources, and apprenticeships, we offer our children *more than traditional schooling could ever provide*. Our kids are learning that answers aren't always black and white. They are learning about different theories and philosophies and **developing their own beliefs**. In short, we are raising free-thinkers!... **Authoritarian parenting does not meet our needs. It only meets the needs of those in power.**"

John Taylor Gatto, Whistle-blower, Author (1935) -
"You either **write your script in life**, or you become an unwitting actor in the script of someone else's."
"The truth is that **schools don't really teach anything except how to obey orders.**"
"I feel ashamed that so many of us cannot imagine a better way to do things than locking children up all day in cells instead of letting them grow up knowing their families, mingling with the world, assuming real obligations, striving to be **independent and self-reliant and free.**"

Herbert Spencer, Psychologist, Polymath (1820) -
"Not only does the **physical-force system** fail to fit the youth for his future position; *it absolutely tends to unfit him.*"

William Godwin, Philosopher (1756) -
"If **self-respect** is one of the most desirable results of a well-conducted education, that, as we should not humble the pupil in his own eyes by disgraceful and humiliating language, so **we should abstain, as much as possible, from personal ill-treatment**, and the employing towards him the measures of an owner towards his purchased or indentured slave."
"*Modern education not only corrupts the heart of our youth, by the rigid slavery to which it condemns them*, it also undermines their **reason**, by the unintelligible jargon with which they are overwhelmed in the first instance, and the little attention, that is given to the accommodating their pursuits to their capacities in the second."
"The argument against **political coercion** is equally strong against the infliction of private penalties, between master and slave, and between parent and child."
"Their obedience should be the **obedience of the heart, and not that of a slave.**"
"Punishment undoubtedly may change a man's behaviour. It may render his external conduct beneficial from injurious, though *it is no very promising expedient for that purpose.* But it cannot improve his sentiments, or lead him to the form of **right** proceeding but by *the basest and most despicable motives*. It leaves him a slave, devoted to an exclusive self-interest, and actuated by **fear**, the meanest of the *selfish* passions."
"Of all the sources of unhappiness to a young person the greatest is a *sense of slavery*. How grievous the insult, or how contemptible the ignorance, that tells a child that youth

is the true season of felicity, when *he feels himself checked, controlled, and tyrannised over in a thousand ways?"*

Auberon Herbert, Philosopher (1838) -
"To have our wants supplied from without by a huge **State machinery**, to be regulated and inspected by great armies of officials, **who are themselves slaves of the system** which they administer, will in the long run **teach us nothing, will profit us nothing.** The true education of children, the true provision for old age, the true conquering of our vices, the true satisfying of our wants, can only be won as we learn to form a society of free men, in which individually and in **our own self-chosen groups** we seek the truest way of solving these great problems. Before any real progress can be made, the great truth must sink deep into our hearts, that we cannot in any of these matters be saved by machinery, **we can only be saved by moral energy in ourselves and in those around us.**"

Noam Chomsky, Philosopher (1928) -
"For those who stubbornly seek freedom, there can be no more urgent task than to come to understand the mechanisms and practices of **indoctrination. These are easy to perceive in the totalitarian societies, much less so in the system of 'brainwashing under freedom' to which we are subjected** and which all too often we serve as willing or unwitting instruments."
"The general population doesn't know what's happening, and **it doesn't even know that it doesn't know.**"

Josiah Warren, Abolitionist (1798) -
"If the human race is destined to any true civilization, the means of attaining it have yet to be learned by old and young. The problem rests in **education**. The **knowledge** of the philosophy of governments, of **laws**, of money, being no

part of general education, the masses become mere dupes and helpless victims of **ignorant and unprincipled** politicians, speculators, and impostors of all kinds, who, from deficiency of education are tempted into such modes of **preserving their worthless existence**."

Are Runaway Slaves Considered Criminals?
According to the 1800s in America, runaway slaves and those who help them, are considered criminals. However, are they immoral just because they break the law or the commands of "authority"? Abolitionists would call them "freedom seekers." Perhaps the *real immorality, the real criminal,* as we explore the nature of slavery, is the law and "authority" itself. The greatest criminal acts have been committed in the name of "authority" as we know with studying *Democide,* and those who have gladly taken up the role of "authority" to do it we may call psychopathic or sociopathic. As famously said, "power corrupts and absolute power corrupts absolutely." It is *good* people allowing *evil* people to take power through their *statism* or belief in "authority." The statist takes an individual out of their natural humanity and rights, just as much as the pro-slavery advocate does. As the book and seminar *TAO: The Full Return To Nature* shares an ancient Taoist story affirming this, "Zhuangzi was fishing, relaxing at a river bank. Two individuals approach him and offer to him a position in power. He observes the river's motion and states that a turtle is taken away from his natural habitat and draped in silk, enshrined for the royal palace; but which condition is preferable? Well-being tells us the natural habitat. 'When all men do not carry their nature beyond its normal condition, nor alter its characteristics, the good government of the world is secured.'" Nonetheless, as what may also be reflective within society, a sociopath is an individual with an enduring pattern of behavior

characterized by the disregard for, and violation of, the rights of others, disregarding right and wrong. Whereas, psychopaths tend to be more deceiving and planned in their actions, therefore making better criminals. Sociopaths and psychopaths, especially in holding slaves, will not *care* for *abolitionism* in ending slavery. Think about yourself, why take the place of slave-master or slave if you want to end *the very role* of these fictions? Similarly, why should you be deemed a "criminal" for committing *no actual crime* to others? **You are free and nothing shall claim otherwise.**

Larken Rose, Philosopher, Author -
"The terms 'crime' and 'criminal' do not, by themselves, even hint at what 'law' is being disobeyed. It is a 'crime' to slowly drive through a red light at an empty intersection, and it is a 'crime' to murder one's neighbors, A hundred years ago it was a 'crime' to teach a slave to read; in 1945 Germany it was a 'crime' to hide Jews from the SS. In Pennsylvania, it is a 'crime' to sleep in or on top of a refrigerator outside. Literally, committing a 'crime' means disobeying the commands of politicians, and a 'criminal' is anyone who does so. Again, such terms have an obviously negative connotation. Most people do not want to be called a 'criminal,' and they mean it as an insult if they call someone else a 'criminal.' Again, this implies that the 'authority' issuing and enforcing the 'laws' has the **right** to do so."

What Makes Slavery Different From Gang Captivity?
When we think of the slave-master and many of his supporters, we may liken it to a gang or mafia, where immoral behavior is taking place among a group of people holding captives. However, there is a difference between the two relying on *perception*. A figure we perceive to be an "authority" with our *Mental Slavery* or *statism*, will *not* be

perceived as immoral when committing an immoral action due to their position. This *enables* the immorality. Whereas, most people perceive gangs and mafias as wrong, not claiming the *justification* for their behavior is due to any "authority." This will have many people working to *disable* the immorality. Yet, both the slave-master or government and mafia or gang, commit crimes, create captives and claim ownership over different pieces of land. *They aren't different*, but we *think* they are due to our indoctrinated superstition to see "authority" as necessary.

Larken Rose, Philosopher, Author -
"What distinguishes a street gang from 'government' is how they are perceived by the people they control the trespasses, robbery, extortion, assault and murder committed by **common thugs are perceived by almost everyone as being immoral, unjustified, and criminal.** Their victims may comply with their demands, but not out of any feeling of **moral obligation** to obey, merely out of **fear**. If the intended victims of the street gang thought they could resist without any danger to themselves, they would do so, without the slightest feeling of guilt. **They do not perceive the street thug to be any sort of legitimate, rightful ruler**; they do not imagine him to be 'authority.' The loot the thug collects is not referred to as 'taxes,' and his threats are not called 'laws.'"
"What literally happens is that one group of people issues a command, and their enforcers impose it upon the masses, by **punishing disobedience**. This is what the Mafia does, what street gangs do, what schoolyard bullies do, and what *all* 'governments' do. The difference is that when 'government' does it, it uses *not only* **threats** but also **indoctrination**, of both the enforcers and the general public. Where the message of most thugs is usually direct and honest ('Do what I say or I hurt you'), the 'government'

message involves a great deal of **psychology and mind control**, which is essential to making the state mercenaries feel **righteous about inflicting oppression** on others. The controllers in 'government' portray themselves as 'lawmakers' who have the **right** to 'govern' society, portray their commands as 'laws,' and portray any who disobey as 'criminals.' And, unlike Mafia 'heavies,' those who administer retribution against any who disobey the politicians are portrayed, not merely as hired thugs, but as noble 'law enforcers,' who are righteously *protecting* society from all the uncivilized, contemptuous 'law-breakers.'"
"Even a gang with tanks, planes, bombs and other weapons has *no power* to control an armed populace for long unless it first **dupes the people into believing that it has the right to control them.**"
"*Only* a gang imagined to be 'authority' can get away with long-term oppression and enslavement. As a result, 'government' (or the **belief** in it), instead of being essential to the protection of individual rights, is essential only for the prolonged and widespread **violation of individual rights.**"

What Are Related Problems To Slavery?
Aside from the *mental* and *moral* problems at the core to slavery, there may be *more* symptoms that are related to the presence of *Political Slavery*. It is said among voluntaryists who study economics, that when a government is able to control what businesses can or cannot do, giving privileges and handouts to certain businesses or sabotaging other businesses *(ex. Raw Milk industry, taxation, regulation, incentives, tariffs, etc.)*, they crush competition in an otherwise free market, therefore enabling monopolies and reducing the *voluntary* solutions that could help innovate society. A monopoly, more specifically defined, is when there exists only one supplier for a type of commodity, creating dependency. Many will

actually define government as what creates monopolies, and the monopolies that have existed, are said to have *all* received assistance from government. Similarly, it is also said that the *only* lasting cartels have been government cartels, referring to collusion and domination in markets. There wouldn't be a "black market" if it weren't for the controlled market, as we notice people desire to be free when it comes to choosing what to do with the fruits of their *Own* labor, just like anything else that an individual has *ownership* over. The Taoist term "spontaneous order" is also an economic term, in sharing the idea of *laissez faire* which translates to "leave people alone to do as they wish," or that with demand, there will be supply, and therefore order will manifest itself by allowing the market and people to *voluntarily* negotiate and trade. A popular definition of government is that it is a monopoly on violence, nonetheless *legitimized* violence *(Max Stirner, Leo Tolstoy, Max Weber etc.)*, as tantamount to *Democide*. 19th century abolitionist Lysander Spooner would attempt to open his own *American Postal Service* and even argued that he broke no laws in the process since he was a lawyer, yet the government shut down his business in order to maintain their monopoly with the *U.S. Postal Service*. Despite this, the price of postal stamps went down because he was able to provide competition. Without competition we cannot have a choice or allow better options to show themselves for *any* services and products. **Freedom provides choice, slavery provides no choice.**

Jeremey Locke, Author -
"All **economic** control is slavery"

Another perspective upon the slave and master relationship is the imbalances among the masculine and feminine, or what may be called the left brain versus right brain. In short, a left brain or masculine imbalanced individual will seek more power and control. Whereas, a right brain or feminine imbalanced individual will be more naive and follow orders. Perhaps it is that we want to be masculine for being in control of ourselves and taking right action, while feminine in following the principle of self-ownership and *not* taking wrong action, as we may say this leads to an energetic or brain balance. While the science of brain imbalance may have disputes, learning mastery therein control and the lack thereof, still holds true. With applying our understanding of *Mental Slavery*, we may argue that dependence or **mind control** comes from a weakened, ill or imbalanced *(unstable)* mind. As the Hermetic philosophy text "The Kybalion" describes, **"The majority of people are more or less the slaves** of heredity, environment, etc., and manifest very little Freedom. They are swayed by the opinions, customs and thoughts of the outside world, and also by their emotions, feelings, moods, etc. They manifest no Mastery, worthy of the name. They indignantly repudiate this assertion, saying, 'Why, I certainly am free to act and do as I please–I do just what I want to do,' but they fail to explain whence arise the 'want to' and 'as I please.' What makes them "want to" do one thing in preference to another; what makes them 'please' to do this, and not do that? Is there no 'because' to their 'pleasing' and 'wanting'? The Master can change these 'pleases' and 'wants' into others at the opposite end of the *mental* pole. He is able to 'Will to will,' instead of to will because some feeling, mood, emotion, or environmental suggestion arouses a tendency or desire within him so to do."

If we look at slavery under the context of illness or disease, we may consider the slave-master as "sick" for their actions or the slave "sick" for their suffering. The word "ill" is defined from *The Etymology Online Dictionary* as "*morally evil or*

hurtful, unhealthy, sick." In a similar way, the word
"unnatural" is defined as "at variance with *moral* standards."
Considering the fact that *Mental Slavery* is a more powerful
tool than *Physical Slavery* for control, as the slave has
enslaved thyself by legitimizing *hurtful* behavior, *statism*
may be argued as a form of *mental illness*. This statement
would not be unfounded upon merely observing the way
Carl Jung describes "state doctrine" or the concept of Mass
Psychosis and Mass Hysteria, then relating it to the Stanley
Milgram psychology experiments. His work also warns us
about the nature of *all governments, continuously forming
into that of autocracy or oligarchy*. Additionally, the mental
health crisis seen in the world and the impacts of diet and
environment will play a toll in regards to slavery and *vice
versa*, as **an unhealthy slave will be easier to control,
mentally and physically.** As with any illness, it must be
diagnosed, *dia-gnosis* "by way of *knowledge*," and treated
at the root cause, by asking *why*.

Carl Jung, Psychoanalyst (1875) -
"The seemingly omnipotent **State doctrine** is for its part
manipulated in the name of State policy by those occupying
the highest positions in the *government*, where all the
power is concentrated. Whoever, by election or caprice,
gets into one of these positions is no longer subservient to
authority, for he is the State policy itself and within the limits
of the situation can proceed at his own discretion. With
Louis XIV he can say, "L'état c'est moi." ["*The State is Me*,"
or perhaps "I am the State."] He is thus the only individual
or, at any rate, one of the few individuals who could make
use of their individuality if only they knew how to
differentiate themselves from the State doctrine. **They are
more likely, however, to be the slaves of their own
fictions.** Such one-sidedness is always compensated
psychologically by *unconscious subversive tendencies*.

Slavery and rebellion are inseparable correlates. Hence, rivalry for power and exaggerated distrust pervade the entire organism from top to bottom."

"The bigger the crowd the more negligible the individual becomes. But if the individual, overwhelmed by the sense of his own puniness and impotence, should feel that his life has lost its meaning – which, after all, is not identical with public welfare and higher standards of living – then **he is already on the road to State slavery** and, without knowing or wanting it, has becomes its proselyte. The man who looks only outside and quails before the big battalions has no resource with which to combat the evidence of his senses and his reason. But that is just what is happening today: we are all fascinated and overawed by statistical truths and large numbers and are daily apprised of the nullity and futility of the individual personality, since it is not represented and personified by any mass organization. Conversely, those personages who strut about on the world stage and whose voices are heard far and wide seem, to the uncritical public, to be borne along on some mass movement or on the tide of **public opinion** and for this reason are either applauded or execrated. Since mass suggestion plays the predominant role here, it remains a moot point whether their message is their own, for which they are personally **responsible**, or whether they merely function as a megaphone for collective opinion."

"Under these circumstances it is small wonder that individual judgment grows increasingly uncertain of itself and that responsibility is collectivized as much as possible, i.e., is shuffled off by the individual and delegated to a corporate body. In this way the individual becomes more and more a function of society, which in its turn usurps the function of the real-life carrier, whereas, in actual fact, **society is nothing more than an abstract idea like the State**. Both are hypostatized, that is, have become

autonomous. **The State in particular is turned into a quasi-animate personality from whom everything is expected.** In reality it is only a *camouflage* for those individuals who know how to manipulate it. Thus, **the constitutional State drifts into the situation of a primitive form of society, namely, the communism of a primitive tribe where everybody is subject to the autocratic rule of a chief or an oligarchy."**
"The ethical decision of the individual human being no longer counts – what alone matters is the **blind movement** of the masses, and **the lie has thus become the operative principle of political action.** The State has drawn the logical conclusions from this, as the existence of many millions of **State slaves** completely deprived of all *rights* mutely testifies."

Herbert Spencer, Psychologist, Polymath (1820) - **"Autocracy presupposes inferiority of nature on the part of both ruler and subject**: on the one side a cold, unsympathetic sacrificing of other's wills to self-will; on the other side a mean, cowardly abandonment of the claims of manhood. Our very language bears testimony to this. Do not dignity, independence, and other words of approbation, imply a nature at variance with this relation? Are not tyrannical, arbitrary, despotic, epithets of reproach? and are not truckling, fawning, cringing, epithets of contempt? Is not slavish a condemnatory term? Does not servile, that is, serf-like, imply littleness, meanness? And has not the word villain, which originally meant bondsman, come to signify everything which is hateful? That language should thus inadvertently embody dislike for those who most display the instinct of subordination, is alone sufficient proof that this instinct is associated with evil dispositions. It has been the parent of *countless crimes*. It is answerable for the torturing and murder of the noble-minded who would not submit—for the horrors of Bastiles and Siberias. It has ever been the *represser of knowledge, of free thought, of true progress."*

Stanley Milgram, Psychologist (1933) -
"A *substantial* proportion of people do what they are told to do, irrespective of the content of the act and without limitations of **conscience**, so long as they **perceive** that the command comes from a **legitimate authority."**
"I would say, on the basis of having observed a thousand people in the experiment and having my own intuition shaped and informed by these experiments, that **if a system of death camps were set up in the United States of the sort we had seen in Nazi Germany, one would find sufficient personnel for those camps in any medium-sized American town."**
"Each individual possesses a **conscience** which to a greater or lesser degree serves to restrain the unimpeded flow of **impulses destructive to others**. But when he merges his person into an **organizational structure**, a new creature replaces autonomous man, *unhindered by the limitations of individual morality, freed of humane inhibition,* **mindful only of the sanctions of authority."**
"Some people treat *systems of human origin* [and maintenance] as if they existed above and beyond any human agent, beyond the control of whim or human feeling. **The human element behind agencies and institutions is denied."**
"In democracies, men are placed in office through popular elections. Yet, once installed, they are *no less in authority than those who get there by other means.* And, as we have seen repeatedly, the demands of democratically installed authority may also come into conflict with **conscience.** The importation and enslavement of millions of black people, the destruction of the American Indian population, the internment of Japanese Americans, the use of napalm

against civilians in Vietnam, all are harsh policies that originated in the *authority* of a democratic nation, and were responded to with the **expected obedience.** In each case, voices of **morality** were raised against the action in question, but **the typical response of the common man was to obey orders."**

From "Government Is Unnatural, Anarchy Is Natural" - "The controversial and shocking psychological studies known as the Stanley Milgram experiment and the Stanford Prison experiment, proves the danger of this belief system. In the Stanley Milgram experiment, the average person of any demographic was willing to torture their fellow man just because an 'authority' figure told them to do so. They would then attempt to give away their own **responsibility**, and place the blame on the victim or the order-giver, when *they* were the ones who actively carried out the order. The common excuse is 'I was just following orders,' as if it is not in their **nature** to think for themself what is right and wrong, or as if they weren't acting as their self. In other words, it's an attempt to give away one's own nature. If it's not with them, who is it with? This is the importance in knowing thyself. Very few individuals were willing to say 'no' because they know... This also explains why many of the order-followers were laughing with insecurity and nervousness in the experiments, because they were feeling uncontrollable of themself. With the Stanford Prison experiment, average individuals of well respected demographics were given the role of 'guard', becoming an 'authority' figure for a prison. Within just a matter of days, their rulership became tyrannical and cruel, that the experiment had to be ended because they embraced the identity of ''authority' and put themself above their fellow man in nature, in **rights**. These individuals would then come out of the experiment to talk about how they never expected to do what they did, how they couldn't believe that they acted in such a manner. Therefore, it shall be known that *humans cannot continually act like a monster without eventually becoming one*... These same experiments proved to demonstrate that an individual can refuse to be a prison guard or refuse to be an order follower, however on the basis that they *know* they shouldn't."

The Conscious Resistance, Danilo Cuellar -
"The **illusion of freedom** is a more powerful tool to manipulate and subjugate a populace than any gun or stick can ever be. Guns can run out of ammunition and sticks can be broken, but **mental enslavement to authority** endures the ages. By this method the people will submit because they have been bred and programmed to do so since before they could talk or reason. *They know of no other relationship than that of master and slave or ruler and subject.* They grow to **adore their servitude and reproach anyone who would seek to criticize their master** just as a dog jumps with excitement when his master fills his food bowl and faithfully guards him against invaders. The main difference is that we far outnumber our oppressors and yet we tolerate their abuses because we cannot conceive of a world without their **arbitrary restrictions** and sundry taxes. We genuinely believe that it is **necessary and moral for a society to rob its brothers and sisters** to fund projects that are neither wanted nor useful. To deny the people the freedom to do with their currency what they will is the foundation for tyranny of the most egregious form, for with that currency 'government' may fund it's own expansion and thereby continually justify it's own existence through the Hegelian Dialectic." *(Hegelian Dialectic: controlled opposition of one side against another; divide and conquer; intentionally creating a problem, expecting a reaction, to implement an agenda-oriented solution)*

Joost Meerloo, Psychoanalyst (1903) -
"In the totalitarian regime the doubting, inquisitive, and imaginative mind has to be **suppressed**. The **totalitarian slave** is only allowed to memorize, to salivate when the bell rings."
"Totalitarian strategy covers **inner chaos** and conflict by the strict order of the police state. So does the compulsive schizophrenic patient, by his inner routine and schedules. These routines and schedules are a defense against painful occurrences in external reality. This **internal robotization** may lead to denial of internal realities and internal needs as well. The citizen of Totalitaria, *repressing and rejecting his inner need for freedom*, may even **experience slavery as liberation**. He may go even one step further - yearn for an escape from life itself, a delusion that he could become omnipotent through utter destruction."
"Spread fear, terror, and hunger, inflict penetrating pain, and finally, as a result of **mental coercion** and growing confusion, many will succumb and even betray their own families. In many of the concentration camps, the victims themselves were in charge of the gas chamber killings and kept their gruesome jobs until their own turns came. **Fear and terror had made will-less slaves out of them.**"

It is worth saying again, that it is *not* an easy recognition to realize you may have been wrong, despite how evident the truth may seem to others. *Cognitive dissonance* may be observed as *Mental Slavery* to our own thoughts. If a slave master was long as slave master, and long promoting it, it's unlikely they will give it up easily. The same goes for a slave, if they have long been legitimizing their slavery and trained into such, it's unlikely they will want to embrace *real freedom*. Since the slave has never lived real freedom, it is *fearful*, especially if the slave master can convince the slave that freedom is chaos, to be avoided in the comfort of "security." When facing *statism*, there will undoubtedly be denial and contradictions. Most people at heart know that violence and slavery is wrong, yet they will allow it through the form of "government," creating a contradiction in need of self-assessment. This assessment will be harder with the more blockades in regards to the psyche. For instance, **self-loathing** may prevent an order-following from escaping their *Mental Slavery*. *Self-loathing* is known as the underlying psychological condition that causes people to attempt to give away their own personal responsibility to exercise conscience *(common sense)* in choosing right over wrong, and fall into patterns of order following and *justification*. Just as it is *not* possible for an order-follower to truly be exercising conscience and *self-ownership*, it is *not* possible for an order-follower to truly love themselves. *Self-loathing* is created when an earlier trauma has been suppressed and buried into the subconscious mind, instead of being confronted, dealt with and healed. Such trauma could take the form of feeling inadequacy, whether real, suggested, or imagined. It is said that "they are in the cage, and they love being in the cage," thus having no desire for real freedom. **Self-respect**, *re-spectare* "to take another look," heals *self-loathing*. Another way of looking at respect, is that if you don't have $10 in your pocket, you can't give it to someone else. In the same way, you must obtain respect first, before you can give it to others. Just as slavery will *never* provide real freedom or respect, *it cannot provide real security*, as there will never be sovereignty, self-ownership and self-defense for property that belongs with you. Even J.R.R Tolkien, author of *The Lord Of The Rings*, who calls himself an "anarchist" within his journals, shares with us through the "ring of power" that no matter who wields it, this ring will corrupt even the best of people, themes of which can be explored among the seminar *The Lord Of The Rings Dethroned*. The average person generally does not want to rule over their fellow man, for usually good reason, yet they may be the ones who still rule over them *unconsciously* through *statism*. As much as people may want to blame those "in power," the blame or culpability belongs on those who "give power," that being the everyday mass public. A slave-master can give an order to a hundred slaves, and it is ultimately the choice of the slaves if they should carry out the order. If they do, they are the ones responsible, since they carried it out. They may even know how bad the condition of slavery is, talking about how it must be changed, akin to explaining or changing all the details of the cage they are in but never thinking about *simply escaping the cage*. What they don't realize is that it *is* slavery and the *only* way it can be changed is through *abolitionism*. Among self-loathing is also the idea of a controlling person, who by definition, demonstrates abusive behavior, coercion and violence. Narcissism is similarly the sense of superiority, the need for admiration, and a lack of empathy, valuing some people less than others. Overall, there may be an abundance of mindsets to diagnose and characterized behavior in effect for both the slave master or government and the slave or subjects. Understanding this through the context of rights, people shall never give someone the right to be a slave master or an owner of another individual, because in reality, that is wrong and can never be legitimately done, as history will also continually demonstrate. **As you must exercise your body, so also your mind; make up your own mind, it's only yours.**

Martin Luther King Jr, Activist, Author (1929) -
"There is *nothing* in all the world greater than **freedom**. It is worth paying for; *it is worth going to jail for*. I would rather be a free pauper than a rich slave. I would rather die in abject poverty with my convictions than live in inordinate riches with the lack of **self-respect**."

"The **greatest purveyor of violence** in the world today is my own **government**."

Albert Camus, Philosopher (1913) -
"A living man can be enslaved and reduced to the historic condition of an object. But if he dies in **refusing to be enslaved**, he reaffirms the existence of another kind of human nature which *refuses to be classified as an object.*"
"The very moment the slave refuses to obey the humiliating orders of his master, he simultaneously rejects the condition of slavery. The act of rebellion carries him far beyond the point he had reached by simply refusing. He exceeds the bounds that he fixed for his antagonist, and now demands to be treated as an **equal.** What was at first the man's obstinate resistance now becomes the whole man, who is identified with and summed up in this resistance. The part of himself that he wanted to be respected he proceeds to place above everything else and proclaims it preferable to everything, even to life itself. It becomes for him the supreme good. Having up to now been willing to compromise, the slave suddenly adopts ('because this is how it must be') an attitude of All or Nothing. **With rebellion, awareness is born**... The slave who opposes his master is not concerned, let us note, with repudiating his master as a human being. He repudiates him as a master. He denies that he has the right to deny him, a slave, on grounds of necessity. The master is discredited to the exact extent that he fails to respond to a demand which he ignores. **If men cannot refer to a common value, recognized by all as existing in each one, then man is incomprehensible to man.** The rebel demands that this value should be clearly recognized in himself because he knows or suspects that, without this **principle**, crime and disorder would reign throughout the world. An act of rebellion on his part seems like a demand for clarity and

unity. **The most elementary form of rebellion, paradoxically, expresses an aspiration to order**... The rebel slave will help us to throw light on this point. He established, by his protest, the existence of the master against whom he rebelled. But at the same time he demonstrated that his master's power was dependent on his own subordination and he affirmed his own power: the power of continually questioning the superiority of his master. In this respect master and slave are really in the same boat: the temporary sway of the former is as relative as the submission of the latter... Undoubtedly the master enjoys total freedom first as regards the slave, since the latter recognizes him totally, *and then as regards the natural world*, since by his work the slave transforms it into objects of enjoyment which the master consumes in a **perpetual affirmation of his own identity**... One leader, one people, signifies one master and millions of slaves... The slave and those whose present life is miserable and who can find no consolation in the heavens are assured that at least the future belongs to them. **The future is the only kind of property that the masters willingly concede to the slaves**... Every act of creation, by its mere existence, denies the world of master and slave... **It is impossible to speak and communicate with a person who has been reduced to servitude**... The rebel undoubtedly demands a certain degree of freedom for himself; but in no case, if he is consistent, does he demand the right to destroy the existence and the freedom of others. He humiliates no one. **The freedom he claims, he claims for all; the freedom he refuses, he forbids everyone to enjoy.** He is not only the slave against the master, but also man against the world of master and slave. Therefore, thanks to rebellion, there is something more in history than the relation between mastery and servitude... **No man considers that his condition is free if it is not at the same time just**, nor just

unless it is free."
"The only way to deal with an unfree world is to **become so absolutely free that your very existence is an act of rebellion**"

Among the many accusations, the abolitionists were attacked as being "rebels" though often their method and intent were both based in love and peace, or the mere practice of *self-ownership*. We don't need to look at famous rebellious figures in history, nor former slaves, and especially not the reactive "rebels" who throw fire in the streets to project their own hatred, in order to understand the rebel *who is actually themself*. Abolitionists such as Bronson Alcott, Henry David Thoreau, Robert Purvis, John Brown, Samuel Adair, W.W. Brown, John Collins, Charles Remond, and Charles Lane were willing to go to jail for not paying taxes, and many of them did, sometimes even worse things happened. In addition, William Lloyd Garrison would go to jail refusing to pay the state in a court case about his journalism against slavery. One should not be surprised to see lists of hundreds and thousands of "tax resisters" in history, especially when we may observe people we may now call "heroes" for the simple act of keeping their *Own* property for the sake of also helping others to keep their *Own* property.

Voltairine de Cleyre, Philosopher (1866) -
"Be men first of all, not held in slavery by the things you make; let your gospel be, '**Things for men, not men for things.**'"

Victor Yarros, Lawyer, Philosopher (1865) -
"No man has ever died through devotion to ideas. Those that had too much **self-love** and too much love of independence to suit the despots now enthroned in this

world very frequently were forced to accept death as a less evil than a life of slavery, suffering, degradation, and **mental anguish**."

Felix Pignal, Philosopher (approx. 1854) -
"**Down with governments**, down with tyranny, and long live independence! Long live love and friendship."

Benjamin Tucker, Philosopher (1854) -
"To establish **Anarchy** nothing is needed except a little **knowledge**, some brains, some will-power, and a determination to stick to the plumb-line."

Are You In Control Or Is Someone Controlling You?
Dependence is characterized as a lack of self-control, a lack of independence, and therefore the seeking of external control, giving-in to an oppressor or provider. It is therefore in the context of slavery, similarly said as *Mental Slavery*. When security is placed externally, it may imply a lack of security internally, creating a false sense of security that is an attempt to abdicate *self-responsibility*. If a slave never comes to secure their *Own* self, their *Own* freedom, their *Own* ownership, they will *never* be free. Freedom relies on the idea that the slave no longer needs a slave master to live their own life. Since government "authority" provides no actual resource to society, and only acts to forcibly transfer resources already made by everyday people, everything that government provides to someone has been *stolen* from someone else. Therefore, people who are dependent upon their government are slaves who are dependent upon their slave-master, as they honor a thief that continuously *steals* from them and others without end. People can help *voluntarily*, but they may be giving you help at the expense of another, *involuntarily*, if one does not know *how* they are being helped and *why*. This is why individuals may speak

as if government partakes in "hidden violence." To reiterate, *why* does government provide? To keep people's trust with their *Mental Slavery*. Their good faith nature is essentially being played on. *How* does government provide? Through the use of theft, by keeping people in fear or *Mental Slavery*, of punishment or *Physical Slavery*, if they do not comply with demands. If government exists and grows out of *Mental Slavery* leading to *Physical Slavery*, at what point do we simply say "government *is* slavery"? If we refer to the notion of self-government, this is would be akin to simply self-control, much like self-mastery. We are *not* fully instinctual or barbaric animals always seeking for power, we have a moral conscience to choose moral behavior and if we choose to continue to develop it as a species, we would create the *opposite condition of slavery*, where individuals are able to control themselves, *real* self-government. Self-slavery or slavery to god and nature negates the nature of slavery just as self-government negates the nature of government or "authority." We can put the past behind as we are developed beings with the capacity of *reasoning*, unless we are to stay suppressed in our ability, making us more susceptible to government slavery. The moral obligation is on *you*, and your own ignorance to act on what you *now know* will be your *karma*. Those who do not put in the effort of making real freedom possible because they *think* humans will never be able to be sovereign, are enforcing *Mental Slavery* in their hopelessness, a slave that will never truly be free. Life is much more than this physical body, are we not to have a higher cause beyond our egoic selfish desires and attachments? Is the needed *abolitionism not* a reason to have a purpose and cause in life? Life without liberty is not worth living, as it is not *real* life. Government creates slavery, and government depends upon statism, but statism depends upon you. We are *free by nature, slaves by government.*

Benjamin Tucker, Philosopher (1854) -
"**Personal government is the only true government**, but
the difference between a free people, so governed, and a
slave people governed, is that the government instituted by
the former proceeds only by the constant **consent** of all
interested, while the latter is carried on in the name either of
one absolute monarch, or, as we of America say, in the
name of 'the majority,' whether those who are governed
consent or not."

Victor Yarros, Lawyer, Philosopher (1865) -
"The patriarch giving way to absolute monarchy, absolute
monarchy to limited, constitutional monarchy, which, in its
turn, was succeeded by a republican form of government
and then a democratic, *we must now go a step farther* and
establish **Anarchy, or self-government**... Sociology is a
science, and that its laws must be gradually discovered. Set
the masses free, and **let them act according to their own
reason**, stimulated by their wants and needs, and we will
soon see the good result... **While government exists, the
people will be slaves**... Trust to human nature. Trust to
common sense and self-interest. Abolish all written, man-
made laws and regulations, and you will find a **higher,
unwritten law** operating and working in the field of human
relations."
"**The State** is a conspiracy of running schemers to enslave
the people and live on the fruits of their toil. Legislation is its
instrumentality; it grants **rights** and privileges to the few at
the expense of the many, it fosters monopolies and kills
competition by protective taxes, and, finally, it defends the
rich criminals and protects them in their 'rights.' **The ballot**
is a cunning device of the conspirators, by which the slaves
are made to tighten their own chains. But *when the radical*

reformer raises his voice, he is voted down as a theorist, dreamer, crank."
"The Government is the master, **we are the slaves.**"
"Besides, so far as this blessed republic is concerned, which, as Mr. Swinton assures us, enjoys a government of the people, for the people, and by the people, what sense is there in saying that the government — that is, the people — is the final owner of all the people? If I, a private citizen, own myself, and every other citizen, individually, owns himself, then, if we, in the aggregate, are really the government, **we, of course, own ourselves.** Obviously, it was not this commonplace which Mr. Swinton insisted upon. Was the idea, then, that each citizen becomes, the moment he consents *(for this government is theoretically based on consent)* to be part of the government, the **property** of the rest of the citizens? But in that case each citizen is at the same time both master and slave, owner of others and property owned by others."

George Fitzhugh, Leading Pro-Slavery Advocate (1806) - "With thinking men, **the question can never arise, who ought to be free? Because no one ought to be free. All government is slavery.** The proper subject of investigation for philosophers and philanthropists is, 'Is the existing mode of government adapted to the wants of its subjects?'"
"It is the duty of society to **protect** all its members, and it can only do so by subjecting each to that degree of **government constraint or slavery**, which will best advance the good of each and of the whole."
"**Liberty is an evil which government is intended to correct.** This is the sole object of government."
"Adopt **the slavery principle**, vindicate the institution in the abstract, **tighten the reins of government**, restrain and punish licentiousness in every form, scout and **repudiate**

the doctrines of let alone... and govern much and rigorously. This is the *new world* that we want."

"There is no such thing as **natural human liberty**, because it is unnatural for man to live alone and **without the pale and government of society.**"

"**The slavery principle is almost the only principle of government**, the distinctive feature of man's social and dependent nature, and the only cement that binds society together and **wards off anarchy.**"

"The **need of law and government** is just in proportion to man's wealth and enlightenment. Barbarians and savages need and will submit to but few and simple laws, and little of government. The **love of personal liberty and freedom** from all restraint, are distinguishing traits of wild men and wild beasts."

"No wonder the abolitionists loved to quote the Declaration of Independence! Its precepts are wholly at war with slavery and equally at war with **all government, all subordination, all order**... Life and liberty are not inalienable. Jefferson in sum, was the architect of ruin, the inaugurator of **anarchy.**" *Although agreeing that government never is made with consent and that "all governments must originate in force, and be continued by force," Fitzhugh actively states this in encouraging the action.*

Robert Lewis Dabney, Pro-Slavery Advocate (1820) - "**Domestic servitude, as we define and defend it, is but civil government in one of its forms.** All government is restraint; and this is but one form of restraint."

Jeremey Locke, Author - "**Democracy is about making slaves and masters of slaves.** The teachings of the world's great democracies are those of liberty and a voice for every person. They teach us that democracies are the greatest possible form of government. The reason they give is that democracy offers a voice for the common man. Unlike kings, dictators and communists, democracy allows most people to have say in the affairs of their neighbors. The evil of democracy knows no freedom. A free person has none to enslave him. Instead, *democracies offer everyone the opportunity to enslave you.* Democratic culture teaches the rule of law. It teaches that **law created by majority** rule *is* morality. Any law, any demand, any punishment is moral when implemented by the majority. Perversions of democracy such as democratic republics and super-majorities are no different. Any law able to be passed by representative, majority, super-majority or any other group becomes morality. If you can convince 50% of a people to enslave themselves or their neighbors, is it moral? If you can convince 66%, 75%, 99% or everyone, is it morality?... All other forms of tyranny are *obviously* evil because they allowed a few to control the lives of all."

"But Without Slavery...?"
Any *covert slavery* is not a "necessary evil" as some people may claim, because the same argument could've been made for more *overt slavery* in the past. It is no coincidence that the same exact arguments against the abolition of *chattel slavery* are essentially the same exact arguments against the abolition of *political slavery* and governments. The following example arguments would be made by an individual who is *mentally enslaved* with *statism*. In other words, these are claims made against the efforts of *abolitionism*, often merely *justifications* made in ignorance of conscience, morality and ownership.

- Slavery is natural – Government is natural
- Slavery has always existed – Government has always existed

- Every society has Slavery – Every society has Government
- Slaves are not capable of taking care of themselves – People are not capable of taking care of themselves
- Without masters, the slaves will die off – Without Government, the people will die off
- Where the common people are free, they are even worse off than slaves – Where the common people have no government, they are much worse off
- Without Slavery, the former slaves would cause chaos and other evils – Without Government, the people would cause chaos and other evils
- Trying to get rid of Slavery is foolishly Utopian and impractical – Trying to get rid of Government is foolishly Utopian and impractical
- Forget *abolition*, a far better plan is to keep the slaves sufficiently well fed, clothed, housed, and occasionally entertained and to take their minds off their exploitation by encouraging them to focus on the better life that awaits them in the hereafter - Forget *anarchy*, a far better plan is to keep the slaves sufficiently well fed, clothed, housed, and occasionally entertained and to take their minds off their exploitation by encouraging them to focus on the better life that awaits them in the hereafter
- Without Slavery, who will pick the cotton – Without Government, who will build the roads
- There will be slavery anyways – There will be Government anyways
- The slaves can go to a better plantation – The people can go to a better government
- We can change who runs the plantation or how it runs, so that the slaves have more freedom – We

can change the leaders or the laws, so that the people have more freedom

William Lloyd Garrison, Journalist, Abolitionist (1805) - (Speaking satirically) "The slaves are kept in bondage **for their own good**. Liberty is a curse to the free people of color—their condition is worse than that of the slaves!" In *The Liberator* newspaper edited by Garrison, they found four main arguments used among pro-slavery advocates thereof the common people, church and state. "1. That **a man might hold a slave, and not do wrong.** 2. That immediate emancipation is impossible. 3. That a slaveholder may be a good Christian. 4. That the influence of slavery is not always evil." Are these arguments not also synonymous with government and politicians? In 1846, Garrison also had a specific list of arguments presented against him, such as: "**The condition of the slaves is better** here than that of the Africans, or the lower of classes all other nations." "Because the evils of Slavery were entailed by the mother country upon the Colonies against their will, and the inheriting States **must bear with the evil**, as irremediable." "Because the Slaves cannot be benefited by freedom, but must ever be reduced below the whites, for the two races **cannot live in peace** on the ground of equality; and while they are in the same country, the one will be the master of the other." Most of the time, churches and governments would try to avoid the conversation in the first place, with churches saying that they should in "**no way intermeddle with that question** while in the commission of this Society" or that "slavery is a *political* question, with which we have nothing to do." In response, Garrison states about their views, "the relation of master to slave, is not only *not* necessarily sinful, it is often innocent, and may be beneficent and **virtuous.**"

"I go for **free trade** and **free inter-communication** the world over, and deny the **right** of any body of men to erect geographical or national barriers in opposition to these **natural**, essential and sacred rights. **Every government must be regarded as a tyranny**, and unworthy of approbation, that erects or maintains such barriers."

Stefan Molyneux, Philosopher, Author (1966) -
"The abolition of slavery was a moral imperative, because slavery as an institution is **innately evil.** The abolition of slavery was not conditional upon the provision of jobs for every freed slave. In a similar manner, anarchic theory does not have to explain how every conceivable social, legal or economic transaction could occur in the absence of a coercive government. What is important to understand is that the initiation of the use of force is a moral evil... **When slavery was abolished for the first time in human history, there was no prior example of a successful slave–free society** — if that had been a requirement, then slavery would be with us still... the honest population is violently **enslaved by the State**, and the dishonest provided with cash incentives and protection... **The majority of those in jail are nonviolent offenders**, enslaved and in chains because they used recreational drugs, or gambled, or went to a prostitute, or did not pay all their taxes, or other such innocuous nonsense – or turned to crime because State 'vice' prohibitions made crime so profitable, and State 'education' kept them so ignorant... **Those who first dreamed of a world free of slavery lived only to see slavery increase and worsen, not diminish and collapse.** Those who dreamed of reason, evidence and science in the late Middle Ages saw their dreams go up in endless flames."
"If the **basic truths** of history, logic, ethics and reality are inconvenient to those in power – as they inevitably are –

those paid by those in power will almost never talk about
them. We would not expect a Stalinist-era teacher to speak
of the glories of capitalism; we would not expect an
Antebellum teacher to teach the children of slave-owners
about the evils of slavery; we would not expect an instructor
at West Point to talk about the evils and corruption of the
military-industrial complex, any more than we would expect
the Vatican to voluntarily initiate a discussion of child abuse
by Catholic priests... By pretending that the evils inherent in
slavery could be mitigated or eliminated through voluntary
internal reform, these 'moralists' actually slowed or stalled
the progress towards **abolition** in many areas. By holding
out **the false hope that an evil institution could be
turned to goodness**, these sophists blunted the power of
the argument from morality, which is that slavery is an
inherent evil, and thus **cannot be reformed.**"

William Blake, Philosopher (1757) -
"The ancient poets animated all objects with Gods or
Geniuses, calling them by the names and adorning them
with the properties of woods, rivers, mountains, lakes,
cities, nations, and whatever their enlarged & numerous
senses could perceive. And particularly they studied the
genius of each city & country, placing it under its mental
deity; **Till a system was formed, which some took
advantage of, & enslav'd the vulgar by attempting to
realize or abstract the mental deities from their objects:
thus began priesthood**; Choosing forms of worship from
poetic tales. And at length they pronounc'd that the Gods
had order'd such things. Thus men forgot that all deities
reside in the human breast."
"I must Create a System, or be **enslav'd by another Man's**"
"The soldiers are *all* slaves."

Theodore Dwight Weld in his historic writing "Slavery As It Is," details main objections to abolitionism in detail, and the main titled points are as following: "Such cruelties are incredible" *(hard to believe)* "Slaveholders protest that they treat their slaves well" "**Slaveholders are proverbial for their kindness**, hospitality, benevolence and generosity" "Northern visitors at the south testify that the **slaves are not cruelly treated**" "It is for the interest of the masters to **treat their slaves well**" "The fact that the slaves multiply so rapidly proves that they are **not inhumanly treated**, but are **in a comfortable condition**" "Public opinion is a protection to the slave"

Frederick Douglass, Former Slave, Abolitionist (1817) - "What shall be done with the four million slaves if they are emancipated?... Primarily, it is a question less for man than for God – less for human intellect than for the **laws of nature** to solve. It assumes that nature has erred; that the law of liberty is a mistake; **that freedom, though a natural want of the human soul, can only be enjoyed at the expense of human welfare**, and that *men are better off in slavery than they would or could be in freedom*; that slavery is the natural order of human relations, and that *liberty is an experiment*. What shall be done with them? Our answer is, do nothing with them; **mind your business**, and let them mind theirs. Your doing with them is their greatest misfortune. They have been undone by your doings, and all they now ask, and really have need of at your hands, is just to let them alone. **They suffer by every interference**, and succeed best by being let alone."

Larken Rose, Philosopher, Author - "Silly arguments are never made in situations where 'authority' is not involved. No one would accept a claim that it is okay for a restaurant to **force** someone to pay for food he did not order, on the grounds that otherwise the person might starve. No one would accept a claim that it is okay for a builder to force someone to pay for a building he did not order, on the grounds that otherwise the person might be homeless. But even more ridiculous would be to claim that it is okay for one street gang to run a 'protection' racket so that they have the resources to keep all the other dangerous street gangs out of their city. Yet that is exactly the attempted **justification** for *all* 'government': that it must be allowed to **commit aggression against everyone, so that it can protect them from others who might commit aggression against them.**"

Excerpts from "What Anarchy Isn't" (Recommended) - "Consider, for example, your favorite grocery store. Everyone involved in the hugely complex operation of growing, processing, transporting, displaying and selling food, participates voluntarily. Customers choose where to shop and what to buy, and all the other people involved— truck-drivers, stock boys, checkout clerks, administrators, etc.—do things in exchange for getting paid. This purely **voluntary arrangement** allows for an amazingly complex degree of organization and cooperation without anyone being forced to participate. This is literally **anarchy in action**. In contrast, whenever government does something, a very small group of people *(politicians)* comes up with an idea, and *forces* everyone else to go along with it. In the authoritarian version of a supermarket, the ruling class would tell people what to produce and how much, and would tell customers what they must buy and what they *must* pay for it. Anyone who did not comply would be punished in some way. That is *always* how government does things."

"One does not need a badge or special 'authority' to have the right to defend himself or others, against attackers and thieves. Everyone already has the right to use defensive force—on his own, or with others for mutual protection. **Anarchy** means no one has the **right to rule** (i.e., no one has special rights); it doesn't mean people can't get together to *exercise* rights that everyone already has. In a stateless society, even professional protectors would only have the *same rights* as everyone else."

"Most people see government domination as necessary and valid, and so they **cooperate with their own victimization.** That is why *government gets away with far more oppression and extortion than private gangs ever could.*"

"The lack of an authoritarian ruling class makes the people far less susceptible to being extorted and dominated, and far more likely to disobey and resist any would-be thieves and thugs... Relying on government to prevent theft and oppression is completely ridiculous, since **government is the biggest thug and thief there is**, confiscating far more wealth than all other crooks and criminals combined."

"A **sociopath** doesn't care about laws or social rules; he cares only about avoiding pain and hardship for himself. And that is true regardless of whether government exists or not. It makes no difference whether the threat comes from the police, or another citizen, or even another criminal."

"**Political authority** is not about people coming together to do something that everyone already has the **right** to do; political authority is about one group of people claiming the right to do things which normal people do *not* have the right to do, such as taxing and controlling everyone else. Organized defense can be very effective without anyone claiming any special right to rule—in other words, without having any special 'authority' and without being government."

"Either we normal people have no idea what is right and wrong unless and until politicians tell us, or the only reason we want to do the right thing and co-exist peacefully is because politicians command us to. A quick examination of your own motivations and behaviors proves that neither of those things is actually true. If the people themselves have no **moral code** and no **conscience**, and are just stupid, violent animals, why does *almost everyone* want government to keep the peace and protect the innocent?.. If people are so short-sighted and selfish that they can't be trusted to **voluntarily** organize and fund whatever they deem important, then how can those same people be trusted to decide who should be in power?"

William Pitt, Activist (1759) -
"Necessity is the plea for every infringement of human freedom. It is the argument of tyrants; it is the creed of slaves."

Richard J. Maybury, Author (1946) -
"Before the slaves were freed in 1863, no one knew how cotton could be harvested without them. But slavery was wrong and it was abolished, and **today cotton is harvested more efficiently than it ever was by slaves.** Not only are the blacks better off but the plantation owners are, too. That's how the world is made. **Liberty and free markets not only work, they work better.**"

Joseph Dejacque, Abolitionist (1821) -
"Will the activity of my nature be developed all the more by being restrained? It is absurd to assert such a thing. The so-called free workman even in the present state of society, produces more and does his work better than the negro slave. How would it be if he were really and universally free? His productive power would increase one-hundred fold."
"We are an original work and not a copy. The slave models himself upon the master, he imitates. The free man does not produce his type, he creates... **They don't want to be**

slaves, nor would they be masters. Being free, they have the cult of Liberty and practice it from their infancy and confess it at *all moments* to the ends of their lives."

"To dare manifest an **abolitionist** opinion, it's prison, it's affronting the power, it's the dagger, the revolver, being tarred and feathered, atrocities and barbarous punishments, Lynch Law inflicted by bands of loafers on the side of the planters and of their mob of lackey politicians, the legislative bodies, and state executives... **All compromise with slavery is a crime.**"

"**No more government**, and thus no more of these destructive ambitions that only use the shoulders of the people, ignorant and credulous, to make of them a step-stool for its covetousness. No more of these candidates-acrobats dancing on the rope of the *professions of faith*, with the right foot for this one and the left foot for that. No more of these political prestidigitators juggling the three words of the republican motto, Liberty, Equality, Fraternity... No more government, and then **no more army to oppress the people by the people. No more University to level the young intelligences under the yoke** of cretinism, manipulating their brains and hearts, and knead and mold them in the image of an obsolete society. No more magistrate-inquisitors to torture on the rack of examination and to condemn to the stifling of prison or exile the voice of the press and the clubs, the manifestations of **conscience** and thought. **No more executioners, no more jailers, no more gendarmes, no more city constables, no more snitches to track, seize, detain and put to death all who are not devoted to the authorities.** No more directing centralization, no more prefects, no ordinary or extraordinary envoys to spread the state of siege through *all* the departments. No more budgets to recruit, arm, equip, to fatten with potatoes or truffles, to intoxicate with schnick or champagne that uniformed domestic staff from the soldier to the general, from the prefect to the policeman and from the executioner to the judge."

Stephen Pearl Andrews, Abolitionist (1812) -
"Individual **property** is based on the **right** of the Individual to the **products of his own labor**. But if the product of my labour is my own, no one can decide the terms on which I shall part with it but myself. The right of exchanging it at pleasure is involved in the right of **ownership**. The attempt to establish a **compulsory law** for this purpose is a gross violation of my acknowledged **Sovereignty**"
"*Government of all sorts is adverse to freedom.* It destroys the freedom of the subject, directly, by virtue of the fact that he is a subject; and destroys equally the freedom of the governor, indirectly, by devolving on him the necessity of overlooking and attempting, hopelessly, to regulate the conduct of others,—a task *never* yet accomplished, and the attempt at which is sufficiently harassing to wear the life out of the most zealous advocate of order."

Benjamin Tucker, Philosopher (1854) -
"**Man, especially when he is superstitious, is always afraid to change anything that exists**; he generally reveres that which is old. 'Our fathers did so; they managed to live in one way or another; they brought you up; they were not unhappy; do you the same!' say the old to the young whenever the latter wish to change anything. **The unknown frightens them; they prefer to cling to the past, even though that past stands for misery, oppression, slavery.** It may even be said that, the unhappier man is, the more he fears to change any thing whatever through fear of becoming still more unhappy; a ray of hope and a few glimpses of *comfort* must penetrate his sorrowful hut before he can begin to wish for something better, to criticise his former manner of life, and to *be willing*

to risk something in the hope of changing it. Until this hope has penetrated his being, until he has freed himself from the *tutelage* of those who utilize his superstitions and his fears, he prefers to remain as he is. *If the young desire a change, the old utter a cry of alarm against the innovators."*
"Mr. Ball,— to his honor be it said,— during antislavery days, was a steadfast abolitionist. He earnestly desired the **abolition** of slavery. Doubtless he remembers how often he was met with the argument that slavery was *necessary* to keep the unlettered blacks out of mischief, and that it would be *unsafe* to give freedom to such a mass of ignorance. Mr. Ball in those days saw through the sophistry of such reasoning, and knew that those who urged it did so to give some color of **moral justification** to their conduct in living in luxury on the enforced toil of slaves. He probably would answer them in this fashion: '**It is the institution of slavery that keeps the blacks in ignorance, and to justify slavery on the ground of their ignorance is to reason in a circle and beg the very question at issue.**'"
"War and authority are companions; **peace and liberty are companions.**"

Anarchy has received a reputation for meaning "chaos," with many people using the term also as a means of rebellion and protest, or using it as a means for violence and identity. Whereas, here we are observing anarchy as **philosophical anarchism**, more specifically as *voluntaryism,* which often advocates the exact opposite of it's fallacious presumptuous portrayal. From Greek *an-archon*: "the absence of rulers," it does *not* mean without rules, as we may know that to even attain the condition of anarchy, one must *know* the rules, past the *belief* that rules must *only* come from man-made rulers. As this is of the aims to abolish *political slavery*, "anarchist" is simply another word for *modern abolitionist*. Much like voluntaryism, using the word abolitionism may help to emphasize that freedom isn't free, that there *are* rules and that this *is* indeed a fight against slavery. We are merely following the path paved by previous *abolitionists*. Therefore, the *real* condition of anarchy is the absence of slavery, where *knowledge* (of *rules* concerning ownership, responsibility, rights etc.) is in circulation by the mass public without *fear*, where because there are no slaves as they have freed themselves, there can be no masters. This means that there is no **master plan** (hence "master") to how society should operate, as no one person or few people get to decide how other people should live their *Own* lives. Thus the condition of a stateless society or freedom, cannot be expected to be exactly described by any individual, though people may observe many different plans within a *voluntary* world due to our natural creativity. People will *voluntarily* make things work without violence, just as they do with *everything* else outside of politics. Similar to the *justifications* made against abolitionists, are also the attacks, which may be expected due to the *cognitive dissonance*; hence, be wary but stand on your principles with love as best as you may.

Thomas Hodgskin, Philosopher (1787) -
"When conceited politicians ask me what I would substitute for their systems, my answer is, that I propose no substitute. My argument is, that **individual man does not make society, and that man cannot organize it**... Men revolt against it, and inflict misery on themselves and others, in **their blind efforts to correct wrong**."

Benjamin Tucker, Philosopher (1854) -
"The doctrines of the Anarchists are taking a more rapid hold upon thinking **minds**, considering the time they have had to travel, than can be said of any other agitation yet set

in motion over the world. History is playing into our hands every day, and the swindle of reigning politics is daily out-preaching to sober-minded people the capacity of our types and pockets"

"**Anarchy** means the absence of **compulsory rulership**; hence, the absence of slavery,— Liberty."

Albert Parsons, Philosopher (1848) -
"**Government is for slaves**; free men govern themselves. Law, statute, man-made law is license. **Anarchy — natural law — is liberty.** Anarchy is the cessation of **force**. Government is the rulership or control of man by men."

"The natural and the imprescriptible **right** of all is the right of each to **control oneself.** Anarchy is a free society where there is no concentrated or centralised power, no State, no king, no emperor, no ruler, no president, no magistrate, no potentate of any character whatever. **Law is the enslaving power of man.**"

"Originally the earth and its contents were held in common by all men. Then came a change brought about by violence, robbery and wholesale murder, called **war.** Later, but still way back in history, we find that there were but two classes in the world — slaves and masters."

Among misconceptions, when we think of **limited government**, ask yourself if there is such a thing as limited slavery. Does limiting slavery make slavery right? If we legitimize any slavery, is it not given a free pass to grow in size? Any limit put upon government, as done in history countless times, never works and is simply a waste of time, short of *abolitionism*, what is *actually* destined for freedom. Another misconception is that anarchy is against *all* forms of hierarchy. However, *voluntary* hierarchies will always exist and is not of the nature of slavery. Many people confuse society with government, since they presume slavery to be natural. Involuntary interaction and authoritarianism, being hierarchies based on violence for compliance, *is* slavery. There will always exist crime, the question is how crime becomes *aggregated*, for which only with government can there be slavery or the aggregation of crime, since it is *permitted*.

John Henry Mackay, Philosopher (1864) -
"Ages had to pass before the idea of **Anarchy** could arise. *All the forms of slavery had to be passed through.* Ever seeking liberty only to find the same despotism in the changed forms, so had the people staggered. Now was the truth found to **condemn all forms which were force. Authority began to yield.**"

Frederick Douglass, Former Slave, Abolitionist (1817) -
"The limits of tyrants are prescribed *by the endurance of those whom they oppress.*"

James Madison, American Independence (1751) -
"If men were angels, **no government** would be necessary."
Mark Passio, De-Occultist, Philosopher (1974) -
"Since humans aren't angels, **none are fit to rule.**"

Lysander Spooner, Abolitionist, Lawyer (1808) -
"The highwayman takes solely upon himself the **responsibility**, danger, and crime of his own act. He does not *pretend* that he has any rightful claim to your money, or that he intends to use it for your own benefit. He does not pretend to be anything but a robber. He has not acquired impudence enough to profess to be merely a 'protector,' and that he takes men's money against their will, merely to enable him to 'protect' those infatuated travelers, who feel perfectly able to protect themselves, or do not appreciate his peculiar system of protection. He is too sensible a man

to make such professions as these. Furthermore, having taken your money, he leaves you, as you wish him to do. He does not persist in following you on the road, against your will; assuming to be your rightful 'sovereign,' on account of the 'protection' he affords you. He does not keep 'protecting' you, by commanding you to bow down and serve him; by requiring you to do this, and forbidding you to do that; by robbing you of more money as often as he finds it for his interest or pleasure to do so; and by branding you as a rebel, a traitor, and an enemy to your country, and shooting you down without mercy, if you dispute his *authority*, or resist his demands. He is too much of a gentleman to be guilty of such impostures, and insults, and villainies as these. In short, he does not, in addition to robbing you, attempt to make you either his dupe or his slave."

Herbert Spencer, Psychologist, Polymath (1820) -
"Be it or be it not true that Man is shapen in iniquity and conceived in sin, it is unquestionably true that **Government is begotten of aggression and by aggression.**"
"We should take the ground that *no human being, however wise and good, is fit to be sole ruler over the doings of an involved society*; and that, with the best intentions, **a benevolent despot** is very likely to produce the most terrible mischiefs which would else have been impossible."
"**As fast as voluntary cooperation is abandoned compulsory cooperation must be substituted.** Some kind of organization labour must have; and if it is not that which arises by agreement under **free competition**, it must be that which is imposed by *authority. Unlike in appearance and names* as it may be to the old order of slaves and serfs, working under masters, who were coerced by barons, who were themselves vassals of dukes or kings, the new order wished for, constituted by workers under foremen of small

groups, overlooked by superintendents, who are subject to higher local managers, who are controlled by superiors of districts, themselves under a central government, must be essentially the same in principle."

Gustave de Molinari, Philosopher (1819) -
"Everywhere we see the races invested with the **monopoly on security** devoting themselves to bitter struggles, in order to add to the extent of their market, the number of their **forced consumers**, and hence the amount of their gains. **War** has been the necessary and inevitable consequence of the establishment of a monopoly on security. Another inevitable consequence has been that this monopoly has *engendered all other monopolies*... after long centuries of suffering, as **enlightenment** spread through the world little by little, the masses who had been smothered under this nexus of privileges began to rebel against the privileged, and to demand liberty, that is to say, the suppression of monopolies... Could it conceivably be relegated to **free competition**? The response to this question on the part of political writers is unanimous: No. Why? We will tell you why. Because these writers, who are concerned especially with **governments, know nothing about society.** They regard it as an *artificial* fabrication, and believe that the mission of government is to modify and remake it constantly... in order to modify or remake society, it is necessary to be empowered with an *authority* superior to that of the various individuals of which it is composed... the fiction of **divine right**. This fiction was certainly the best imaginable. If you succeed in persuading the multitude that God himself has chosen certain men or certain races to give laws to society and to govern it, no one will dream of revolting against these appointees of Providence, and everything the government does will be accepted... It was free inquiry that demonetized the fiction of divine right...

Just as war is the natural consequence of monopoly, **peace is the natural consequence of liberty**... *the natural organization of the security industry would not be different from that of other industries*. In small districts a single entrepreneur could suffice. This entrepreneur might leave his business to his son, or sell it to another entrepreneur. In larger districts, one company by itself would bring together enough resources adequately to carry on this important and difficult business. If it were well managed, this company could easily last, and security would last with it. In the security industry, just as in most of the other branches of production, the latter mode of organization will probably replace the former, in the end."

"**All history** attests that it was **force**, and in no sense a **voluntary agreement** of both parties, which erected the associations called **political States**... The strongest members of the species, usually hordes subsisting by the *chase and pillage*, seized the territories occupied by weaker members. The **conquerors** effected a partition of these lands, and compelled the inhabitants to work for their benefit, whether by reducing the conquered population to a state of slavery or by leaving them in possession of the land, but subject to a system of serfdom or of simple subjection. **The origins of a political State** were a commercial speculation in agriculture or industry, and profits naturally depended upon the administrative capacity of their owner, the industry and productive aptitudes of the subject population, the fertility of the soil, and other similar conditions. Taken as *forced labour*, or as imposts in kind or in money, these profits constituted the owners' revenue, and were, as such, subject to no limitation but that of the entire nett production of which the labours of the slaves, serfs, or subjects were capable... Thanks to many **moral and material advances**, and a whole series of transitions, the servant, serf, or slave became his own proprietor. But, although freed from the domination of a master, he remained member of a community or nation, and consequently subject to the power erected by this community or nation for its better preservation from the risks of destruction or subjection, which are consequences of a State of War. This power was, for these purposes, invested with an unlimited right of disposition over the lives and goods of all members—a subjection effectively negativing the **sovereignty** of the individual. However seriously he might be declared sovereign **master of himself**, his goods and life, the individual was still controlled by a power invested with **rights** which took precedence of his own." *(from among the first texts to discuss how defense and the market would operate among the end of political slavery)*

Louise Michel, Philosopher (1830) -
"**Man will only be conscious when he is free.** Anarchy will therefore be the complete separation between the human flocks, composed of slaves and tyrants, as they exist to day, and the free humanity of tomorrow. As soon as man, whoever he may be, comes to power, he suffers its fatal influence and is corrupted; he uses **force** to defend his person. He is the State; and he considers it a **property to be used for his benefit**, as a dog considers the bone he knaws."

Larken Rose, Philosopher, Author -
"To expect *the master to serve the slave* – to expect power to be used solely for the benefit of the one being controlled, not the one in control – is ridiculous. What makes it even more insane is that **statists** claim that appointing rulers is the only way to overcome the imperfections and untrustworthiness of man. Statists look out at a world full of strangers who have questionable motives and dubious

morality, and they are afraid of what some of those people might do. That, in and of itself, is a perfectly reasonable concern. But then, as protection against what some of those people might do, the statists advocate giving some of those same people of questionable virtue a huge amount of power, and societal **permission** to rule over everyone else, in the vain hope that, by some miracle, those people will happen to decide to use their newfound power only for good."

"If 'legal' **theft** is legitimate and just, why couldn't 'legalized' torture and murder be legitimate and just? If some 'collective need' requires society to have an **institution** that has an **exemption from morality** why would there be any **limits** on what it can do? If exterminating an entire race, or outlawing a religion, or forcibly enslaving millions is deemed necessary for the 'common good,' by what moral standards could anyone complain, once they have accepted the premise of 'authority'? All belief in 'government' rests on the idea that the 'common good' justifies the 'legal' initiation of **violence** against innocents to one degree or another. And once that premise has been accepted, there is no objective moral standard to limit 'government' behavior. History shows this all too clearly."

"For slaves to concede that they are the **rightful property** of someone else, only to then claim that there are **limits** on what their owners may do to them, is a logical contradiction. For a subject to accept any master (including one called 'government'), and to then imagine that he – the subject – will decide the extent of the master's powers, defies logic and reality. Yet that is what all believers in 'representative government' seek to do."

"The life of a caged animal is, in many ways, easier than life in the wild. Likewise, **life as an unthinking human slave can be more predictable and feel safer than a life of responsibility.** But, just as living in the wild makes animals stronger, smarter, and far better able to care for themselves, letting go of the 'authority' myth will force human beings to be smarter, more creative, more compassionate, and more **moral.** That is not to say that all people will, without the belief in 'government,' be wise, kind and generous. But if millions of individuals each understood that it is up to them personally to make the world a better place, instead of merely obediently playing an assigned part in someone else's **master plan** while crying to 'government' to fix everything, it would unleash a level of human creativity, ingenuity, and cooperation beyond what most people could possibly imagine."

Jeremey Locke, Author -
"**Protection**, as always, is slavery."
"They teach that **freedom is depravity, and insecurity**. Such attacks have nothing to do with the people being attacked. They are about maintaining the grip of *cultural slavery* over oppressed peoples."

J. L. W. (from Liberty newspaper, approx. 1881) -
"I claim that **Anarchy will accomplish in a more true and scientific manner the aim of protection, which is all that attaches republicans to government.** I claim this with the same confidence as you claim that natural morality will develop all the virtues — and develop them far better for not having a mixture or leaven of authority foreign to the meritorious element in the case."

William Godwin, Philosopher (1756) -
"Above all we should not forget that **government is an evil**, a usurpation upon the private judgement and individual **conscience** of mankind."

"Whenever government assumes to deliver us from the trouble of **thinking for ourselves**, the only consequences it produces are those of torpor and imbecility."

It must be known that it cannot be expected that *every* abolitionist understood slavery to the fullest extent, like Lysander Spooner or Josiah Warren understood it, since their ideas were the first of it's kind and they are not living in an age of mass information and history. The advent of such technology was only just beginning, but that also may explain the change in *mindset*. The same could be said for the American Revolution—if they recognized that everyone was equal, why did they have slaves? The transition is a timely process, as long as people are putting in the *care* and effort toward that transition. For Ancient Taoists, this was so evident that the effort was quite literally a *lack of effort* or wu-wei, in seeing that we are acting unnecessarily by creating systems in which we think we can *make* people good, when they *can* be fundamentally good working with their innate nature. We can now recognize the full nature of slavery with no contradictions as we understand our full nature, if we truly live and act according to *principle*, seeing past our *conditioning*. For not just the colonies away from the British, or the negro living with the whites, but for real freedom and for everybody. It is known that many abolitionists were called quasi-anarchists or "no-government" men or "comeouters" by their critics, as *many* different "anarchists" and individuals of "antinomianism" (Greek *anti-nomos:* against law) were actually attending meetings, active abolitionists in the 19th century, people of names that were not often recognized or kept out of history, like Jeremiah Hacker.

Lysander Spooner, Abolitionist, Lawyer (1808) -
"All these cries of having 'abolished slavery,' of having 'saved the country,' of having 'preserved the union,' of establishing 'a government of consent,' and of 'maintaining the national honor,' are all gross, shameless, transparent cheats—so transparent that they ought to **deceive** no one—when uttered as **justifications for the war**, or for the government that has succeeded the war, or for now compelling the people to pay the cost of the war, or for compelling anybody to support **a government that he does not want.**"
"**A man's natural rights are his own, against the whole world**; and any infringement of them is equally a crime, whether committed by one man, or by millions; whether committed by one man, calling himself a robber, (or by any other name indicating his true character) or by millions, calling themselves a **government.**"

William Batchelder Greene, Abolitionist (1819) -
"**Slave-propagandism and abolitionism both ended in 'federalism' — 'nationalism;'** the first in a federalism which tended to the subordination of Northern rights and interests to the advantage of the dominant faction at the South, and the second in a federalism which tended to the subordination of Southern rights and interests to the advantage of the dominant faction at the North. The temporary triumph of the first was followed by a temporary triumph of the second; and *the effort on both sides has been productive of nothing but disaster.*"
"The power of the commander-in-chief extends to the liberation of slaves, but *not to the abolition of slavery.*"
"The rule of **God is not tyranny, for it does not partake of a political or governmental character** — it is not a rule of authority... I must deny to civil government, as such, *all* **moral authority** whatever."

As an example testimony from 1844, Roger Moses Sargent writes of anti-slavery meetings, "Last August when I was at home I found there was quite an excitement about slavery and *non-resistance*. They had an anti-slavery discussion as they called it every Monday night, and a lot of... **no-governments** and no-church and no-nothing men deemed to take the lead."

Dyer Lum (from Liberty newspaper, approx. 1881) -
"The anti-slavery sentiment gave the government power to *secure* **ideal freedom**."
"In slavery the master had to sustain life in his slave, or lose him. The minimum cost of subsistence therefore became a *necessary expense* to the master."

Henry Demarest Lloyd, Philosopher (1847) -
"**Social love abolished the horrors of slavery**, not by telling the masters to be loving owners but by ordering them not to be owners at all. The **law of love** is not good owners but free men, not good kings but enfranchised citizens, not good employers but self-employing workingmen... They have cried Peace when there was no Peace, Love when there was no Love, because they knew how potent was the mere sound of the words to charm the heart of the multitude always thirsting for love. The depredators used to rob with the tools of hate; now they rob with the tools of love... **To love the King, dethrone him. To love the slave owner, free his slaves**... Did it destroy society to abolish slavery? 'This is revolution!' *No, it is the remedy*."

Charles Lane, Abolitionist (1800) -
"As the word **revolutionary** is rather alarming to some friends' nerves, it is of importance that the reader's mind should be disabused of any imagination, that violent proceedings are recommended or contemplated. In as

much as the **principle** of universal charity is quite opposed to the principle of **brute force**, the proposed new basis for social action may be said to involve a revolution; that is to say, a something on the other side of the **moral** wheel. But nothing can be more clear, than that if the new plan is to be brought into the actual world, it must be only by kind, orderly, and moral means. I am not unaware that it may require some time to render this thought familiar to the **public mind**; but I see very plainly, that the more the practicability of **immediate abolition** of colored slavery is considered, the sooner all will be brought to see that really there is little hope for its success, until we entertain this question of **the larger evil, of which colored slavery is, in fact, but a consequence.** Let us suppose that success should attend the present abolition efforts, and all the colored population are liberated, or are at least what we call set free; still, this master evil, this monster tyrant will remain. Whereas, *if we could but penetrate, at once, to this deeper, this more radical vice, the shallower crime would at the same time be dried up...* In comprehending white freedom as well as black, the white man as well as the black will be heartily engaged in the great cause of human freedom. Coadjutors, who feel deeply because the question comes vitally home to them, will be actively enlisted. This, Sir, is the little wicket gate, by which we must enter the straight and narrow way which leads to *universal liberty.* As soon as we see this, we shall vigorously and successfully struggle out of the slough of despond. Every abolitionist must perceive, by this time, that the great obstruction to colored freedom consists in this very fact of **government, not of charity, but of force.** The State and its intrigues, its place-hunting, its office-seeking, is at this moment the *only* serious obstacle to that freedom, in favor of which **public opinion** is even now strong enough, if this hard, compacted hindrance did not stand in the way. *Moral feeling*, I declare,

Sir, is at this hour clear enough, potent enough, to carry this small step, this triffling section of personal freedom, were but our brute force government superseded by a **voluntary** government. *The State, not being a person, can be carried to any tyrannic action without any remorse.* There is none to blush for it. It imprisons without inquiry. It punishes without trial, either by jury or solitary judge. It converts and perverts an anti-slavery constitution into pro-slavery conduct. It does things daily without shame, *which no individual in it could do without soul-stirring contrition.* It involves a system which absolutely shuts out the best men from public life, and selects only the mediocre, such as are capable of *being used as tools and instruments.* **It pretends to defend person and property, and is the first to invade them, and that also in a more brutal manner than it allows to any of its individual members.** Let the people recollect that it is *themselves* who have made and who sustain this dragon, which respects or disrespects, holds up or tramples down written constitutions, just as slaveholders shall suggest. Away, then, with such a delusion! *There is no safety for a person or property, while a government by force exists.* Let us supersede it by one of charity. Let us have a voluntary State, as well as a voluntary Church, and we may possibly then have some claim to the appellation of free men. *Till then, at least, we are slaves.*" In response, Nathaniel Peabody Rogers stated, "**Can government be voluntary? Is it not compulsory in its nature?** Men may regulate themselves, possibly – but can they govern one another, or rather be governed, voluntarily?… Can we get along on earth without fetters and handcuffs on?… I am sure we can't get along with, *for we have tried it.*" A. Brooke, president of the *Society for Universal Inquiry and Reform* founded in 1842, posed a similar question: "C.L. says a great many sensible things in his essays upon a 'voluntary political government,' but I am free to confess I do not exactly comprehend the point to which his lucubrations tend... I claim the right to **govern myself**, and my *rights* are certainly infringed by a *compulsory obedience* to the dictates of a few as of many, and the vassalage is not a whit more 'voluntary.' With my ignorance, the term 'voluntary political government' passes for a solecism [grammatical contradiction]. So much of the truth however is conveyed in these writings, and in so sensible a manner, that I guess their author holds to the abrogation [end] of *all* government, save self-government."

Is There A Particular Strategy To End Slavery?

Aside and among moral suasion and nonviolent resistance, we may want to get more specific as to what we can do to have slavery *abolished,* but also to ensure that it is *gone for good*. The slave-trade was almost everywhere in society in the 19th century, and the word of morality and ownership had to spread from the 1% to the majority of the population until the *overt* practice was gone away with in the majority for it to be considered "abolished." It is important to note that *abolitionism* was a **movement**. With a movement, a common issue can be aggregated in awareness, to provide mass action. For many successful movements of the past, that action was disobeying *taxation*. This is an observed action shared among many of those we have studied, such as Mahatma Gandhi, the American founding fathers, the Quakers and the Abolitionists. This is not the only way, but it does serve as a simple powerful example. If just one community or town got together and committed to not pay any more taxes, for which is *involuntary* and *a claim of ownership over another's property*, and they show *why* they are doing this to the rest of the world via the movement of *abolitionism*, it would spark the domino effect of other communities being willing to *stop condoning slavery*. Is it a guarantee? Such mass-efforts being demonstrated would certainly leave an impression to say the least, that many around the world would talk about. People are looking for a purpose, and dramatic stories often get highlighted. If their "own" government is supposedly "by the people, for the people," what a demonstration it would show that they would use their "own" people, man's law enforcement, to stop their "own" people from being free, by use of violence for compliance. If their "own" people are not slaves, then why can't they freely choose what to do with the products of their own labor? The media or the many people surrounding these communities, with the help of technology, would pick up on this, creating a moment in history to remember. It isn't the peaceful *voluntary* community that is the problem, it would be the presumed "authority" of government **initiating violence** upon them with their order-following *mental slaves*, exposing their own "authority." The voluntary community would have every right to self-defense against the self-presumed slave master, as did the slaves who had to free themselves in the 19th century, or they may strictly adhere to the nonresistance promoted among many abolitionists and successful movements in history. People think of economics and other topics as problematic or as solutions, however the *moral and principled* cause is *always* at the deepest of roots that determines the rest. Nonetheless, economic solutions such as utilizing permaculture and alternative currencies may be integral to the effort. From immorality comes *every* evil and from enslavement comes *every vulnerability* to evil. To realize this, is *not* a revolution, it is an inevitable world-wide awakening, where may it be some places recognize this, their next effort would be to share it with other places, and make it known everywhere, exactly as done with *abolitionism* in the past. Lysander Spooner would even emphasize how different communities across America could organize in "leagues" in order to abolish slavery, though this was also implemented in different "societies," therefore let us speculate upon the same methodology. This involves you and your input, therefore rely not on this text. These real-world issues require real-world experience, and every town has it's own issues in complication thereof the slavery we all endure. There is no one exact blueprint to action, but together in the shared pursuit for ending slavery, we may do what we can within our own lives. The following may be a blueprint for *abolitionist* movement change.

Mahatma Gandhi, Indian Independence (1869) -
"Many people, especially **ignorant** people, want to punish you for speaking the truth, for being correct, for **being you**. Never apologize for being correct, or for being years ahead of your time. If you're **right** and you know it, **speak your mind.** Even if you are a minority of one, the truth is still the truth."
"First they ignore you, then **they laugh at you**, then they fight you, then you win." This is similar to Arthur Schopenhauer in his saying of how "all truth passes through three stages. First, it is **ridiculed**. Second, it is violently opposed. Third, it is accepted as being **self-evident.**"
"You assist an evil system most effectively by obeying its orders and decrees. An evil system never deserves such allegiance. Allegiance to it means partaking of the evil. A good person will resist an evil system with his or her whole soul."
"Parliaments are really emblems of slavery... **Slaves ourselves**, it would be a mere *pretension* to think of freeing others... **a petition from a slave is a symbol of his slavery**... So long as the **superstition** that men should obey unjust laws exists, so long will their slavery exist."

Martin Luther King Jr, Activist, Author (1929) -
"Mahatma Gandhi never had more than one hundred persons absolutely committed to his philosophy. But with this small group of devoted followers, he galvanized the whole of India... This then must be our present program: **nonviolent resistance** to all forms of [racial] injustice, *including state and local laws* and practices, even when this means *going to jail*; and imaginative, bold, constructive action to **end the demoralization caused by the legacy of slavery**"

Elijah Parish Lovejoy, Abolitionist (1802) -
"Slaveholding has been justly designated as *the sum of all villainy*. Put every crime perpetrated among men into a **moral** crucible, and dissolve and combine them all, and the resultant amalgam is slaveholding. It has the violence of robbery."

Rose Wilder Lane, Philosopher (1886) -
"Any slavery in this world today is a surviving remnant of the ancient slavery. The use of man's **natural freedom** creates the industrial revolution and makes this New World in which individuals must use their natural freedom."
"**Individual liberty is individual responsibility**. Whoever makes decisions is responsible for results. When common men were slaves and serfs, they obeyed and they were fed, but they died by thousands in plagues and famines. Free men paid for their freedom by leaving that **false and illusory security**."

Anselme Bellegarrigue, Philosopher (1813) -
"**The government**, the men of the government, the manner of constituting the government, the antecedents and doctrines of various individuals, the preeminence this system or that one: all that is of little importance to the

people. What matters to them is well-being, and it is clear
that no one can realize well-being except for *themselves*; it
is proven that it cannot be obtained by delegation, and it is
established in fact that it is independent of the form. It is
thus with full and complete reason that people become
indifferent with regard to the form, with the government, and
they pay attention to the content, which is nothing but the
people themselves, and their own business."
"If governing is called a job, I ask to examine the products
of this job, and if those products don't suit me, I declare that
forcing me to consume them would be the strangest abuse
of power a man could exercise on another man. It is true
that this abuse is done by force and that I am the one who
supports, *on my own coins*, this force I am complaining
about. That said, I'm coiling back on myself and recognize
that though I am a victim, I am also an idiot. But my idiocy
only stems from my isolation, which is why I say to my
fellow citizens: Let's rise up; let's only trust in ourselves;
let's say: **let freedom be, and freedom shall be.**"
"**Government is not a fact, but a fiction.** The only
permanent and eternal fact is people."
"Here, in its *true* colors, is what governmental control
accomplishes: slavery and ruin."

William Godwin, Philosopher (1756) -
"The advocates of *revolution* usually remark 'that there is no
way to rid ourselves of our oppressors, and prevent new
ones from starting up in their room, but by inflicting on them
some severe and memorable retribution.' Upon this
statement it is particularly to be observed that there will be
oppressors as long as there are individuals inclined, either
from perverseness, or rooted and obstinate prejudice, to
take party with the oppressor. We have therefore to terrify
not only the man of crooked ambition but all those who
would support him, either from a corrupt motive, or a well

intended error. Thus, we propose to make men free; and the method we adopt is to influence them, more rigorously than ever, by the **fear** of punishment. We say that government has usurped too much, and we organize a government tenfold more encroaching in its **principles** and terrible in its proceedings. **Is slavery the best project that can be devised for making men free?** Is a display of terror the readiest mode for rendering them fearless, independent and enterprising?"

Henry David Thoreau, Abolitionist, Philosopher (1817) - "If a thousand [citizens] were not to pay their tax-bills this year, that would not be a violent and bloody measure, as it would be to pay them, and enable the State to commit violence and shed innocent blood. This is, in fact, the definition of a *peaceable revolution*, if any such is possible."

Larken Rose, Philosopher, Author - "The notion of 'a government of the people, by the people, and for the people,' while it makes nice feel-good political rhetoric, is a logical impossibility. *A ruling class cannot serve or represent those it rules any more than a slave owner can serve or represent his slaves.* The *only* way he could do so is by ceasing to be a slave owner, by freeing his slaves. Likewise, the *only* way a ruling class could become a servant of the people is by ceasing to be a ruling class, by relinquishing all of its power. 'Government' cannot serve the people unless it ceases to be 'government.'"

The Two Objectives:
  - *Why We Are Slaves (The Truth)*
  - *How We Can't Be Slaves (The Truth → In Action)*

We should already be grounded upon universal ideas, such as that of *equality* and *rights*, thus the focus should be on talking about action. However both are needed and interwoven, as *the main action* is *moral suasion*. We may stray off course to different ideas, not looking at the root-cause problem needing to be addressed. We may at times, only focus on the "current news" and we ought to be careful to not simply focus on symptoms or not focusing on action or not inspiring others to find what actions they can partake in within their own life. If we do look at symptoms, we may connect it to the root-cause problem. For reference, holistically healing the body is how we shall heal the world, especially since the subject is touchy and may require great *care* to address. Most people know what they need to do with their own health just as most people know what is wrong in the world and what they should do in their own lives to not contribute to problems, they simply need motivation and inspiration past their own *justifications* to go and do it. Therefore, *the why and how* may otherwise be said as *the moral and morale*.

Larken Rose, Philosopher, Author -
"No one recognizes the **underlying problem**, and as a result, no one ever gets any closer to a solution. *They remain slaves, because their thoughts and discussions are limited to the pointless question of who should be their master.* They never consider – and dare not allow themselves to consider – the possibility that they should have **no master at all.** As a result, they focus entirely on *political action* of one kind or another, But the foundation of *all* political action is the belief in 'authority,' which is the problem itself. So the efforts of statists are, and always will be, *doomed to fail*."

Henry David Thoreau, Abolitionist, Philosopher (1817) -
"There are a thousand hacking at the branches of evil to one who is **striking at the root**"

"If the tax-gatherer, or any other public officer, asks me, as one has done, 'But what shall I do?' my answer is, 'If you really wish to do anything, **resign your office**.' When the subject has refused allegiance, and the officer has resigned his office, *then the revolution is accomplished*."

The Two Problems:
- *Not Starting*
- *Not Going All The Way*

When we permit wrong-doing, we are not going all the way. This can include talking about the truth of what's happening right now but still reinforcing slavery, or refusing to acknowledge such slavery. Additionally, we cannot make this as an "us versus them" scenario either, because the whole point of dismantling *statism* is to say we are all of a shared humanity, not to be slaves or masters of slaves. We aren't to make more enemies of the world, however sure to defend truth, we come with peace and love, to *embody the message we hold*. We must continually question ourselves to improve upon our own efforts.

Benjamin Tucker, Philosopher (1854) -
"The slave who is so utterly destitute of an idea, so thoroughly incapable of a generalization, in short, so entirely and exclusively practical, that he cannot appreciate the remoter fact that his oppression rests upon an almost **universal belief in mastership**, but can see no further than the concrete master whose lash he feels. If one of his fellows were to reason from the latter back to the former and seek some method of striking at **the foundation of the tyranny**, this slave would sneer at him."

The Main Focus:
- *Select Relevant Ideas*
- *Not Select People*
- *Not Select Events*

Where our attention goes, our energy goes. Do we want to focus on the temporary and limited? On the divisive and symptomatic? As the saying goes "teach a man to fish" or learn how to grow food rather than give him a fish or some food, for this ensures long-term sustainability. We see in politics the emphasis on promoting "candidates," and not only do we see this as problematic in the case of *statism*, it is also short-term, not focusing on the ideas itself, where we also assume this one person must carry the ideas and implement them *for* us. It may be that slavery, statism and voluntaryism as definitive concepts *has not even been presented* to the every-day person. If it was at least presented, it's akin to giving someone multiple choices in their health, even if they may be ignorant of them or convinced away from them *at first*. Additionally, there may be emphasis on those "in the dark," who perhaps *need this knowledge the most*. We should not form echo-chambers and a domino effect should be encouraged. Furthermore, real-life action may be integrated with online and technological use, to inspire and create *direct change*, as well as to stand *invulnerable to censorship*. We may utilize all the resources we can, wary of counter-intuitive methods. Learning from the programming into slavery, we may learn how to de-program out of slavery, and therefore optionally utilize political action as non-political action *(ex. putting up signs, having unique flags, knocking on doors, etc.)*.

Larken Rose, Philosopher, Author -
"The truth is, one who seeks to achieve **freedom by petitioning** those in power to give it to him has already

failed, regardless of the response. To **beg** for the blessing of 'authority' is to accept that the choice is the master's alone to make, which means that the person is already, by definition, a slave."

"Their trained-in desire to have the approval of 'authority' creates in them a mindset not unlike the mindset of a slave: they literally *feel bad about keeping their own money* and making their own choices without first getting the master's **permission** to do so."

"The truth is, one cannot believe in 'authority' and be free, because accepting the myth of 'government' is accepting one's own obligation to obey a master, which means accepting one's own enslavement. Sadly, many people believe that begging the master, via '**political action**,' is all they can do, So they forever engage in rituals which only *legitimize the slave-master relationship*, instead of simply disobeying the tyrants. The idea of disobeying 'authority,' 'breaking the law,' and being 'criminals' is *more disturbing to them than the idea of being a slave.*"

"When, in the history of the world, anywhere on the planet, has 'working within the system' achieved freedom? To put it another way, when has a slave ever achieved freedom by **whining to his master**, or by **getting a new master**?"

"Anarchists know better. They know that **human society will never be perfect**, but that it would be a whole lot better if evil deeds were committed only by genuinely nasty, sociopathic people, rather than being advocated and committed by *many millions of basically good people*"

Gertrude B. Kelly (from Liberty newspaper, approx. 1881) - "They are glad to see **one slave fighting another slave** on a question of a few cents, because it keeps your attention away from **the main issue**, as to who are your **real enemies**."

Herbert Spencer, Psychologist, Polymath (1820) -
"Pictures of the slave and the tyrant are exhibited to excite
its abhorrence; a state of **pure freedom** is described to it as
the one to be loved and hoped for; and it is made sensible
of the sacredness of **human rights.** After men's minds
have been for many years thus *exercised and stimulated*, a
sufficiently intense manifestation of feeling is produced, and
then comes the reform. But this feeling, mark, proceeds
from that same combination of faculties by which, as we
have seen, free institutions are upheld and made
practicable. One of these agitations, therefore, is a kind of
apprenticeship to the liberties obtained by it. The power to
get freedom becomes the measure of the power to use it.
The law of social forms is that they shall be expressive of
national character; they come into existence bearing its
impress; and they live only so long as it supplies them with
vitality. Now a general dissatisfaction with old arrangements
is a sign that the national character requires better ones."

The Main Problem:
- *Slavery (or ignorance thereof)*
  - *Political Slavery via Statism
    or Mental Slavery*

Involuntary systems, due to the *lack* of *the main action*.

The Main Action:
- *Freedom (or knowledge thereof)*
  - *Self-Ownership via Voluntaryism
    or Moral Suasion*

Voluntary systems, due to *prevent the main problem*.

Change relies in the masses, not in any select few. Our
intent should be simple, we don't need freedom by any

other name, we simply need freedom, so we simply shall stand for what *is, the truth*. It may be observed in manifestation as courage for love, conversation for knowledge, responsibility for sovereignty, and guidance for freedom. Guidance may even include forming communities and becoming more self-sufficient *(ex. permaculture food forestry, parallel institutions, constructive programs, etc.)*. Therein our moral suasion with individuals, we may ask curious questions about morality, supporting them coming to their own conclusions *(The Socratic Method)*. This process is psychologically detailed and exampled among Larken Rose's *Candles In The Dark* seminar, road-map and worksheet.

The Abolitionism "Movement":
- *Freedom (Liberty), Equality, Sovereignty (Self-Ownership), Humanity, Voluntaryism (Agorism, True Anarchism), Nature (Natural Law, Taoism), Nonviolence (Non-Violent Religion)*

Your action creates the movement and the movement creates more action. Many outcasts may be skeptical of different "movements" because it may entail having shared symbolism, materials or knowledge, but self-input may be encouraged and multiple movements may manifest for a similar cause. Real impact can occur quickly depending on the active participants. Not every movement of the past was necessarily perfect in form, as they may have emphasized one individual which ended up getting targeted or depended upon, or their ideas were not universally grounded. If the truth gets out to more people, we may see this as fulfilling since the truth rises above all, even if the methodology isn't "perfect," thus there is a level of trust we must have with the process of doing our best to share what we find important.

Frederick Douglass, Former Slave, Abolitionist (1817) -
"It is the **righteous** of the **cause**—the humanity of the cause—which constitutes its potency."

F. A. Harper, Author (1905) -
"Not in government or force, not in slavery or war, but in the **creative**, and thereby spiritual, power of **freedom**, shall our **inspiration** be found."

Movements may be exampled through the abolitionist cause. There were thousands of members of different societies and groups all across America, with many newspapers as well. Garrison, who is often credited among the leading organizers, said that we need "to concentrate the moral energies of the nation. Auxiliaries must be formed in every State; every town and village must have an Association." It must be known that more efforts could be used with the help of technology. Upon studying this, *TheLiberatorFiles* also provides a list of strategies that the abolitionists used: "Fairs and bazaars were often annual events, involving weeks of planning. Celebratory events were planned on important historical dates, like July 4. Anti-slavery Choirs were formed, such as the Hutchinson Family Singers. Abolitionist music united people at many large gatherings. People were urged to raise or sell only Anti-Slavery Produce. Some gathered around a Peace Pledge, with an anti-slavery theme. Anti-Slavery Wafers were used to attach to mail, each with an Abolition theme. Anti-Slavery Sewing Circles gathered, and read Abolition literature. Cent-a-Week Societies formed, providing a way for modest contributions." Garrison actively connected with different groups that many were afraid of reaching out toward, therefore we may do the same, for the sake of love, unification and impact.

Questions For Action:

Can we save humanity through awareness, before we need to learn through harmful experience? Is our simple needs being compromised? What would happen if you did *not* tell the truth that nobody else saw? Are there mindsets telling people "what to think" *(by way of propaganda)* instead of "how to think" *(asking questions like this)*? If any alternative arises to the mainstream as there has been, what happens when there exists many, but they are not unified against slavery? If you want to make a difference, are you really creating the difference? Does having something to aspire to within our personal lives, contribute to our health and happiness, which in turn helps us *walk the talk*? Is it more likely that people are to become a whistle-blower if they have a growing movement backing them? Are we seeking a better tomorrow? If we see a clear path for humanity, do we follow it? If at the end of the day, we can all agree upon the principles of *self-ownership*, will we stand on it? Can there be a message as mission, a movement based on upholding self-ownership for all the generations to come?

The Speed Of Change:

Change can happen rapidly if we have the courage to truly act on it. If the understanding of slavery reaches audiences which are *already* freedom-oriented, a movement can consist of an almost-immediate hundreds, to thousands, to millions of people. From one individual sharing to another, and on, numbers will amass. It may be as simple as the sharing of this material, or it's concepts, both online and in-person. The movement for *abolitionism* simply exists to share knowledge, to show we are all on the same path, never alone, making organized action easier. Allow your creative expression to flow. Actions are not to be simply limited to joining meetings or being active out there, it can be as simple as having a yard sign, one that is totally different from promoting candidates or *statism*. As a thought experiment, think of the "do not tread on me flag" *(Gadsen Flag of 1775)* and imagine how much influence it would have, if it had a website in the corner or actually led people to learn about freedom. The strategies of old may be mixed with the innovation of now. Those who put in the most effort toward these ideas may also become the *leaders* or *abolitionists* that people or slaves *voluntarily* look up to.

Core Political Slavery Signs & Corresponding Solutions
Also known as "The Statist Criterion"
<u>*Statist:*</u>
  – Makes "End Justifies Means" Statements
    "What Will Stop Me or Someone..." "It'll Just Happen Again" "What About Other Countries?" "Why Don't You Leave?" "Violence Is Necessary" "Wouldn't Warlords or Gangs Take Over?" "It Would Be Chaos" "It's Impossible." "How Will _ Get Done?" "Somebody Needs To Lead" "People Are Not Capable" "It Has Always Existed" "There's Nothing We Can Do" etc.
  – Contradictive Morality and Actions *(Violates The Golden Rule, Twists Basic Or Common Morality)*
  – Avoiding Discussion *(Cognitive Dissonance)*
  – Disregards Education *(Never Seen or Read Voluntaryist or Abolitionist Material)*
  – "We Should Obey" *(Indoctrination, Mind Control)*
  – Follows Related Trends *(Includes Voting, Use of Terminology, Reliance on "Experts")*

<u>*Abolitionist/Voluntaryist:*</u>
- Free-Thinker *(Has Own Views, Not To Impose)*
- Self-Responsible *(Recognizes Self-Ownership)*
- "We Should Do What's Right" *(Use of Principles)*
- Knows About Statism *(Recognizes Slavery)*
- Regards Education *(Has Seen or Read Voluntaryist, Philosophical Anarchist or Abolitionist Material)*
- Encourages Discussion *(Socratic, Moral Suasion)*
- Always Sees Evil As Evil *(No Justifications, Excuses or Contradictions)*
- Disciplined Morality and Actions *(Applies The Golden Rule, Basic Or Common Morality)*

The Three Factors:
- *Representation (Creativity)*
- *Education (Presentation, Conversation)*
- *Networking (Guidance, Demonstration)*

The Two Factors:
- *Integration (for Disintegration)*
- *Promotion (for Demotion)*

These factors are based on dozens of books you may find in regards to social change. Everyone has different environments, one specific action cannot apply to everyone, and these guidelines may manifest in many different forms. In summary, we may observe that the greatest change comes from changing and connecting the minds of people, whilst influencing the culture through creativity. Do the inner work, connect with love, practice small acts everyday, express your gifts. It may also be known that appeals to influential individuals may be made to further the cause, just as Francis Jackson gave substantial financial support to William Lloyd Garrison in the abolitionist effort.

William Lloyd Garrison, Journalist, Abolitionist (1805) - (Letter from 1838) "The American Anti-Slavery Society had *in the past year* receipts totaling forty-three thousand dollars, but expenditures of more than forty-five thousand, 'leaving the Society somewhat in debt.' Total number of publications, printed during the same time, came to 646,000! Thirty-eight traveling agents had been in the field." It has been noted that Garrison printed a total of 1,820 weekly issues during 35 years (1831 to 1865), and that is just *The Liberator* newspaper alone.

"It is time for the friends of bleeding humanity to make a demonstration of their strength. It is idle for them to sigh over the degradation and misery of the slaves, while they neglect to coalesce. To effect this union, agents are indispensable... **It is much easier to convince a hundred men in a large audience, than half a dozen by detail.** In this manner I may be able to disarm whole communities of their antipathies, and rally them around the standard which has been lifted up in Boston."

The Four Steps:
1. *Represent (communities and connections reached with the ideas of the movement and it's material; presence, the overlooked step)*
2. *Educate (moral suasion, upon addressing statism with voluntaryism, successfully takes place in at least one community; the strategic step)*
3. *Ground (the educated community together stops committing a vital statist act, ex. taxation, there is no offense, it is just saying "no"; the freedom step)*
4. *Show (embracing freedom, simply record it as a demonstration for others, displaying or leading to "why" materials; the historic step)*

U.S. Declaration of Independence (1776) -
"Whenever **any form of government** becomes destructive
of these ends, it is the **Right of the People** to alter or to
abolish it."

Larken Rose, Philosopher, Author -
"If every slave sold into bondage had **refused** to work,
there would soon have been no slave trade. If the IRS had
to calculate the tax due and then directly take it from each
'taxpayer,' there would be no more federal 'taxation.'"

Upon the use of self-defense, as we may know it's use but
also risks, from the Liberty newspaper, detailing the side of
Abolitionist John Brown, "Garrison's 'moral suasion' had its
good side, and produced certain strong and telling effects
upon the North. But the South would never yield by
persuasion. A 'forcible separation of the connection
between master and slave' he believed the inevitable, the
only, solution of the problem possible. 'I believe in *the
Golden Rule* and *the Declaration of Independence*. I think
they both mean the same thing; and it is better that a whole
generation should pass off the earth — men, women, and
children — by a violent death than that one jot of either
should fail in this country. I mean exactly so, sir.' This more
forceful method and demonstration was also supported by
individuals such as Lysander Spooner and Frederick
Douglas.

J. Wm. Lloyd (from Liberty newspaper, approx. 1881) -
"Anarchy says, 'carry your sword only for **protection**, and
use it only when your shield will not avail.' In brief, the
position of Anarchy is that in the relations of man with man
there is no right in might except where might is right, and
that might is only right when used in *defence of Liberty*."

Elisee Reclus (from Liberty newspaper, approx. 1881) -
"If great human evolutions are always followed by sad
outbreaks of personal hatreds, it is not to these bad
passions that well-wishers of their kind appeal when they
wish to rouse the motive virtues of enthusiasm, devotion,
and generosity. If changes had no other result than to
punish oppressors, to make them suffer in their turn, to
repay evil with evil, the transformation would be only in
seeming. What boots it to him who truly loves humanity and
desires the happiness of all that the slave becomes master,
that the master is reduced to servitude, that the whip
changes hands, and that money passes from one pocket to
another? It is not the rich and the powerful whom we devote
to destruction, but the institutions which have favored the
birth and growth of these malevolent beings. It is the
medium which it behooves us to alter, and for this great
work we must reserve all our strength; to waste it in
personal vindications were merest puerility."

As the fourth step occurs, the domino effect may occur.
This is strengthened with more media coverage. In other
words, through the four steps, the movement carries the
message and mission on to free different areas of the world
and to uphold the history and knowledge through
generations of time. The material may overtime stand as a
reminder for *why* a generation did what they did. The
courage in taking step 3 would demonstrate that an
individual should *always* stand up for their *self-ownership*.
To the benefit of our cause, being with the modern
centuries, technology is able to preserve history exactly and
share a message far and wide. Think of "the people"
disobeying, and "their own government" going to stop
them? The evils of *Political Slavery* would expose itself,
with the governments of the world going against their "own"
populace, and rulers using other human beings as pawns to

do it. In broad daylight, it would highlight the true nature of order-following and how the systems that be are based on violence for compliance in reaffirming the message of this entire work and former *abolitionists.*

William Lloyd Garrison, Journalist, Abolitionist (1805) -
"Those who take up the sword shall perish by the sword."

Adin Ballou, Abolitionist (1803) -
"So long as men will indulge the lust of dominion, they shall be filled with the fruits of slavery; that they who will not be obedient to the **law of love**, shall bow down under the law of **physical force**; that they who take the sword shall perish with the sword... So **if men will not be governed by God, it is their doom to be enslaved by one another.**"
"What is human government. It is the will of man whether of one, few, many or all, in a state or nation exercising absolute *authority* over man, by means of **cunning and physical force**. This will may be ascertained, declared and executed, with or without written constitutions and laws, regularly or irregularly, in moderation or in violence; still it is alike **human government under all forms and administrations**... It may be patriarchal, hierarchical, monarchical, arislocratical, democratical, or monocratical, still it answers to this definition. It originates in man, depends on man, and **makes man the lord, the slave of man.**"
"1. When God requires one thing and men requires the contrary. In this case, whom ought we to obey? All Christians must answer, with the faithful apostles of old, 'We ought to obey God rather than men.' But must we disobey parents, patriarchs, priests, kings, nobles, presidents, governors, generals, legislatures, constitutions, armies, mobs, all rather than disobey God? We Must and then patiently endure the penal consequences. Then surely

human government is nothing against the government of God. 2. Human government and divine government sometimes agree in prescribing the same duty; i.e. God and man both require the same thing. In this case ought not the reverence of human authority to constitute at least a part of the motive for doing right. We will see. Did man originate this duty? No. Did he first declare it? No. Has he aided one iota of obligation to it? No. God originated it, first declared it, and made it in the highest possible degree obligatory. Human government has merely borrowed it, re-echoed and interwoven it, with the tissue of its own enactments... How can he divide his reverence between the divine and mere human authority? How can he perform this duty any more willingly or faithfully, because human government has re-enacted it? Evidently he cannot. He will feel that it is the Creator's law, not the creature's; that he is under the highest possible obligation to perform it from reverence to God alone. Man has adopted it, and incorporated it with his own devices, but he has added nothing to its rightfulness or force. Here again **human government is virtually nothing.** It has not even a claim of joint reverence with that of the divine... What, therefore, is demonstrably right, he will feel bound to approve and scrupulously practice, not for human government's sake, but *for righteousness' sake...* The conclusion is therefore unavoidable, that the will of man **human government whether in one, a thousand, or many millions, has no intrinsic authority no moral supremacy and no rightful claim to the allegiance of man. It has no original, inherent authority whatsoever over the conscience.** What then becomes of human government, as contra-distinguished from the divine government? Is it not a mere cypher? When it opposes God's government it is nothing; when it agrees with his government it is nothing and when it discovers a new item of duty a new application of the general law of God it is nothing... Our principles forbid us to take any part in the management of its machinery. **We can neither fight for it, legislate in it, hold its offices, vote at its elections, nor act any political part within its pale.** To purify, to reform it if such were our object we must actively participate in its management. Moreover, if human government, properly so called, is what I have shown it to be, there can be no such thing as purifying it... We have nothing to do with nations, states and bodies politic merely as such; for they have neither souls nor conscience. We address ourselves to individuals, who have both soul and conscience, and expect to affect organized masses of men only through their individual members."

"They shall be filled with the fruits of slavery; that they who will not be obedient to the **law of love**, shall bow down under the yoke of **physical force**."

"It is not by the poor test of **numbers** that righteousness can gain its deserved respect in the world. It is not by getting into places of **worldly power** and emolument, that Christians are to promote human welfare. It is not by fighting with carnal weapons, and wielding the instruments of legal vengeance, that they can hope to strengthen the bonds of moral restraint. Majorities often decree folly and iniquity. Power oftener corrupts its possessor, than benefits the powerless. **The real power which restrains the world is moral power.**"

"He, therefore, who has the fewest outward ensigns of *authority*, will, if wise and holy, contribute most to the good **order** of mankind. Besides, even **unprincipled** men in office are compelled to bow to a strong **public sentiment**, super-induced by the efforts of good men in private life."

"Towards promoting a **sound morality**, as we hope to do, we shall make our influence felt without envy, not only in the lowest depths of society, but in the high places of political power"

"Declare the truth, walk in love, and deserve the gratitude of the world, *though we never receive it*"
"The only strife will be-who shall do most for the promotion of every good work"
"**The heart is right** though the head may err."

From The Herald of Freedom newspaper (1835) -
"If it be true, as your correspondent argues, that government cannot exist without the mass of the people, each one consenting to do something he thinks wrong, then government had better cease. **If we can't have government without smothering our moral convictions, as individuals, I am a no-government man.**"
"For it is an understood thing, that **taxes are an imposition, to which government does not ask the assent of each individual.**—She collects them equally of non-votes, and aliens, and women... What is the difference between giving your purse to a highwayman, and letting him take it out of your pocket with his own hand?"
"**Non-Voting** Theory thus: 'It is wrong to give our votes for any man, who as a public officer, will do any thing unjust.' He should say, 'who, as a public offer, **will be bound to do any thing unjust.'**"
"*Abolitionists have been accused of being 'no government men.'* Let these who bring the charge, show if they can, what reason abolitionists have to respect our government."
"Something like this, no doubt, was **the origin of civil governments.** A spirit of master and oppression on one side, and of retaliation and liberty on the other. And *all* governments in their origin, too, were naturally simple democracies. A union of individuals in the most simple form of combination. But **governments, whatever their original form, always became in a short time avaricious and oppressive.**"

"**Civil government**—it gives aspiring men the opportunity to **throw off the responsibility of their villainous conduct upon others.** And this result is the same, let the form of government be what it may."
"Governments always live on the people. *They never do any thing for the good of the people*."
"The people can get any thing done cheaper by **private enterprise** than the government can do it. Private ingenuity and skill would have removed the Seminoles from Florida, and for one fortieth part of the actual expense; and now we have got Texas to support and protect, I wish the government would let out the job."

Victor Yarros, Lawyer, Philosopher (1865) -
"All Anarchist workers devote their energies in the direction of spreading the light of **true social principles**, popularizing political and economic science, and illustrating the beauty and excellence of **voluntaryism** and general recognition of the **right of individual self-government**. All forces are concentrated on the work of creating a strong **anti-State tendency**,— a tendency that shall prepare the conditions and pave the way for the carrying out, on an extensive scale, of the Anarchists' plan of **passive resistance** to the State, through which the emancipation is to be principally realized and the great change introduced."
"**The anarchists... work not for a perfect social state, but for a perfect political system.** A perfect social state is... totally free from sin or crime or folly; a perfect political system is merely a system in which justice is observed, in which nothing is punished but crime and nobody coerced but the invader."

William Godwin, Philosopher (1756) -
"A human being, suddenly emancipated from a state of subjection, if we may not call it slavery, and transported into

a state of freedom, *must* be expected to be guilty of some extravagancies and follies."

Understanding more of the role of **nonviolent resistance** or non-resistance on the mass scale, and the problems with an immediate instinct to only *self-defense*, we may observe what Mahatma Gandhi called the "law of suffering." It may be known that *fear* leads to submission or aggression, with each being based on instinct or survival, loss or gain. Therefore, it may be argued that love and peace, which takes us out of *fear*, is the path of nonviolence. Gandhi states, "I am not a visionary. I claim to be a practical idealist. The religion of nonviolence is not meant merely for the Rishis and saints. It is meant for the common people as well. **Nonviolence is the law of our species as violence is the law of the brute.** The spirit lies dormant in the brute and he knows no law but that of physical might. The dignity of man requires obedience to a **higher law** to the strength of the spirit... I have therefore ventured to place before India the ancient law of self sacrifice. For Satyagraha and its off-shoots, non-cooperation and civil resistance, are nothing but new names for the law of suffering. The Rishis, who discovered the law of nonviolence in the midst of violence, were greater geniuses than Newton. They were themselves greater warriors than Wellington. Having themselves known the use of arms, they realized their uselessness and taught a weary world that its salvation lay not through violence but through nonviolence... Nonviolence in its dynamic condition means conscious suffering. It does not mean meek submission to the will of the evil-doer, but it means the putting of one's whole soul against the will of the tyrant. Working under this law of being, it is possible for a single individual to defy the whole might of an unjust empire to save his honor, his religion, his soul and lay the foundation for the empire's fall or its regeneration." Similarly, Tolstoy makes the bold statement that "as soon as men live entirely in accord with the **law of love** natural to their hearts and now revealed to them, which excludes *all* resistance by violence, and therefore hold aloof from *all* participation in violence - as soon as this happens, *not only will hundreds be unable to enslave millions, but not even millions will be able to enslave a single individual.*" Even Sun Tzu from *The Art of War* tells us that "supreme excellence consists in breaking the enemy's resistance *without fighting*." Laozi of Taoism similarly states, "for every force there is a counter-force. Violence, even well intentioned, always rebounds upon oneself. The Master does his job and then stops. He understands that the universe is forever out of control, and that trying to dominate events goes against the current of the Tao. Because he believes in himself, he doesn't try to convince others. Because he is content with himself, he doesn't need others' approval. Because he accepts himself, the whole world accepts him" and that "the best soldier does not attack. The superior fighter succeeds without violence. The greatest conqueror wins without struggle. The most successful manager leads without dictating. This is **intelligent non-aggressiveness**." Biblical studies point to a similar conclusion, stating "but if anyone slaps you on the right cheek, turn to him the other also" or "don't *react* violently against the one who is evil" or "love your enemies and pray for those who persecute you." Gandhi clarifies, "I contemplate a **mental**, and therefore a **moral opposition** to immoralities. I seek entirely to blunt the edge of the tyrant's sword, not by putting up against it a sharper-edged weapon, but by disappointing his expectation that I would be offering physical resistance. **The resistance of the soul** that I should offer instead would elude him. It would at first dazzle him, and at last compel recognition from him, which recognition would not humiliate him but would uplift him. It may be urged that this is an ideal state. And so it is...

Suffering is infinitely more powerful than the law of the jungle for converting the opponent and opening his ears, which are otherwise shut, to the voice of reason. Nobody has probably drawn up more petitions or espoused more forlorn causes than I, and I have come to this fundamental conclusion that, if you want something really important to be done, **you must not merely satisfy the reason, you must move the heart also.** The appeal of reason is more to the head, but the penetration of the heart comes from suffering. It opens up the **inner understanding** in man. Suffering is the badge of the human race, not the sword... **I object to violence because when it appears to do good, the good is only temporary; the evil it does is permanent.**" Being a Jurist, Marshall McConkie shares with us that "as a prosecutor, I would know what justice and sentencing demanded and then I would read the background of the defendant, and I would get sick. **I couldn't bear the thought of doing justice, when justice would bring further harm.** Justice in and of itself is straightforward— make right what you made wrong. Receive the punishment that you deserve. You know, an eye for an eye, and a tooth for a tooth. Let's balance the scales and move forward. But Tevye [from *Fiddler on the Roof*] wasn't kidding that the end result of that type of justice is a bunch of blind and toothless people... balanced scales don't always result in fixed situations—*very often* justice makes two sides broken instead of one. The scales are balanced, but they aren't balanced in peace, they are balanced in pain. Blood cries out for blood, and justice without mercy, without forgiveness results in a world soaked in blood and drowning in 'justice.' I've seen justice without love—it balances scales and it equalizes pain. I've seen justice with mercy, and it ennobles, lifts, and balances justice's scales with a healing balm in the flow of its gentleness. To paraphrase Shakespeare, mercy blesses both the extender and the receiver of it. Mercy is godly, and it allows us to function more like Him. In a world where true justice is impossible—can you be truly just without omniscience?—mercy allows for others that which we would beg for ourselves. **Mercy allows for mistakes, for growth, and for progress. It does not demand suffering, but it does make room for healing**... Justice is essential to make society work, to ensure equal treatment, to give us all a steady footing and starting point. A society without justice is horrifying, a nightmare. But to have justice with no mercy, whether for those whom you love, those whom you hate, for those who live or those who are dead, is to unleash a sword that can only be matched with another sword. Blind and toothless." Martin Luther King Jr. tells us that "**returning violence for violence multiplies violence**, adding deeper darkness to a night already devoid of stars. Darkness cannot drive out darkness; only light can do that. Hate cannot drive out hate; only love can do that." Even in mere conversation with others we may apply these principles, so to sympathize and connect, for a real change in heart and mind, rather than being overbearing and controversial.

We may also observe how the historic efforts of Abolitionist John Brown can help and inspire us to take action for freedom nowadays, as Benjamin Tucker explains, "John Brown acted under **his own authority**, or, as he himself said, 'under the auspices of John Brown,' by the power of his own manhood, in behalf of **right** and man's rights. He took the **responsibility**, seeking no sanction other than that of his own **conscience**. He did not refrain from action because he was weak, nor wait till the majority was on his side. **'I acknowledge no master in human form,' said John Brown.** John Brown did not hesitate to confront the government and all its menaces. He stood by himself against all the established shows of the day — political, ecclesiastical, and pecuniary. **John Brown violated law and the laws.** John Brown believed in destroying wrongful institutions by the sword, *when no other way was available*. John Brown believed in fighting for others, in giving his life for the freedom of slaves. John Brown took no heed of self interest, obloquy, petty prudence, or the condemnation and vengeance of the times. John Brown put his whole soul in his work, and gave it all he had, his own life and his four sons, three of whom fell by his side. Yet withal, John Brown was a practical and sensible man, the attestation of which are his work and his success. If it be not for us of to-day to imitate John Brown's action, well were it for us to possess the qualities of soul that underlay it. *Other times need other work and ways of other men.* Man rises to each occasion. For every emergency, bountiful nature furnishes the man."

What If Slavery Is Tried?

You may worry about slavery occuring in another form. For instance, *technocracy* or *technological slavery (especially with the merge between robotics and humanity, as the word rabu is defined as "slave")* may become concerning, however the principles of *self-ownership* and our definitions still remain very much the same. The *abolitionist* movement may simply be applied in different times to focus on different matters, with the concept of *nature* and naturalness or humanization growing more relevant adjacent to the growth of the contrary and confused or dehumanized. The goal of the slave-master shall always be to have you *never* realize that you are in fact a slave. Just as overt slavery or chattel slavery isn't tried in the general circulation of the world as it is accepted as wrong, covert slavery or political slavery will not be tried when it is accepted as wrong. **No slave master will succeed without submissive slaves.** People will be more on the outlook for it, if it ever persists, since it is a *known* evil, rather than allowing it to persist because it is *believed* to be legitimate. Presumed "authority" will always claim that some form of violence, or violation of rights, is *necessary* for the "common good," as done with the *justifications* for slavery. You may now know the signs to pay attention toward. There is no such thing as the *right to enslave* just as there is no such thing as the *right to rule*. If we are enslaved, what is your *real* responsibility? Do you value truth, justice, equality, freedom, health, peace, love, fun and sovereignty for all peoples, above all other so-called "work"? You are not simply responsible for yourself, you are in part-responsible for the world around you for this work. It is your responsibility to share what you know, that others do *not* know, often intentionally because it's kept *hidden* from them. By merely arming people with *knowledge*, you give them the *power* to no longer be slaves.

Oscar Wilde, Poet, Playwright (1854) -
"Human slavery is **wrong, insecure, and demoralising**. On mechanical slavery, on the slavery of the machine, the future of the world *depends*."

Mahatma Gandhi, Indian Independence (1869) -
"We should not use machinery for producing things which we can produce without its aid and have got the capacity to do so. As machinery makes you its slave, we want to be independent and self-supporting; so we should not take the help of machinery when we can do without it. We want to make our villages free and self-sufficient and through them achieve our goal - **liberty** - and also protect it. I have no interest in the machine nor [do] I oppose it. **If I can produce my things myself, I become my master and so need no machinery.**"

Anonymous -
"People were created to be loved. Things were created to be used. The reason the world is in **chaos** is because things are being loved and **people are being used**."

David Icke, Philosopher (1952) -
"**Artificial intelligence** will do more and more of human thinking until human thinking as we know it now will be negligible. Now, I'd like someone to define a more extreme level of slavery than to have your entire perceptual processes externally controlled and dictated so that you not only have your body enslaved you have your *mind enslaved* and you know, when we talk about **slavery, enslaving the mind is the whole foundation of it**... People won't even have their opinions manipulated or their opinions silenced, they will be *given* their opinions through AI's connection to the brain." *(Icke refers to this as "the ultimate slavery")*

Joost Meerloo, Psychoanalyst (1903) -
"The growth of technology may confuse man's struggle for **mental maturity**. The practical application of science and tools originally were meant to give man more **security** against outside physical forces. It safeguarded his inner world; it freed time and energy for meditation, concentration, play, and creative thinking. Gradually *the very tools man made took possession of him* and pushed him back into serfdom instead of toward liberation. Man became drunk with technical skill; he became a **technology addict**. Technology calls forth from people, *unknown to themselves*, an infantile, servile attitude. We have nearly all become slaves of our cars. Technical security paradoxically may increase cowardice. There is almost no challenge any more to face the forces of nature outside us and the forces of instinct within us. Because the very technical world has become for us that magical challenge which nature

originally afforded." Meerloo goes on to tell us about how technology creates a disconnect between ourselves and nature, and how it's enslavement works, similar to other forms of slavery: the lack of self-awareness and sensibility or natural reality. Despite being truthful in regards to psychology, like many other strong minds, Meerloo also succumbed to the *political slavery* of *statist mind control* by believing in Democracy. It would be tempting to blame great thinkers for this folly, but knowing how deeply hypnotizing *mental slavery* can be, could we? He even tells us in regards to "the future age of psychology" that "many of the victims of thought control, brainwashing, and menticide that we have talked about were strong men whose minds and wills were broken and degraded... Compared with the million-year span of human existence and evolution, **civilization is still in its infancy.**"

What Happens When Slavery Is Gone For Good?
No longer will there be interference for *voluntarily* trading with anyone. No longer will you be interfered with the security of your own home by invaders who are seen as legitimate. No longer will there be any "war" to identify, as no mass amount of slaves will have orders to carry out on behalf of few slave masters. No longer will there be any compulsory government propagandized schooling. No longer will you be summoned by your rulers in their own *arbitrary* justice system. No longer will you be spied on by government agencies. No longer will people be punished for victimless "crimes." There would be more variety than ever when it comes to products, medicines, education, media and businesses, with competition to inspire more innovation. Natural medicine can actually be encouraged when it works, with less censorship. Family businesses and farms will inevitably prosper and grow more authentically. Talk about imaginary country-borders and other divisive

and collectivized concepts will not matter, as only ever more real property *ownership* will matter. People and businesses will *voluntarily* pay for the services that they need, choosing what to do with their own products of their own labor. Hidden knowledge, whistle-blowers, inventions and history will finally come more to light. One can speculate long about what will happen, but as done with previous *abolitionism*, if we ensure the end of slavery, people will make the world work as much as they already do and with even more productivity without violence. The many solutions proposed by people will be far better than violently imposed solutions proposed by slavery. You can ask anyone about their ideas on what should be done about different things in the world, then follow-up asking if they would want it done with violence, to see this apparent reality. People shall know of that better tomorrow which is totally possible, with their simple "no" in mass. This simple effort may seem difficult in a complex world, present of much slavery, but your own standing upon the fundamental truth is destined to grow overtime as others come to see how important it really is, just as you saw for yourself. We are all *ex-statists* helping our fellow man escape their own *statism*. Your efforts will not be forgotten, we are making history by the day, improving upon the past and for the future, a world of more creativity and love than ever, especially as we adapt to embrace our *deserved freedom*.

Larken Rose, Philosopher, Author -
"War could not happen at all without soldiers putting their devotion and loyalty to their own gang, tribe or 'country' above doing what is **right"**
"People are not perfect, and some are downright malicious and dangerous. And **some people mistakenly view anarchism as a utopian idea** that would only work if everyone were generous and compassionate. But if people

are too stupid, greedy and malicious to be free, aren't they also too stupid, greedy and malicious to be trusted with power? If you don't trust some stranger to have control over his own life, why would you trust him to have control over yours? Whether people are inherently good, bad, or some of each, giving a small group of people power and control over everyone else is *never* the answer... What if instead of deciding what the throne should look like, and who should sit on it, all people of good-will embraced the non aggression principle? **What if instead of looking to a ruling class to forcibly impose our values onto society, we embraced the concept of self-ownership?**... You need to choose which you want: peaceful coexistence among equals ('anarchism'), or authoritarian domination, with some ruling over everyone else ('government'). The two are mutually exclusive... **Anarchism means that no one is your master, and that no one is your slave.**"

Richard Price, Philosopher (1723) -
"Happy will the world be when these truths shall be every where acknowledged and practised upon. Religious bigotry, that cruel demon, will be then laid asleep. **Slavish governments** and slavish hierarchies will then sink and the old prophecies be verified, 'that the last universal empire upon earth shall be the **empire of reason and virtue**, under which the gospel of peace (better understood) shall have free course and be glorified, many will run to and fro and knowledge be increased, the wolf dwell with the lamb and the leopard with the kid, and **nation no more lift up a sword against nation.'**... **No wise people will trust their defence out of their own hands, or consent to hold their rights at the mercy of armed slaves.**"

Auberon Herbert, Philosopher (1838) -
"The great choice lies before you. No nation stands still. It must move in one direction or the other. Either the State must grow in power, imposing new burdens and **compulsions**, and the nation sink lower and lower into a helpless quarreling crowd, or the individual must gain his own **rightful freedom**, become **master of himself**, creature of none, confident in himself and in his own qualities, confident in his power to plan and to do, and determined to end this old-world, profitless and worn-out system of restrictions and compulsions, which is not good or healthy even for the children. Once we realize the waste and the folly of striving against each other, once we feel in our hearts that the worst use to which we can turn human energies is gaining victories over each other, then we shall at last begin in true earnest to **turn the wilderness into a garden**, and to plant all the best and fairest of the flowers where now only the nettles and the briars grow."
"May the day come, for us and for every other nation, when the *politician*, as we know him at present, shall be numbered amongst the fossils of the past, when **we shall cease to desire to rule each other either by force or by trick**, when we shall dread for the sake of our own selves the possession of power, when we shall recognize that there are such things as **universal rights.**"

Benjamin Tucker, Philosopher (1854) -
"**The soul cries out from it's enslavement of past ages for broader, higher, greater Liberty, for complete moral, physical, and political freedom**, not only in its aspirations, but in its limitless capabilities of thought and power. In every direction the force which is to break down the barriers of the past is gathering."

Oscar Wilde, Poet, Playwright (1854) -
"Is this Utopian? A map of the world that does not include Utopia is not worth even glancing at, for it leaves out the one country at which Humanity is always landing. And when Humanity lands there, it looks out, and, seeing a better country, sets sail. **Progress is the realisation of Utopias**... It will be what the Greeks sought for, but could not, except in Thought, realise completely, because they had slaves, and fed them; it will be what the Renaissance sought for, but could not realise completely except in Art, because they had slaves, and starved them. It will be complete, and through it each man will attain to his perfection."

Henry David Thoreau, Abolitionist, Philosopher (1817) -
"I heartily accept the motto, 'That government is best which governs least;' and I should like to see it acted up to more rapidly and systematically. Carried out, it *finally* amounts to this, which also I believe- '**That government is best which governs not at all**;' and *when men are prepared for it*, that will be the kind of government which they *will* have."

In concluding...

Who Are You If You Don't Want Slavery?
To not be a slave, is to be **sovereign**. From the Latin adverb *super*, "above" and the Latin noun *regnum*, "ruler-ship." To be sovereign, means to be above the ruler-ship of another, to not have a slave-master, as you *know* yourself, you have achieved mastery, control and ownership over yourself. "Royalty" in the past used this term to represent only themselves. However, we are all the rulers of ourselves, if it isn't also nature, god or truth. To want freedom, as by *voluntaryism* and *self-ownership* for all peoples including yourself, you are an **abolitionist** or voluntaryist in the cause against *all* slavery.

Josiah Warren, Abolitionist (1798) -
"When one's person, his **labor**, his **responsibilities**, the soil he rests on, his food, his **property**, and all his interests are so disconnected, disunited from others, that he can control or dispose of these at all times, **according to his own views and feelings, without controlling or disturbing others**; and when his premises are sacred to himself, and his person is not approached, nor his time and attention taken up against his inclination, then the individual may be said to be practically **sovereign** of himself and all that constitutes or pertains to his individuality."

Arthur Schopenhauer, Philosopher (1788) -
"**Every true thinker for himself is so far like a monarch; he is absolute, and recognises nobody above him.** His judgments, like the decrees of a monarch, spring from his own sovereign power and proceed directly from himself. He takes as little notice of *authority* as a monarch does of a command; nothing is valid unless he has himself authorised it. On the other hand, those of vulgar minds, who are swayed by all kinds of current opinions, authorities, and prejudices, are like the people which in silence *obey the law* and commands."

William Godwin, Philosopher (1756) -
"We should endeavour to **make them wise, not to make them slaves.** The depriving men of their **self-government** is, in the first place, unjust, while, in the second, this self-government, imperfect as it is, will be found *more salutary than anything that can be substituted in its place.*"

John Stuart Mill, Philosopher (1806) -
"Over himself, over his own **body and mind**, the individual is sovereign"

Bryan J. Butts, Abolitionist (1826) -
"Man should be a **law unto himself**, and prove to the world, by a life of **truth** and **virtue**, that **all outward laws are superfluous.**"

William Batchelder Greene, Abolitionist (1819) -
"The fundamental right of a man is the right to be himself; and this right is his **sovereignty**. No man has a **right** to confiscate the sovereignty of any other man. *No man can delegate to another man, or to society, any right which he does not himself possess.* A man may wickedly forfeit his sovereignty by the commission of crime; he may perversely turn his back upon the Blazing Star, and abdicate his individuality and his manhood. But no man can rightfully abdicate his sovereignty. It is the duty of every man of sane mind, who supports himself, and is not convicted of crime, to vindicate his essential dignity as rightful sovereign of himself and of everything that pertains to his individuality. Every able-bodied man has a natural right, and a natural duty, to forcibly repel, and to combine with others to forcibly repel, any and all wrongful invasions of his sovereignty."

Henry Clarke Wright, Abolitionist (1797) -
"Thus each human being, man and woman, is invested with **sovereignty** over himself—and *no one over another.*"

Lysander Spooner, Abolitionist, Lawyer (1808) -
"The *only* real 'sovereignty,' or right of 'sovereignty,' in this or any other country, is that **right of sovereignty which each and every human being has over his or her own person and property**"

Gustave de Molinari, Philosopher (1819) -
"The **sovereignty** of the individual will—to conclude—be the basis of the political system of *the future community.*

This sovereignty no longer belongs to the associated owners of a territory and its inhabitants, slave or subject; nor to an idealised entity inheriting from the *political establishment* of its predecessor, and invested with his unrestricted *claims upon the life and property of the individual.* It will belong to the individual himself, no more a subject but proper master and sovereign of his person, free to labour, to exchange the products of his labour; to lend, give, devise, do all things as his will directs him. He will dispose, as he pleases, of the forces and materials which minister to his physical, intellectual, and moral needs."

Larken Rose, Philosopher, Author -
"Government, rather than serving as a cheek against the imperfections of our nature, instead drastically amplifies our greed, resentment, irresponsibility and malice, by giving us a 'legal,' risk-free way to forcibly interfere with the lives and choices of our fellow man. **In short, politics brings out the bully and meddling busy-body in everyone.** In contrast, without a ruling class, people wouldn't be forever asking 'law-makers' to interfere with their neighbors' lives, and thugs and thieves wouldn't be able to deny *responsibility* for their evil deeds by saying they were just *following orders.*"

What If The Truth About Slavery Is Censored?
This work and the cause for Abolitionism may get censored and suppressed, however by utilizing the many peaceful methods to our disposal with persistence and courage, we may ensure the message is delivered to all whom *must* hear it for *good* to prevail, for *good.* And finally, for those who may attack this work by deceitful or ignorant means, we shall ask the simple question, *"but is it wrong?"*

Frederick Douglass, Former Slave, Abolitionist (1805) -
"To suppress free speech is a double wrong. It violates the
rights of the hearer as well as those of the speaker."

William Godwin, Philosopher (1756) -
"Granting, for a moment, the utmost weight to the
objections of those who remind us of the mischief of
political experiments, it is proper to ask, Can we suppress
discussion? Can we arrest the progress of the **enquiring
mind**? If we can, it must be by the most unmitigated
despotism. *Intellect has a perpetual tendency to proceed.* It
cannot be held back, but by a power that counteracts its
genuine tendency, through every moment of its existence.
Tyrannical and sanguinary *must* be the measures employed
for this purpose. Misereable and disgustful must be the
scene they produce. Their result will be barbarism,
ignorance, superstition, servility, hypocrisy... Such has
been, for the most part, **the policy of governments
through every age of the world. Have we slaves?**"

Francis Dashwood Tandy, Philosopher (1867) -
"In spite of all our vaunted freedom we are still **enslaved by
the State.** Even the freedoms of speech and press, which
we hear glorified on every hand, are but shams after all.
You doubt it? Then go into any court room and criticize a
decision of the Judge, and see how much freedom of
speech you are allowed. Tell a lot of strikers that they will
never gain anything by peaceful methods. Publish a paper
for the promotion of suicide. Expose certain of the evils that
result from the present marriage system. Then you will see
how much the liberty of the press is respected in this 'land
of the free and home of the brave.' 'But these are
dangerous doctrines,' it is said. How do you know that they
are dangerous? Christianity was considered dangerous
once. Protestantism was considered dangerous. Free-

thought was considered dangerous. That is why stringent laws against the promulgation of such doctrines were passed. **The only freedom of speech that is worth having is the freedom to preach dangerous doctrines.** In no age, no matter how benighted, in no country, *no matter how tyrannical its form of government*, has the freedom to preach harmless doctrines ever been denied. It was for preaching dangerous doctrines that Jesus of Nazareth was crucified, that Bruno was burnt, that the Chicago Communists were hanged. Thousands of others have been tortured and put to death for a similar reason. Nothing but the freedom to preach all doctrines, no matter how dangerous they may seem, is worthy of the name of liberty. Evidences of the tyranny of the State abound on every hand. In spite of all our progress we have far to travel before the goal of Equal Freedom can be reached. **All the laws, which prohibit or restrict the free exchange of commodities, or services, between individuals of the same or different countries, are inconsistent with the fundamental law of progress.** The protective tariff, the laws prohibiting private individuals from carrying the mails, those compelling a man to pay for the education of another's children, or to supply gratuitous novel-reading for gum-chewing school girls, copyrights, patents, the laws regulating intercourse between the sexes, all these and many other similar forms of coercion will be found on close analysis to be reversions to the militant type of society."

Thomas Hodgskin, Philosopher (1787) -
"Those who controul and restrict the press, are **conscience-stricken criminals**.

Slavery Gone For Good
A Voluntary World, For Actual Freedom

Unknown digitally-remastered abolitionist flag from 1860

Josiah Warren, Abolitionist (1798) -
"A 'Union' not only on paper, but rooted in the heart, whose members, trained in the constant reverence for the **inalienable right of sovereignty in every person**, would be habituated to forbearance towards even wrong opinions and different educations and tastes, to patient endurance of irremediable injuries, and a **self-governing** deportment and gentleness of manner, and a *prompt but careful resistance* to wanton aggression *wherever* found, which would meet with a ready and an affectionate welcome in any part of the world."

NEAS Convention (from The Liberator newspaper) -
"**No equal union can exist between a slaveholding and a free community**; that under *any form of government*, a large body of slaveholders must necessarily control the policy and character of the nation; and that it is the great fault of the *United States Constitution*, that it assists and facilitates this result."

William Lloyd Garrison, Journalist, Abolitionist (1805) -
"No compromise with slavery! No union with slaveholders!"

Nature Is The Answer (NITA.ONE) flag

An individual may simply utilize a white flag, if it may help warrant more support or if material is limited. For instance in China of 2022, protestors used white pieces of paper as they had nothing else. White, being contrary to most flag symbolism, may memorialize all who died all throughout the world by slavery, and those who have surrendered due to state encroachment. It may represent the light of truth, the surrendering to truth, unity, clarity, completion (evolution, enlightenment or consciousness), awakening, and simplicity (naturalness).

Learn More About Slavery & Abolitionism:

The Best Freedom Videos (Compilation) – <u>nita.one/docu</u>

The Most Dangerous Superstition (Book) – Larken Rose
The Jones Plantation (Movie & Book) – Larken Rose

For A New Liberty (Book) – Murray Rothbard
Anatomy Of The State (Book) – Murray Rothbard
Economics (Resource) – <u>Managainstthestate.com</u>

Natural Law (3-Part Seminar) – Mark Passio
The End Of All Evil (Book) – Jeremey Locke
"Government": Biggest Scam (Book) – Etienne de la Boetie²
Practical & Everyday Anarchy (Books) – Stefan Molyneux

Natural Health (Resource) – Weston A. Price Foundation
Growing Food (Resource) – Food Forest Abundance

Radical Unschooling (Book) – Dayna Martin
Underground History (Book) – John Taylor Gatto

End Of Slavery Summit (50+ Speakers) – <u>nita.one/summit</u>
TAO: The Full Return To Nature (Book) – <u>nita.one/tao</u>

The Liberator 2 News (All-In-One Platform)
Includes Collaborative Projects, Networking, Interviews,
Events, Strategies, Quizzes, Activism, Weekly Newspapers
<u>TheLiberator.us</u>

To Share This Book – <u>TheLiberator.us/book</u>

If you found this book valuable, please feel free to review it
online so that it can reach more people. You may share or
re-print this work freely. Credit would be appreciated.

Excerpts from "Slavery As It Is"
Theodore Dwight Weld, 1839

They were made slaves and are held such by force, and by being put in fear, and this for no crime! Reader, what have you to say of such treatment? Is it right, just, benevolent? Suppose I should seize you, rob you of your liberty, drive you into the field, and make you work without pay as long as you live, would that be justice and kindness, or monstrous injustice and cruelty? Now, every body knows that the slaveholders do these things to the slaves every day, and yet it is stoutly affirmed that they treat them well and kindly, and that their tender regard for their slaves restrains the masters from inflicting cruelties upon them. We shall go into no metaphysics to show the absurdity of this pretence. The man who robs you every day, is, forsooth, quite too tender-hearted ever to cuff or kick you! True, he can snatch your money, but he does it gently lest he should hurt you. He can empty your pockets without qualms, but if your stomach is empty, it cuts him to the quick. He can make you work a life time without pay, but loves you too well to let you go hungry. He fleeces you of your rights with a relish, but is shocked if you work bareheaded in summer, or in winter without warm stockings. He can make you go without your liberty, but never without a shirt. He can crush, in you, all hope of bettering your condition, by vowing that you shall die his slave, but though he can coolly torture your feelings, he is too compassionate to lacerate your back--he can break your heart, but he is very tender of your skin. He can strip you of all protection and thus expose you to all outrages, but if you are exposed to the weather, half clad and half sheltered, how yearn his tender bowels! What! slaveholders talk of treating men well, and yet not only rob them of all they get, and as fast as they get it, but rob them of themselves, also; their very hands and feet, all their muscles, and limbs, and senses, their bodies and minds, their time and liberty and earnings, their free speech and rights of conscience, their right to acquire knowledge, and property, and reputation;--and yet they, who plunder them of all these, would fain make us believe that their soft hearts ooze out so lovingly toward their slaves that they always keep them well housed and well clad, never push them too hard in the field, never make their dear backs smart, nor let their dear stomachs get empty.

But there is no end to these absurdities. Are slaveholders dunces, or do they take all the rest of the world to be, that they think to bandage our eyes with such thin gauzes? Protesting their kind regard for those whom they hourly plunder of all they have and all they get! What! when they have seized their victims, and annihilated all their rights, still claim to be the special guardians of their happiness! Plunderers of their liberty, yet the careful suppliers of their wants? Robbers of their earnings, yet watchful sentinels round their interests, and kind providers for their comfort? Filching all their time, yet granting generous donations for rest and sleep? Stealing the use of their muscles, yet thoughtful of their ease? Putting them under drivers, yet careful that they are not hard-pushed? Too humane forsooth to stint the stomachs of their slaves, yet force their minds to starve, and brandish over them pains and penalties, if they dare to reach forth for the smallest crumb of knowledge, even a letter of the alphabet!

It is no marvel that slaveholders are always talking of their kind treatment of their slaves. The only marvel is, that men of sense can be gulled by such professions. Despots always insist that they are merciful. The greatest tyrants that ever dripped with blood have assumed the titles of "most gracious," "most clement," "most merciful," &c., and have ordered their crouching vassals to accost them thus. When did not vice lay claim to those virtues which are the opposites of its habitual crimes? The guilty, according to their own showing, are always innocent, and cowards brave, and drunkards sober, and harlots chaste, and pickpockets honest to a fault. Every body understands this. When a man's tongue grows thick, and he begins to hiccough and walk cross-legged, we expect him, as a matter of course, to protest that he is not drunk; so when a man is always singing the praises of his own honesty, we instinctively watch his movements and look out for our pocket-books. Whoever is simple enough to be hoaxed by such professions, should never be trusted in the streets without somebody to take care of him. Human nature works out in slaveholders just as it does in other men, and in American slaveholders just as in English, French, Turkish, Algerine, Roman and Grecian...

The bloody atrocities of Philip II., in the expulsion of his Moorish subjects, are matters of imperishable history. Who disbelieves or doubts them? And yet his courtiers magnified his virtues and chanted his clemency and his mercy, while the wail of a million victims, smitten down by a tempest of fire and slaughter let loose at his bidding, rose above the Te Deums that thundered from all Spain's cathedrals. When Louis XIV. revoked the edict of Nantz, and proclaimed two millions of his subjects free plunder for persecution, when from the English channel to the Pyrennees the mangled bodies of the Protestants were dragged on reeking hurdles by a shouting populace, he claimed to be "the father of his people," and wrote himself "His most Christian Majesty."... *(Author note: this relates to World War 2, the praising of Hitler, Stalin, Mao, etc.)*

We shall show, not merely that such deeds are committed, but that they are frequent; not done in corners, but before the sun; not in one of the slave states, but in all of them; not perpetrated by brutal overseers and drivers merely, but by magistrates, by legislators, by professors of religion, by preachers of the gospel, by governors of states, by "gentlemen of property and standing," and by delicate females moving in the "highest circles of society." We know, full well, the outcry that will be made by multitudes, at these declarations; the multiform cavils, the flat denials, the charges of "exaggeration" and "falsehood" so often bandied, the sneers of affected contempt at the credulity that can believe such things, and the rage and imprecations against those who give them currency. We know, too, the threadbare sophistries by which slaveholders and their apologists seek to evade such testimony...

Sometimes the master will hire some of his most trusty negroes to secure any stray negroes, who come on to their plantations, for many come at night to beg food of their friends on the plantations. The slaves assist one another usually when they can, and not be found out in it. The master can now and then, however, get some of his hands to betray the runaways. Some obtain their living in hunting after lost slaves... *(Author note: this relates to policing, as it's roots is with the slave patrol)* Some slaves run away who never mean to be taken alive. I will mention one. He run off and was pursued by the dogs, but having a weapon with him he succeeded in killing two or three of the dogs; but was afterwards shot. He had declared, that he never would be taken alive. The people rejoiced at the death of the slave, but lamented the death of the dogs, they were such ravenous hunters... Some masters boast that their slaves would not be free if they could. How little they know of their slaves! They are all sighing and groaning for freedom...

Author note: texts as these, describe in great detail, the brutality of slavery and how people, no matter how esteemed in society, were willing to go along with the most atrocious and inhumane acts imaginable. This will not be detailed here, just as bloody as the history of governments have ever been, since slavery has always been the accomplice. Weld goes on to tell us how Masters give themselves an excuse to abuse their power:

Old slaves: It would be for the interest of the masters to shorten their days. Worn out slaves: Multitudes of slaves by being overworked, have their constitutions broken in middle life. It would be economical for masters to starve or flog such to death. The incurably diseased and maimed: In all such cases it would be cheaper for masters to buy poison than medicine. The blind, lunatics, and idiots: As all such would be a tax on him, it would be for his interest to shorten their days. The deaf and dumb, and persons greatly deformed: Such might or might not be serviceable to him; many of them at least would be a burden, and few men carry burdens when they can throw them off. Feeble infants: As such would require much nursing, the time, trouble and expense necessary to raise them, would generally be more than they would be worth as working animals. How many such infants would be likely to be 'raised,' from disinterested benevolence? To this it may be added that in the far south and south west, it is notoriously for the interest of the master not to 'raise' slaves at all. To buy slaves when nearly grown, from the northern slave states, would be cheaper than to raise them. This is shown in the fact, that mothers with infants sell for less in those states than those without them. And when slave-traders purchase such in the upper country, it is notorious that they not unfrequently either sell their infants, or give them away. Therefore it would be for the interest of the masters, throughout that region, to have all the new-born children left to perish. It would also be for their interest to make such arrangements as effectually to separate the sexes, or if that were not done, so to overwork the females as to prevent childbearing. Incorrigible slaves: On most of the large plantations, there are, more or less, incorrigible slaves,--that is, slaves who will not be profitable to their masters--and from whom torture can extort little but defiance. These are frequently slaves of uncommon minds, who feel so keenly the wrongs of slavery that their proud spirits spurn their chains and defy their tormentors.

They have commonly great sway over the other slaves, their example is contagious, and their influence subversive of 'plantation discipline.' Consequently they must be made a warning to others. It is for the interest of the masters (at least they believe it to be) to put upon such slaves iron collars and chains, to brand and crop them; to disfigure, lacerate, starve and torture them--in a word, to inflict upon them such vengeance as shall strike terror into the other slaves. To this class may be added the incorrigibly thievish and indolent; it would be for the interest of the masters to treat them with such severity as would deter others from following their example. Runaways: When a slave has once runaway from his master and is caught, he is thenceforward treated with severity. It is for the interest of the master to make an example of him, by the greatest privations and inflictions...

Author note: Weld also details how economy and societal identity are used as a justification for the evils of slavery.

The enormities inflicted by slaveholders upon their slaves will never be discredited, except by those who overlook the simple fact, that he who holds human beings as his *bona fide* property, regards them as property, and not as persons; this is his permanent state of mind toward them. He does not contemplate slaves as human beings, consequently does not treat them as such; and with entire indifference sees them suffer privations and writhe under blows, which, if inflicted upon whites, would fill him with horror and indignation. He regards that as good treatment of slaves, which would seem to him insufferable abuse, if practised upon others; and would denounce that as a monstrous outrage and horrible cruelty, if perpetrated upon white men and women, which he sees every day meted out to black slaves, without perhaps ever thinking it cruel. Accustomed all his life to regard them rather as domestic animals, to hear them stormed at, and to see them cuffed and caned; and being himself in constant habit of treating them thus, such practices have become to him a mere matter of course, and make no impression on his mind. True, it is incredible that men should treat as chattels those whom they truly regard as human beings; but that they should treat as chattels and working animals those whom they regard as such, is no marvel. The common treatment of dogs, when they are in the way, is to kick them out of it; we see them every day kicked off of sidewalks, and on Sabbaths out of churches—yet, as they are but dogs, these do not strike us as outrages; yet if we were to see men, women and children—our neighbors and friends—kicked out of stores by merchants, or out of churches by the deacons and sexton, we should call the perpetrators inhuman wretches.

We have said that slaveholders regard their slaves not as human beings, but as mere working animals, or merchandise. The whole vocabulary of slaveholders, their laws, their usages, and their entire treatment of their slaves, fully establish this. The same terms are applied to slaves that are given to cattle. They are called 'stock.' So, when the children of slaves are spoken of prospectively, they are called their 'increase;' the same term that is applied to flocks and herds. So the female slaves that are mothers are called 'breeders,' till past child-bearing; and often the same terms are applied to the different sexes that are applied to the males and females among cattle. Those who compel the labor of slaves and cattle have the same appellation, 'drivers;' the names which they call them are the same, and similar to those given to their horses and oxen. The laws of slave States make them property, equally with goats and swine; they are levied upon for debt in the same way; they are included in the same advertisements of public sales with cattle, swine and asses; when moved from one part of the country to another, they are herded in droves like cattle, and like them urged on by drivers; their labor is compelled in the same way. They are bought and sold, and separated like cattle; when exposed for sale, their good qualities are described as jockeys show off the good points of their horses; their strength, activity, skill, power of endurance, &c., are lauded, and those who bid upon them examine their persons, just as purchasers inspect horses and oxen; they open their mouths to see if their teeth are sound; strip their backs to see if they are badly scarred, and handle their limbs and muscles to see if they are firmly knit. Like horses, they are warranted to be 'sound,' or to be returned to the owner if 'unsound.' A father gives his son a horse and slave; by his will he distributes among them his racehorses, hounds, game-cocks and slaves. We leave the reader to carry out the parallel which we have only begun. Its details would cover many pages.

The idea of property having a will, and that too in opposition to the will of its owner, and counteracting it, is a stimulant of terrible power to the most relentless human passions; and from the nature of slavery, and the constitution of the human mind, this fierce stimulant must, with various degrees of strength, act upon slaveholders almost without ceasing. The slave, however abject and crushed, is an intelligent being: he has a will, and that will cannot be annihilated, it will show itself, if for a moment it is smothered, like pent up fires, when vent is found, it flames the fiercer. Make intelligence property, and its manager will have his match; he is met at every turn by an opposing will, not in the form of downright rebellion and defiance, but yet, visibly, an ever-opposing will. He sees it in the dissatisfied look, and reluctant air, and unwilling movement; the constrained strokes of labor, the drawling tones, the slow hearing, the feigned stupidity, the sham pains and sickness, the short memory; and he feels it every hour, in innumerable forms, frustrating his designs by a ceaseless, though perhaps invisible countermining. This unceasing opposition to the will of its 'owner,' on the part of his rational 'property,' is to the slaveholder as the hot iron to the nerve. He raves under it, and storms, and gnashes, and smites; but the more he smites, the hotter it gets, and the more it burns him. Further, this opposition of the slave's will to his owner's, not only excites him to severity, that he may gratify his rage, but makes it necessary for him to use violence in breaking down this resistance— thus subjecting the slave to additional tortures. There is another inducement to cruel inflictions upon the slave, and a necessity for it, which does not exist in the case of brutes. Offenders must be made an example to others, to strike them with terror. If a slave runs away and is caught, his master flogs him with terrible severity, not merely to gratify his resentment, and to keep him from running away again, but as a warning to others.

So in every case of disobedience, neglect, stubbornness, unfaithfulness, indolence, insolence, theft, feigned sickness, when his directions are forgotten, or slighted, or supposed to be, or his wishes crossed, or his property injured, or left exposed, or his work ill-executed, the master is tempted to inflict cruelties, not merely to wreak his own vengeance upon him, and to make the slave more circumspect in future, but to sustain his authority over the other slaves, to restrain them from like practices, and to preserve his own property...

From the nature of the case, from the laws of mind, such power, so intensely desired, griped with such a death-clutch, and with such fierce spurnings of all curtailment or restraint, cannot but be abused. Privations and inflictions must be its natural, habitual products, with ever and anon, terror, torture and despair, let loose to do their worst upon their helpless victims. Slaveholders organize themselves into a tribunal to adjudicate upon their own conduct, and give us, in their decisions, their estimate of their own character; informing us with characteristic modesty, that they have a high opinion of themselves; that in their own judgment, they are very mild, kind, and merciful gentlemen!...

When men speak of the treatment of others as being either good or bad, their declarations are not generally to be taken as testimony to matters of fact, so much as expressions of their own feelings towards those persons or classes who are the subjects of such treatment. If those persons are their fellow citizens; if they are in the same class of society with themselves; of the same language, creed, and color; similar in their habits, pursuits, and sympathies; they will keenly feel any wrong done to them, and denounce it as base, outrageous treatment; but let the same wrongs be done to persons of a condition in all respects the reverse, persons whom they habitually despise, and regard only in the light of mere conveniences, to be used for their pleasure, and the idea that such treatment is barbarous will be laughed at as ridiculous. When we hear slaveholders say that their slaves are well treated, we have only to remember that they are not speaking of persons, but of property; not of men and women, but of chattels and things; not of friends and associates, but of vassals and victims; not of those whom they respect and honor, but of those whom they scorn and trample on; not of those with whom they sympathize, and co-operate, and interchange courtesies, but of those whom they regard with contempt and aversion, and disdainfully set with the dogs of their flock.

Excerpts from "The Non-Resistant"
19th Century Abolitionist Newspaper

Human governments are opposed to the government of God, and true liberty, which is to be found only in the kingdom of God, will be obvious to all who will consider their origin and true character. They are vain attempts by man to establish an order of things by which those who live in rebellion against God and in continual opposition to the principles of truth and love may secure to themselves by physical force that which can be found and enjoyed only by yielding to the influence and acting in accordance with these holy principles. They are the vain efforts of men to rival God and live independent of his government, and this is to make their wisdom answer better than the wisdom of God. The vain attempts of mankind, while determined upon living in open rebellion against the great moral governor of the universe, to make laws by which they may govern one another. And what has been the influence of these efforts and these laws? Have they ever had the effect of changing men's characters? Do they not always 'work wrath' and increase crime in every community? Is it not sufficiently obvious that legal penalties and outward restraints cannot produce inward purity and obedience? It is their natural and universal tendency to excite and redouble the strength of those very passions and propensities that they are intended to restrain. Man was designed to be governed by a law within himself, the Moral Law of God, implanted in his moral nature, engraved on his heart, or affections; and if he lives in rebellion against this law and thus sets at naught the government of God, he is not to be governed at all. If he will not be governed by God, he is not to be governed by his fellow men, who are equally rebellious against God as he is himself. While men are rebels against God's government, they are in reality rebels against all governments, for there is in reality but one government in the universe, and that is the government of God. All attempts to establish human government are but so many rebellious combinations of men, which will be scattered and brought to naught. All the attempts at governments by men are unwarranted assumptions of power, without right or authority. Vain and impious efforts of men to set up substitutes for the perfectly wise, holy, and righteous government of God, which they are openly rebelling against, and thus to exalt their wisdom above the wisdom of God. Will it be said that they all acknowledge allegiance to God and his government? It is solemn mockery for them to make any such pretensions, since every man of them lives in continual rebellion against God and his government. Every individual who is living in violation of God's law, and who of them is not? is living in open rebellion against God's government, the only righteous and real government upon earth. Every individual who is thus living is living without any government at all. And all the pretension he may make to being under a human government is but a 'refuge of lies' a retreat to which he retreats to quiet the rebukes of his own conscience and to secure and serve his selfish purposes. Human governments are an invention of men, by which they are vainly endeavoring to live independent of God and to exalt and aggrandize themselves with the toil and servitude of their more ignorant fellow men. What are the distinguishing characteristics of all the human governments upon earth— pride and arrogance, iniquity, and injustice? What is their history, but a history of wrongs and injuries? What is their standard of proceeding as invariably exhibited in their practice, but the principle that might make it right? What is their main spring to action, but self-interest, cupidity, and self-aggrandizement? What their trust for defense and security, but physical strength and military prowess, mere brute force? All human governments make it a point of honor to kill their enemies, and thus vainly strive to correct and overcome wrong with wrong. He has only to choose between tacitly assenting to be one of a confederacy that violates the principles of truth and righteousness, or preserving his individual integrity, his peace of conscience, and his liberty of soul by speaking out fearlessly and then going, if need be, cheerfully to prison or to death...

It is impossible for him to be a loyal subject of the government of God, at the same time that he is in allegiance to a government that is in open rebellion against the government of God and which tolerates and encourages selfishness, pride, revenge, and cruelty. He cannot be a loyal subject of the kingdom of God and, at the same time, be in league with a combination of men who openly practice and whose laws sanction iniquity, injustice, and oppression. If he acts upon the principles of truth and righteousness and his trust is in the moral power of truth and love, he cannot silently consent to be one of a confederacy of men who violate these principles continually. The whole influence of the institution attempted to be imposed upon men under the name of human governments goes to prevent them from entering the kingdom of God and enjoying the peace and confidence, the light, liberty, and happiness that it is their right and privilege to enjoy. It tends to blind, deceive, and keep them ignorant of the truth by leading them to rely upon physical instead of moral power: to act with slavish regard to outward laws and external restraints instead of acting freely and voluntarily from the inward and perfect Law of God, written upon their own hearts. But the powers of darkness are beginning to be shaken. The time is at hand when the sincere and honest are no longer to be deceived and cheated out of that true self-government, which is to be found and enjoyed only by entering into that kingdom of light and love, which God is establishing on earth as a state of perfect liberty and happiness, because it is the foil emancipation of man from the bondage of his own evil inclinations, by a complete predominance of the moral and spiritual over the sensual and. animal nature, a full and everlasting deliverance from the restraints of human authority, by an entire conformity of the whole man to the moral law and righteous government of God. What has been so long and so much talked of as self-government can scarcely be considered an approach to it. How can they be said to govern themselves when they pay so dearly for others to govern them? Others too, who are equally violators of God's Law and equally rebel against all government as they are themselves! It is the perfect absurdity! A gross and palpable delusion! And he who aids in sustaining and perpetuating this delusion, aids in sustaining and perpetuating that which interferes with the prerogatives of God and imposes upon the ignorance of men by hindering their entrance into that state of true liberty which God would have them to enjoy...

A man has fallen into the hands of a band of robbers. The band leaves it to their leader to say what will be done with him. We petition that leader, as one invested with power to let the victim go, to let him go without injury to his property. A man has fallen into the hands of a band of murderers. The band has invested their leader with the power to kill or to pardon. We address that leader by the title with which his followers address him and as one who has the power of life and death, derived from his associates in blood, over this man, and petition for his pardon. In doing this, we do not sanction the existence of these robbers as robbers or these murderers as murderers, nor do we justify or countenance their leaders in being leaders of robbers or murderers or in consenting to be clothed with such powers. We petition them not to use the power vested in them to do any evil, and in doing this, we do not assume that they are rightfully vested with the power...

Congress is not only a slaveholder and a supporter of the slave system, but it also has power over other slaveholders.

The Pro-Slavery Argument
"But Who Will Pick the Cotton?" by Larken Rose

Plantation Owner (1815): "This whole 'abolitionist' movement is just another silly, impractical, idealistic fad that will pass. Show me one successful example of a country functioning without slavery! Sure, there are problems with it, and there are abuses, but to think that humanity will ever exist without it is utopian and ridiculous! This is just human nature-this is how things are, and how they will always be, and the whining and complaining of these abolitionists isn't going to change that!"

Statist (2023): "This whole 'voluntaryist' movement is just another silly, impractical, idealistic fad that will pass. Show me one successful example of a country functioning without government! Sure, there are problems with it, and there are abuses, but to think that humanity will ever exist without it is utopian and ridiculous! This is just human nature-this is how things are, and how they will always be, and the whining and complaining of these voluntaryists isn't going to change that!"

Pro-Slavery Advocate: "Well sure you can say that slavery is bad and all, and that people shouldn't be forcibly robbed of the fruits of their labors, and I don't necessarily disagree but I mean we can't just do away with it with nothing to replace it. We have to gradually transition from slavery to no slavery and I wouldn't even go for that unless and until you can describe for me just how every aspect of society will work without slavery. You can't just say it's wrong and suddenly end it. I mean, who will pick the cotton? You have to ease into these things; maybe we can start by petitioning slave owners to allow their slaves to have more free time and maybe ask them to not whip the slave so hard or so often but we can't be extreme, we can't just say 'it's bad so end it right now.' Think of the chaos that would ensue if tomorrow there was suddenly no slavery. You know, just because some slave masters are really nasty, yeah I guess it's pretty much all of them, but it still doesn't mean that slavery in and of itself is inherently bad, yeah we definitely need rules limiting how nasty the slave owners can be to their slaves but that doesn't mean that the institution has to be done away with entirely. I mean no slavery? Come on, that's that's kooky and extreme, it's utopian, I mean just think of slavery as a necessary evil."

Statist: "Well sure you can say that government is bad and all, and that people shouldn't be forcibly robbed of the fruits of their labors, and I don't necessarily disagree but I mean we can't just do away with it with nothing to replace it. We have to gradually transition from government to no government and I wouldn't even go for that unless and until you can describe for me just how every aspect of society will work without government. You can't just say it's wrong and suddenly end it. I mean, who will build the roads? You have to ease into these things; maybe we can start by petitioning congress to reduce or eliminate certain taxes and to repeal unjust laws but we can't be extreme, we can't just say 'it's bad so end it right now.' Think of the chaos that would ensue if tomorrow there was suddenly no government. You know, just because some governments are really nasty, yeah I guess it's pretty much all of them, but it still doesn't mean that government in and of itself is inherently bad, yeah we definitely need rules limiting how nasty these governments can be to the people but that doesn't mean that the institution has to be done away with entirely. I mean no government? Come on, that's kooky and extreme, it's utopian, I mean just think of government as a necessary evil."

Author Note: With great pleasure, I dedicate the rest of this text to my good friend of humanity, William H. Douglas, whom shares laboring in *The Liberator 2 News* with me, for the cause of *modern abolitionism*. His words are profound and to my understanding, deserves great attention and respect for anyone who seeks justice and spiritual growth. We met spontaneously and unintentionally through the shared research upon the abolitionists and their close relationship with philosophical anarchism or voluntaryism.

~ **Epilogue** *by* **William H. Douglas** ~

Introduction

Though Cory refers to the following section as an epilogue, I prefer to think of it more as an application. As a historian, both by trade and by hobby, I know that it is not merely enough to read rousing speeches and great ideas from the past, we must have some framework for understanding and implementing their lessons into our lives. One of the most meaningful ways to do this is to learn about how those ideas were implemented into the lives of great figures in the past. We do not want to merely be reinventing the wheel, rediscovering every generation the obvious truths known to our forefathers, but building on the discoveries of the past to create a brighter, freer, and more prosperous tomorrow for all people.

That is the purpose of this section – to show by example how the application of historical truths can not only allow us to avoid the pitfalls of the past but to transform tomorrow for the better for everyone.

In the essay *Great Profiles in Courage: William Lloyd Garrison in Baltimore Jail* you will read about the great abolitionist William Lloyd Garrison and his refusal to back down from the truth even though it landed him in prison. Decades before Thoreau set pen to paper, Garrison was practicing civil disobedience and noncompliance with wicked and corrupt laws that protected liars, thieves, and monsters while punishing the good, just, and true. In this article you will find an example of the kind of men and women we must be if we hope to slay the monster of the State and establish societies based on true equal rights for all.

In the essay *The Most Revolutionary Text In American History* you will read about the alternative to the State. Written by Garrison, this text explodes the myths of the government as the purveyor of justice and establishes government upon the only solid foundation upon which it can exist, morality and liberty. The purpose of government is to act morally in order to protect liberty and when it violates this purpose then it is a necessity that the people refuse to comply with or enforce such injustice. Garrison also does a great deal to demonstrate the anarchist nature of true Christianity as the antithesis of the State. When one belongs to the Kingdom of God he cannot bow before the idols of man. Religious or not, here you will find a grand example of anarchy enunciated years before that word was used to coopt the movement towards atheism and Socialism.

In the essay *The U.S. Constitution: A Covenant With Death, An Agreement With Hell* you will read as Garrison reveals the true nature of the Constitution of the United States of America. Far from a document protecting liberty and individual humanity, the Constitution was crafted by an aristocratic elite to ensure their continued hold on the levers of power and means of controlling the populace. Founded on robbery and oppression, justifying the continual rape, torture, and destruction of millions held in slavery, the Constitution has been rotten at its core from the very start. Garrison further enunciates and proclaims the right of secession as the solution to many of its evils, demonstrating that he better understood what the "consent of the governed" is and how it operates.

Finally, in the essay *Socialism is Slavery In All But Name* you will read the words of George Fitzhugh, one of America's earliest and most ardent defenders of Socialism and Marxism. He is also the most vociferous defender of slavery that ever existed. And if those things seem contradictory to you, it is only because you have been indoctrinated into ignorance and imbecility by a political/educational system that wants you just smart enough to operate a forklift but too dense to ask questions about the true meaning of liberty and the function of government. Fitzhugh though, he understood the true nature of Marxism-Socialism and slavery. And in his book Sociology for the South, Fitzhugh explains how slavery is the ultimate, most perfected form of Socialism that could ever exist and how the implementation of Socialism inexorably leads to slavery. Socialism, Fitzhugh explains, is just the name people give to slavery to make it more palatable to embrace and promote

May the wisdom of the past light the way for your feet as you trod the path of liberty to the better tomorrow.

Happy Reading.

Great Profiles in Courage: William Lloyd Garrison in Baltimore Jail

"Delicacy is not to be consulted. Slavery is a monster, and he must be treated as such-hunted down bravely and despatched at a blow."

So spoke[1] the editor, journalist, avowed enemy of slavery, and proponent of racial equality William Lloyd Garrison when a colleague of his warned him to moderate his views, words, and actions when it came to his abolitionism and his denouncement of slavery as an absolute evil that should be immediately ended no matter what the consequences to the rich and power or even to the nation itself. Evil was evil and could never be justifiable. Compromising with it only gave it power and weakened the cause of justice. Anything that collapsed because of the ending of such evils was founded upon wickedness and either needed to be demolished or purged as by fire in order to create something good for humanity.

This scaled up to the macro level, where Garrison was a secessionist who would have rather seen the North leave the Union so that it could be a bastion of liberation instead of the enabler of slavery, all the way down to the personal level, where Garrison would be willing to give his life and his liberty for the cause of justice. In his conviction and his courage, Garrison reminds me of another quote from a latter-day proponent of freedom, Karl Hess, who wrote, "Extremism in defense of liberty is no vice. Moderation in pursuit of justice is no virtue."[2]

---

[1] Wendell Phillips Garrison and Francis Jackson Garrison, William Lloyd Garrison, 1805-1879. the Story of His Life Told by His Children, in Four Volumes, 1st ed., vol. 1, 4 vols. (Boston, MA: Houghton, Mifflin and Company, 1889). pp. 151-152

[2] Times Staff Writer, "Karl Hess; Goldwater's Speech Writer in 1964," Los Angeles Times, April 26, 1994

This too seems to be how Garrison lived. He not only supported the immediate ending of slavery, he was also a vocal supporter of women's suffrage, to the point that he was willing to split the abolitionist movement over the issue because he would not exclude women from the organization. Likewise, when later in his life the United States government began to limit the immigration of Chinese people to the nation, Garrison spoke out against the evil, racism, and lies used to justify this anti-immigration law (and all others as well.)[3] Upon his death, no less a lion of a man than Frederick Douglass eulogized Garrison, saying that despite his human faults, Garrison's unwillingness to compromise was a virtue that gave him the power to stand unmoved and lead out in the cause of liberty:

> It was the glory of this man that he could stand alone with the truth, and calmly await the result.
>
> …He had faith in the simple truth and faith in himself. He was unusually modest and retiring in his disposition; but his zeal was like fire, and his courage like steel, and during all his fifty years of service, in sunshine and storm, no doubt or fear as to the final result, ever shook his manly breast or caused him to swerve an inch from the right line of principle.[4]

One of the storms that arose to shake Garrison's life occurred early in his career. Years before he had begun his famous (and infamous) abolitionist newspaper, *The Liberator*, Garrison edited and wrote for another abolitionist newspaper, the cumbersomely titled *Genius of Universal Emancipation*. His time

---

[3] William Lloyd Garrison, "Chinese Exclusion," The Advocate of Peace, February 1902, 64 edition, sec. 2.

[4] Frederick Douglass, "Speech on the Death of William Lloyd Garrison," ibiblio, accessed March 23, 2024. Originally publish 1879.

at this newspaper, under the tutelage of its owner Benjamin Lundy, proved important for Garrison as it was during the years that he served as its editor (1829-1830) that helped him to realize that "gradual emancipation" over an uncertain number of years and deportation of the free black population from the United States was immoral, unethical, and foolish.

It was during these years that he was moved intellectually, morally, and emotionally to embrace universal abolitionism and damn everything that called for anything less than the immediate liberation of all slaves from slavery. He denounced every argument which justified the robbery, rape, torture, and murder of slaves even one second more. It was also during this time in his life that he faced the reality that his advocacy could cost him his liberty or even his life and courageously judged the sacrifice worthy of the reward.

During his tenure editing and publishing the *Universal Genius*, Garrison introduced a new feature of the paper which he, perhaps in a moment of dark humor, titled *The Black List*. Each week in this section, Garrison published "some of the terrible incidents of slavery-instances of cruelty and torture, cases of kidnapping, advertisements of slave auctions, and descriptions of the horrors of the foreign and domestic slave trade."[5] It was in this section on November 13th, 1829 that Garrison wrote about the transportation of 75 slaves from Baltimore to New Orleans on the ship *Francis*, owned by New England merchant Francis Todd and managed by "Yankee captain" Nicholas Brown. In a November 20th follow up article, Garrison denounced both men and the society that allows their business saying:

---

[5] Wendell Phillips Garrison and Francis Jackson Garrison, William Lloyd Garrison, 1805-1879. the Story of His Life Told by His Children, in Four Volumes, 1st ed., vol. 1, 4 vols. (Boston, MA: Houghton, Mifflin and Company, 1889). p. 163

I do not repeat the fact because it is a rare instance of domestic piracy, or because the case was attended with extraordinary circumstances; for the horrible traffic is briskly carried on, and the transportation was effected in the ordinary manner. I merely wish to illustrate New England humanity and morality. I am resolved to cover with thick infamy all who were concerned in this nefarious business.

…It is no worse to fit out piratical cruisers, or to engage in the foreign slave trade, than to pursue a similar trade along our own coasts; and the men who have the wickedness to participate therein, for the purpose of heaping up wealth, should be **sentenced to solitary confinement for life**; *they are the enemies of their own species—highway robbers and murderers;* and their final doom will be, unless they speedily repent, *to occupy the lowest depths of perdition.* I know that our laws make a distinction in this matter. I know that the man who is allowed to freight his vessel with slaves at home, for a distant market, would be thought worthy of death if he should take a similar freight on the coast of Africa; but I know, too, that this distinction is absurd, and at war with the common sense of mankind, and that God and good men regard it with abhorrence

…[After explaining how people used to wonder how Todd managed to maintain a profitable merchant business Garrison states,] The mystery seems to be unravelled. Any man can gather up riches if he does not care by what means they are obtained. …Capt. B., we believe, is a *mason*. Where was his charity or brotherly kindness?[6]

More than the mere facts of the case, it is Garrison's incisive statements of truth that will cause Todd to sue him for libel. Garrison's taking New England to task for not just its complacency in regards to slavery but its actual enabling of the slave trade is damning – after all, no matter how many laws you pass against slavery in your territory as long as you engage in the slave trade you will still be enabling slavery and slave masters. Garrison rightfully noted that it doesn't matter what the law says, or what society says, or what the government says. Evil is evil even when it is legal, and any person of morality will not only reject it but work to end it.

A law which allows a domestic slave trade while making the international trade illegal is absurd, the former is just as bad as the latter and there is no difference between those who kidnap men from Africa and those who kidnap them from Virginia. And yes, the slave trade is always kidnapping and piracy. It doesn't matter what the slave master says, the opinion of the man, women, or child actually being stolen is the only opinion that matters, and they do not wish to be slaves.

In the Todd case, those engaged in this frightful evil pretend to be Christians and Masons who believe love and charity are the foundation of human conduct?

Balderdash.

You can be a Christian and/or a Mason or you can be involved in the slave trade.

You cannot be both.

---

[6] Wendell Phillips Garrison and Francis Jackson Garrison, William Lloyd Garrison, 1805-1879. the Story of His Life Told by His Children, in Four Volumes, 1st ed., vol. 1, 4 vols. (Boston, MA: Houghton, Mifflin and Company, 1889). pp. 165-166.

Enraged at having himself revealed for what he truly was, for having the cloak he used to cover his lies stripped away from him, Todd accused Garrison of, "contriving and unlawfully, wickedly, and maliciously intending, to hurt, injure and vilify [Todd] and to deprive him of his good name, fame and reputation, and to bring him into great contempt, scandal, infamy, and disgrace, to the evil example of all others in like manner offending, and against the peace, government and dignity of the State."[7]

Todd's libel trial against Garrison started on February 19th, 1830. Multiple witnesses testified to the facts of Garrison's accusation. The ship's "pilot," which I take to mean the person who actually drove the ship day to day, testified that there were actually *eighty-eight slaves* on the ship, thirteen more than what Garrison had published, and Todd's agent in Baltimore testified that he (the agent) had notified Todd that he would be transporting slaves on behalf of Todd and that Todd willingly accepted this, thus making him a knowing and willing participant in the slave trade.

Todd's defense quoted from Garrison's article, defended Todd's role in taking part in a legally acceptable practice, and accused Garrison of 'fanaticism and virulence.'[8] It took 15 minutes for the jury of Baltimore citizens to find Garrison guilty and the court ended up sentencing him to a fine of $50 plus costs amounting to about $100, which in modern present-day dollars amounts to **$2904.33**.[9] This was far more than Garrison could afford to pay just as many today could not afford to pay. So, on April 17th, 1830, William Lloyd Garrison was sentenced to six months in prison and entered Baltimore Jail.

---

[7] Wendell Phillips Garrison and Francis Jackson Garrison, William Lloyd Garrison, 1805-1879. the Story of His Life Told by His Children, in Four Volumes, 1st ed., vol. 1, 4 vols. (Boston, MA: Houghton, Mifflin and Company, 1889). p. 168

[8] Ibid. p. 171

[9] "The Inflation Calculator," Westegg, January 26, 2024.

Garrison spent forty-nine days in jail before a wealthy and generous abolitionist named Arthur Tappan would pay Garrison's costs. During his time in prison Garrison was regularly confronted with slave masters or their agents who came to claim runaway slaves who had been captured and were being held in the jail until they were reclaimed. He saw the complacency of the local population to slavery and the essential role that the government played in making the recapture and forcible return of slaves to slavery possible. Even though he was behind bars in a hostile land, he did not back down from challenging evil and speaking the truth.

Garrison's confrontation with one such slave master is recorded by his sons as he related it to them, and includes this wonderful exchange:

> "Why, sir," exclaimed the slavite ["slave-ite," i.e. the slave master], with unmingled astonishment, "do you really think that the slaves are beings like ourselves? -that is, I mean do you believe that they possess the same faculties and capacities as the whites?"

> "Certainly, sir," I [Garrison] responded; "I do not know that there is any moral or intellectual quality in the curl of the hair or the color of the skin. I cannot conceive why a black man may not as reasonably object to my color, as I to his. Sir, it is not a black face that I detest, but a black heart—and I find it very often under a white skin."

> "Well, sir," said my querist, "how should you like to see a black man President of the United States?"

> "As to that, sir, I am a true republican, and bow to the will of the majority. If the people prefer a black President, I shall cheerfully submit; and if he

be qualified for the station, may peradventure give him my vote."[10]

To those who live in a world where racism is understood to be wrong and slavery is recognized as a horrific evil, Garrison's response that he would gladly welcome a Black man as President of the United States and vote for him may seem a little blasé. In 2024, it seems obvious. But in 1830? In 1830, was a statement of racial equality so radical that it could have gotten him killed. Garrison promoted racial equality in an era that racial inferiority was taught as scientific fact! Remember, he was sentenced to prison for simply stating facts about a slave trader. Even among the radical abolitionists this would have been seen as extremist.

No one was saying this in 1830.

No one except the courageous and brilliant William Lloyd Garrison.

No wonder the "man and his crew were confounded." Garrison was a radical ahead of his time by a century if not a century and a half. Like many prophets and great minds, he was largely hated by the masses of his country and beloved only by the few who had the vision to see and ears to hear the truth. Because he refused to submit and be silenced, because they could not prove he was wrong when all the logic and evidence were on his side, they hated him. Like very true great men in history, their hatred did not stop him. He knew what was right and heroically would not give an inch.

While in prison Garrison continued to write a great deal. One of these letters were to Francis Todd and demonstrates both Garrison's magnanimity, but also his keen sense of justice:

---

[10] Wendell Phillips Garrison and Francis Jackson Garrison, William Lloyd Garrison, 1805-1879. the Story of His Life Told by His Children, in Four Volumes, 1st ed., vol. 1, 4 vols. (Boston, MA: Houghton, Mifflin and Company, 1889). pp. 177-178

How could you suffer your noble ship to be freighted with the wretched victims of slavery? Is not this horrible traffic offensive to God, and revolting to humanity? You have a wife—Do you love her? You have children—If one merchant should kidnap, another sell, and a third transport them to a foreign market, how would you bear this bereavement? What language would be strong enough to denounce the abettor? You would rend the heavens with your lamentations! There is no sacrifice so painful to parents as the loss of their offspring. So cries the voice of nature!

…Sir, I owe you no ill-will. My soul weeps over your error. I denounced your conduct in strong language—but did not you deserve it? Consult your Bible and your heart. I am in prison for denouncing slavery in a free country! You, who have assisted in oppressing your fellow-creatures, are permitted to go at large, and to enjoy the fruits of your crime! *Cui prodest scelus, is fecit.* [He who benefits from the crime has done it.][11]

In addition to the many letters that Garrison wrote, he also was able to write more poetry than he had in the past. In contrast to a large part of the late 20th century wherein men were often taught to deny their feelings and to avoid at all costs expressing their feelings, the 19th century was an era of emotional masculinity. Men were encouraged to write and recite poetry which, along with music and dancing, was considered one of the manliest arts.

---

[11] Wendell Phillips Garrison and Francis Jackson Garrison, William Lloyd Garrison, 1805-1879. the Story of His Life Told by His Children, in Four Volumes, 1st ed., vol. 1, 4 vols. (Boston, MA: Houghton, Mifflin and Company, 1889). pp. 180-181

While Garrison was no Byron, one of Garrison's favorite poets, Garrison's works still demonstrate the courage and peace he felt in his course, which in turn testify to his determination to do the same again even if it meant facing the same punishments. Fear would not prevent him from pursing truth. He knew how to, "Do what is right and let the consequences follow,"[12] as can be seen in this poem he wrote:

To Sleep

Written After a Night's Incarceration In Prison

Thou art no fawning sycophant, sweet Sleep!

Who turn'st away if fortune rudely frown,

Leaving the stricken wretch alone to weep,

And mourn his former opulent renown:

O, no! but here - even in this desolate place -

Thou com'st, as t'were a palace trimmed with gold;

Its architecture of Corinthian grace;

Its gorgeous pageants, dazzling to behold.

No prison walls nor bolts can thee affright;

Where dwellest innocence, thou art found:

How pleasant and serene wast thou last night!

What blissful dreams my morning slumber crowned!

Health-giving Sleep! than mine a nobler verse

---

[12] Anonymous, "Do What Is Right," Hymn 237, accessed March 22, 2024.

Must to the world thy matchless worth rehearse.[13]

––––––––––

As Garrison understood, peace and rest in life are not obtained through wealth and ease. Thereby many men have gained the world only to torture and lose their own soul. Peace in this life, rest from the cares and woes and travails of this world, can only be found in righteous and noble living. Such living may end one up in the goal, the ghetto, or the gully, but if so then you will have lived a life worth living, one valuable to yourself and your fellowman.

Whether you find rest in a good nights rest or the long sleep of years, you will find the riches of peace denied to the haunted who find that they have sold themselves for a mess of pottage. When one does what is right, he is free even when behind bars. When one does wickedly, he is bound by the shackles of sin and the repercussions of his evil, placing him in prison even when he is apparently walking freely.

Once released from jail thanks to the kindness (and money) of Arthur Tappan, who would remain a patron of Garrison for another decade, Garrison shortly left Baltimore and began a speaking tour which would eventually culminate in his settlement in Boston and the founding of *The Liberator*.

Lessons To Be Learned

Courage is not measured in how much one is willing to maim, brutalize, or kill others. Heroism is not determined by one's waging war, destroying homes, and leveling civilizations. Heroes are not people who murder men, women, and children, who stack up bodies of babies and declare it victory.

––––––––––

[13] William Lloyd Garrison, "Poem: To Sleep, Written after a Night's Incarceration in Prison," Digital Commonwealth, accessed March 22, 2024.

Heroism and courage are found in the willingness to sacrifice of yourself. Heroism is doing what is right even when it requires you to suffer for the good of others even, especially, your enemies. Garrison demonstrated these qualities again and again in his life. His willingness to go to prison in protest against one of the most ancient evils in human history has him teaching by example what Henry David Thoreau would later develop as a maxim: "Under a government which imprisons any unjustly, the true place for a just man is also a prison."[14] And so Garrison went to prison.

Garrison understood that noncompliance and noncooperation with evil, no matter its source, must ever be our guide, even if that means refusing to comply with or intentionally breaking the law. Even if that means going to jail. To do otherwise would be to balk before the monster, be silent when what was required was the truth, and to become quietly complicit in its evil.

It did not matter to Garrison that the government was involved, or what laws he may have broken, or whose power he was defying. The government's willingness to enforce wickedness by law meant that it too must be defied by those who sought to save those who were suffering under and by its power.

This is as true today as it was then, whether the subject be slaves or the multitude of oppressive, corrupt, and often brutal laws and actions of government today. Defiance, not compliance, is what is called for in the face of wickedness in places high and low. To do otherwise would make us, like Francis Todd, "highway robbers and murderers, the enemies of our own species."

---

[14] Henry David Thoreau, On the Duty of Civil Disobedience (Adelaide, Australia : The University of Adelaide Library, 2004). p. 14. Though largely ignored by professional history, Garrison exemplified what Thoreau wrote decades before Thoreau ever put pen to paper. This is another way in which Garrison was long ahead of his time.

Sometimes this will require us to stand alone. Then alone we must stand. As Garrison shows, when we do so our courage will often win to our side the support of those who can enable us to do more for the good of our fellow man, just as Garrison's stand brought him to the attention of Arthur Tappan and eventually gave him the ability to begin *The Liberator*. This in turn allowed Garrison to become the most important voice in the nation calling for the immediate liberation of all slaves, the ending of racism, and the granting of equal rights to all men and women. But, even if it does not win us fame, even if we stand alone and win no allies and are unable to magnify our example, the stand itself is still worth taking.

As Garrison notes in his poem *To Sleep*, written when he thought he would be in prison for many more months and before anyone appeared to help him, the only way that a man can rest easy is with a conscious free from the burden of sin and evil. The knowledge that you have done right is itself a great reward. No man can think himself a true Man[15] and no woman can think of herself as a true Woman if he or she has betrayed virtue for ease.

At the same time, Garrison shows us the proper attitude that we should have towards our persecutors. He does not hate Francis Todd, even though he has taken part in the slave trade and even though his persecutions have caused Garrison to be imprisoned. Instead of anger and hatred, Garrison responds with sorrow and mercy.

Garrison is truly saddened that Todd has chosen evil over good and seeking to convince him of the error of his ways that he may repent and redeem himself. If you want a good example of what it means to be a Christian, to love your enemy, to forgive all men, and to seek to overcome evil with good, there are fewer better examples than this one.

---

[15] Richard C. Edgley, "Behold the Man," Ensign, October 2, 1999.

It is this forgiveness and this love which animates Garrison, both in his denunciations of and opposition to slavery as well as his appeal to Todd in an attempt to get him to recognize the evil of his actions and repent, that I find so appealing about the man, not just here but throughout the rest of his life. Whereas so much of the world is driven by anger, hatred, and vengeance, Garrison was doing his utmost to be a true Christian and was motivated by Faith, Hope, and Love. His example and his courage are what the world needs more of today as much as ever before.

The Most Revolutionary Text
in American History

William Lloyd Garrison authored and published the most revolutionary text in American history. Yes, most revolutionary, even more so than the Declaration of Independence, a text which cemented a rebellion, announced a revolution, and whose ideals are still held to be insane and radical when enunciated today. The Declaration was merely the repetition of ideas first formulated by John Locke in his historic *Two Treatise on Government*, and took for granted that a formal political society, a minarchist state, would be necessary.

The below text, written by Garrison to be the formal declaration of the founding ideals of the New England Non-Resistance Society, rejects the very foundation of the state - violence- and forms a society dedicated to the principles of Christ to such a degree that Dr. William O. Reichert, former chair of the Political Science Department at Bowling Green State University, explained that the basic outlook of the Society:

> The basic outlook of the New England Non-Resistance Society was that of philosophical anarchism. Though acknowledging that some authority may be essential to collective social life, its members agreed that this should come from within the individual rather than from without and that the use of force was to be completely avoided in the maintenance of social order. In its Declaration of Sentiments, which was largely written by Garrison, the Non-Resistants pronounced themselves to be opposed to all

human law and government, which they proposed to replace with a spontaneous social order founded upon a pure love of God and the Golden Rule. This goal was to be achieved through nonviolent resistance (Reichert, *The Philosophical Anarchism of Adin Ballou*)

This Christian anarchism is seen clearly in the Declaration. In it Garrison locates all authority on Earth in the only source worth obeying, the Lord Jesus Christ, rejects both war and violence justified as self-defense, exposes the violent nature of the state[16] and pledges to disobey any state order that violates the commandments of the Gospel, no matter what the consequences.

Though Garrison himself announces that they are not interested in overthrowing the American government, his program of loyalty to God and civil disobedience to unjust laws challenges the very authority of the State and if followed by every man would dissolve every nation-state without conflict. While Jefferson was trying to perfect Babylon, Garrison declared for Zion and would settle for nothing less. This masterful work on the supremacy of God, the liberty of man, and the power of peace and nonviolence is commended to everyone. The emphasis in the text replicates the original as it appeared in *The Liberator* in Sept. 1838.

Declaration of Sentiments
Adopted by the Peace Convention

Held in Boston, September 18 – 20, 1838

---

[16] William H. Douglas, "What Is 'The State'?," The Latter-day Liberator, September 8, 2020.

Assembled in Convention, from various sections of the American Union, for the promotion of peace on earth and good-will among men, we, the undersigned, regard it as due to ourselves, to the cause which we love, to the country in which we live, and to the world, to publish a **DECLARATION**, expressive of the principles we cherish, the purposes we aim to accomplish, and the measures we shall adopt to carry forward the work of peaceful, universal reformation.

We cannot acknowledge allegiance to any human government; neither can we oppose any such government by a resort to physical force. We recognize but one **King** and **Lawgiver**, one **Judge** and **Ruler** of mankind. We are bound by the laws of a kingdom which is not of this world; the subjects of which are forbidden to fight; in which **Mercy** and **Truth** are met together, and **Righteousness** and **Peace** have kissed each other; which has no state lines, no national partitions, no geographical boundaries; in which there is no distinction of rank, or division of caste, or inequality of sex; the officers of which are **Peace**, its exactors **Righteousness**, its walls **Salvation**, and its gates **Praise**; and which is destined to break in pieces and consume all other kingdoms.

Our country is the world, our countrymen are all mankind. We love the land of our nativity only as we love all other lands. The interests, rights, liberties of American citizens are no more dear to us than are those of the whole human race. Hence, we can allow no appeal to patriotism, to revenge any national insult or injury. The **Prince of Peace**, under whose stainless banner we rally, came not to destroy, but to save, even the worst of enemies. He has left us an example, that we should follow his steps. **God commandeth his love toward us, in that while we were yet sinners, Christ died for us.**

We conceive, that if a nation has no right to defend itself against foreign enemies, or to punish its invaders, no individual possesses that right in his own case. The unit cannot be of greater importance than the aggregate. If one man may take life, to obtain or defend his rights, the same license must necessarily be granted to communities, states, and nations. If *he* may use a dagger or a pistol, *they* may employ cannon, bomb-shells, land and naval forces. The means of self-preservation must be in proportion to the magnitude of interests at stake and the number of lives exposed to destruction. But if a rapacious and bloodthirsty soldiery, thronging these shores from abroad, with intent to commit rapine and destroy life, may not be resisted by the people or magistracy, then ought no resistance to be offered to domestic troublers of the public peace or of private security. No obligation can rest upon Americans to regard foreigners as more sacred in their persons than themseles, or to give them a monopoly of wrong-doing with impunity.

The dogma, that all the governments of the world are approvingly ordained of God, and that **the powers that be** in the United States, in Russia, in Turkey, are in accordance with his will, is not less absurd than impious. It makes the impartial Author of human freedom and equality, unequal and tyrannical. It cannot be affirmed that **the powers that be**, in any nation, are actuated by the spirit or guided by the example of Christ, in the treatment of enemies; therefore, they cannot be agreeable to the will of God, and therefore, their overthrow, by a spiritual regeneration of their subjects, is inevitable.

We register our testimony, not only against all wars, whether offensive or defensive, but all prepations for war; against every naval ship, every arsenal, every fortification; against the militia system and a standing army; against all military chieftains and soldiers; against all monuments commemorative of victory over a fallen foe, all trophies won in battle, all celebrations in honor of military or naval exploits; against all appropriations for the defence of a nation by force and arms, on the part of any legislative body; against every edict of government requiring of its subjects military service. Hence, we deem it unlawful to bear arms, or to hold a military office.

As every human government is upheld by physical strength, and its laws are enforced virtually at the point of the bayonet, we cannot hold any office which imposes upon its incumbent the obligation to compel men to do right, on pain of imprisonment or death. We therefore voluntarily exclude ourselves from every legislative and judicial body, and repudiate all human politics, worldly honors, and stations of authority. If *we* cannot occupy a seat in the legislature or on the bench, neither can we elect *others* to act as our substitutes in any such capacity.

It follows, that we cannot sue any man at law, to compel him by force to restore anything which he may have wrongfully taken from us or others; but if he has seized our coat, we shall surrender up our cloak, rather than subject him to punishment.

We believe that the penal code of the old covenant, **An eye for an eye and a tooth for a tooth**, has been abrogated by **JESUS CHRIST**; and that, under the new covenant, the forgiveness instead of the punishment of enemies has been enjoined upon all his disciples, in all cases whatsoever. To extort money from his enemies, or set them upon a pillory, or cast them into prison, or hang them upon a gallows, is obviously not to forgive, but to take retribution. **Vengeance is mine—I will repay, saith the Lord.**

The history of mankind is crowded with evidence proving that physical coercion is not adapted to moral regeneration; that the sinful disposition of men can be subdued only by love; that evil can be exterminated from earth only by goodness; that it is not safe to rely on an arm of flesh, upon a man whose breath is in his nostrils, to preserve us from harm; that there is great security in being gentle, harmless, long-suffering, and abundant in mercy; that it is only the meek who shall inherit the earth, for the violent who resort to the sword are destined to perish with the sword. Hence, as a measure of sound policy—of safety to property, life, and liberty—of public quietude and private enjoyment—as well as on the ground of allegiance to **HIM** who is **King of kings and Lord of lords**, we cordially adopt the non-resistance principle; being confident that it provides for all possible consequences, will ensure all things needful to us, is armed with omnipotent power, and must ultimately triumph over every assailing force.

We advocate no jacobinical doctrine. The spirit of jacobinism is the spirit of retaliation, violence, and murder. It neither fears God nor regards man. *We* would be filled with the spirit of **Christ**. If we abide by our principles, it is impossible for us to be disorderly or plot treason, or participate in any evil work; we shall submit to every ordinance of man, **for the Lord's sake**; obey all the requirements of Government, except such as we deem contrary to the commands of the gospel; and in no case resist the operation of the law, except by meekly submitting to the penalty of disobedience.

But, while we shall adhere to the doctrine of non-resistance and passive submission to enemies, we purpose, in a moral and spiritual sense, to speak and act boldly in the cause of **God**; to assail iniquity, in high places and in low places; to apply our principles to all existing civil, political, legal, and ecclesiastical institutions; and to hasten the time when the kingdoms of this world will have become the kingdoms of our **Lord** and of his **Christ**, and he shall reign for ever.

It appears to us a self-evident truth, that, whatever the gospel is designed to destroy at any period of the world, being contrary to it, ought now to be abandoned. If, then, the time is predicted when swords shall be beaten into ploughshares, and spears into pruning-hooks, and men shall not learn the art of war any more, it follows that all who manufacture, sell or wield these deadly weapons, do thus array themselves against the peaceful dominion of the **Son of God** on earth.

Having thus briefly, but frankly, stated our principles and purposes, we proceed to specify the measures we propose to adopt, in carrying our object into effect.

We expect to prevail through **the foolishness of preaching**—striving to commend ourselves unto every man's conscience, in the sight of **God**. From the press, we shall promulgate our sentiments as widely as practicable. We shall endeavour to secure the co-operation of all persons, of whatever name or sect. The triumphant progress of the cause of **Temperance** and **Abolition** in our land, through the instrumentality of benevolent and voluntary associations, encourages us to combine our own means and efforts for the promotion of a still greater cause. Hence, we shall employ lecturers, circulate tracts and publications, form societies, and petition our State and national governments, in relation to the subject of **Universal Peace**. It will be our leading object to devise ways and means for effecting a radical change in the views, feelings, and practices of society, respecting the sinfulness of war and the treatment of enemies.

In entering upon the great work before us, we are not unmindful that, in its prosecution, we may be called to test our sincerity, even as in a fiery ordeal. It may subject us to insult, outrage, suffering, yea, even death itself. We anticipate no small amount of misconception, misrepresentation, calumny. Tumults may arise against us. The ongodly and violent, the pround and pharisaical, the ambitious and tyrannical, principalities and powers, and spiritual wickedness in high places, may combine to crush us. So they treated the **Messiah**, whose example we are humbly striving to imitate. If we suffer with him, we know that we shall reign with him. We shall not be so afraid of their terror, neither be troubled. Our confidence is in the **Lord Almighty**, not in man. Having withdrawn from human protection, what can sustain us but that faith which overcomes the world? We shall not think it strange concerning the fiery trial which is to try us, as though some strange thing had happened unto us; but rejoice, inasmuch as we are partakers of **Christ's** sufferings. Wherefore, we commit the keeping of our souls to God, in well-doing, as unto the faithful Creator. **For every one that forsakes houses, or brethren, or sisters, or father, or mother, or wife, or children, or lands, for Christ's sake, shall receive a hundred fold, and shall inherit everlasting life.**

Firmly relying upon the certain and universal triumph of the sentiments contained in this **DECLARATION**, however formidable may be the opposition arrayed against them—in solemn testimony of our faith in their divine origin—we hereby affix our signatures to it; commending it to the reason and conscience of mankind, giving ourselves no anxiety as to what may befall us, and resolving in the strength of the **Lord God** calmly and meekly to abide the issue.

Perhaps you think the ideas espoused here are too idealistic. The reason you believe you need a political regime to beat, cage, and kill others in order to have peace is a result of your indoctrination into the Cult of the State, the beliefs that justify the apparatus of violent government power and thereby secures the position and wealth of those parasites which sit atop it.

If we want a society where the ability of all people to be free and peace is universal, then we have to reject these lies. We have to stop trying to perfect Babylon. No matter how much gold and fine scarlet you dress a Whore in, she is still a Whore. The State will always be the State. It will always operate on extortion, violence, and death. The way to escape the lies of the State, to get rid of it altogether for something better, is to follow Garrison's example. We must reject the beliefs and practices upon which it is built and maintained. As Garrison understood, we must choose something else, Someone else.

Socialism is Slavery In All But Name

George Fitzhugh is a name that means very little today. But in the mid-19th century, Fitzhugh was one of America's loudest and most vocal proponents of slavery. Fitzhugh did not defend slavery, he argued that it was the most moral and just form of society.

Fitzhugh argued that a society based on individualism and free labor was one destined to class warfare, social collapse, and chaos. In its stead, Fitzhugh proposed a society based on slavery which he argued solved the problems of social discord by establishing a league of leaders who would care for all the needs of workers and ensure all people were well cared for in all aspects of life in exchange for their labor. If slavery doesn't exist in fact, he argued, people would just reinvent it under a different name.

In his defense of slavery, Fitzhugh explicitly explains how it and Socialism/Communism are the same thing in all but name. Note: Herein I will used Socialism to refer to both Socialism and Communism because most of everyone and every nation ever labeled Communist has in fact been Socialist. And by Socialism, I mean the ideas of Karl Marx, also known as Marxism or Marxist Socialism. Marx's *The Communist Manifesto* was first published in 1848 and Fitzhugh's 1854 book, *Sociology for the South, or the Failure of Free Society* was written as a response to Marx. Fitzhugh even references and paraphrases Marx in *Sociology*.

Fitzhugh, a slaveowner not only understood Socialism, but he explained clearly how the function, goals, and outcomes of Socialism were the exact same thing as those of slave owners and how slavery fulfilled all the goals of Socialism. Fitzhugh explains in detail that slavery isn't just *like* Socialism.

Slavery *is* Socialism.

Socialism *is* slavery.

In this essay, I will share with you the relevant excerpts from *Sociology for the South*, and I will do so with very little commentary. I don't need to add much commentary. Fitzhugh himself clearly explains the truth that Socialism is slavery better than I ever have been able to do so.

Anyone doubting the truth of his claims needs but look at the history of Socialism in the world and the presence of absolute slavery on a massive scale in every single Socialist state – from the gulags of the U.S.S.R. to the collective farms of Communist China and everything in between. At their heights of power, the Socialist nations were the largest slave empires in history. Just compare the numbers – 5 to 10 million slaves in the Roman Empire,[17] 10 million slaves in pre-1865 America,[18] while there were 25 million slaves in the Soviet gulags[19] during Stalin's rule alone and there is no way of knowing how many Chinese were enslaved on the collective farms, but we do know that 45 million were murdered by them.[20]

These iceberg tip numbers hint at a horrific and terrible truth. Slavery is not just an undesirable outcome of the failures of Socialism and Socialists to understand economic and political reality. As Fitzhugh makes clear here, slavery is embedded in the very nature of Socialism itself, to the point that the terms slavery and Socialism are but synonyms for one another.

Excerpts from *Sociology for the South*

---

[17] "Slavery in Ancient Rome," The British Museum, accessed March 22, 2024.

[18] Diego Lopez and Craig LeMoult, "Project Seeks to Name the 10 Million People Enslaved before the Civil War," GBH, August 18, 2023.

[19] Emily Buder, "The Truth about Stalin's Prison Camps," The Atlantic, accessed March 22, 2024.

[20] Frank Dikötter, "Mao's Great Leap to Famine," The New York Times, December 15, 2010.

The excerpt below is proceeded by an extensive quotation from an article in the January 1851 edition of *The Edinburgh Review* on the topic of Socialism. It is to this quotation that the first paragraph below refers to and then continues to quote from, which here is the second paragraph. Fitzhugh is quoting other pro-Socialist writers to show that the nature of Socialism and slavery is the same.

No association, no efficient combination of labor can be effected till men give up their liberty of action and subject themselves to a common despotic head or ruler. This is slavery, and towards this socialism is moving. The above quotation and the succeeding one go to prove the positions with which we set out: that free trade or political economy is the science of free society, and socialism the science of slavery. The writer from whom we are quoting sees and thus exposes the tendency of socialism to slavery:

…'The working classes and their advocates must decide on which of the two positions they will take their stand: whether they will be cared for as dependents and inferiors, or whether, by wisdom, self-control, frugality and toil, they will fight their independent way to dignity and well-being; whether they will step back to a stationary and degraded past, or strive onward to the assertion of their free humanity? But it is not given to them, any more than to other classes, to combine inconsistent advantages: they cannot unite the safety of being in leading strings, with the liberty of being without them; the right of acting for themselves, with the right to be saved from the consequences of their

actions; they must not whine because the
higher classes do not aid them, and refuse to
let these classes direct them; they must not
insist on the duty of government to provide
for them, and deny the authority of
government to control them; they must not
denounce laissez-faire, and denounce a
paternal despotism likewise.'

…Now listen to the conclusion, and see whether
the practical remedy proposed be not Slavery. We
believe there is not an intelligent reformist in the
world who does not see the necessity of slavery—
who does not advocate its re-institution in all save
the name. Every one of them concurs in
deprecating free competition, and in the wish and
purpose to destroy it. To destroy it is to destroy
Liberty, and where liberty is destroyed, slavery is
established.

[Fitzhugh then gives an extended quotation about
the general acceptance of Socialism in England
and the organization of workers by Socialist ideals
of organizing labor.]

Now strip these and the extracts from Blackwood
of their pompous verbiage, and they become
express assertions that free society has failed, and
that that which is not free must be substituted.[21]

It is worth noting here that, unlike the Socialist ideologues
who refuse to acknowledge the obvious truth, Fitzhugh clearly
understood that Socialism's rejection of the elements of a free
society would inevitably lead to oppression. "Free competition,"

---

[21] George Fitzhugh, *Sociology for the South: Or the Failure of Free Society* (Richmond,
Virginia: A. Morris, 1857). pp. 62, 66-67

that is to say the free market, is the foundation of liberty and the destruction of the free market is the destruction of liberty. Once that is accomplished, slavery is inevitable no matter what you choose to call it. This pro-slavery Southerner of the early 19th century predicted the inevitable development of the Socialist dictatorships that arose in the 20th century. How? Because he recognized the inevitable outcome of rejecting liberty is slavery.

After explaining that European societies were rejecting liberty and free labor for Socialism, and explaining that the rejection of liberty naturally led to *de facto* subjugation, the rule of one group over another and the establishment of slavery, Fitzhugh now goes on to explain how slavery fulfills all the promises of Socialism.

> Every Southern slave has an estate in tail,[22] indefeasible by fine and recovery, in the lands of the South. If his present master cannot support him, he must sell him to one who can. Slaves, too, have a valuable property in their masters. Abolitionists overlook this—overlook the protective in-fluence of slavery, its distinguishing feature, and no doubt the cause of its origin and continuance and abuse it as a mere engine of oppression. Infant negroes, sick, helpless, aged and infirm negres [*nègres* is French for black], are simply a charge to their master; he has no property in them in the common sense of the term, for they are of no value for the time, but they have the most invaluable property in him. He is bound to support them, to supply all their wants, and relieve them of all care for the present or future. And well, and feelingly and faithfully does he discharge his duty.

---

[22]Inc. US Legal, "Find a Legal Form in Minutes," Estate Tail Law and Legal Definition, accessed March 22, 2024.

What a glorious thing to man is slavery, when want, misfortune, old age, debility and sickness overtake him. Free society, in its various forms of insurance, in its odd-fellow and temperance societies, in its social and communistic establishments, and in ten thousand other ways, is vainly attempting to attain this never failing protective, caretaking and supporting feature of slavery.

…This, the noblest sentiment ever uttered by uninspired man, recognizes the great truth which lies at the foundation of all society – *that every man has property in his fellow-man*! It is because that adequate provision is not made properly to enforce this great truth in free society, that men are driven to the necessity of attempting to remedy the defects of government by voluntary associations, that carry into definite and practical operation this great and glorious truth. It is because such defects do not exist in slave society, that we are not troubled with strikes, trade unions, phalansteries, communistic establishments, Mormonism, and the thousand other isms that deface and deform free society. Socialism, in some form or other, is universal in free society, and its single aim is to attain the protective influence of slavery.[23]

Socialism is founded on the idea that one human has a right to the product of another's labor – and the life, energy, and time it took to produce that work. This, as Fitzhugh points out here by saying that humans have a right in property to other people, is the very basis of slavery – that the master has the right

---

[23] George Fitzhugh, *Sociology for the South: Or the Failure of Free Society* (Richmond, Virginia: A. Morris, 1857). pp. 67-68, 69

to the life, energy, time, and product of the slave's labor. Fitzhugh argues that slavery provides (or could provide) everything everyone wants out of Socialism – universal medical care, old age care, disability care, emergency care, etc., all from cradle to grave no matter their age by the caring master. In turn, the slave provides the labor the master needs.

In contrast, in all free societies the people are constantly in danger of illness and injury that they cannot afford so they innovate different ways to get others to help them pay their costs- including humorously enough Mormonism (and by implication, religion generally.) In all these ways, Fitzhugh argues, free societies are only trying to achieve for workers what slavery does for slaves. Socialism, he argues, is the free society's attempt to establish slavery and its benefits without naming it as slavery.

In the next quotation, Fitzhugh argues that while Socialists say that wage labor is slavery, this is actually an insult to slavery. He emphasizes the ideological connection between Socialism and slavery while showing how slavery fulfills the ideals of Socialism regarding caring for laborers and the abolishing of wages:

> More than half of the white citizens of the North
> are common laborers, either in the field, or as body
> or house servants. They perform the same services
> that our slaves do. They serve their employers for
> hire; they have quite as little option whether they
> shall so serve, or not, as our slaves, for they cannot
> live without their wages. Their hire or wages,
> except with the healthy and able-bodied, are not
> half what we allow our slaves, for it is wholly
> insufficient for their comfortable maintenance,
> whilst we always keep our slaves in comfort, in
> return for their past, present, or expected labor.
> The socialists say wages is slavery. It is a gross
> libel on slavery. Wages are given in time of

vigorous health and strength, and denied when
most needed, when sickness or old age has
overtaken us. The slave is never without a master
to maintain him. The free laborer, though willing
to work, cannot always find an employer. He is
then without a home and without wages! In a
densely peopled country, where the supply of
laborers exceeds the demand, wages is worse than
slavery. [24]

Socialists continue the ridiculous wage labor is
slavery[25] argument today and demand the abolishing of wages
and wage labor. No one yet has been able to define what makes it
exploitative when two people or groups agree to work in a
mutually beneficial degree. Of course, this argument is nonsense.
You might as well argue that laborers exploit employers by taking
advantage of their need for laborers to accomplish all the work
the employer could not do on his own as alike arguing that
employers take advantage of the laborers need to work for money.
When laborers and employers voluntarily agree to a labor contract
it is because the agreement is mutually beneficial, it helps them
both achieve their goals.

The Socialist wage slavery argument begs the question
"Outside of science fiction,[26] what happens to people when you
abolish wages?"

What do you call it when people are no longer able to
freely engage in buying and selling their labor at will and instead

---

[24] George Fitzhugh, *Sociology for the South: Or the Failure of Free Society* (Richmond,
Virginia: A. Morris, 1857). pp. 250-251

[25] Anthony Leonardi, "'Slaves in Many, Many Ways': Bernie Sanders Once Compared
Vermont Workers to Black Slaves," Washington Examiner, January 23, 2020.

[26] Daniel Kowalski, "Is Star Trek's Society Really Socialist?," Foundation for
Economic Education, February 6, 2024.

must answer to another agency or organization (whether a government or a worker's union of some sort) for work and in order to get food, clothing, and shelter? What do you get when some other organization uses force to control where you work, what work you do, when you work, and what you get paid as the product of your labor?

Fitzhugh's answer is clear and correct. The inevitable reality is that you become a slave to those who control the necessities of life, having to do what they command in order to get what you need to survive.

Socialism, by abolishing wages and forcing you into complete dependence on a political elite of officials, institutes universal slavery. The Socialist protests that their leaders will be elected, and this will ensure freedom. That this rulership is democratic or autocratic is irrelevant. History has taught us that democracy and slavery are fully compatible. Ancient Athens was a democracy with a mass slave population. The Roman Republic was a republic with millions of slaves. The United States was a democratic-republic for nearly a century with millions of slaves. The great abolitionist lion Lysander Spooner explained exactly how democratic slavery functions:

> A man is none the less a slave because he is allowed to choose a new master once in a term of years. Neither are a people any the less slaves because permitted periodically to choose new masters. What makes them slaves is the fact that they now are, and are always hereafter to be, in the hands of men whose power over them is, and always is to be, absolute and irresponsible.
>
> The right of absolute and irresponsible dominion is the right of property, and the right of property is the right of absolute, irresponsible dominion. The two are identical; the one

necessarily implies the other. Neither can exist
without the other. If, therefore, Congress have that
absolute and irresponsible law-making power,
which the Constitution – according to their
interpretation of it – gives them, it can only be
because they own us as property. If they own us as
property, they are our masters, and their will is our
law. If they do not own us as property, they are not
our masters, and their will, as such, is of no
authority over us.[27]

Fitzhugh understood this truth, too. He knew that the
abolition of liberty, the centralization of power into the hands of
any leaders chosen in any manner was but the institution of
slavery by another name because its turns humans into objects,
into property. This is why Fitzhugh the slave master attacked
wages and wage labor as great evils. He understood that they
were the tools of independence and liberation. In contrast,
Fitzhugh proudly explained how slavery abolishes wages and
ensures that all slaves are cared for and provided for by their
master(s), achieving the ends Socialism strives to obtain.

Socialists even try and induce you to embrace slavery by
promising to do for you what slave masters do for their slaves,
which is the topic of the next excerpt. Below, Fitzhugh directly
explains how slavery fulfills the property ideals of Socialism and
is based on the Socialist ideal of holding all property in common
and dividing it according to Marx's maxim: "from each according
to his ability, to each according to his needs."[28] Fitzhugh writes:

But the chief and far most important enquiry is,
how does slavery affect the condition of the slave?

---

[27] Lysander Spooner, *No Treason. No. VI. The Constitution of No Authority* (Boston:
Lysander Spooner, 1870). p. 26

[28] Karl Marx, Critique of the Gotha Programme (Moscow: Progress Publishers, 1960).
Originally printed in 1875. p. 20.

One of the wildest sects of Communists in France proposes not only to hold all property in common, but to divide the profits, not according to each man's in-put and labor, but according to each man's wants. Now this is precisely the system of domestic slavery with us. We provide for each slave, in old age and in infancy, in sickness and in health, not according to his labor, but according to his wants. The master's wants are more costly and refined, and he therefore gets a larger share of the profits.

A Southern farm is the beau ideal of Communism; it is a joint concern, in which the slave consumes more than the master, of the coarse products, and is far happier, because although the concern may fail, he is always sure of a support; he is only transferred to another master to participate in the profits of another concern; he marries when he pleases, because he knows he will have to work no more with a family than without one, and whether he live or die, that family will be taken care of; he exhibits all the pride of ownership, despises a partner in a smaller concern, "a poor man's negro" boasts of "our crops, horses, fields and cattle;" and is as happy as a human being can be.

And why should he not? —he enjoys as much of the fruits of the farm as he is capable of doing, and the wealthiest can do no more. Great wealth brings many additional cares, but few additional enjoyments. Our stomachs do not increase in capacity with our fortunes. We want no more clothing to keep us warm. We may create new wants, but we cannot create new pleasures. The intellectual enjoyments which wealth affords are probably balanced by the new cares it brings along with it.

There is no rivalry, no competition to get employment among slaves, as among free laborers. Nor is there a war between master and slave. The master's interest prevents his reducing the slave's allowance or wages in infancy or sickness, for he might lose the slave by so doing. His feeling for his slave never permits him to stint him in old age. The slaves are all well fed, well clad, have plenty of fuel, and are happy. They have no dread of the future—no fear of want. A state of dependence is the only condition in which reciprocal affection can exist among human beings —the only situation in which the war of competition ceases, and peace, amity and good will arise. A state of independence always begets more or less of jealous rivalry and hostility.[29]

Fitzhugh's explanation of slavery as the slave providing more labor because what he or she is capable of physically producing is greater than the masters, but giving the slave master more of the final product because the slave master's needs are greater than the slave's need – which are provided for by the master – is one of the most damning critiques of Socialism ever written.

In a Socialist society property is held communally. Fitzhugh even explains how property is held in common and a plantation operates as a joint venture. And your access to it is not based upon your wants or what you've "earned," but what you "need." The illusion of the master having more comes only from the fact that his share is concentrated while the share of the slaves

---

[29] George Fitzhugh, Sociology for the South: Or the Failure of Free Society (Richmond, Virginia: A. Morris, 1857). pp. 254-246.

is diffused among them all. And if the master *does* have more, well that is only because the needs of the master and his family are greater than the needs of the slaves. Therefore, under the influence of Socialist ideals, the master will get more than the slaves – after all in a Socialist society property is given to everyone according to his *needs*, not according to what he has earned, and the master needs more.

Slavery perfectly fits the Socialist mold and here, by comparing the two, Fitzhugh even prefigures what Socialist nations would be like in the future. After all, what was the Soviet Union other than one massive plantation system where the few political empowered masters profited from the labor of the many who did the lion's share of the work but always received less because their needs were lesser than those of the "nation" and those in power? Is this not also true of Socialist China, Socialist North Korea, Socialist Venezuela, and Socialist Vietnam?

It is, and just as the plantation was a miniature dictatorship with the master having absolute power over the slaves, so too have all Socialist nations been totalitarian dictatorships where those in power ruled over society with absolute power – the slave plantation writ large. And the conditions for the slaves are the same. All you have to do in order to gain release from the fear of want is to surrender all your liberty.

Final Thoughts

Socialist nations have universally been nations full of slaves. This is because Socialism *is* slavery. It is that startlingly simple. And yes, I know that this will not convince the Socialists that they are only slave masters, that just because they (like Fitzhugh) have dressed the whore of slavery up in the lady's finery of benevolence it doesn't change who she is underneath the nice dress and fancy jewelry. That is fine. This wasn't for them anyway. Not even Jesus could make the intentional deaf hear or give sight to the willfully blind.

This article is for those who are just being entranced by the lies of Socialism. They haven't imbibed so deeply of the poison of Socialist propaganda yet and therefore can still hear and see the truth. I beg you, pay attention to the warning in Fitzhugh's words. He understood slavery like no other man today. When he says that slavery and Socialism are the same thing, he knew what he was talking about, as he proved by showing how slavery and Socialism have the same goals, use the same rhetoric, and come to the same ends.

Just as slavery promised utopia but delivered Hell, so too does Socialism today. No matter what sweet words Socialists whisper with honeyed lips, the outcome of their philosophy is always the same. Socialism produces nothing but, poverty, oppression, and slavery for all those subjected to it, because Socialism *is* Slavery.

The U.S. Constitution:

A Covenant with Death, An Agreement with Hell

The Constitution nationalized slavery, forcing its funding and protection onto even those who opposed it and making it a federal crime to help slaves escape being robbed, raped, tortured, and murdered. The Constitution also made it impossible to truly end slavery anywhere as the Constitution used the national power of the centralized government to ensure it could be practiced everywhere.

The Constitution didn't just permit slavery. It actively promoted it, protected it, funded it, and expanded it. In doing so, the Constitution promoted the grossest of sins and the worst violations of the commandments of Jesus Christ to love one another in one of the most oppressive and bloodthirsty ways possible. Further, the Constitution continues to encourage sin, corruption, and evil today as it sanctions state violence, government theft, and the violation of individual human liberty.

Since early in American history there have been people whose vision and understanding of the U.S. Constitution and the American Founding Fathers has been clearer than those around them and whose dedication to the Higher Law of the Gospel of Jesus Christ have led them to make more powerful denunciations of the document and system itself. William Lloyd Garrison was just such a man.

Garrison was the beating hard and thunderous voice of the abolitionist movement through his abolitionist newspaper *The Liberator*. While men and women around him equivocated and compromised with the evils of slavery and its political supporters, Garrison was a granite mountain of truth, immoveable, impassable and implacable in his dedication to the immediate liberty of all slaves and their immediate enfranchisement as equal citizens. As. historian Dr. Ronald Osborn has said, "Garrison did more to force the issue of slavery into public debate and to galvanize the nation around the slavery issue than any other individual."[30]

It was Garrison who branded the U.S. Constitution "the source and parent of all the other atrocities – a covenant with death, and an agreement with hell,"[31] for the way in which it condemned millions of men, women, and children, to the brutality, rape, robbery, torture, humiliation, and dehumanization of slavery with no recourse for salvation and which beat, caged, robbed, and killed any of those who tried to live the Gospel of Jesus Christ by helping their brothers and sisters escape slavery.

Garrison was also one of the earliest practitioners of what has come to be known as anarchy, Christian voluntaryism, nonviolence, and civil disobedience.[32] Garrison understood the truth that God and His Law was and is supreme to all the laws, traditions, and edicts of men. Further is a quotation from an article Garrison wrote in December 1832 titled *The Great Crisis*. In the power of its truth, it denounces all those who would perpetuate evil for political and national causes.

One may ask how this is relevant when slavery has been illegal for so long here today. The explanation is simple. Everything Garrison says about slavery applies to the State[33] today. The governments of the world rob people of their labor and the worth that they produce by extorting money from them in the name of taxation. The governments of the world will

---

[30] Ronald Osborn, "William Lloyd Garrison and the United States Constitution: The Political Evolution of an American Radical," Journal of Law and Religion 24, no. 1 (2008): 66.

[31] "A Covenant with Death and an Agreement with Hell," Massachusetts Historical Society, accessed March 22, 2024.

[32] See *The Most Revolutionary Text in American History* in this volume.

[33] William H. Douglas, "What Is 'The State'?," The Latter-day Liberator, September 8, 2020.

destroy your life and/or murder you if you refuse to obey its unjust laws.

The governments of the world claim your life and your liberty, your body, and your mind as their property to use and destroy as they choose. They claim the authority to tell you when you can enter and leave the plantation nation, what clothes you can and cannot own by regulating trade, who you can or cannot befriend through immigration controls, the ability to decide what you eat and drink through food regulations, what kind of things you watch, read, or play through trade regulations, what kind of medicines you can take through medical regulations, what money you get to keep through taxation, who you love and marry through marriage licenses, what kind of jobs you can or cannot do through business licenses, where you can live and work through zoning laws, and so on *ad infinitum*.

Every aspect of your life is domination, regulated, controlled, and dictated by the rules, regulations, laws, and edicts of the politicians that control the nation and the corporate parasites that do their bidding. And if you don't like it, then government agents will beat you, cage you, rob you, and murder you for resisting. As Dr. Stephen Carter succinctly explained:

> Law professors and lawyers instinctively shy away from considering the problem of law's violence. Every law is violent. We try not to think about this, but we should. On the first day of law school, I tell my Contracts students never to argue for invoking the power of law except in a cause for which they are willing to kill. They are suitably astonished, and often annoyed. But I point out that even a breach of contract requires a judicial remedy; and if the breacher will not pay damages, the sheriff will sequester his house and goods; and

if he resists the forced sale of his property, the
sheriff might have to shoot him.[34]

It isn't just the violent force that we are threatened with
that places us in horrific danger. Sexual molestation and rape are
a part of almost every police arrest across the world. What else
would you call someone else using violence to force you into
submission as they run their hands over every part of your body,
including your genitalia and other private areas? What else do you
call it when they strip you naked in order to search you, forcing
their fingers inside your mouth, anus, and vagina as part of cavity
search other than sexual harassment, molestation, sexual assault,
and rape?

The police murder people in the streets for even the most
minor of offenses or no violation of the law at all. They sexually
assault you and rape you for the most minor of offenses. You
cannot leave the tax farm, the country, without the State's
permission and if you try it will imprison you or kill you.

But we have elections, you will say! We have democracy!
This gives us liberty! Hogwash. In the words of the immortal
Lysander Spooner:

> Neither is it any answer to this view of the
> case to say that the men holding this absolute,
> irresponsible power, must be chosen by the people
> (or portions of them) to hold it. A man is none the
> less a slave because he is allowed to choose a new
> master once in a term of years. Neither are a
> people any the less slaves because permitted
> periodically to choose new masters. What makes
> them slaves is the fact that they now are, and are
> always hereafter to be, in the hands of men whose

---

[34] Conor Friedersdorf, "Enforcing the Law Is Inherently Violent," The Atlantic, June 27, 2016.

power over them is, and always is to be, absolute
and Irresponsible.[35]

Elections don't matter when the whole nation has become
a plantation where we work only to have our wealth, our liberty,
and our safety stolen from us by a parasitic class of political
elites. Just because we get to choose a new parasite to lord over us
every few years neither grants nor protects freedom. The violence
and brutality of the State is as prevalent and evil as ever, if not
more so. It victimizes every person in the world in every country
on the planet. And until its tyranny is overthrown, we will not be
free and our work will only ever be half done.

So, as you read below replace all the references to slavery
with the State or the government. And don't be misled by the
mental conditioning you've been exposed to all your life[36] which
has trained you to look at your national charter – whether it be the
U.S. Constitution or any other – as if it were some noble,
inspired, text laid out to ensure your rights and liberties, to
establish justice, or unite humanity. Instead regard it as it truly is,
a document that enables a small group of elites to profit from the
robbery, abuse, and oppression of the public under the color of
the law and grant a false sense of legitimacy to what Frédéric
Bastiat called the Great Fiction of the State as it legalizes its
plundering of the public.[37]

As Garrison argues, no government can bind anyone in his
day or ours to obey it by the words of others. Thus, the
Constitution (and any other legal compact) has no legitimate
authority over your life unless you freely wish it so, unless you

---

[35] Lysander Spooner, No Treason. No. VI. The Constitution of No Authority (Boston: Lysander Spooner, 1870). p. 26

[36] William H. Douglas, "The Death Cult of the State," The Latter-day Liberator, January 2, 2020.

[37] Frédéric Bastiat, "The State," Foundation for Economic Education, originally published in 1848. Accessed March 22, 2024.

consent to it. Any legal compacts which authorize the committing of sin, oppression, and evil are of no authority or force to begin with and must be disobeyed. To do anything else would be to prosper the cause of injustice and corruption in the world.

In the excerpts from *The Great Crisis* below I have altered the text slightly by introducing paragraphs to make it more readable. Garrison was working with limited space on his news sheets and as a result his spacing is not very good by present standards. Otherwise, the entire text, including all emphasis, is original.

The excerpt below picks up right after a long section where Garrison has rehearsed the arguments of those who don't want to immediately end slavery because it was more convenient to continue in sin and because ending slavery might tear the country apart – in other words the same justifications that people use today for supporting the government, the State, despite its manifold evils.

———————————

Could we make such a plea at the bar of God? Would not his blazing eye strike terror into our guilty souls, and his retributive thunders sink them to perdition? If this plea will not avail aught in the day of judgment, it is good for nothing here. Now, then, let those beware who would make us believe it a valid one, or who are thus trying to deceive themselves. God is not mocked—and he may cut them down with the plea on their lips and summon them before him.

It is highly probable that many who read these lines will never live to see another year—perhaps we may all be in our graves ere another week: if, then, we ever intend to plead for the bleeding, dying slaves, we must plead now, and pray now, and labor now, and humble ourselves before God now, for our past indifference and slothfulness.

There is much declamation about the sacredness of the compact which was formed between the free and slave states, on the adoption of the Constitution. A sacred compact, forsooth! We pronounce it the most bloody and heaven-daring arrangement ever made by men for the continuance and protection of a system of the most atrocious villany ever exhibited on earth. Yes—we recognize the compact, but with feelings of shame and indignation, and it will be held in everlasting infamy by the friends of justice and humanity throughout the world.

It was a compact formed at the sacrifice of the bodies and souls of millions of our race, for the sake of achieving a political object—an unblushing and monstrous coalition to do evil that good might come. Such a compact was, in the nature of things and according to the law of God, null and void from the beginning. No body of men ever had the right to guarantee the holding of human beings in bondage.

Who or what were the framers of our government, that they should dare confirm and authorise such high-handed villainy—such flagrant robbery of the inalienable rights of man—such a glaring violation of all the precepts and injunctions of the gospel—such a savage war upon a sixth part of our whole population?—They were men, like ourselves—as fallible, as sinful, as weak, as ourselves. By the infamous bargain which they made between themselves, they virtually dethroned the Most High God, and trampled beneath their feet their own solemn and heaven-attested Declaration, that all men are created equal, and endowed by their Creator with certain inalienable rights—among which are life, liberty, and the pursuit of happiness.

They had no lawful power to bind themselves, or their posterity, for one hour—for one moment—by such an unholy alliance. It was not valid then—it is not valid now. Still they persisted in maintaining it—and still do their successors, the people of Massachusetts, of New-England, and of the twelve free

States, persist in maintaining it. A sacred compact! A sacred compact! What, then, is wicked and ignominious?

This, then, is the relation in which we of New-England stand to the holders of slaves at the south, and this is virtually our language toward them—Go on, most worthy associates, from day to day, from month to month, from year to year, from generation to generation, plundering two millions of human beings of their liberty and the fruits of their toil—driving them into the fields like cattle—starving and lacerating their bodies—selling the husband from his wife, the wife from her husband, and children from their parents—spilling their blood—withholding the bible from their hands and all knowledge from their minds—and kidnapping annually sixty thousand infants, the offspring of pollution and shame!

Go on, in these practices—we do not wish nor mean to interfere, for the rescue of your victims, even by expostulation or warning—we like your company too well to offend you by denouncing your conduct—although we know that by every principle of law which does not utterly disgrace us by assimilating us to pirates, that they have as good and true a right to the equal protection of the law as we have; and although we ourselves stand prepared to die, rather than submit even to a fragment of the intolerable load of oppression to which we are subjecting them— yet, never mind—let that be—they have grown old in suffering and we iniquity—and we have nothing to do now but to speak *peace, peace,* to one another in our sins.

We are too wicked ever to love them as God commands us to do—we are so resolute in our wickedness as not even to desire to do so—and we are so proud in our iniquity that we will hate and revile whoever disturbs us in it. We want, like the devils of old, to be let alone in our sin. We are unalterably determined, and neither God nor man shall move us from this resolution, that our colored fellow subjects never shall be free or happy in their native land.

Go on, from bad to worse—add link to link to the chains upon the bodies of your victims—add constantly to the intolerable burdens under which they groan—and if, goaded to desperation by your cruelties; they should rise to assert their rights and redress their wrongs, fear nothing—we are pledged, by a sacred compact, to shoot them like dogs and rescue you from their vengeance! Go on—we never will forsake you, for their is honor among thieves—our swords are ready to leap from their scabbards, and our muskets to pour forth deadly vollies, as soon as you are in danger. We pledge you our physical strength, by the sacredness of the national compact—a compact by which we have enabled you already to plunder, persecute, and destroy two millions of slaves, who now lie beneath the sod; and by which we now give you the same piratical license to prey upon a much larger number of victims and all their posterity.

Go on—and by this sacred instrument, the Constitution of the United States, *dripping as it is with human blood*, we solemnly pledge you our lives, our fortunes, and our sacred honor, that we will stand by you to the last.

People of New-England, and of the free States! is it true that slavery is no concern of yours? Have you no right even to protest against it, or to seek its removal? Are you not the main pillars of its support? How long do you mean to be answerable to God and the world, for spilling the blood of the poor innocents? Be not afraid to look the monster **Slavery** boldly in the face. He is your implacable foe—the vampyre who is sucking your life-blood—the ravager of a large portion of your country, and the enemy of God and man. Never hope to be a united, or happy, or prosperous people while he exists. He has an appetite like the grave—a spirit as malignant as that of the bottomless pit—and an influence as dreadful as the corruption of death. Awake to your danger! the struggle is a mighty one—it cannot be avoided—it should not be, if it could.

It is said that if you agitate this question, you will divide the Union. Believe it not; but should disunion follow, the fault will not be yours. You must perform your duty, faithfully, fearlessly and promptly, and leave the consequences to God: that duty clearly is, to cease from giving countenance and protection to southern kidnappers. Let them separate, if they can muster courage enough—and the liberation of their slaves is certain. Be assured that slavery will very speedily destroy this Union, *if it be left alone*; but even if the Union can be preserved by treading upon the necks, spilling the blood, and destroying the souls of millions of your race, we say it is not worth a price like this, and that it is in the highest degree criminal for you to continue the present compact. Let the pillars thereof fall—let the superstructure crumble into dust—if it must be upheld by robbery and oppression.

––––––––––

We must not idolize the nation, the country, or the government. Its only means of survival are extortion, theft, violence, and the violation of the rights of individuals. It is a tool of horrific barbarism and we do much evil by continuing to prop it up. Instead, we must, as Garrison said, let the pillars justifying it fall and lets its foundations of manipulation and lies crumble into dust. Let us, like Samson of old, tear down the Temple of the State[38] and wreck its idols so that we may build something better in its place – the Kingdom of Our God and His Christ.

––––––––––

[38] William H. Douglas, "On Signs, Symbols, and Statist Sacraments," The Latter-day Liberator, July 29, 2020.

If this leads to "disunion," that is to separation and secession, then so be it. It is only indoctrination and lies that has led us to believe these things evil. Disunion and secession are just different terms for the consent of the governed. People have the right to give and withdraw consent from the governments that claim authority over them and, in doing so, to legitimize or reject those governments. When that consent is recognized and people can leave any government they deem unjust then it not only allows them to adopt the best forms of government to meet their needs, but it compels governments to act justly or otherwise lose the resources of the individual or groups in question who choose to secede.

A government so constructed would not have the power to enforce mass oppression and evil. As soon as it did the masses would turn against it and leave it for better forms of government. Thus, what Garrison called disunion and what we call secession, both of which are actually the consent of the governed in action, are absolutely necessary to building a just, prosperous, and free society for all people. Indeed, it is the only basis upon which a just society could be built.

Anything else is just another Covenant with Death, another Agreement with Hell.

When You Should
Overthrow the Government

What is the purpose of government?

What separates a just government from an unjust government?

What is the difference between a good government and a bad one?

What ideas should a good government be based upon?

How can you tell when a government has gone bad?

When should you be loyal to a government?

How long does it command your loyalties?

When should you resist it?

When should you rebel against it?

When should you tear it down entirely?

These ideas have long been examined and debated by insightful men all across history. One such man was William Lloyd Garrison. As I have introduced who Garrison is in a previous essay, I will not repeat myself here. Instead, I want to get right to what he wrote that matters so much to us today in our quest to understand the nature of the State and when we should dissolve the government that rules over us.

In his newspaper, *The Liberator*, Garrison exposed the corruption and lies of the political system and called upon people

to reject all the justifications not only for slavery but of any kind
of oppressive, unjust political system. In doing so he outlined the
exact purpose of government, how to tell when it was just or
unjust, legitimate or illegitimate, and what we should do when
faced with an illegitimate government, one that violates any of the
the sacred, natural, and unalienable rights of the individual.

In his article, *The American Union*, published in *The
Liberator* on January 10, 1845, Garrison very clearly answers all
these questions with a clarity of understanding that will benefit
and enlighten the understanding of anyone who reads it today just
as much as when it was originally published.

Tyrants of the old world! contemners of the rights of man!
disbelievers in human freedom and equality! enemies of mankind!
console not yourselves with the delusion, that
REPUBLICANISM and the AMERICAN UNION are
synonymous terms—or that the downfall of the latter will be the
extinction of the former, and, consequently, a proof of the
incapacity of the people for self-government, and a confirmation
of your own despotic claims! Your thrones must crumble to dust;
your sceptre of dominion drop from your powerless hands; your
rod of oppression be broken; yourselves so vilely abased, that
there shall be "none so poor to do you reverence."

The will of God, the beneficent Creator of the human
family, cannot always be frustrated. It is his will that every form
of usurpation, every kind of injustice, every device of tyranny,
shall come to nought; that peace, and liberty, and righteousness,
shall "reign from sea to sea, and from the rivers to the ends of the
earth"; and that, throughout the earth, in the fulness of a sure
redemption, there shall be "none to molest or make afraid."

Humanity, covered with gore, cries with a voice that pierces the heavens. "His will be done!"

Justice, discrowned by the hand of violence, exclaims in tones of deep solemnity, "HIS WILL BE DONE!"

Liberty, burdened with chains, and driven into exile, in thunder-tones responds, "HIS WILL BE DONE!"

Tyrants! know that the rights of man are inherent and unalienable, and therefore, not to be forfeited by the failure of any form of government, however democratic. Let the American Union perish; let these allied States be torn with faction, or drenched in blood; let this republic realize the fate of Rome and Carthage, of Babylon and Tyre; still those rights would remain undiminished in strength, unsullied in purity, unaffected in value, and sacred as their Divine Author. If nations perish, it is not because of their devotion to liberty, but for their disregard of its requirements.

Man is superior to all political compacts, all governmental arrangements, all religious institutions. As means to an end, these may sometimes be useful, though never indispensable; but that end must always be the freedom and happiness of man, INDIVIDUAL MAN. It can never be true that the public good requires the violent sacrifice of any, even the humblest citizen; for it is absolutely dependent on his preservation, not destruction. To do evil that good may come, is equally absurd and criminal. The time for the overthrow of any government, the abandonment of any alliance, the subversion of any institution, is, whenever it justifies the immolation of the individual to secure the general welfare; for the welfare of the many cannot be hostile to the safety of the few. In all agreements, in all measures, in all political or religious enterprises, in all attempts to redeem the human race, man, as an individual, is to be held paramount: —

"Him first, him last, him midst, and without end."

The doctrine, that the end sanctifies the means, is the maxim of profligates and impostors, of usurpers and tyrants. They who, to promote the cause of truth will sanction the utterance of a falsehood are to be put in the category of liars. So, likewise, they who are for trampling on the rights of the minority, in order to benefit the majority, are to be registered as the monsters of their race. Might is never right, excepting when it sees in every human being, "a man and a brother," and protects him with a divine fidelity. It is the recognition of these truths, the adoption of these principles, which alone can extirpate tyranny from the earth, perpetuate a free government, and cause the dwellers in every clime, "like kindred drops, to mingle into one."

Tyrants! confident of its overthrow, proclaim not to your vassals that the AMERICAN UNION is an experiment of Freedom, which, if it fail, will forever demonstrate the necessity of whips for the backs, and chains for the limbs of the people. Know that its subversion is essential to the triumph of justice, the deliverance of the oppressed, the vindication of the BROTHERHOOD OF THE RACE. It was conceived in sin, and brought forth in iniquity; and its career has been marked by unparalleled hypocrisy, by high-handed tyranny, by a bold defiance of the omniscience and omnipotence of God. Freedom indignantly disowns it, and calls for its extinction; for within its borders are three millions of Slaves, whose blood constitutes its cement, whose flesh forms a large and flourishing branch of its commerce, and who are ranked with four-footed beasts and creeping things.

To secure the adoption of the Constitution of the United States, it was agreed:

First, that the African slave-trade, —till that time, a feeble, isolated colonial traffic, — should for at least twenty years be prosecuted as a national interest under the American flag, and protected by the national arm

Secondly, that a slaveholding oligarchy, created by allowing three-fifths of the slave population to be represented by their taskmasters, should be allowed a permanent seat in Congress

Thirdly, that the slave system should be secured against internal revolt and external invasion, by the united physical force of the country

Fourthly, that not a foot of national territory should be granted, on which the panting fugitive from Slavery might stand, and be safe from his pursuers—thus making every citizen a slave-hunter and slave-catcher.

To say that this "covenant with death" shall not be annulled—that this "agreement with hell" shall continue to stand—that this "refuge of lies" shall not be swept away—is to hurl defiance at the eternal throne, and to give the lie to Him who sits thereon. It is an attempt, alike monstrous and impracticable, to blend the light of heaven with the darkness of the bottomless pit, to unite the living with the dead, to associate the Son of God with the prince of evil.

Accursed be the AMERICAN UNION, as a stupendous republican imposture!

Accursed be it, as the most frightful despotism, with regard to three millions of the people, ever exercised over any portion of the human family!

Accursed be it, as the most subtle and atrocious compromise ever made to gratify power and selfishness!

Accursed be it, as a libel on Democracy, and a bold assault on Christianity!

Accursed be it, as stained with human blood, and supported by human sacrifices!

Accursed be it, for the terrible evils it has inflicted on Africa, by burning her villages, ravaging her coast, and kidnapping her children, at an enormous expense of human life, and for a diabolical purpose!

Accursed be it, for all the crimes it has committed at home—for seeking the utter extermination of the red men of its wildernesses—and for enslaving one-sixth part of its teeming population!

Accursed be it, for its hypocrisy, its falsehood, its impudence, its lust, its cruelty, its oppression!

Accursed be it, as a mighty obstacle in the way of universal freedom and equality!

Accursed be it, from the foundation to the roof, and may there soon not be left one stone upon another, that shall not be thrown down!

Henceforth, the watchword of every uncompromising abolitionist, of every friend of God and liberty, must be, both in a religious and political sense-"NO UNION WITH SLAVEHOLDERS!"

The answer to all our questions on government can be found in Garrison's article and be summarized thusly:

Governments exist because they are formed by individuals to protect the rights of said individual. As a consequence, the rights of the individual supersedes all supposed authority of the government and the root of all government authority is the rights of the individual. Therefore, whenever and however any government violates the rights of man in any manner it immediately becomes illegitimate.

Whenever a government demands that any human life be sacrificed for its sake it immediately becomes illegitimate. This is because in both instances it violates its specific purpose, to protect the life, liberties, and properties of man. When any violation of these rights occurs the government immediately becomes unjust and illegitimate, a bastard monster to be disowned and dismantled. Just men, good men, intelligent men, would never sanction nor support such evil. They will always rebel against it and destroy it. Dissolving the government is always justified. Secession is always justified. Individuals, not government power or maintenance, is what matters.

Imagine if we today truly understood and lived by these truths. People wouldn't idolize democracy as if voting for a new master every few years means you're free. The ritual human sacrifice that is war would be obliterated. The ritual human sacrifice that is law enforcement would be obliterated. The natural right of secession would ensure government by consent and stand as a mass bulwark against authoritarianism. Totalitarianism would be impossible. The Death Cult of the State[39] would be obliterated

---

[39] William H. Douglas, "The Death Cult of the State," The Latter-day Liberator, January 2, 2020.

and its propaganda and its indoctrination systems would be wiped
out.

In place we would have a true protection of human liberty
and a truly free society that would maximize prosperity and
liberty for all people. Garrison understood this in 1845 but people
didn't listen to him. Our contemporary society of dueling partisan
secular political religions and burgeoning authoritarianism is the
result. If we hope to prevent the inevitable collapse into
totalitarianism this all forebodes, then we have to stop it now,
before the hour grows too dark, the minds of men grow too dim,
the hearts of humans grow too cold, and it becomes too late. In
preventing dystopia from coming to pass, putting Garrison's ideas
into action is an essential place to start.

Bibliography

Anonymous. "Do What Is Right." Hymn 237. Accessed March 22, 2024. https://www.churchofjesuschrist.org/study/manual/hymns/do-what-is-right?lang=eng.

Bastiat, Frédéric. "The State." Foundation for Economic Education. Accessed March 22, 2024. https://fee.org/articles/the-state/.

Buder, Emily. "The Truth about Stalin's Prison Camps." The Atlantic. Accessed March 22, 2024. https://www.theatlantic.com/video/index/607546/gulag-stories-russia/.

Dikötter, Frank. "Mao's Great Leap to Famine." The New York Times, December 15, 2010. https://www.nytimes.com/2010/12/16/opinion/16iht-eddikotter16.html.

Douglas, William H. "The Death Cult of the State." The Latterday Liberator, January 2, 2020. https://thelatterdayliberator.com/the-death-cult-of-the-state/.

Douglas, William H. "On Signs, Symbols, and Statist Sacraments." The Latter-day Liberator, July 29, 2020. https://thelatterdayliberator.com/signs-symbols-and-statist-sacraments/.

Douglas, William H. "What Is 'The State'?" The Latter-day Liberator, September 8, 2020. https://thelatterdayliberator.com/the-state/.

Douglass, Frederick. "Speech on the Death of William Lloyd Garrison." ibiblio. Accessed March 23, 2024.

https://www.ibiblio.org/ebooks/Douglass/Douglass_Garris
on.pdf.

Edgley, Richard C. "'Behold the Man.'" Ensign, Oct. 1999,
October 2, 1999.
https://www.churchofjesuschrist.org/study/general-
conference/1999/10/behold-the-man?lang=eng.

Fitzhugh, George. *Sociology for the South: Or the Failure of Free
Society*. Richmond, Virginia: A. Morris, 1857.

Friedersdorf, Conor. "Enforcing the Law Is Inherently Violent."
The Atlantic, June 27, 2016.
https://www.theatlantic.com/politics/archive/2016/06/enfo
rcing-the-law-is-inherently-
violent/488828/?utm_source=atlfb.

Garrison, Wendell Phillips, and Francis Jackson Garrison.
*William Lloyd Garrison, 1805-1879. the story of his life
told by his children, in four volumes*. 1st ed. Vol. 1. 4 vols.
Boston, MA: Houghton, Mifflin and Company, 1889.

Garrison, William Lloyd. "Chinese Exclusion." *The Advocate of
Peace*, February 1902, 64 edition, sec. 2.

Garrison, William Lloyd. "Poem: To Sleep, Written after a
Night's Incarceration in Prison." Digital Commonwealth.
Accessed March 22, 2024.
https://www.digitalcommonwealth.org/search/commonwe
alth:2z110c421.

"The Inflation Calculator." Westegg, January 26, 2024.
https://westegg.com/inflation/?money=100&first=1830&fi
nal=2023.

Kowalski, Daniel. "Is Star Trek's Society Really Socialist?"
Foundation for Economic Education, February 6, 2024.

https://fee.org/articles/is-star-trek-s-society-really-socialist/.

Leonardi, Anthony. "'Slaves in Many, Many Ways': Bernie Sanders Once Compared Vermont Workers to Black Slaves - Washington Examiner." Washington Examiner - Political News and Conservative Analysis About Congress, the President, and the Federal Government, January 23, 2020. https://www.washingtonexaminer.com/?p=1898162.

Lopez, Diego, and Craig LeMoult. "Project Seeks to Name the 10 Million People Enslaved before the Civil War." GBH, August 18, 2023. https://www.wgbh.org/news/2023-08-18/project-seeks-to-name-the-10-million-people-enslaved-before-the-civil-war.

Marx, Karl. *Critique of the Gotha Programme*. Moscow: Progress Publishers, 1960.

Osborn, Ronald. "William Lloyd Garrison and the United States Constitution: The Political Evolution of an American Radical." *Journal of Law and Religion* 24, no. 1 (2008): 65–88. https://doi.org/10.1017/s0748081400001934.

"Slavery in Ancient Rome." The British Museum. Accessed March 22, 2024. https://www.britishmuseum.org/exhibitions/nero-man-behind-myth/slavery-ancient-rome#:~:text=This%20would%20mean%2C%20for%20an,urban%20areas%20and%20in%20Italy.

Spooner, Lysander. *No Treason. No. VI. The Constitution of No Authority*. Boston: Lysander Spooner, 1870.

Thoreau, Henry David. *On the Duty of Civil Disobedience*. Adelaide, Australia : The University of Adelaide Library, 2004.

Times Staff Writer. "Karl Hess; Goldwater's Speech Writer in 1964." Los Angeles Times, April 26, 1994. https://www.latimes.com/archives/la-xpm-1994-04-26-mn-50436-story.html.

US Legal, Inc. "Find a Legal Form in Minutes." Estate Tail Law and Legal Definition . Accessed March 22, 2024. https://definitions.uslegal.com/e/estate-tail/.

"A Covenant with Death and an Agreement with Hell." Massachusetts Historical Society. Accessed March 22, 2024. https://www.masshist.org/object-of-the-month/objects/a-covenant-with-death-and-an-agreement-with-hell-2005-07-01.

~ **End of Epilogue** *by* **William H. Douglas** ~

The state creates "authority" in *man over man*.
The state will *always* violate, not protect.
The state will *always* steal, not create.
The real "slave state" is the state.

It was war that made people slaves under government; then it was indoctrination and laws that conditioned their slavery; then it was different forms of government, psychological manipulation and lesser forms of slavery (ie. chattel slavery) that made them liken their slavery and see the lesser forms as the greater, changing one system to the next, until they never saw they were under slavery. Yet to strike at the foundation of slavery, the rest will fall with it.
If war and government creates slavery and chaos,
then love and voluntaryism creates freedom and order.

Freedom looks impossible to the slave, and when they start to see it's possible, they are no longer a slave. To see past evils as so obvious now, be not surprised to see present evils as not so obvious. Slavery keeps us from freedom, but freedom keeps us from slavery. Abolitionism as the missing link, helps us escape the feedback loop of slavery, by learning to practice freedom directly without compromise.

Were you were created to be free or to be a slave?
Are you nurtured into being free or being a slave?

This book is dedicated to those who want to change the world. If this book ever gets attacked in the mainstream, know that it is likely making a positive impact. All the culture will simply remind us of our former history, as does the abolitionism of the past. If government were allowed to justify slavery, then it could justify any form of crime. Take heed of these warnings. If society has chosen slavery, they have chosen death over liberty.

If *our minds create the world and the masses give power to the few* **then** *change the minds of the masses.*
We are all just people. A voluntary world is possible.

When making this work, I could not but help feel a deep sinking feeling in my heart, for the importance of this knowledge. We owe our lives to those before us who warned us of slavery, and we owe our lives to those after us for the abolition of slavery in the aggregate. The book "Radical Abolitionism" by Lewis Perry, alongside my knowledge of voluntaryism, helped me see what eventually led to this work. It is your turn to follow up, and create the greater work beyond this book just as I did.

The core message is this:
Ending the belief in slavery is not a utopian ideal, it is a reality we must learn to embrace.

Index of Terms (A-Z)
Approximate References, More Included In Quotes

Quotation Index (A-Z)

Date By Birth

Larken Rose (approx. 1900s) - 31-32, 36, 53, 68, 74, 90, 117, 121,
137, 152, 201, 223, 246, 255-256, 282,
295, 308-309, 311, 320, 335, 341

Leo Tolstoy (1828) - 4-5, 7, 28, 31, 193, 214, 238, 327

Liberty newspaper (1881) - 79, 83, 89, 126, 134, 320

Lizzie M. Holmes (1850) - 68

Louise Michel (1830) - 295

Luc de Clapiers (1715) - 65

Lucretia Mott (1793) - 32, 227

Lysander Spooner (1808) - 15, 24, 54, 109, 121, 135, 165, 172, 196,
226, 243, 291, 299, 340, 399, 408

Mahatma Gandhi (1869) - 34, 62, 86, 135, 198, 225, 233, 305, 327,
332

Manly Palmer Hall (1901) - 69

Marcus Aurelius (121 AD) - 64, 73

Maria Weston Chapman (1806) - 54, 209, 222, 227

Mark Passio (1974) - 28, 132

Mark Twain (1835) - 73, 95

Marshall McConkie - 329

Martin Luther King Jr. (1929) - 62, 268, 306, 330

Mary Harris Jones (1837) - 225

Mary Wollstonecraft (1759) - 68, 179, 223

Max Nettlau (1865) - 223

Maxim Gorky (1868) - 77

Mikhail Bakunin (1814) - 110, 198

Miles Davis (1926) - 31

Mortimer Adler (1902) - 39, 53

Murray Rothbard (1926) - 172

N.Y. Evangelist (1856) - 18

Nathaniel Peabody Rogers (1794) - 302

Nelson Mandela (1918) - 83

Noam Chomsky (1928) - 253

Oscar Wilde (1854) - 142, 147, 150, 190, 242, 332, 338

P.J. O'Rourke (1947) - 138

P.W. Grayson (approx. 1830) - 162

Parker Pillsbury (1809) - 149, 152, 169, 183

Patsy Mitchner (approx. 1800s) - 198

Percy Shelley (1792) - 25, 50

Pierre-Joseph Proudhon (1809) - 188

Plato (427 BC) - 233

Ralph Waldo Emerson (1803) - 6, 8, 35, 83, 177

Richard J. Maybury (1946) - 234, 285

Richard Price (1723) - 150, 193, 219, 336

Richard W. Wetherill (approx. 1900s) - 78

Robert A. Heinlein (1907) - 64

Robert Anton Wilson (1932) - 74

Robert Lewis Dabney (1820) - 276

Rod Taylor (from 1996) - 173

Roger Moses Sargent (approx. 1800s) - 300

Rose Wilder Lane (1886) - 34, 42, 138, 306

Rudolph Steiner (1861) - 65

S. Mitchell (approx. 1800s) - 180

Salmon Chase (1808) - 149

Samuel May (1797) - 50, 135, 205

Samuel Seabury (1729) - 234

Samuel Taylor Coleridge (1772) - 68

Sarah E. Holmes (1847) - 37

Sarah Grimke (1792) - 243

Seneca (4 BC) - 64, 72

Sojourner Truth (1797) - 225

Stanley Milgram (1933) - 263

William Godwin (1756) - 69, 75, 80, 84, 111, 126, 164, 207, 252, 297, 307, 326, 339, 342

William Goodell (1792) - 228

William Graham Sumner (1840) - 142, 167

William Lloyd Garrison (1805) - 8, 14, 27, 34, 40, 45, 132, 176, 181, 192, 224, 229, 279, 319, 322, 344, 369, 383, 405, 416

William Molyneux (1656) - 233

William Pitt (1759) - 285

William Sloane Coffin Jr. (1924) - 54

William Still (1821) - 141

Wordsworth Donisthorpe (1847) - 35, 95

Zygmunt Bauman (1925) - 59